America's

Miracle Man

in Vietnam

American Encounters/

Global Interactions

A SERIES EDITED BY

GILBERT M. JOSEPH AND

EMILY S. ROSENBERG

America's Miracle Man in Vietnam

DUKE UNIVERSITY PRESS

DURHAM AND LONDON 2004

Ngo Dinh Diem,

Religion, Race, and

U.S. Intervention in

Southeast Asia,

1950–1957

Seth Jacobs

FOR DEVORA

AMERICAN ENCOUNTERS/
GLOBAL INTERACTIONS
*A series edited by Gilbert M. Joseph
and Emily S. Rosenberg*

This series aims to stimulate critical
perspectives and fresh interpretive
frameworks for scholarship on the
history of the imposing global presence of the United States. Its primary
concerns include the deployment and
contestation of power, the construction and deconstruction of cultural
and political borders, the fluid meanings of intercultural encounters, and
the complex interplay between the
global and the local. American Encounters seeks to strengthen dialogue
and collaboration between historians
of U.S. international relations and
area studies specialists.

The series encourages scholarship
based on multiarchival historical research. At the same time, it supports a
recognition of the representational
character of all stories about the past
and promotes critical inquiry into
issues of subjectivity and narrative.
In the process, American Encounters
strives to understand the context in
which meanings related to nations,
cultures, and political economy are
continually produced, challenged,
and reshaped.

Contents

Acknowledgments

It is hard to believe that the researching and writing of this book took only six years, not only because I feel at least two decades older now than when I began but also because of the innumerable debts I have accumulated since my dissertation proposal was approved in 1997. Most of these debts are intellectual and spiritual, which makes them difficult to quantify. I am certain, though, that I will never be able to repay the many people—family, friends, colleagues, and instructors—who gave so generously of their time and talent.

Let me begin with the more tangible—that is, financial—debts. A dissertation year fellowship from Northwestern University provided funding for my research trips to Abilene, College Park, Lubbock, Missoula, Princeton, St. Louis, Washington, Cambridge, and Boston. The Cushwa Center at Notre Dame furnished a grant that covered the costs of a rewarding visit to South Bend. To cite an extreme instance of the openhanded beneficence that graced this project from the beginning: the staff of the Maureen and Mike Mansfield Library at the University of Montana has yet to bill me for the hundreds of dollars in photocopies I made, despite several phone calls and letters reminding them of my now four-year-old tab. Senator Mansfield could not have asked for a more accommodating group of archivists to oversee his papers.

Archivists in general, I have discovered, are a unique breed. James Arnold dedicates his fine monograph *The First Domino* "to the archivists, . . . custodians of democracy's greatest treasure, truth." I think that's making the eagle scream a bit. My appreciation of archivists owes less to the nobility of their profession than to the courtesy they inevitably display, their seemingly inexhaustible patience, and the countless hours of searching that their advice to look at this or that file has saved me. Among a stellar assortment, I would like to single out five archivists for special thanks. Tom Branigar and Herb Pankratz of the Eisenhower Library are simply the best record keepers I have ever encountered, having an encyclopedic knowledge and capacity to provide insight into personality and politics that beggars description. Ron Frankum was a shrewd, engaging guide to the American Friends of Vietnam Papers and helped make my stay in Lubbock far more pleasant than it would otherwise have been. Finally, John Waide and Randy McGuire led me through Tom Dooley's correspondence with an admirable mix of forbearance and good cheer.

My dissertation committee was all that a graduate student could hope for. Michael Sherry, Laura Hein, and Nancy MacLean's perceptive criticisms of the dissertation, their bracing insights into the problems it addressed, and most of all the example of their own scholarship inspired, facilitated, and greatly improved my work at every stage. My colleagues at Boston College provided an intellectually stimulating but not intimidating environment as I was revising the dissertation for publication. David Quigley, Robin Fleming, James O'Toole, and Lynn Johnson contributed well-informed criticism of parts of the manuscript. Lynn Lyerly deserves particular credit not only for investing a remarkable amount of time in reviewing my often congested prose but also for offering the most original and incisive commentary it has been my privilege to receive. Panel presentations at two meetings of the Society for Historians of American Foreign Relations gave me the opportunity to air some of the themes in this book, and the response those panels elicited—from such formidable scholars as David Anderson, Anne Foster, Fredrik Logevall, and especially Andrew Rotter—was invaluable. The three anonymous reviewers at *Diplomatic History* were also helpful, as was the critical feedback I received when my article linking America's midcentury religious revival to the "Diem experiment" appeared in that journal. Mark Bradley, Christina Klein, and Edward Miller interjected needed guidance during the final stages of revision when I ran up against a series of evidentiary and methodological roadblocks. Finally, I am grateful to Valerie Millholland of Duke University Press for her interest in publishing this work and her encouragement.

My two daughters, Miranda and Sophie, were born while I was working on this project, and while I cannot in good conscience thank them for their patience—a virtue not normally associated with newborns and toddlers—I can thank them for being the most incandescent, magical children imaginable and for providing me with a constant reminder of why I am the luckiest man alive. For my wife, Devora . . . well, the debt that writers acknowledge to their spouses has become a cliché. This book is dedicated to her, for reasons too profound and personal for me to cheapen by trying to put into words.

Introduction

"The Winston Churchill of Southeast Asia" was a pitiful figure at the end. Shortly before 10 A.M. on 2 November 1963, South Vietnamese President Ngo Dinh Diem stumbled out of a Catholic church in Cholon, Saigon's Chinese district, to face the martyrdom he had courted ever since assuming command of his country in the mid-1950s. Eyes glazed from lack of sleep, trademark white sharkskin suit spattered with mud and soaked with perspiration, he hardly looked like a chief of state, much less the demigod eulogized by Washington policymakers and the American media. Diem's brother Ngo Dinh Nhu followed him down the church steps and into a narrow, dead-end street. Almost immediately, the two men were set upon by a contingent of soldiers who bound their hands behind their backs and ordered them into an armored personnel carrier. Diem did not protest the rough treatment but expressed disappointment that the cabal of generals who presently constituted South Vietnam's government had not sent a limousine befitting his rank. One of the soldiers responded that the armored car had been deliberately chosen to protect its distinguished passengers against "extremists." This appeared to satisfy Diem, but Nhu snarled, "You use such a vehicle to drive the *president?*" The soldiers had to force Nhu's head down as they shoved him into the car.[1]

During the trip to army headquarters in Saigon, Diem and Nhu were sprayed with bullets and repeatedly stabbed with knives and bayonets. Their bodies were buried in a prison cemetery. The officer who typed the brothers' death certificates inflicted a further, posthumous indignity upon Diem, describing him not as "head of state" but as "chief of province," a position he had held years earlier during the French colonial period. Even more degrading, in light of Diem's Catholic faith, was the official cause of death: "suicide," later amended to "accidental suicide" when published photographs of the president's corpse showed his hands tied behind his back.[2]

As news of the assassinations went out over the radio, Saigon exploded in jubilation. An American correspondent reported, "Everybody seemed to be in the streets, singing, dancing, shouting, waving banners, or just standing by, watching. There were smiles on practically every face."[3] Tens of thousands flocked around the tanks of rebel soldiers to shower their heroes with presents and expressions of gratitude. Nightclubs threw open their doors, and revelers danced the twist, the tango, and all the other dances Diem had banned. Saigon's Buddhists congregated at Xa Loi Pagoda for a daylong service of thanksgiving. Students stormed the shell-scarred Presidential Palace, screaming "Freedom!" and "Long live the junta!" When newly released political prisoners began relating stories of torture, outraged mobs laid waste to the National Assembly Building and set fire to the homes of government officials. A few resourceful citizens used a power winch from a ship in Saigon harbor to pull down a statue of Diem's sister-in-law, Madame Nhu. The offices of the *Times of Vietnam,* a pro-Diem newspaper funded by the United States, were burned to the ground. Crowds lit bonfires in front of the residences of American diplomats, ransacked buildings and business establishments owned by the Ngo family, and ripped up Diem's portrait wherever it was displayed.[4] The cathartic rioting lasted less than a day, and then calm settled over the city. "After the crisis had passed," Frances FitzGerald writes, "the people of Saigon rarely spoke of the Diem regime again. There was nothing more to be said."[5]

Thus ended America's nine-year attempt to turn Ngo Dinh Diem into a popular leader capable of posing a noncommunist alternative to North Vietnam's Ho Chi Minh. The Eisenhower and Kennedy administrations had invested billions of dollars in Diem in the conviction that he, and he alone, represented South Vietnam's best hope for national survival. A slew of American political advisers had traveled to Saigon to assist Diem in everything from public relations to constitution writing; American military advisers had trained South Vietnam's armed forces to resist communist insurgencies and any neutralist threat to Diem's paramountcy; mainstream American newspapers and magazines had touted Diem as the "Tough Miracle Man of Vietnam" for whom "freedom is the very breath of life, . . . a man history may yet adjudge as one of the great figures of the twentieth century."[6] For almost a decade, American policymakers adhered to a strategy that the journalist Homer Bigart caustically dubbed "sink or swim with Ngo Dinh Diem."[7] After the drama of the Diem era played itself out, all the United States had to show for nine years of support was a whopping list of expenditures and

1. Rioters drag the head of a demolished statue through the streets of Saigon after the overthrow of the Diem regime. © AP/WORLDWIDE PHOTOS, 2 November 1963

a South Vietnamese republic in greater chaos than it had been in during the tempestuous early months of its creation.

While every historical phenomenon is subject to waves of revision and counterrevision, it would be difficult to characterize America's "sink or swim" policy as anything other than a disaster. When Diem became prime minister of South Vietnam in 1954, there were several dozen American advisers in that fledgling nation. By the time of his murder in 1963, U.S. personnel "in country" exceeded sixteen thousand. France, the dominant Western power in Vietnam for almost a century, refused to endorse Washington's so-called Diem experiment and relinquished its former colony within months of Diem's assumption of office, thereby conferring upon the United States primary responsibility for stemming the red tide in Southeast Asia. Diem's regime marked America's crossover point from advice and support to cobelligerency in a Vietnamese civil war. The commitment to Diem was the essential precondition for the ensuing measures that led to the defeat and humiliation of the United States.[8]

Vietnam War historians usually ascribe this fateful partnership to the regnant anticommunist ethos of the American cold war and the anonymity of most Saigon politicians. Diem's virulent anticommunism, so the argument goes, made him the logical free world proxy for U.S. cold warriors seeking to quarantine Soviet and Chinese influence behind Vietnam's 17th parallel, especially insofar as Washington was unaware of any credible rivals for the South Vietnamese premiership.[9] Yet anticommunism and ignorance of local political realities are insufficient to explain why America opted to sink or swim with *Diem* rather than some other South Vietnamese. As the record of administrative deliberations in the mid-1950s makes plain, several popular, qualified, and irreproachably anticommunist politicians in Saigon presented attractive alternatives to Diem, and every member of President Dwight Eisenhower's policy-making coterie was aware of their existence; indeed, one aspirant, former defense minister Phan Huy Quat, came close to unseating Diem, as J. Lawton Collins, Eisenhower's "special representative" in Vietnam, relentlessly badgered Washington to effect such a change in command. Other suitable candidates included Foreign Affairs Minister Tran Van Do and General Nguyen Van Hinh. These men had all established their anticommunism, and all had greater political experience than Diem. Yet none was able to secure the backing of the Eisenhower administration.

Moreover, the contention that Diem initially governed South Vietnam as a liberal reformer and became an autocrat only in the final months of his reign—a narrative that the Kennedy and Johnson administrations promulgated in the early to mid-1960s—is simply false. Evaluations composed by American observers during Diem's first days in office identified the very same qualities that would bring about his assassination nine years later: discrimination against non-Catholics, refusal to share power, and easy resort to violence to quell dissent. None of these idiosyncrasies ought to have come as a surprise to Eisenhower, his chief advisers, or those molders of American public opinion—the press lords Henry Luce and DeWitt Wallace, Senators Mike Mansfield and John F. Kennedy, "celebrity saint" Tom Dooley, and others—who championed Diem in the 1950s and helped bankroll his despotism. Diem never pretended to be anything other than what he was, and he never changed.

This indicates a shortfall in Vietnam War scholarship. Traditional explanations cannot account for the launching of the Diem experiment by men who, on the face of it, ought to have known better. The 1954 Geneva Accords that came out of multilateral peace talks on the Indochina War allowed the United States only two years in which to build up its Vietnamese candidate into a figure capable of challenging Ho Chi Minh in a nationwide election. Why did Eisenhower and Secretary of State John Foster Dulles gamble on a devout Catholic in a country 90 percent Buddhist? Why stake America's future in Southeast Asia on an individual deprived of the flexibility necessary to deal with the problems he confronted? Why, to paraphrase Barbara Tuchman, would intelligent statesmen behave in a manner so contrary to the way reason pointed and enlightened self-interest suggested?[10]

This book attempts to answer those questions. Neither a traditional work of diplomatic history nor what is commonly designated cultural history, it straddles both genres, drawing from such time-honored founts as government archives and presidential libraries as well as more unorthodox sources like television and radio broadcasts, movies and newsreels, fiction and nonfiction best-sellers, and the papers of citizens and private organizations whose nongovernmental status has frequently rendered them invisible to historians of the Vietnam War. There is no generally accepted label for such noncanonical inclusiveness, but I have chosen, despite misgivings, to call it ideological history—or history of the power of ideas. I propose to demonstrate how a particular body of ideas about religion and race helped cement the Eisenhower administration's alliance with Diem. Taking this approach does not mean I discount ostensibly more tangible factors like economics and "national security," although I join with Michael Hunt and Anders Stephanson in questioning whether such familiar explanatory devices can be isolated from the elusive realm of culture.[11] It does mean that I heed Frank Ninkovich's admonition not to "treat . . . ideas as second-order phenomena, derivations of the generative *Realfaktoren* that make the world go round."[12] Ideas matter. They can drive people to murder or martyrdom, catapult them into outer space, and conscript them into wars fought far from their national territory for no discernible pecuniary or strategic purpose. "Ideas," Terry Eagleton reminds us, "are what men and women live by, and will occasionally die for."[13] Thousands of Americans and millions of Vietnamese died in the 1960s and 1970s largely because of ideas governing the calculations of U.S. policymakers in the 1950s.

My unease in dubbing this approach ideological history stems from the fact that *ideology* is a difficult term to pin down.[14] An essay in a journal of political science catalogs no fewer than twenty-seven definitions of *ideology,* and while historians tend to select from a narrower range of meanings, they still disagree profoundly about what ideology is and how it works.[15] The diplomatic historian William Appleman Williams seems to view ideology in functional terms, as an instrument employed by political actors to achieve and maintain positions of power and whip up popular support for their policies.[16] By contrast, Eric Foner adopts a sweeping construction, describing ideology as "the system of beliefs, values, fears, prejudices, reflexes, and commitments—in sum, the social consciousness—of a social group, be it a class, a party, or a section."[17] Other scholars, notably Emily Rosenberg and Michael Latham, incorporate both specificity and expansiveness. Ideology, Latham writes, "function[s] in diverse contexts," both as a "rhetorical tool employed to justify particular actions" and as a "perceptual framework through which much broader, widespread understandings of America's national identity, mission, and world role [a]re apprehended."[18] Given such disagreement and the potential for confusion, anyone attempting to prove the importance of ideology in a crucial episode in the history of U.S. foreign policy needs to define his or her terms and come to grips with a number of methodological problems.

First, let me address the issue of what ideology is not. Ideology is not the same thing as discourse, although several diplomatic historians use those words more or less interchangeably.[19] I accept Gail Bederman's definition of discourse as "a set of ideas and practices which, taken together, organize both the way a society defines certain truths about itself and the way it deploys social power."[20] In my view, ideology does not encompass either those practices or the observable manifestations of that power; it does not refer to physical actions like firing a gun or material institutions like the Pentagon. Those phenomena, however, are dependent upon ideology for their existence because ideology provides the concepts, values, and language that enable people to make sense of the world and act within it, whether by pulling a trigger or building a fortress. Ideology is also not the same thing as propaganda, by which I mean government-sponsored publicity calculated to sway people into fulfilling their leaders' (usually hidden) agenda. To qualify as ideology, public statements must echo private deliberations, as they did with regard to Vietnam in the fifties. While Washington certainly used ideologically charged rhetoric to sell its Vietnam policy to the American people, statesmen described that policy in almost identical terms in top-secret conferences and correspondence. There was a high degree of continuity, for example, between the Dulles millions of Americans saw on their television screens and the man who dominated National Security Council meetings. "[T]o a considerable extent, the rhetoric *is* the reality," Robert Packenham notes in his study of U.S. foreign aid programs for a number of third world countries, including Vietnam. "Much rhetoric was in fact firmly and widely believed by the officials."[21] That is because the rhetoric reflected those officials' ideology; it was not just window dressing.

At the same time, ideology is never the sole force driving policy. Single-issue explanations seldom suffice for any geopolitical endeavor, and they definitely fall short with respect to America's plunge into Southeast Asia, which David Anderson astutely describes as a "multilane freeway."[22] U.S. policy toward Vietnam in the mid-1950s was impelled and constrained by a number of political, social, and strategic factors that cannot be completely disentangled from ideology but that were not entirely coincident with it: American defense commitments to Western Europe, the Middle East, and Latin America as well as Indochina; the administration's tacit pledge not to violate the Geneva Accords prohibiting introduction of new forces into Vietnam; co-occurring cold war crises in Guatemala and the Formosa Straits; and so on. The fact that U.S. statesmen had the military and financial *means* to keep an anticommunist client regime afloat in South Vietnam was also critical. French policymakers may have experienced similar ideological impulses, but they lacked America's awesome arsenal and booming economy. Stephanson's conclusions about Americans' nineteenth-century "national ideology" of Manifest Destiny are equally applicable to the notions Eisenhower and Dulles carried in their heads while inaugurating the Diem experiment. "Manifest Destiny did not 'cause' President [James] Polk to go to war against Mexico," Stephanson declares. "No particular policy flowed from [it] as such: though certainly conducive to expansionism, it was not a strategic doctrine. . . . What I do argue, however, is that Manifest Destiny is of signal importance in the way the United States came to understand itself in the world . . . and that this understanding has determinate effects."[23] I make a similar case in this book. While the roots of American activities in Vietnam were many and complex, the ideological assumptions identified herein facilitated those activities by making them seem logical and necessary and blinding policymakers to their consequences.

Finally, ideology is not monolithic in the sense of being uncontested or exerting equal influence over all members of a community, much less a nation. Even during the earliest years of the cold war, when there was general concurrence among policymakers about how and why Washington ought to meet the communist threat to Southeast Asia, not all Americans shared the deeply persistent beliefs of their leaders. Well-known iconic figures like the journalist I. F. Stone and the singer Paul Robeson critiqued policymakers' condescending perceptions of the developing world; the political scientist Hans Morgenthau argued that Asian communism did not derive from the same sources as European communism; and even Secretary of Defense Charles Wilson occasionally questioned whether a noncommunist South Vietnam was essential to U.S. security.[24] Although the ideology that gave Eisenhower and Dulles a conceptual handle on Vietnam pervaded all sectors of American society in the 1950s, it did not eliminate the possibility of resistance or dissent. Nonetheless, as this book demonstrates, contrary points of view were exceedingly rare—in academe, in the mass media, in the entertainment industry, and especially where it mattered most: in the White House, State Department, Pentagon, and Congress. Senior policymakers, all wealthy, white men of middle age or older, tended to draw upon the same constellation of mutually reinforcing ideas when coping with Vietnam. There were no ideological mavericks in this select group, and to that extent, at least, recollections of the Eisenhower years as an age of conformity and consensus have substantial basis in fact.

What, then, is ideology? Among the many competing definitions, I favor that of the cultural anthropologist Clifford Geertz, who calls ideology a "symbolic framework" that "attempt[s] . . . to render otherwise incomprehensible social situations meaningful, to so construe them as to make it possible to act purposefully within them."[25] Even more helpful is Hunt, who explicitly relates Geertz's formulation to American foreign policy. Ideology, Hunt claims,

> [i]s an interrelated set of convictions or assumptions that reduces the complexities of a particular slice of reality to easily comprehensible terms and suggests appropriate ways of dealing with that reality. . . . To move in a world of infinite complexity, individuals and societies need to reduce that world to finite terms. Only then can they pretend an understanding of their environment and have the confidence to talk about it and the courage to act on it. Policymaking, like any other individual or collective activity, requires that simplifying clarity.[26]

Put in terms more relevant to U.S.–Vietnam relations in the Eisenhower era: ideology gave American policymakers their keys to Vietnamese "reality." It allowed men like Mansfield to look at Vietnam and believe they understood what they observed. Because of "an interrelated set of convictions or assumptions," Mansfield could bring order (at least in his own mind) to events that would otherwise have been indecipherable. His ideology isolated certain features of Vietnam in the mid-1950s as salient and crucial, screened out discordant information, and applied some basic principles to determine what Washington's response should be; he was then able to make policy appropriate for the situation as he comprehended it. Unfortunately for him and other U.S. officials, to say nothing of the Vietnamese, much of America's ideological scaffolding in the fifties rested on shifting sand; it bore little relation to actual conditions in Southeast Asia and proved catastrophic as a guide to action. Crafting policy less to fit the facts than their own preconceptions, American officials went from blunder to blunder in Vietnam during the Eisenhower years. Their greatest mistake was their choice of strongman.

Hunt's Geertzian definition of ideology is capitally suited to the historical problem of Diem's deputation by the United States not only because of its commonsensical breadth and the precision of its language —"pretend an understanding"—but also because Dulles, the South Vietnamese leader's most powerful American advocate, anticipated Hunt in an address to a gathering of State Department officials in April 1955. This after-dinner talk has been ignored by historians (even Dulles's most accomplished biographer does not mention it) and this is hardly surprising.[27] A U.S. secretary of state makes dozens of speeches a year; unless he or she is proposing a Marshall Plan, threatening "massive retaliation," or announcing "peace is at hand," these orations are soon forgotten. But if one is willing to allow that religion, shaping as it does the deepest values of life, might play some part in shaping policy, then what Dulles said to his audience of fellow policymakers after a day of struggling to shore up American support for Diem is of legitimate concern to scholars. The themes Dulles stressed, his choice of illustrative examples, and above all the manner in which he resolved the dilemma he posed suggest he was engaged in more than the fulfillment of a tiresome social obligation. Rather, his words may have been the most revealing articulation of his ideological frame of reference ever set down on paper, and their implications for the study of foreign policy in the Eisenhower era are profound.

Dulles began by acknowledging, as Hunt would over three decades later, the infinite complexity of the modern world. "There is hardly any international problem which lends itself to easy or sure solution," he declared. "I have the impression that, in the days before the world became so unified, it was easier to take decisions. The issues were, or seemed to be, simple. . . . Today, almost every problem has many complications." Even maps, the diplomat's most basic guide, no longer realistically portrayed a planet on which "time and space" had been "almost annihilated." Dulles noted that traditional geographical concepts like the nation-state had "lost much of their former forbidding significance" as a result of global information technology, near-instant communications, and air power. Furthermore, many people did "not want to be contained by the lines which statesmen have drawn." Dulles offered two cases in point:

> In Korea, the 38th parallel became famous as a line between the free and communist-dominated parts of Korea. But the line did not demarcate the hopes and aspirations of the people. I recall being in Korea in June 1950 and addressing at Seoul a religious gathering of thousands of refugees. They had fled from the North and crossed the parallel to the South in the hope of finding the freedom of religion which they cherished. In Viet-Nam a line was drawn at the 17th parallel. But hundreds of thousands of refugees have crossed it, fleeing to the South. Again, the driving force was a longing for religious freedom.

These were among the most vivid recent demonstrations that, in the convoluted international environment of the cold war, "geographical solutions rarely coincide with human solutions."

Some policymakers, Dulles observed, were defeated by the volume of information they felt obliged to master. Their effort to see all sides of a problem before acting on it tended to "deprive decisions of the dynamic quality which is needed to make them effective. The mainspring of action is a sense of certainty. Unhappily, those who are best informed are often deprived of that satisfaction." How was a geopolitician to overcome the paralysis brought on by information overload? Dulles's solution could not have been farther removed from the unsentimental realism normally attributed to statesmen of his generation. "The great deeds of history," he argued, "were wrought primarily by men with deep conviction and dynamic faith. They were sure that they were right. It seems today that sureness can be dependably found only in the spiritual realm. . . . Certainty is not readily found in the mundane realm, at least when there is full knowledge of the facts. The yearning for more certainty and precision than is compatible with the complexity of affairs encourages . . . ultimate disillusionment." If policymakers were to avoid such inhibitive anomie, Dulles counseled them to set their sights on a higher goal than "immediate political expediency." Stop trying to absorb every piece of intelligence that flows into your department, he in effect advised, and remember a few maxims: "It was said by Jesus that material things will be added unto those who seek first the Kingdom of God and His righteousness. . . . Men who feel a sense of duty to some Higher Being strive here to do His will. Because of their faith, they have power and virtue and simple wisdom." In conclusion, and without naming Ngo Dinh Diem or any other American ally, Dulles reminded his audience, "Our policies must be dependably embraced by . . . our people, who are essentially religious."[28]

The sentiments expressed in Dulles's speech—the mistrust of facts and data, the preference for doctrinal certainty—were those of a Savonarola, not a Metternich. As we will see in chapter 5, Dulles spent much of the day prior to delivering this address opposing Special Representative Collins's campaign to strip Diem of office, going so far as to obstruct transmission of a presidential message authorizing the appointment of a new South Vietnamese premier. In conniving to rescue Diem, Dulles may, to appropriate his own phraseology, be said to have cast America's lot with "dynamic faith" against "disillusionment" and "full knowledge of the facts." It was an astonishing display of statecraft as faith act, of religious fervor trumping evidence and common sense, and it was hardly inconsistent with the spirit of the times. More than in any other period in modern American history, policymakers in the 1950s tended to view events at home and abroad through a religious lens.

Religion is accordingly one of two categories of analysis under the rubric of ideology that this book employs in making sense of America's covenant with Diem. Although many historians and sociologists have addressed the theological renaissance of the Eisenhower era,[29] this mid-century religious revival has been absent from studies of Eisenhower's foreign policy, for reasons that may be guessed at. Americans are presumed to separate church and state. Those self-styled realists who dominated much of policymaking during the fifty-year standoff with the Soviet Union—the George Kennans, Robert McNamaras, and Henry

Kissingers—would protest that religious ideals and the principles of conduct derived therefrom have no place in geopolitics.[30] If this were the case, however, Americans would dare elect and appoint only irreligious public servants, a condition that did not obtain in the 1950s, when over 80 percent of respondents to a Gallup poll claimed they "would refuse to vote for an atheist for president under *any* circumstances."[31] Dulles, who served as U.S. secretary of state for most of that pious decade, once responded to mild criticism of North Korean President Syngman Rhee and Nationalist Chinese leader Chiang Kai-shek by defending them as "Christian gentlemen who have suffered for their faith."[32] Scholars would do well not to dismiss such statements as hyperbole and pay greater heed to Dulles's choice of analogy when, for example, he repeatedly compared the communist menace to "the tide of Islam [that] swept over much of Christendom . . . in the tenth century after Christ."[33]

For Dulles and many other statesmen and pundits of the 1950s, religious metaphors, symbols, icons, keywords, and clichés provided much of the "simplifying clarity" identified by Hunt as ideology's prime function. As Dulles's biographer Townsend Hoopes notes, "Dulles, along with most Americans, was magnificently ignorant of Vietnamese history and culture."[34] The secretary had never encountered a more alien state of affairs than the wars-within-wars maelstrom that raged in South Vietnam in 1954–55. He could not begin to fathom this cauldron of competing ethnic, economic, and political groups, but he *could,* as Hunt puts it, "pretend an understanding" by referring to whatever exegetic paradigm was most familiar. The fact that Diem was a Christian and his rivals were not proved to be the organizing principle that Dulles and other policymakers seized upon in solving the riddle of Vietnam. Phan Huy Quat and Tran Van Do may have been more seasoned politicians than Diem, but they were also Buddhists, and American ethnocentrism linked that faith to certain assumed traits, including passivity, weakness, selfishness, depravity, impracticality, and cowardice. Those candidates for the premiership who were members of Vietnam's Cao Dai and Hoa Hao religious groups fared even worse. American officials and the American media reviled them as atheists at best, devil-worshipers at worst, and in any event unsuitable allies for a superpower that, in the jingoistic words of Senator Edward Martin, "must move forward with the atomic bomb in one hand and the cross in the other!"[35]

In my archival research, I have encountered countless examples of policymakers' bias against "Eastern" faiths like Buddhism, Confucianism, and Taoism. These attitudes are amplified in such artifacts of American popular culture as the Luce publications—*Time* and *Life* magazines—best-selling books, and television programs. It is impossible to connect attitudes precisely to deeds—ideological histories always leave the relationship between belief and action in the realm of the problematic[36]—but there is considerable evidence that American delimitation of what did and did not constitute a real religion regulated the manner in which Washington selected its allies. As H. W. Brands muses in his popular survey of U.S. cold war foreign policy, "It was convenient, and not completely coincidental, that three of America's principal protégés in Asia—Chiang [Kai-shek], [Syngman] Rhee, and South Vietnam's Ngo Dinh Diem—were Christians."[37] Brands does not follow up on his insight, but this book does. The Diem disaster is here reconceptualized as symptomatic of a religious ethos that also manifested itself in alliances with Rhee and Chiang, two other Christian statesmen who presided over largely non-Christian nations on the front lines of the cold war.

If, however, American solipsism mandated endorsement of a disciple of a recognized Western faith over any Buddhist, Cao Dai, or Hoa Hao alternative, religion alone cannot account for the durability of the Diem–U.S. affiliation. After almost one million North Vietnamese Catholics fled south in the "Passage to Freedom" exodus of 1954–55, Diem appointed thousands of his émigré coreligionists to key posts in his regime. The South Vietnamese government was soon well stocked with Catholic politicians—indeed, Catholics were overrepresented in both the civil and military bureaucracy. If the Eisenhower administration merely wished to see American interests in Southeast Asia defended by a Christian executive, many South Vietnamese met that requirement by the time Eisenhower began his second term in 1956. Yet America stuck by Diem, despite periodic reports by U.S. representatives in Saigon that he was making no attempt to cultivate a base of popular support and was, in fact, a dictator who regularly ordered the execution of political opponents, shut down dissident newspapers, and violated every article in South Vietnam's constitution.

In order to understand why Washington clung in paralyzed attachment to the policy of sink or swim for so long, then, one must incorporate another ideological proclivity, superimposing it upon religion in the manner of an optometrist combining lenses of different concavities to produce a sharper image. For over two decades, following Edward Said's pioneering work, historians labeled this category of analysis Orientalism, but Melani McAlister has recently made a powerful case for the limited utility of that term in explaining U.S. foreign policy after 1945. McAlister correctly notes that *Orientalism* refers to the presumption of a "generalized 'East'" in which nations as dissimilar as China, Saudi Arabia, and Vietnam are conflated by the Western observer into "a single world deemed 'Oriental.'"[38] Certainly, the Eisenhower administration engaged in this type of crude nation lumping when fashioning U.S. policy toward Vietnam, but Washington's conceptualization of Asia was more complex. Policymakers, especially Dulles, alternated to suit their purposes between positing a homogenous, monolithic "Orient" and drawing distinctions between Asian nations. Frequently, they justified U.S. support of Diem's regime on the grounds that the South Vietnamese were different from other Asians, then, often within the same breath, excused Diem's trampling of civil liberties as being necessary throughout "the Orient." As Barbara Fields observes, racial stereotypes are "promiscuous creatures," and a central survival mechanism of the various sets of beliefs classifying humanity into racial hierarchies is their malleability and capacity to accommodate contradictory notions.[39] I find the well-worn term *racism*, inexact and tendentious as it unquestionably is, still the best locution to describe those many-faceted attitudes and perceptions that contorted Americans' view of Asian societies and played a formative role in the conduct of U.S. foreign policy.

Few diplomatic historians would deny that racism pervaded Washington's postwar relations with Asia. Kennan, the "father of containment" and arguably the cold war's most influential intellectual, referred to "Oriental secretiveness and conspiracy" in his famous "long telegram" of 1946 and advertised his anti-Asian bias on many other occasions.[40] The muster roll of Dulles's generalizations about "Orientals" is long, as this book demonstrates.[41] Eisenhower, while more temperate than his secretary of state, also made numerous public and private remarks that smacked of a deep-seated racist condescension toward America's allies and adversaries in the East. These men grew up in a culture shaped by more than a century of stereotypical depictions of Asians, and when they looked at Vietnam in the mid-1950s, they saw what their background had conditioned them to see.

What they did not see were a people ready for democratic self-government. A number of historians have documented the American tendency to invest the citizens of predominantly nonwhite countries with the symbolic characteristics of childhood: immaturity, unreliability, excitability. Mary Renda's superlative study of U.S.–Haitian relations is perhaps the most rigorous unpacking of the "ideology of paternalism" that "encouraged" Americans "to take up the role of father to what was considered a child nation." Not only did the ideology Renda identifies legitimate U.S. intervention in nations like Haiti; it also "justified violence committed under the guise of necessary discipline."[42] From the perspective of American policymakers, it was absurd to expect backward, childlike people to responsibly conduct their own political affairs. Rather, they needed a strict, even ruthless national paterfamilias, either in the form of an occupying Western army or a native tyrant, to avoid degenerating into anarchy. With regard to Vietnam, this paternalistic construct was confirmed by supposed experts like Professor Wesley Fishel of Michigan State University, a close friend of Diem employed by both the State Department and the Central Intelligence Agency to advise policymakers on Vietnamese politics and culture. As Fishel wrote in a 1959 *New Leader* article, "The peoples of Southeast Asia are not sufficiently sophisticated to understand what we mean by democracy and how they can exercise and protect their own political rights. . . . That individual human rights may often be neglected or sacrificed in this period of national infancy should not be surprising."[43] Such reasoning played into Diem's hands. Officials stationed in Saigon might occasionally question whether he was the most *fitting* superintendent for South Vietnam, but no high-level U.S. policymaker ever doubted that autocracy was the best form of government for a recently liberated Asian colony, and no prominent American journalist or authority on Vietnam raised the issue either.

As well as legitimating Diem's centralization of power, American racism explained away his more disturbing traits—paranoia, violent temper, and vainglory—as being customary in Asia. Behavior that would have been interpreted as evidence of a psychopathic personality if indulged in by a Western statesman was not only tolerated but encouraged by U.S. officials as a means of demonstrating that America was not interested in foisting an obeisant puppet upon the South Vietnamese. Responding to French premier Edgar Faure's denunciation of Diem as "not only incapable but mad," Dulles asserted, "Diem is not a person to whom one can dictate. [The] U.S. cannot undertake to force upon him [a] govt. or policies which he does not like. . . . Any man who would blindly accept U.S. bidding would not be worth supporting."[44] In one of the bitterest ironies of the Vietnam War, Diem's supporters in the United States often charged those who criticized his suppression of human rights with neocolonialist leanings and insensitivity to Asian ways of thinking.

As significant as Diem's conformity to policymakers' concepts of Asianness was the extent to which he violated those clichés. The journalist Marguerite Higgins spoke for many Americans when she contrasted Diem favorably with "Asian leaders who punctuate smiles and protocol politeness with pointed reminders of their neutralist creed." After tortuous dealings between the United States and Jawaharlal Nehru, Higgins noted, "it is a refreshing—almost startling—experience to hear this Asian hero assert forthrightly: 'communism isn't neutral, therefore we cannot be neutral.' "[45] A recurring theme in the treatment accorded Diem in government correspondence and in the American media was how unique he was among Asian heads of state: anticommunist whereas most were neutral, incorruptible whereas most were mercenary, congenial toward U.S. business interests whereas most were suspicious, a staunch Catholic whereas most worshiped their ancestors or practiced some "fatalistic" religion like Buddhism. Colonel Edward Lansdale, Diem's principal American advocate in South Vietnam, emphasized this uniqueness prior to Vice President Lyndon Johnson's visit to Saigon in 1961. "Diem's feet barely seem to reach the floor when he is seated," Lansdale noted in a Pentagon communiqué. "However, he is not defensive about his short stature and is at ease around tall Americans. He has a very positive approach to Westerners, not the least bit concerned about differences such as Asian-Caucasian background. When the vice president sees him, he will find him as interested in cattle as any Texan, and as interested in freedom as Sam Houston."[46] (LBJ was indeed taken with Diem, dubbing him "the Winston Churchill of Southeast Asia.")[47] Viewed through the prism of American racism, Diem was not an inflexible reactionary with a Christ complex but rather that rarest of commodities: a straight-shooting, God-fearing, two-fisted *man* in the inscrutable, un-Christian, effeminate East. Diem, Supreme Court Justice William O. Douglas remarked to Senator Mansfield in early 1954, was "the kind of Asian we can live with."[48]

As American propagandists like Tom Dooley and Joseph Buttinger published their widely read paeans to Diem in the mid- to late 1950s, and as members of Congress like Mansfield, Walter Judd, and Edna Kelly delivered speeches extolling his accomplishments, the Vietnamese people as a whole came to be viewed in America as the kind of *Asians* we can live with. This projection of Diem's perceived strengths onto the population of his country was never complete; he retained a privileged status as the Miracle Man who alone could galvanize an otherwise simpleminded people for holy war against the communists. American writers never credited the Vietnamese in general with such qualities as rugged individualism or creativity—these attributes were reserved for Diem—but a distinction was drawn, by degrees, in American minds between Vietnam and "the rest" of Asia. While Diem's subjects were saddled with such putatively "Oriental" shortcomings as backwardness, inscrutability, and obtuseness, they were nonetheless, Americans learned, exceptional in their adaptability to Western political and economic procedures and their gratitude for American tutelage. The fact that a small but significant percentage of them were Catholics, making Diem's so-called republic the most Catholic country on mainland Asia, only reinforced the popular American notion of the Vietnamese as a superior breed of Asians who might one day fulfill in some measure Senator Kenneth Wherry's quintessentially fifties pledge: "With God's help, we will lift Shanghai up and up, ever up, until it is just like Kansas City!"[49]

By examining Americans' impressions of Vietnam and relating them to the contemporaneous religious revival in the United States and to racist patterns of perception, this book historicizes a connection between domestic culture and foreign policy. It demonstrates that, in addition to the incontestably important anticommunist factor, two mutually reinforcing ideologies shaped America's covenant with Diem: religion and race. These conceptual frameworks disposed policymakers like Eisenhower and Dulles to interpret events in South Vietnam in a fashion cataclysmic for the United States but remarkably favorable to Diem. The book documents how Diem's reign of terror and error was filtered through a lens of American ethnocentrism that translated the South Vietnamese dictator's shortcomings into merits, and how Washington's "Vietnam" became, from at least 1950 through 1957, a projection of American religious and racial preconceptions.

Those preconceptions overlapped and interpenetrated, and any attempt to pull them apart for purposes of analysis runs the risk of implying a discreteness that did not exist. Still, they may be usefully enumerated as follows: (1) America's conflict with the Soviet Union was an all-consuming religious crusade against an adversary who rejected God's universal moral law and sought to enslave humanity under an atheistic creed; (2) the free world needed faith, best exemplified by Christianity, to win its battle against godless communism; (3) foreign leaders who subscribed to a recognized "Western" religion were better allies than followers of "Eastern" faiths whose ethical inconstancy rendered them unable to distinguish right from wrong and whose submissiveness made them easy prey for the reds; (4) communism posed a particular threat to former European colonial possessions in Asia because the inhabitants of those countries had no experience governing themselves, were culturally predisposed to submit to strong leaders, and were so immature as to believe communist blandishments about Marxism's capacity to overcome poverty and desperation; (5) given Asian unfamiliarity with and incapacity for popular self-rule, it was necessary for Washington to countenance Asian allies who eschewed democratic politics provided they shared America's religious opposition to communism.

Schematizing ideology in this fashion has the advantage of pointing up a feature of U.S. attitudes toward Vietnam that is easy to miss: the degree to which anticommunism grew out of and was predicated on religiosity and racism. This contingent relationship tends to be obscured in conventional accounts of the Vietnam War that stress the primacy of American anticommunism; indeed, I anticipate that diplomatic historians from the realist camp and other more traditional scholars will respond to my argument by contending that while conceptions of religion and race may have had some impact on U.S.–Vietnam relations, they played a decidedly subservient role to policymakers' overriding compulsion to contain the global spread of communism.[50] But this misses the point: statesmen like Dulles were so fiercely anticommunist precisely *because* they were so religious, and they supported a South Vietnamese dictator as a direct consequence of their racist assumption that the Vietnamese, being childlike and primitive, required authoritarian government if they were to be kept out of the communist bloc. Both Americans' motivation for opposing communism and the manner in which they sought to halt its Asian advance derived in large part from their religious and racial views. To privilege anticommunism over religion and race in interpreting the Eisenhower administration's Vietnam policy is to assume a false hierarchy. The question of whether, for example, Dulles was more anticommunist than Christian—or whether his anticommunism outran his paternalism where the Vietnamese were concerned—is, I submit, unanswerable and frankly misguided. America's Diem experiment rested on an ideological tripod, all three legs of which were necessary to elevate Diem to high office and keep him there for so long.

A word on sources is in order. As Bruce Cumings observes in a famous article entitled "The Poverty of Theory in Diplomatic History," "An unsystematic, nearly random survey of articles in the popular press, sermons by Fulton J. Sheen, speeches in the *Congressional Record*, etc., is no way to judge how 'profound' was the impact of domestic politics."[51] Perhaps. But I would counter that if the same loaded imagery appears in both the *Congressional Record* and a popular book—if, for example, both Senator Mansfield of the Senate Foreign Relations Committee and Tom Dooley, author of the great early best-seller on Vietnam, refer to the Vietnamese as clay needing to be molded by American sculptors[52]— then a broad-scope process of value ascription is at work that cannot help but play a part in fashioning foreign policy. Similarly, if the National Security Council, a justice of the Supreme Court, America's most widely read magazine, and a scholarly monograph all characterize Vietnamese Buddhism as passive and thus vulnerable to communist influence,[53] such like-mindedness is indicative of the climate of opinion in which policy is made, and this legitimate subject of historical inquiry cannot be discerned, let alone investigated, unless the historian is willing to be eclectic in his or her choice of sources. In this regard I am persuaded by John Dower, who defends his wide-ranging research into the "stereotyped and often blatantly racist thinking" exhibited by Americans and Japanese in the Pacific War as necessary to establish the ideological context of policymaking:

> This is not the tidiest way to do history, but it is satisfying. . . . To understand how racism influenced the conduct of the war in Asia has required going beyond the formal documents and battle reports upon which historians normally rely and drawing on materials such as songs, movies, cartoons, and a wide variety of popular as well as academic writings published at the time. In some academic circles these are not respectable sources. . . . But they are invaluable for re-creating the ethos which underlay the attitudes and actions of men and women during these years.[54]

Neither Dower nor I would assert that the actors in our respective studies were helpless prisoners of an "ethos" that dictated their "attitudes and actions." One of the most arresting passages in Dower's *War without Mercy* involves a middle-aged Charles Lindbergh, who, having overcome his prewar isolationist sentiments, flew several missions in 1944 as a civilian observer with U.S. forces based in New Guinea. Although in many respects as xenophobic as the men he accompanied, the famous "Lone Eagle" was appalled by the atrocities American soldiers committed. Unable to reconcile his observation that GIs "were as cruel and barbaric . . . as the Japs themselves" with the interpretive dichotomy of "Oriental barbarian[s]" versus "civilized" Americans, Lindbergh attempted (unsuccessfully) to persuade his superiors to adopt a more humane means of prosecuting the war. This did not constitute an escape from the racist paradigm Dower identifies; rather, it represented an instance of "the same stereotypes that fed . . . outright race hate" being "turned about . . . to legitimize . . . [a] purpose contradictory" to that of most U.S. commanders in the last year of Japanese-American conflict.[55] Similarly, while the American Catholic Joe Collins was just as disdainful of Vietnamese Buddhism, Hoa Haoism, and Cao Daism as his contemporaries in the Eisenhower administration—and no more willing than a French rubber plantation baron to concede to the Vietnamese rights of self-government—he managed to bend the terms of hegemonic ideological notions about "the Orient" and "non-Western" faiths to argue against America's investment in Diem. The "Collins mission" to Vietnam in 1954–55 lends credence to Gail Bederman's proposition that "ideology, although coercive, does not preclude human agency."[56] But individuals like Collins were in the minority, and their counsel proved insufficient to deter more powerful statesmen from embracing the devouring incubus of the Diem regime.

Ultimately, the same rewards that spurred earlier studies sustain and justify this entry in what Robert McMahon calls the "Why Vietnam sweepstakes"[57]: I hope to arrive at a fuller understanding of the origins of America's longest and most divisive war and of why the United States expended so much blood and treasure in an area of such apparent strategic and economic insignificance. I believe historians can achieve this understanding only by charting fresh directions and becoming more cross-disciplinary in their research. If there is one thing that the ever-expanding secondary literature on the Vietnam War makes clear, it is that traditional balance-of-power and materialist interpretations cannot explain America's thirty-year military involvement in Southeast Asia. The answers will not be found on maps or in bankbooks. Room must be made for what Richard Slotkin calls "the activities of symbol-making, interpretation, and imaginative projection [that] continuously interlock with the political and material processes of social existence."[58]

Happily, several historians of diplomacy have expanded their horizons to accommodate these activities. The field of diplomatic history is entering a new and exciting stage in which categories of analysis perennially consigned by more conservative scholars to cultural history are enabling scholars like Laura McEnaney, Kristin Hoganson, Mary Dudziak, Michelle Mart, Geoffrey Smith, Penny Von Eschen, Brenda Gayle Plummer, Emily Rosenberg, Robert Dean, and Andrew Rotter to illuminate critical dimensions of policymaking long overlooked.[59] This book contributes to that trend. Conceptually, it represents a refinement of Loren Baritz's observation that "Americans were ignorant about the Vietnamese not because we were stupid, but because we believe certain things. . . . These things necessarily distorted our vision and confused our minds in ways that made learning extraordinarily difficult. To understand our failure, we must think about what it means to be an American."[60] *Pace* Baritz: to understand the Diem commitment, we must think about what it meant to be an American in the Eisenhower years—a time of unprecedented religious revival and global interventionism during which detailed knowledge of the Far East was almost completely lacking. Consideration of the ideology that shaped policymakers' consciousness in this pivotal time can help explain why the strategy of "sink or swim with Ngo Dinh Diem" was adopted and pursued for so many years, and why America's experiment in nation building in Southeast Asia was doomed from the outset despite the investment of billions of dollars, the sacrifice of hundreds of thousands of lives, and the application of more firepower than had previously been deployed in all of American history.

We live in a post–cold war world of snowballing nuclear proliferation, where it is more rather than less likely that America will face geopolitical crises involving unfamiliar peoples. In light of these sobering facts, the significance of the Diem experiment for the study and conduct of U.S. foreign relations is self-evident. It is a superb vehicle for exhibiting the effects of cultural insularity upon the crafting of policy and vividly demonstrates the need for periodic testing of policymakers' preconceived notions and emotional fixations against the evidence. Dower may be correct when he asserts that "fantasy and sensationalism shape the mind in ways beyond measure, undoubtedly a great deal more than most scholarship does."[61] Still, this does not absolve historians of the responsibility of challenging those public servants—presidents, secretaries of state, senators—who view complex international events with rigid ideological tunnel vision. As Clifford Geertz declared in one of the earliest defenses of ideology as a proper concern for scholars, "The social function of science vis-à-vis ideologies is first to understand them—what they are, how they work, what gives rise to them—and second to criticize them, to force them to come to terms with (but not necessarily to surrender to) reality."[62]

America's
Miracle Man
in Vietnam

1

"Colonialism,

Communism, or

Catholicism?":

Mr. Diem Goes to

Washington

On 7 July 1954, Jean Baptiste Ngo Dinh Diem formally took over the government of the young, besieged State of Vietnam. Diem's appointment as prime minister represented the culmination of many years of campaigning, a time during which, like most politicians, he cultivated the support of influential patrons by seeking out their company and telling them what they wanted to hear. He was also fortunate in that certain features of his background and character, over which he had no control, appealed to many government officials and well-connected private citizens. Through a classic mix of networking and luck, Diem had built up such an effective power base by the summer of 1954 that the emperor of Vietnam had no choice but to offer him the premiership.

What made Diem's rise to prominence noteworthy was the fact that none of his prestigious sponsors were Vietnamese. Indeed, Diem was not widely known in his native land, where he had held no public office for more than twenty years. He was likewise unable to command any meaningful support in France, Vietnam's longtime colonial overlord. It was in the United States that Diem won his post. His piety and his appeals to Americans' paternalistic and missionary impulses favorably impressed statesmen like Senator Mike Mansfield and Representative Walter Judd, among others. Not merely Diem's Christianity but his Catholicism endeared him to elite figures in the Eisenhower administration and made him stand out among possible candidates for America's cold war surrogate in Saigon. Moreover, widespread assumptions that Asians were culturally, and perhaps racially, unready for democratic self-government predisposed U.S. policymakers to excuse Diem's overtly dictatorial ambitions as appropriate for Vietnam.

From the beginning, Diem's government was an American creation. As a Central Intelligence Agency (CIA) operative stationed in Saigon in the mid-1950s recalled, Diem was "so wholly dependent on American support that he would have fallen in a day without it. . . . What he did was inspired by Americans, planned by Americans, and carried out with close American guidance."[1] Those Vietnamese who disparaged the Diem regime as "*My-Diem*"—"American Diem"—were more insightful than they could have known, as was the British novelist Graham Greene, who in 1955 called Diem "The Patriot Ruined by the West."[2] The same qualities that enabled Diem to acquire South Vietnam's highest office through the agency of the Eisenhower administration also ensured that he would never establish a government of any popular legitimacy and doomed his so-called republic to permanent, quasi-colonial reliance upon Western aid—a cruel paradox for a man who, whatever his faults, must be counted among Vietnam's staunchest nationalists.

"An Exceptionally Serious Catholic"

Diem first set foot on American soil in late August 1950, less than two months after the outbreak of the Korean War. While hardly the most distinguished Asian statesman to visit the United States that year, he came with impressive references. Edmund Gullion of the American embassy in Saigon informed Secretary of State Dean Acheson that Diem was "the chief leader of the Vietnamese Catholics" and speculated that his visit might heighten Catholic awareness of "the communist danger to Viet-Nam."[3] Charles Spinks, the U.S. ambassador to Japan, saw Diem during the latter's stopover in Tokyo and alerted his superiors that Diem was "anti-French, anti-communist, progressive, liberal, [and] a good possibility as an American tool in Indo-China."[4] Ever on the lookout for potential tools to arrest the communist advance in Asia, Washington took heed of these reports. The State Department's Bureau of Far Eastern Affairs made arrangements for a reception for Diem at the capital.[5]

Diem arrived in Washington accompanied by his brother, Bishop Ngo Dinh Thuc, who ironically made a better impression on State Department representatives than Diem did. James Webb, acting secretary of state, cabled the Saigon embassy, "We were impressed that Thuc, through the Catholics, might be [an] important figure in [the] present IC [Indochina] complex. . . . [The i]nfluence of Thuc's clerical background and position[,] with its evident bearing on his thinking[,] was apparent." Diem, on the other hand, struck officials as "less precise, realistic, and authoritative. . . . He fits more into [the] mold of [a] present-day Vietnamese politician, steeped in Oriental intrigue." Both Diem and Thuc stressed the need for greater Vietnamese autonomy from France, criticized the Vietnamese emperor, Bao Dai, for his inability to rally popular support to the anticommunist cause, and argued for more direct American involvement in the war raging in Vietnam. They were, however, incapable of advancing any strategy whereby the United States could displace the French in Indochina without damaging the recently inaugurated North Atlantic Treaty Organization (NATO), and proved similarly unable to explain how American forces, nearly expelled from the Korean peninsula just weeks before, could fight two land wars in Asia at the same time. Diem in particular irritated Webb with his "resort to generalities." "Like other prominent Vietnamese," the acting secretary complained, "Diem is . . . either incapable or unwilling to [sic] offer any constructive solution to [the] current dilemma other than vague and defamatory ref[erence]s to Fr[ance] and implications that only [the] U.S. can solve [the] problem, thru him of course."[6]

The Ngo brothers remained in America for almost a month, occasionally meeting with lower-level functionaries in the Truman administration but associating primarily with clergymen and other individuals active in Catholic circles. They left for Europe in mid-October to lobby for Diem's installation as Vietnamese prime minister.[7] Shortly after their departure, Dean Rusk, then assistant secretary of state for Far Eastern affairs, wrote to Father Frederick McGuire, a former Vincentian missionary to Indochina who often advised the State Department on Asian matters. Rusk thanked McGuire for his "cooperation and assistance . . . in receiving Mr. Diem" and called Diem and Thuc "valuable allies in our common endeavor to preserve the rights of free men in Indochina." While Rusk did not anticipate that Diem and Thuc would return to America, he assured McGuire that "they have expressed themselves eager . . . to remain in touch with the Catholic clergy of the United States."[8]

No American newspaper mentioned Diem's visit, and a contemporary observer could be forgiven for assuming that the stocky little man from the other side of the world would soon fade into obscurity. Indeed, Diem's life prior to 1950 suggested a personality ill-suited to politics, at least by Western standards.[9] Born in 1901 near the imperial city of Hue in central Vietnam, Diem was one of nine children in a wealthy family headed by Ngo Dinh Kha, the highest-ranking mandarin in the court of Emperor Thanh Thai. The Ngo family had been Catholic for generations, converting in the seventeenth century. They paid a heavy price for their faith under emperors Minh Mang and Tu Duc, who encouraged the persecution of Catholics. Around 1880, when Kha was studying for government service in Malaya, Buddhist monks led an anti-Catholic riot that nearly wiped out the Ngo family. More than a hundred Ngo—including Kha's parents, sisters, and brothers—were burned alive. Such oppression only intensified Kha's devotion to the Catholic Church, a sentiment he passed on to his six sons and three daughters.[10]

Diem grew up in a household in which, according to one biographer, "Catholicism and Confucianism went hand in hand."[11] Kha was not a nurturant or forgiving father. Through harangue, catechization, and frequent beatings, he impressed upon his children the importance of self-denial and conformity to the moral and social order.[12] Diem stood out for his piety, rising every morning before dawn to pray and flying into a rage if interrupted by his siblings. At six, he won his first school prize—for "assiduousness."[13] At fifteen, he entered a monastery and considered becoming a priest but dropped the notion because, as he informed Stanley Karnow, "the discipline was too rigorous."[14] Denis Warner is probably nearer the mark when he concludes that Diem "found the Church too pliable for his own unbending will."[15]

A year after leaving the monastery, Diem took competitive examinations for French Indochina's equivalent of a high school diploma. He scored so high that the French offered him a scholarship in Paris, but he declined, enrolling instead in Hanoi's School of Public Administration and Law. While a student there, he had a fleeting romance with the daughter of one of his instructors, but she jilted him and joined a convent. He probably remained celibate for the rest of his life.[16] Diem performed well at school, graduating first in his class and moving into government service. Within a few years, he became provincial chief of a district containing over three hundred villages. It was here that he first encountered local communist agents distributing propaganda. Revolted by the Marxist doctrines of social revolution and atheism, he helped the French suppress the first communist-inspired peasant revolts. By 1933, when he was only thirty-two years old, the French agreed to his appointment as minister of the interior under Emperor Bao Dai.[17]

It was a decision the French would regret. Shortly after assuming office, Diem was invited to head a commission to examine possible administrative reforms. He submitted a list of proposals, all of which the French rejected. In an act of considerable bravery, he publicly resigned, denounced Bao Dai as "nothing but an instrument in the hands of the French," and returned all of the decorations the emperor had bestowed on him.[18] The French threatened him with deportation. Diem retired to his family home in Hue to nurse his wounded pride. He would not work for a living for the next twenty-one years, although he remained politically active, meeting often with nationalist intellectuals and keeping up a diligent correspondence with the legendary Phan Boi Chau, Indochina's most famous anticolonial activist.[19]

Like Ho Chi Minh, Diem recognized that World War II presented a unique opportunity for Vietnam to break free from French control. When Japan completed its occupation of Indochina in 1942, he tried to convince Japanese officials to grant Vietnam its independence, but they preferred to leave the outward form of French colonial administration in place. Three years later, the tide of war having turned, the Japanese relented and asked Diem to serve as prime minister in a nominally sovereign Vietnam. Diem refused. Both the Japanese and the French declared him a subversive and ordered his arrest. Diem fled south to Saigon, where he lay low and managed to avoid capture until the end of the war. His older brother Ngo Dinh Khoi was not so fortunate. The communist Viet Minh apprehended Khoi and his son, tried and convicted them for counterrevolutionary acts, and buried them alive.[20]

Diem himself was seized by Viet Minh agents in late 1945. His anticommunism and prior service in the colonial administration might have sealed his fate, but Ho Chi Minh was anxious to have a Catholic in his first coalition cabinet. Rather than order Diem's execution, he had Diem brought to Viet Minh headquarters in Hanoi. The ensuing dialogue between the two men vividly demonstrated both Ho's political skills—which enabled him to hold a fractious, poorly armed population together through decades of war—and the dogmatism that would hamstring Diem's efforts to pull off a similar feat:

Diem: What do you want of me?

Ho: I want of you what you have always wanted of me—your cooperation in gaining independence. We seek the same thing. We should work together.

Diem: You are a criminal who has burned and destroyed the country, and you have held me prisoner.

Ho: I apologize for that unfortunate incident. When people who have been oppressed revolt, mistakes are inevitable and tragedies occur. . . . You have grievances against us, but let's forget them.

Diem: You want me to *forget* that your followers killed my *brother?*

Ho: I knew nothing of it. I had nothing to do with your brother's death. I deplore such excesses as much as you do. . . . I have brought you here to take a position of high importance in our government.

Diem: My brother and his son are only two of the hundreds who have died—and hundreds more who have been betrayed. How can you dare to invite me to work with you?

Ho: Your mind is focused on the past. Think of the future—education, improved standards of living for the people.

Diem: You speak a language without conscience.

Impressed by his captive's audacity, Ho let Diem depart.[21]

The Viet Minh may have expected Diem to be grateful for his reprieve and beat a hasty retreat south, but Diem was nothing if not courageous. He remained in the hostile Tonkinese countryside for months, trying to organize anticommunist guerrilla bases, and even after he returned to Saigon in late 1946 he did not retire from public life. He founded a political party that attempted to pressure the French into setting up a Vietnamese government under dominion status. These efforts, while unsuccessful, earned Diem some public notice, and when in 1949 the French proposed to bring Bao Dai back from exile and install him as leader of a new government in the south, Diem briefly became the chief negotiator between the Fourth Republic and the exiled Vietnamese emperor. Diem tried to get Bao Dai to insist upon a French commitment to independence, but Bao Dai refused to hold out for Diem's terms. Disgusted, Diem went into seclusion at the home of his brother Thuc, by now bishop of Vinh Long diocese in the Mekong Delta.[22]

The forty-nine-year-old Diem had numerous incentives to leave Vietnam in 1950. He had spent many years in the political wilderness, and the chances of his being offered a post in the present regime were slim. He had no organized popular support. The Viet Minh appeared poised to overrun all of Vietnam, making prospects for a conservative Catholic look ominous. Of greatest importance, Ho Chi Minh decided in early 1950 to reverse his previous clemency and sentenced Diem to death in absentia. When Diem asked the French for protection against Viet Minh agents, he was informed that no police were available. Recognizing that if he remained in Vietnam he would be easy prey for the communists, Diem applied for permission to travel to Rome for the Holy Year celebrations at the Vatican. En route, he changed his itinerary, sailing instead for America. This proved an inspired decision.[23]

Following Diem and Thuc's month-long sojourn in the United States, the Ngo brothers flew to France to urge Bao Dai to appoint Diem prime minister. The emperor declined, after which a disconsolate Thuc returned to Vietnam. Diem, however, sensed Bao Dai's increasing dependence on the deep pockets of the United States and decided to try his luck with the State Department again. By the end of 1950, Diem was back in America.[24] This time, he managed to gain an audience with Secretary of State Acheson, who noted that Diem "spoke with much more balance than heretofore."[25]

Possibly recalling the favorable impression Thuc had made months earlier—when Undersecretary Webb opined that the bishop might "be an important figure . . . through the Catholics"—Diem emphasized his own religious affiliation in meetings with State Department officials. Dallas Coors, director of Indochinese affairs, recorded Diem as stating that the "only truly anti-communist group in Indochina was the Catholics. The nature of their religion and the strength of their faith prevented infiltration by other groups." Coors concluded that a "Catholic leadership in government is the only way to assure a national government free of communist influence."[26] Robert Hoey, the officer in charge of Vietnam-Cambodia-Laos affairs, sounded a similar note. Hoey called Diem "the most influential lay Catholic leader in Indochina today" and warned that unless Vietnam's Catholics were "convinced immediately that their ultimate existence as Christians depends upon the support of the anti-communist forces, . . . the forces of communism, already so powerful, may be ultimately successful."[27] These sentiments were echoed by the embassy in Saigon, which assured Acheson that "the Catholics are patriotic, sympathetic to the West, and have higher standards of probity and conduct than those generally prevailing in Vietnam."[28]

Diem did not restrict his politicking to State Department representatives. He met Francis Spellman, the powerful Roman Catholic cardinal and archbishop of New York, soon after arriving in the United States. The cardinal, having studied with Thuc in Rome during the 1930s, was anxious to see Diem, and Diem had little difficulty winning Spellman's confidence. As the cardinal's biographer notes, Diem's "most strongly held positions were readily apparent. He believed in the power of the Catholic Church and he was virulently anti-communist." Spellman offered his kindred spirit lodging at the Maryknoll seminary in Lakewood, New Jersey, and Diem accepted. For nearly three years, Diem lived off and on as Spellman's guest in Lakewood and at another seminary in Ossining, New York.[29]

Diem's agenda from late 1950 to mid-1953 included regular forays to New York City and Washington, D.C., where he was introduced to an array of political activists, clergymen, journalists, academics, and politicians, the majority of whom came away from these encounters ready to back Diem in his campaign for high office in the Bao Dai regime. That Diem could make a favorable impression on so many Americans of different walks of life seems incongruous, given that he lacked the personality that normally attracts a wide circle of devotees. "Unlike Ho Chi Minh," Frances FitzGerald notes, "he had not a grain of humor."[30] An American journalist remarked after interviewing Diem, "He's sort of a screwball, isn't he? His eyes don't even focus."[31] Diem was painfully shy, especially in the presence of women; an otherwise adulatory *Time* magazine article of 1955 observed that he was "so uncomfortable around women" that he "put up a sign outside his office: WOMEN FORBIDDEN."[32] While Diem's demeanor was customarily formal and remote—"utterly without warmth," in the view of one contemporary—he was prone to periodic fits of temper that frightened even members of his own family.[33] Added to these eccentricities were his physical appearance and body language. David Halberstam remembers Diem as "small and strangely young-looking" with "a funny, open-toed duck walk which bordered on a bustle."[34]

These liabilities notwithstanding, Diem had a number of factors working in his favor. His visit to the United States coincided with a red scare that has come to be identified with the Republican right wing but that extended to American liberals and socialists as well. The fact that Diem had never cooperated with the Viet Minh and had even called Ho Chi Minh a criminal to his face established his anticommunist credentials. Furthermore, Diem's standing as an anti-French nationalist seemed equally unimpeachable. He had, after all, resigned from the colonial administration rather than be a puppet, and his absence from Vietnam during the years of fiercest Franco–Viet Minh combat had spared him the dilemma of having to choose sides, whereas those nationalists who stayed and refused to join the Viet Minh were forced to collaborate with their former colonial masters. Diem's advocates could feel confident that, in backing him, they remained true to the frequently conflicting American creeds of anticommunism and anticolonialism.[35]

Perhaps most important, as Joseph Morgan observes, was the fact that Diem's "pleas appealed to a long-held conviction that the United States could do much to shape Asia's future."[36] Unlike other nationalists who sought to establish an alternative to Ho Chi Minh's Leninist vision of an independent Vietnam, Diem bypassed the anticommunist political parties and religious sects in his own country—along with the decolonizing powers of Western Europe—to take his case directly to the United States. The symbolic significance of that gesture was profound. Here was an Asian nationalist whose choice of mentor seemed to confirm what many Americans had long presumed: that it was America's duty to usher the pagan hordes of the East into the sunlit uplands of Christian civilization. In the best study of this chivalric impulse, three scholars of U.S.–East Asian relations trace how "geography and history combined to give Americans a unique urge . . . toward tutorial benevolence in the twentieth century."[37] Senator H. Alexander Smith delivered a passionate defense of such tutorial benevolence when he reported to the Senate on a junket he made to Indochina in November 1953. Smith, whom the Eisenhower administration lauded as an "expert on the Far East,"[38] declared that "final and lasting victory" over Asian communism could be won only "by convincing the minds of men of the eternal values of freedom under the guiding hand of God. . . . May we pray and strive that our United States will be a beacon of light guiding these suffering, groping people of Asia to join the Great Crusade."[39]

Whether or not Diem purposefully played upon popular notions about America's responsibility to shape Asia's future, the results of his campaign were impressive. Aside from one State Department officer who noted that Diem was "out of touch with developments in [his] own country," the former civil servant inspired fierce loyalty in those Americans whose support he solicited.[40] One of the first to commit himself to

Diem was Peter White, a frequent contributor to liberal and conservative Catholic journals. He initially met Diem at the New York office of Senator William Benton, who had permitted White to use the office for a merchandising program. As White recalled, Diem "blew my mind with jolts and blasts of urgent and slanted language regarding [his] cause, . . . which added up to Diem's expectation of being president of South Vietnam."[41] White soon planted articles about Diem in *Jubilee*, an expensive monthly that the historian Patrick Allitt terms the "Catholic version of *Life* magazine."[42] In one piece, White described Diem as "an exceptionally serious Catholic, an ascetic *'grand initié,'*" and attested that "Catholicism . . . has had much greater success in Vietnam than elsewhere in Asia. . . . [M]issionaries found natives who welcomed the Church and who, in subsequent persecutions, proved willing to die for it by the thousands." In the same article, White made derisory remarks about Vietnam's "Buddhists and ancestor-worshippers" and their "pretty conceits about moonbeams and lotus blossoms."[43]

White also introduced Diem to Christopher Emmet, secretary of the American Friends of Captive Nations, at a dinner in Manhattan in 1951. Shortly thereafter, Emmet wrote on Diem's behalf to Christian Herter, a Massachusetts Republican on the House Foreign Affairs Committee. Emmet praised Diem as "one of the greatest of the Indo-Chinese anticommunist leaders" and asked Herter to introduce Diem to other lawmakers like Judd, Edna Kelly, and Mansfield.[44] In the case of Kelly, Herter evidently complied. Livingstone Merchant, the deputy assistant secretary of state for Far Eastern affairs, recorded in his memorandum a frosty exchange with Kelly over the issue of aid to the French forces in Indochina: "The congresswoman has been sold on the idea . . . that the French must get out completely at once. . . . Among other sources of information, Mrs. Kelly has been talking to, and impressed by, Ngo Dinh Diem."[45]

Diem proved adept at befriending American scholars specializing in Asian affairs, particularly Wesley Fishel of Michigan State University (MSU), who hired Diem as a consultant to the school's governmental research bureau in 1951. An exponent of the fashionable "Third Force" theory of development—a postwar school of thought formulated to help U.S. policymakers deal with revolutionary changes in non-Western countries—Fishel found in Diem's mix of nationalism and anticommunism the ideal prescription for former colonies undergoing struggles for independence. The professor believed that American observers tended to misconstrue the war in Vietnam as a conflict solely between French colonialists and the Viet Minh; consequently, in Fishel's view, Vietnamese like Diem who were equally anticolonialist and anticommunist did not receive the encouragement from Washington they merited. Fishel intended to redress this imbalance by convincing policymakers that, as he put it, "the Third Force is the West's last chance in Indochina."[46] Along with befriending Diem and furnishing him with a forum at Michigan State from which to promulgate his vision of an independent, noncommunist Vietnam, Fishel wrote numerous magazine articles in the late 1950s and early 1960s extolling the virtues of Diem's government. In addition, Fishel spearheaded the assistance program MSU provided the Diem regime after its establishment in 1954.[47]

Other academics who forged ties with Diem during his years in the United States were I. Milton Sacks, a political scientist at Brandeis University, and Father Raymond de Jaegher, regent of Seton Hall University's Far East Institute.[48] In the spring of 1951, de Jaegher introduced Diem to William Donovan, former head of the Office of Strategic Services, who would later become one of the most illustrious members of the American Friends of Vietnam, a pro-Diem lobby.[49] Diem also formed a close association with the journalists Sol Sanders and Gouverneur Paulding. Sanders published articles lauding Diem in the *New Leader,* and Paulding, a senior writer at the *Reporter,* informed readers of that magazine that Diem "spoke to us . . . with earnestness and charm . . . [about] his country's need for absolute independence."[50]

Diem did talk a great deal about Vietnamese independence, but he never spelled out for his American supporters what form his ideal independent state would take. On one of the few occasions when an American engaged him in a discussion of political objectives, the results were disturbing. In 1952, Peter White introduced his Vietnamese protégé to Joseph Calderon, a New York attorney who specialized in Italian affairs. Calderon was a follower of Don Luigi Sturzo, the antifascist, anticommunist leader of the Christian Democratic Party in Italy, and he assumed that Diem's principles were similar to those of the progressive Sturzo. The attorney rhapsodized about Sturzo's commitment to social reforms, civil liberties, and representative government, but Diem proved unsympathetic. As White recalled, "Diem was authoritarian and the lecture didn't take."[51]

"Asian Governments Have Seldom Been Benevolent Governments"

Authoritarian was not an unjust term, but like any single-adjective description—indeed, like much of the literature on Diem—it obscured more than it illuminated. One of the great contributions of recent scholarship dealing with the South Vietnamese side of the Vietnam War has been to rescue Diem's politico-religious philosophy of "personalism" from the dismissive treatment accorded it by many journalists and historians. Typical is the judgment of one writer who calls personalism "a confused mélange of papal encyclicals and kindergarten economics."[52] Diem himself admittedly failed to encourage much public understanding of the credo; he never published a formal treatise on it, and his lectures to curious foreign and Vietnamese interviewers were impenetrable. Yet personalism represented a genuine effort on Diem's part to formulate a counterdoctrine to communism that was authentically Vietnamese rather than an imitation of Western models. Philip Catton, one of the most perceptive students of Diem's philosophy, argues that personalism, as first developed in France during the 1930s, sought a "middle way" between the excesses of dog-eat-dog liberal capitalism and dehumanizing fascism/communism. A personalist society would allow people to grow as individuals and enjoy the inalienable rights guaranteed by Western constitutions, while at the same time directing their energies toward securing the well-being of the group. Although the French founders of personalism, fearing the "tyranny of theory," deliberately refrained from drafting any master plan for building a personalist republic, Diem believed he could draw upon their insights to overcome Vietnam's underdevelopment, legacy of colonialism, and susceptibility to Marxist propaganda.[53]

Personalism appealed to Diem for a variety of reasons, among them its origins in the writings of conservative Catholic philosophers like Emmanuel Mounier and its rejection of communism as a cure for the ills of modern industrialized society. Perhaps most important was its compatibility with Confucianism. The Confucian dimension of Diem's thinking is noted in almost every account of his life and career, but only a few scholars have really tried to tease out the implications of Bernard Fall's famous observation that it was an "open question" whether Diem was "basically a Confucianist with a Catholic overlay, or vice versa."[54] Measuring the relative impact of the two doctrines may be impossible, for the environment in which Diem grew to maturity was intensely Confucian as well as Catholic. It could hardly have been otherwise; Confucianism was the moral philosophy the Vietnamese used to regulate their society—"the intellectual and ideological backbone of Vietnam," according to the historian Nguyen Khac Vien.[55] Vietnam's entire social structure embodied Confucian precepts binding subject to ruler, son to father, wife to husband, and so on. Americans would frequently misinterpret Diem's preoccupation with fealty and rank as an expression of his Catholic faith, but it was equally reflective of another doctrinal and institutional source of inspiration. "[H]is view of the world was Confucian," Ellen Hammer writes. "He believed in the immutability of the social and political order, the incarnation of political and moral authority in the ruler, the subordination of rights to duties."[56]

Yet Diem was not the backward-looking mandarin depicted by many writers.[57] Catton argues that he was a "conservative modernizer [who] . . . possessed a sense of historical change that militated against mere revivalism."[58] While Diem revered Vietnam's history and Confucian tradition, he knew that Confucianism needed to be reformed if it was to be made relevant to postwar Asia; therefore, he was selective in terms of which Confucian teachings he emphasized and which he ignored. Indeed, as Edward Miller demonstrates, Diem did not feel bound by the strictures of any single dogma, borrowing ideas from a variety of sources, including Confucianism, Catholicism, European personalism, and others, in fashioning his program to turn Vietnam into a free, prosperous, and unified state.[59] He even regularly employed a term favored by the Viet Minh, *revolution*, to describe the policies he planned to pursue.[60] But he did not advocate abandoning those cultural traits that made Vietnam unique. Rather, he wanted to strike a balance between progress and tradition. "We are not going to go back to a sterile copy of the mandarin past," he informed the journalist Marguerite Higgins. "We are going to adapt the best of our heritage to the modern situation."[61] Diem was convinced that a Vietnamese version of personalism, capitalizing on indigenous ethical principles, could help his nation modernize without falling victim to the evils of either capitalism or collectivism. A personalist Vietnam would acquire Western-style technology and industry, guarantee its citizens' basic material needs, and foster an ethos of mutual obligation among those citizens, who would thus enjoy the economic security and communal involvement of fully realized persons rather than alienated individuals.[62]

If, however, Diem's ideas were more complex and progressive than many scholars acknowledge, he was still undeniably an autocrat. Even had his American supporters understood the subtleties of Diemist personalism, which was unlikely, since the State Department did not undertake a detailed analysis of the philosophy until 1958, they would have found little in it that valued individual liberties or representative government.[63] For Diem, people attained greatest fulfillment not by the exercise of formal political rights, but through performing their prescribed roles within a hierarchy of social relationships. Indeed, Diem considered Western-style freedoms dangerous, for they provided a platform for citizens to criticize their leader, which was subversive of group cohesion. Diem thought one absolute source of authority was necessary if Vietnam was to make the forced-march transition from colonial ignobility to modern independence. There was no place in his personalist regime for such institutions as a free press or an autonomous national legislature. This is not to say he believed in the divine right of kings. Under certain circumstances, a leader could legitimately be removed. As Diem observed years prior to assuming control of South Vietnam, "The state is founded on the people; the mandate of heaven held by the sovereign is revocable if he proves himself unworthy thereof." If, in other words, the leader failed to properly discharge his obligations to the people, he forfeited the right to command; but if he remained morally correct, he could expect complete obedience. "A sacred respect is due to the person of the sovereign," wrote Diem in a pronouncement that probably owed more to Confucianism than Catholicism. "He is the mediator between the people and heaven as he celebrates the national cult."[64]

Diem's autocratic temperament—which he did little to hide—might have been expected to cause greater consternation among his American backers. Cold war liberals like Fishel and Sanders would never have countenanced such an "I-am-the-state" posture by a potential European leader; certainly they would not have risked their reputations to see that person installed in high office. Diem, however, was Vietnamese, a visitor from a part of the world about which Americans knew almost nothing and upon which they projected preconceptions of "the Orient" as unfit for democratic institutions. Harold Isaacs's classic work of social science *Scratches on Our Minds* demonstrates this proclivity. From early 1954 through the middle of the following year, a time frame that maps out almost perfectly onto the Eisenhower administration's debate over whether or not to sponsor Diem, Isaacs conducted 181 interviews with individuals in the "academic world, mass media, government, ex-government, business, groups concerned with public opinion and education, [and] church-missionary groups." Forty-nine of the interviewees had achieved some distinction as "Asia specialists" by the time they spoke with Isaacs, "almost all" considered themselves "informed" and well-read, and only ten failed to graduate from college. Yet when Isaacs asked them to discuss their impressions of China, India, and Asia in general, "it quickly became clear that a variety of unsupported or unsupportable assumptions . . . floated about, even in such relatively schooled and orderly minds." Some of the most interesting responses from Isaacs's subjects had to do with Asia's presumed unpreparedness for democracy. One man expressed revulsion at the Asian predisposition to behave "like slaves. . . . No dynamism, no feeling of energy, a broken-spirited people." Another worried about America having to cope with "so many people detached from the democratic world." The most sanguine assessment of political conditions in Asia came from a "panel of interviewees" who predicted that, with American prodding, "China will evolve away from Russian communism, but it is optimistic to think that it will become a Jeffersonian democracy. . . . [S]omehow they will come through with a better government, nearer to democratic government than we expect." Nonetheless, a panelist cautioned, "I see this evolution as lasting a couple of hundred years."[65]

The attitudes voiced by Isaacs's interviewees were reflected in area studies prepared by the Operations Coordinating Board (OCB), an agency set up by Eisenhower to coordinate departmental execution of national security policies.[66] In 1954, in a special committee report, the OCB declared that "the people of Southeast Asia are accustomed to the rule of the many by the very few. . . . Their principal national political vitality expresses itself as 'anti-colonialism' rather than in a desire for political democracy."[67] A year later, the board reported that for the Vietnamese "the word 'freedom' has no meaning, . . . but 'good government' does."[68] Authorities outside the Eisenhower administration concurred. Senator J. William Fulbright remarked in 1954 that the Vietnamese were "a people who do not understand democracy." "It seems to me that we . . . have often gone overboard in talking about democracy in countries such as this," the Arkansas Democrat observed. "What you need here is a strong leader comparable . . . to [Kemal] Ataturk in Turkey. . . . [Y]ou cannot expect this country to respond to democratic ideas."[69]

Joseph Buttinger, a millionaire philanthropist and America's leading authority on Vietnam in the mid-1950s, pointed out in a mass mailing from the American Friends of Vietnam that "the first tendency one observes in newly independent states in Asia . . . is a strong executive. One may object to such a development on theoretical grounds that it is essentially undemocratic, but in practice it is a logical consequence of the need of Asian governments to assure their continued existence."[70] Mortimer Graves, president of the American Council of Learned Societies, noted in 1954 that "backward Asian societies" required "a particular form of organization" that was "ruthless, fierce . . . and a throwback to earlier and outmoded patterns of social and political organization. . . . The anarchic form of democracy which happens to suit us does not help them one bit."[71] Diem's American supporters could thus feel confident that the Vietnamese would not object to living under a personalist autocracy.

Congress offered up a graphic example of such Orientalia when Representatives Judd, Marguerite Church, Ross Adair, and Clement Zablocki reported to the House Foreign Affairs Committee on their 1953 "Special Study Mission to Southeast Asia and the Pacific." The report concluded with the assertion that "in the Orient, the idea of a 'loyal opposition' is neither understood nor respected. To be in the opposition is generally regarded not as evidence of political courage but as evidence of weakness. . . . Historically, Asian governments have seldom been benevolent governments, and . . . it is doubtful that they ever will [be]—certainly not in the foreseeable future." Besides, the lawmakers reasoned, "democratic practice as we understand it requires a high sense of public responsibility and the acceptance of values different from those that are the heritage of the Asian nations. . . . To the illiterate masses, the operation of democratic machinery represents confusion."[72] The arguments in this report would be recycled frequently in coming years by Diem's American defenders, among whom Judd and Zablocki assumed places of prominence.

"The Fact that We Were All Catholics Was Just Coincidental"

Diem was gratified by the support of people like Judd, Zablocki, White, and Fishel, but none of these individuals exercised sufficient control over American foreign policy to make him the prime candidate for leadership of a U.S.-backed Vietnamese republic. Not until Diem's final months in America did he make contact with the advocates who would prove most influential in enlisting the support of the Eisenhower administration. The first was Supreme Court Justice William O. Douglas, best known for writing the majority opinion in *Zorach v. Clauson* (1952), in which he stated, "We are a religious people whose institutions presuppose a Supreme Being."[73] Douglas heard of Diem while traveling through Asia in the summer of 1952. Upon his return to the United States, he asked Diem to proofread the sections about Vietnam in *North from Malaya,* an account of the justice's reconnaissance of the Far Eastern front lines of the cold war. When the book was published in 1953, Douglas informed his readers that Diem was "a hero in Central and North Vietnam, with a considerable following in the South, too. . . . Diem is revered by the Vietnamese because he is honest and independent."[74] Unlike some of Diem's early supporters, Douglas never minimized the role he played in bringing the former seminarian to power. Five years after Diem's murder, with America reeling from the effects of the Tet Offensive, Douglas admitted in a letter to a friend, "I think perhaps if there is any one individual who is more responsible than any other, it was myself, and that was by way of introduction of [Diem] to Washington, D.C., and the book I wrote."[75] Of course, Douglas did not introduce Diem to Washington. Diem had numerous contacts with American officials and politicians before he met Douglas. But Douglas did orchestrate the first meeting between Diem and the man who would become known as "Diem's godfather," Senator Mike Mansfield, Democrat from Montana.

Nicknamed "China Mike," Mansfield was Congress's foremost authority on Asia, having been a professor of Far Eastern history before his election to the House of Representatives in 1942. The war in the Pacific generated a demand for individuals with Mansfield's academic background, and he acquired a seat on the House Foreign Affairs Committee despite his lack of seniority. In 1944, President Franklin Roosevelt sent him on a fact-finding trip to India, Burma, and China. Although FDR subsequently showed little interest in Mansfield's report, and despite the fact that Mansfield's criticism of Chiang Kai-shek left him vulnerable to attacks from McCarthyites after the Chinese communists won their civil war, the Montanan gained notoriety from this

2. Senator Mike Mansfield, Democrat of Montana. © CORBIS, ca. 1960s

junketing. A biographer notes that Mansfield's report "established him as a Far Eastern expert in the eyes of the public, the press, his peers, and even American servicemen in the Far East."[76]

While Mansfield enjoyed the limelight, he was candid enough to admit in 1949, "I do not know too much about the Indochina situation. I do not think that anyone does."[77] His history courses had concentrated on Japan and China; nations like Vietnam, Laos, Cambodia, Burma, and the Philippines received scant attention. Professor Mansfield's voluminous lecture notes contain only a page and a half of material on Indochina.[78] Furthermore, his greater familiarity with the big powers of Asia did not preclude Mansfield from referring to the Japanese as "these small, myopic, buck-toothed sons of Nippon" or declaring that "the Chinese smile and mean it; the Japanese smile and do not mean it. The Chinese are reasonable; the Japanese fanatical."[79] An intelligent and moral man, the senator was also a man of his time, when sweeping generalizations about Asian peoples characterized even erudite discourse.[80]

Given the role Mansfield would play in promoting American sponsorship of Diem, his first meeting with the future South Vietnamese leader, at a luncheon hosted by Douglas at the Supreme Court Building on 7 May 1953, may have been one of the most fateful encounters of the postwar era. Also present at Douglas's luncheon were Senator John F. Kennedy, Cardinal Spellman, Gene Gregory of the State Department, and Representative Zablocki, soon to become chairman of the House Foreign Affairs Committee. When asked years later about the apparent religious homogeneity of the gathering, Mansfield insisted, "It wasn't a question of religion—the fact that we were all Catholics was just coincidental."[81]

The senator was doubtless sincere in that assertion. By the standards of the day, Mansfield was not a religious bigot; in fact, he was considered one of the most broad-minded men in Washington. The same, however, could be said for Douglas, who nevertheless followed up his tribute to Diem in *North from Malaya* with a denunciation of the Buddhist church of Vietnam as "remote from the people and the country. . . . It is a passive institution. It teaches very little social or community responsibility. It concerns itself mostly with devotions which women especially practice."[82] This was a dubious assessment: most members of the Viet Minh, after all, were Buddhist, and they could hardly be judged passive or remote from the people and the country. Moreover, any nation that manages to win wars against France, the United States, and the People's Republic of China is not likely to have a church whose impact upon the citizenry is to induce detachment and docility. Although Douglas would have denied it, his book betrayed considerable ethnocentrism toward Buddhism.

This animus may have been reinforced by the trial of the accused traitor John Provoo, which concluded less than a month before Douglas's luncheon at the Supreme Court Building. Provoo had been captured in 1942 by the Japanese when the Allied fortress at Corregidor surrendered, and he remained a prisoner of war until Japan's defeat in 1945. The prosecution in Provoo's trial contended that the former seaman had been an accomplice in the maltreatment of American prisoners in the camp where he was incarcerated. One of the most damaging strikes against Provoo was the widely held but unsubstantiated notion that he was a Buddhist. Naoko Shibusawa documents how "throughout the nearly four-month trial, the press made much of [Provoo's] espousal of Buddhism . . . and did so in ways that questioned his masculinity." Thus the *New York Times* returned repeatedly to the theme of Provoo "delicately slip[ping] out of his khakis into the robes of a Buddhist priest." The *Times* referred to Provoo as the "fan-bearing 'Buddhist priest' from Sausalito, California, . . . with almost effeminate features." Correspondents at the trial reported that Provoo helped other prisoners by doing their laundry, cried when subjected to criticism, and was "touchy" on the subject of his unmarried status. Over the objections of Provoo's lawyers, the judge permitted the jury to hear evidence of Provoo's homosexuality, which prosecutors tried to connect to the defendant's religious beliefs. The conviction of Provoo for treason, and the judge's statement upon passing sentence that Provoo "suffered with certain aberrations which, to say the least, constitute a real . . . deviation from the normal," served to reinforce some of the dominant phobias of America in the 1950s: against gays, certainly, and against allegedly non-Western religions as well.[83]

Whether Mansfield followed the Provoo trial cannot be determined. Certainly, he never drew the knee-jerk association between Buddhism and cowardice that some of Diem's supporters did. Yet Mansfield's correspondence hints at the primacy of religion in fortifying his allegiance to the future South Vietnamese president. Shortly before Diem assumed office, Mansfield received a letter from Augustine Nguyen-Thai, a Catholic Vietnamese graduate student at Cornell. Nguyen-Thai expressed himself "desirous of sharing my views on the situation in my country," and enclosed a copy of an article he had written for the Catholic journal *The Shield*. Titled "Colonialism, Communism, or Catholicism?," the piece was a tribute to Diem, whom Nguyen-Thai described as "a nationalist leader whose integrity is beyond suspicion." Nguyen-Thai claimed that the Catholics were the one group in Vietnam with "a definite philosophy to oppose the materialistic doctrine of communism," and he noted that his fellow "Vietnamese admit, some openly and some implicitly, that Catholicism is Vietnam's only firm opponent to communism." While conceding that Catholics constituted "a minority of less than eight percent of the population," Nguyen-Thai was confident they would play a leading role in "reconstructing their country on a basis of Christian love and justice" because they could count on support from abroad:

Certainly, the notion of international cooperation will not be strange to the Catholics of this country, for they already have a sense of membership in a universal Church. It is essential, therefore, that they be able to feel that they are supported in their Christian crusade by their brother Catholics in other nations. If Catholics of the world are true to the revolutionary implications of their Faith, and offer the exploited and neglected people of Vietnam what has been denied them in the past, a great part of the effectiveness of communism will be lost.[84]

Mansfield agreed to meet personally with Nguyen-Thai, a rare courtesy, and assured him, "I have read the enclosure you sent me with great interest and am in full accord with the views expressed therein."[85]

Nguyen-Thai's interpretation of conditions in his homeland could stand virtually unchallenged in the United States. There were no authorities on Vietnam at the State Department. No courses on Vietnamese culture or history were offered at any American university. No published works on Vietnam in English were in print.[86] The most influential American accounts of Vietnam were Virginia Thompson's *French Indochina* and Thomas Ennis's *French Policy and Developments in Indochina*, both published in the late 1930s.[87] These works were almost twenty years out of date—a virtual millennium given the revolutionary upheavals that had taken place in Southeast Asia since World War II. Moreover, the image of Vietnam promulgated by Ennis and especially Thompson was patently racist, characterized by familiar American presumptions of Asians' laziness, unassertiveness, and political immaturity. Thompson's readers learned that the Vietnamese, or "Annamites," as she called them, "accept the principle of authority . . . so completely that they never even question, or try to mitigate, the most cruel of legal penalties." Perhaps this was due to the "Annamite nervous system," which Thompson found "certainly less sensitive than that of Occidentals." In any event, she concluded that "subservience is only too congenial to the Annamite soul." While Thompson admired Vietnamese Catholics, she noted that "Catholicism runs counter to the social and political fabric of Annamite society. . . . Altruism is conspicuously absent from Oriental psychology, and the Annamite mentality is not propitious for the propagation of Christianity." Far more "congenial" to the Vietnamese "character" were "the tolerance and benign resignation of Buddhism." In fact, Thompson blamed "a strong Buddhistic strain" for the "conspicuous absence of epic virility" in Vietnamese literature, but judged Buddhism as at least preferable to Cao Daism, which, Thompson ventured, "might be communism masking as a religion."[88] Ennis, whose books on Vietnam were required reading for American diplomats in the Far East, was likewise apprehensive about the Cao Dai faith, calling it an "anti-white cult," and similarly contemptuous of Vietnamese unindustriousness. "[T]he Annamite," Ennis noted, "is not inclined to work with regularity."[89]

The memorandum issuing from Douglas's Supreme Court Building luncheon attests to the dearth of reliable information about Vietnam in America in the mid-1950s. When Diem informed the gathering that Ho Chi Minh was "no longer free to make decisions," having handed the reins of foreign policy over to Mao Tse-tung, no one thought to point out how improbable this was, given the centuries of mutual enmity between Vietnam and China. "The trouble in Vietnam," Diem declared, was that "there was no rallying point between the communists and the French." He believed that he could be that rallying point. An independent Vietnam under his leadership, he insisted, "will satisfy the Vietnamese population that they have something to fight for." After fielding a few friendly questions from Douglas and Kennedy, the only two Americans present who had visited Vietnam, Diem announced his intention to leave the United States for France, where he expected to "find understanding among some French groups who had begun to be puzzled and resentful of France's failure in Indochina."[90]

Diem did leave for France in late May 1953, but his lobbying efforts there were unsuccessful. Members of the Vietnamese community in Paris later told the CIA operative Chester Cooper that Diem made "a very bad impression," that he was "obscure" and "murky" and that his ideas were "obsolete." One Vietnamese intellectual found Diem "stupid." Nguyen Nhoc Bich, a prominent anticommunist nationalist whose father was one of the founders of the Cao Dai religion, walked out of a meeting with Diem and refused to associate with him further.[91] Clearly, Diem's American audience would prove more profitable to him than any sympathizers in Europe or in Vietnam itself.

"Capitalize on the Religious Issue"

While Diem campaigned on both sides of the Atlantic, the conflict in his homeland ground on with no end in sight. Despite receiving more than twice the sum it had been given in U.S. aid under the Marshall Plan, France enjoyed little success against the Viet Minh. By late 1953, Ho Chi Minh's forces dominated over two-thirds of Vietnam. Saint-Cyr, the French military academy, was not graduating officers fast enough to replace the ones killed in Vietnam. Public enthusiasm for *la guerre sale* had waned, and the government of Premier Joseph Laniel began to contemplate the possibility of a negotiated peace.[92]

To secure the best possible cease-fire terms, the French general staff sought to maneuver Ho's army into a set-piece battle. General Henri-Eugene Navarre, commander of French forces in Indochina, was confident that greater French firepower would then prove decisive. Mansfield, who made his first visit to Indochina in the fall of 1953, concurred with this assessment, reporting to his colleagues that the French were "doing a very good job." Mansfield described Navarre as "brilliant" and assured the Senate that the newly adopted "Navarre Plan"—which involved staking out "mooring points" like the valley of Dien Bien Phu to draw Ho's guerrillas into conventional assaults—would "change the psychology of the . . . French Union forces . . . from a defensive-minded to an offensive-minded one." Provided the communist Chinese did not intervene, Mansfield believed that French victory was likely "within two years."[93]

Rarely has a forecast been so speedily refuted. Less than four months after the senator delivered his report, Dien Bien Phu fell to the Viet Minh, and America was confronted with the prospect of a communist victory throughout Indochina.[94] Mansfield admitted fourteen years later that when he embarked on his junket to Indochina in 1953 he was so unfamiliar with the region that he had to check a map "to be certain of the capital cities."[95] This did not augur well for his capacity to predict events in an area that was exotic and inscrutable even to well-traveled cold warriors like Eisenhower and John Foster Dulles. Nonetheless, Mansfield retained his reputation as Congress's Indochina specialist. No other prominent American was better informed.

Eisenhower's refusal to risk a unilateral, armed rescue of the French outpost at Dien Bien Phu has been deservedly praised by historians.[96] Unlike his successors in the White House, the president proved sufficiently knowledgeable about military conditions in Southeast Asia to refrain from taking an action that would have resulted in American troops fighting Vietnamese communists ten years before that became their fate. But several intergovernmental documents produced during the Dien Bien Phu crisis and in the months following the garrison's surrender partially illuminate why Eisenhower's restraint was fleeting. As David Anderson notes, the Eisenhower administration's most crucial Vietnam decisions were made after the fall of Dien Bien Phu.[97] For all his circumspection when it came to committing U.S. forces to a land war in Asia, Eisenhower had no intention of allowing Ho Chi Minh to seize all of Vietnam. He understood, moreover, that Dien Bien Phu had shaken France's resolve to continue in its role of principal Western combatant in Indochina and that prominent anticommunist Vietnamese, recognizing they could no longer rely on the French, would seek closer ties with the United States. The question of who among these Vietnamese would lead the opposition to the Viet Minh was now an issue for the Eisenhower administration to decide, and the manner in which it did so testifies to the impact of religious preconceptions upon policy making.

In a National Security Council (NSC) meeting on 4 February 1954, over three months before the red flag was hoisted over Dien Bien Phu, CIA Director Allen Dulles complained that "there was no dynamism in the leadership of the Franco-Vietnamese forces." Eisenhower "interrupted" to "inquire if it would be possible to capitalize on the religious issue." Given that "most of the people of Vietnam were Buddhists," the president wondered whether the United States might "find a good Buddhist leader to whip up some real fervor." The source of the next remark is unnamed, but he clearly voiced a shared sentiment. According to the minutes, "It was pointed out to the president that, unhappily, Buddha was a pacifist rather than a fighter." This led to laughter. Vice President Richard Nixon then "expressed some doubt as to the strength and conviction with which the people of Vietnam clung to their religious views." Eisenhower replied that "he still believed that there was something in the idea of a religious motivation." While conceding that Emperor Bao Dai was an unlikely guiding star for religious passions, Eisenhower "pointed out how Joan of Arc had managed to defeat a large enemy force and place a timid king upon his throne in France." Picking up on the Joan of Arc theme, Secretary of State Dulles remarked that "there were, of course, a million and a half Roman Catholics in Vietnam, and they included some of the best brains of the country." Eisenhower "suggested that the Catholics be enlisted."[98]

These remarks might be dismissed as an example of the president thinking out loud. Robert Bowie, head of the State Department's policy planning staff, insists that Eisenhower often put forward quirky proposals just to see what response they elicited.[99] Yet the theme of cultivating a religious leader for South Vietnam arose again. Twelve days after the 4 February NSC meeting, during an executive session of the Senate Foreign Relations Committee, Undersecretary of State Walter Bedell Smith responded to Senator Fulbright's protest that Bao Dai "is not any good" by assuring the Democrat from Arkansas that a change in command in Vietnam had been considered. "I do not want to go into great detail," Bedell Smith remarked, but volunteered that the administration was thinking of "providing a certain religious leadership or religious cause . . . to fight for."[100] The undersecretary was probably alluding to Diem.

Still more compelling was a study prepared by government tacticians who apparently took heed of the president's injunction to "capitalize on the religious issue." On 13 April 1955, the Operations Coordinating Board, an organization the historian James Arnold calls Eisenhower's "principal source of information" on Southeast Asia in the second half of the 1950s, submitted "Recommendations Concerning Study of Religious Factors in International Strategy."[101] The OCB began with the proposition that "the religious beliefs and usages of any given people afford the surest key to their psychology, culture, and historical conduct." After a brief assessment of "communism as a religion," the major premise of the document was set forth:

[T]he conduct of men, especially in moments of crisis, is very largely determined by what they believe. In other words, human conduct consists of choices which are consciously or unconsciously governed by judgments of value. . . . [I]f we can discover what men really believe, and how firmly they believe it, their behavior under given circumstances will become in some degree predictable. The importance of such knowledge in the preparation of any world-wide strategic plan, and even in the day-to-day conduct of diplomacy, hardly needs to be labored.

There will be hazards in any such venture, the OCB cautioned. In the exigencies of the moment, someone professing certain religious beliefs may engage in behavior irreconcilable with those beliefs. To illustrate this point, the OCB seized upon an obvious example: "It is often assumed that nearly all Italians are Catholics; but if this were strictly true, it would be impossible to explain the present power and prestige of the

Communist Party [in Italy]." The OCB reconciled the Italian Catholic–communist paradox—and the "analogous situation" in France—by postulating that while "a great majority of . . . people is Catholic by both tradition and psychology[,] . . . great numbers . . . who are counted as Catholics have long ceased to be such either in practice or ideological affirmation." What was required, then, for evidence of genuine Catholicism, and of its concomitant, anticommunism, was practice and ideological affirmation. Although neither Diem nor any other American ally was identified by name in the report, the South Vietnamese premier's celibacy, Spartan lifestyle, and repeated declarations of loyalty to the Catholic Church conformed nicely to the OCB's stipulations.

According to the board, such godliness was rare in "the East," where "religion . . . has never been a great positive factor. . . . Taoism and even Buddhism are regarded as philosophies rather than theological systems. . . . In recent decades, however, missionaries have reported an increasing responsiveness to Christianity." The board was more sanguine about the chances of the United States in "enlisting the cooperation and support" of Christians (and especially Catholics) in nations already under communist domination than it was about U.S. efforts to recruit Buddhists, Taoists, and Confucians in countries still ostensibly part of the free world. "Virtually all witnesses have testified to the profoundly religious character of the Russian people," the board reported. "Russia, in short, affords another illustration of the principle that religion thrives upon persecution." The Buddhist monks who self-immolated in the streets of Saigon in 1963 to protest Diem's rule would have concurred with that principle.

The board's concluding recommendation—"that an organization to undertake the study be formed around a nucleus of five to eight chaplains, assisted by a small technical and clerical staff, including translators"—was so depthless as to confirm the unrealizability of the enterprise.[102] Although Eisenhower's fondness for psychological warfare has been well documented, there is no evidence that this project was ever operationalized.[103] But as Barbara Tuchman observes with regard to another policy paper on Indochina moldering in the archives, "The fate of this document, whether discussed, rejected, or adopted . . . does not matter, for the fact that it could be formulated at all reflects the thinking —or what passes for thinking by government—that . . . laid the path for future American intervention in Vietnam."[104]

The OCB generated another document that passed for thinking when its Committee on Buddhism met in the summer of 1956. Composed of representatives from the State Department, the CIA, and the U.S. Information Agency, the committee was charged with studying the "effectiveness of Buddhist organizations" in several Southeast Asian countries so as to discover "ways and means to ensure that the influence of Buddhist monks and lay leaders is exerted in favor of U.S. interests."[105] The OCB's staff representative on the committee, Kenneth Landon, furnished committee members with a list of fifteen subtopics around which to organize their research, including such questions as, "What knowledge does the Buddhist clergy and lay organizations have of the dangers of communism and its potential threat to them?"[106] Kenneth Young, director of the State Department's Division of Philippine and Southeast Asian Affairs and a key player in rescuing Diem's premiership in the spring of 1955, warned the board that Buddhism might not be "a suitable channel for U.S. influence." "Many of the priests of this religion," Young noted, "are essentially reactionary and their tenets are strongly inclined against the kind of competitive enterprise we favor and towards neutralist pacifism. These factors present obstacles to U.S. efforts to utilize contacts with the Buddhist clergy for political purposes."[107]

Despite several months of study, the OCB's final report did little more than recapitulate Young's views. Indeed, "Outline Plan Regarding Buddhist Organizations in Ceylon, Burma, Thailand, Laos, [and] Cambodia" was, for all practical purposes, a forty-three-page tally sheet of the era's Buddhist-bashing, with the board variously affirming: "A few Buddhist monks are well-known communists or fellow travelers, and for some years have been actively promoting communist causes"; "Buddhism, in Cambodia and elsewhere, is essentially quietist and generally pacifist, . . . decidedly anti-Western"; "[T]he intellectual preparation of most monks for instruction on the danger of communism is seriously deficient"; "Devotees of Christianity, Islam, and Hinduism believe in gods to whom they pray, whereas Buddhism does not teach belief in God but in 'man's own efforts to attain perfection'; thus Buddhism is a philosophy and not a religion, which relieves it of the Marxist stigma of being an opiate of the people and makes it appear compatible with communism."[108]

Vietnam's Cao Dai and Hoa Hao religious groups received similar treatment at the hands of administration officials. Robert McClintock, U.S. ambassador to Cambodia and future member of the State Department's policy planning staff, dismissed the Cao Dai pope as a "charlatan . . . with no convictions . . . who is lured by the will-of-the-wisp of neutralism."[109] A 1955 State Department working paper found "considerable Viet Minh collaboration with the Hoa Hao and penetration of the Cao Dai." "Because of the . . . unsystematic structure" of the groups, the paper asserted, "they are heavily penetrated by the V[iet] M[inh]. . . . The V[iet] M[inh] are generally able to manipulate them without interference."[110] By contrast, the department's Bureau of Intelligence and Research noted, "Vietnamese Catholic leaders, although bound only by their common religious faith, exercise a major political influence in Vietnam. Their tendency is strongly nationalistic . . . and anticommunist."[111]

The views expressed by the OCB and other government authorities give some indication why, when on 10 May 1954 analysts at the State Department's Division of Philippine and Southeast Asian Affairs produced a list of sixteen Vietnamese politicians whom they considered reliably anticommunist, Ngo Dinh Diem—who had held no political office for over two decades and who had not participated in the struggle to rid his homeland of colonial oppression—headed the list. The analysts described Diem as "[t]he most prominent Catholic leader in Vietnam, perhaps the most popular personality in the country after Ho Chi Minh." They added, "Probably has Vatican support." At least six of the sixteen candidates for South Vietnamese leadership were Catholics, a high number given that Catholics made up only about 10 percent of the population of Vietnam.[112]

"A Vietnamese Version of Joan of Arc"

As Diem's name was bandied about in Washington as the free world's answer to Ho Chi Minh, the man himself was living in Paris—"in extremely tenuous circumstances," according to Michel Wintrebert of the French High Commissariat. Wintrebert informed Randolph Kidder, U.S. embassy chargé in Saigon, that Diem had "no more than three shirts to his name" and was "supported by friends."[113] A little over a month after this report was filed, Diem was the new prime minister of South Vietnam, having been granted "full civil and military powers" by Bao Dai—more authority than the emperor had ever delegated to any of his premiers.[114] Details of how Diem made his ascent remain shrouded by a snail-like declassification process. Yet it is unduly equivocal to argue, as several historians have, that the absence of a "smoking gun" connecting the Eisenhower administration to Diem's appointment means that the issue of America's contribution to this fateful selection must remain unresolved.[115] In fact, Diem would never have been named premier had he not been Washington's candidate, and the available documentary record makes this plain.

Given Diem's Francophobia, it is inconceivable that the impetus for his premiership could have originated in Paris. As Donald Heath, U.S. ambassador in Saigon, observed after his first meeting with Diem, "The man charged with forming the new government of Vietnam is at an almost insane pitch of hatred against the French."[116] French prime minister Pierre Mendès-France opposed Diem's installation, informing U.S. Ambassador Douglas Dillon that "he expected to have considerable difficulty with the new Vietnamese government." Diem was "a fanatic much like Syngman Rhee," Mendès-France declared. He considered Emperor Bao Dai's decision to appoint Diem "most unfortunate."[117] Defeated on the battlefield in Indochina, France nonetheless nourished hopes of retaining influence in its former colonies. This was the impetus behind the posting in 1954 of Jean Sainteny to Hanoi as official French representative. Sainteny had negotiated French recognition of Ho Chi Minh's government in 1946, and his mission after the Franco–Viet Minh War, as he recalls, was "to act as a continuer and not a liquidator of French interests in the northern zone."[118] Diem, on the other hand, made no secret of his desire to act as a liquidator of French interests in the southern zone. No French politician concerned with sustaining the Fourth Republic's status as a great power could have viewed Diem's appointment with anything other than horror. Furthermore, while it is true that Bao Dai—and not the Americans—officially bestowed the title of premier on Diem, this gesture did not signify Vietnamese initiative. Bao Dai had long disliked Diem intensely; a report from Ambassador Heath sent as early as January 1951 referred to the emperor's "extreme antipathy" toward Diem.[119] As Bao Dai recalls in his memoirs, Diem had a "difficult temperament" and "messianic tendencies." Yet he possessed one virtue that, in Bao Dai's judgment, compensated for his many defects. "He had known some Americans who admired his intransigence," Bao Dai notes. "In their eyes, he was especially suited for this particular juncture; also, Washington would not spare him its support."[120]

The first mention of Diem's potential appointment in diplomatic discussions occurred on 16 May 1954, when Bao Dai boasted to the U.S. delegation at the Geneva Conference on Korea and Indochina that he had "received a message from Ngo Dinh Diem, a leading Catholic lay figure . . . offering to return to Vietnam."[121] Two days later, Ngo Dinh Luyen, Diem's brother, told two American diplomats at Geneva, Undersecretary Bedell Smith and Philip Bonsal of the State Department's office of Philippine and Southeast Asian Affairs, of Bao Dai's intention to name Diem premier if the United States supported his decision. Smith and Bonsal responded noncommittally. Luyen pressed the issue, confiding that "if Bao Dai were in fact free to choose, he would now call Ngo Dinh Diem to power. However, . . . the French would oppose this." Smith and Bonsal reported to the State Department that Bao Dai was "obviously trying to find out whether the U.S. is disposed to replace France in Indochina." They declined to give Luyen any such assurance but recommended that "direct contact with Ngo Dinh Diem be established. . . . Bao Dai . . . might well play the Ngo Dinh Diem card if he could be sure we would support him; otherwise not."[122]

Luyen was more direct the following day when he informed Bonsal that Bao Dai was "most anxious to . . . bring in Ngo Dinh Diem as prime minister." If France "should decide to abandon the struggle" in the event of a Diem premiership, Luyen asked, "would the U.S. intervene directly?" Again, Bonsal dodged the issue, claiming he did not want to jeopardize the negotiations at Geneva.[123] Luyen confronted Bonsal once more on 20 May. "Bao Dai has almost decided to change his government," Luyen reported. "However, he would only do so with U.S. support." Bonsal promised to pass Luyen's message along to his superiors.[124] Walter Robertson, assistant secretary of state for Far Eastern affairs, felt that the U.S. delegation was being too irresolute and "strongly recommended" that Washington give the go-ahead to Bao Dai, "regardless of what course France might take."[125] Secretary of State Dulles agreed with Robertson. "[W]e have given much thought to Bao Dai's offer," Dulles cabled Geneva two days after Luyen's final meeting with Bonsal. "I believe this offer should be discreetly exploited."[126]

Dulles's role in securing Diem's appointment is difficult to determine, but it was certainly important and possibly decisive. Records indicate that Dulles first heard of Diem in early January 1953, less than a month before becoming secretary of state. Senator James Duff of Pennsylvania wrote to Dulles at his Wall Street office to inform him that "Ngo Dinh Diem, former minister of the interior of the imperial cabinet under the present emperor of Indo-China, is anxious to have the privilege of a short talk with you . . . respecting the situation in Indo-China as he perceives it." Duff further advised Dulles that "the Reverend Thomas A. O'Melia, . . . who is requesting this audience for Diem, . . . evidently is a man of standing in the Roman Catholic Church."[127] Preoccupied with supervising the transfer of his effects from New York to Washington, Dulles did not have time to meet Diem; as he related to Duff, "I arranged for him to speak to a member of my personal staff."[128]

Inauspicious though this beginning was, sometime between Eisenhower's inauguration as president and the Geneva Conference in 1954, Dulles became committed to Diem and went to bat for him as energetically as he ever did for an American ally. Dulles's aide John Hanes recalled in 1966,

> The secretary was very impressed by Diem. The secretary was almost alone in this. The French were saying that nobody could do anything there, and particularly not this little upstart Diem. And they were attempting to cut him to pieces, . . . you know, they were all being cynical and saying, "Well, he'll last a few months, but he hasn't got the guts to do it, or the ability." The secretary said, "This guy, I think, has the guts to do it . . . and we're going to back him." And he rammed this one through single-handedly. . . . [W]e did back him, and he survived. And he surprised almost everybody—except the secretary, who always thought that he would.[129]

Bao Dai later claimed that he told Dulles of his intention to appoint Diem before broaching the subject with Diem himself.[130] The publicly available memorandum of Dulles's meeting with Bao Dai in Paris reveals no discussion of Diem, but there may have been other contacts between the secretary and the emperor through clandestine channels.[131] (CIA records for the period remain classified.) Chester Cooper, a CIA officer in the 1950s, lends credibility to Bao Dai's version of events, detailing a meeting between Dulles and Bao Dai that dealt with the role Diem would play in preserving an anticommunist citadel in Vietnam. Cooper speculates that Diem's "devout Catholicism may well have appealed to Secretary Dulles's strong Calvinist character."[132] Whether or not Dulles took the lead in stumping for Diem, it is difficult to dispute the conclusion set forth in a military cable of early June 1954 that "Diem has received support and encouragement from many American official quarters, and this is the reason why Bao Dai is considering him for the post."[133]

3. Secretary of State John Foster Dulles (left) and President Dwight D. Eisenhower
confer. © AP/WORLDWIDE PHOTOS, 12 September 1954

Diem's induction as prime minister was suitably theatrical. According to one account, Bao Dai produced a crucifix and had Diem swear
before his God to defend Vietnam against the communists. Empress
Nam Phuong, like Diem a Catholic, knelt with the new premier and
begged him to save the dynasty for her son.[134] Bao Dai then forced Diem
and the Americans to wait for over a month before announcing the
change in command. While the emperor dawdled, rumors were rampant in Vietnam, Washington, and Geneva. "This may be all unjustified
speculation," U.S. Ambassador David Cameron cabled the State Department from Hanoi. "However, we were told ... that Bao Dai had charged
Ngo Dinh Diem with an important but unspecified mission."[135] Robert
McClintock, American ambassador to Cambodia, likewise reported that
he had been "informed by several usually reliable sources [that] Ngo
Dinh Diem[,] Vietnamese Catholic lay leader presently residing in
France[, is] expected [to] return [to] Vietnam in [the] near future to ...
possibly consider participation in [a] government."[136] Douglas Dillon,
U.S. ambassador to France, heard a different story: "We have [the]
impression that in actual fact it may be Ngo Dinh Diem who is being let

down—in customary Oriental fashion without loss of face—by Bao Dai. . . . Diem is naïve enough not to realize he is being done in."[137]

One of the most striking observations to come out of this liminal period in Vietnamese politics was made by the Catholic bishop of Phat Diem Province, who requested an audience with Ambassador Heath. The bishop advised Heath that Diem had "no popular appeal" and was "temperamentally unfitted to head a government in these trying times." He was "too narrow and too intolerant, and . . . would govern only with his small band of followers."[138] This warning from a prominent Vietnamese Catholic perhaps ought to have been given some consideration in Washington, yet there is no record of a response to Heath's cable. A similarly dire prediction by Dac Khe, deputy chief of the South Vietnamese delegation at Geneva, also went unheeded. Khe cautioned Undersecretary Bedell Smith that Diem was a "mystic of an age that had passed" who "did not believe in popular assembly" and "would not be good in rallying the peasants."[139] Washington received another ominous report about Diem in the days before he assumed office. Describing his first encounter with the premier-designate, Ambassador Dillon cabled from Paris that "much of what Diem said was vague, rambling, and even unintelligible." While the ambassador was inclined to chalk this up to "excitement at the prospect of new responsibilities," he further observed,

> Diem impresses one as a mystic who has just emerged from a religious retreat into the cold world, which is, in fact, almost what he has done. He appears too unworldly and unsophisticated to cope with the grave problems . . . we find in Saigon. . . . On balance, we were favorably impressed, but only in the realization that we are prepared to accept the seemingly ridiculous prospect that this yogi-like mystic could assume the charge he is apparently about to undertake only because the standard set by his predecessors is so low.[140]

Bao Dai finally made his long-awaited pronouncement on 17 June 1954, declaring, "I have charged Ngo Dinh Diem with forming a government, . . . an almost symbolic task which consists in galvanizing, binding, and merging the national energies. He accepts this role. It is up to the country to respond by a vast movement of unanimous adhesion."[141] The country did nothing of the sort. Ambassador McClintock, visiting Saigon at the time, reported that "Bao Dai's action in requesting Ngo Dinh Diem [to] form [a] government has totally failed [to] arouse

[the] enthusiasm [of the] Vietnamese people so essential if [the] war effort [is] to get [the] necessary support. . . . Even though Diem is [a] prominent Catholic, he does not (repeat not) have any great degree [of] support even in [the] Catholic community." McClintock found that those Vietnamese whom he questioned about Diem's appointment "worried . . . that he is too proud, that he is not (repeat not) known to [the] vast majority of [the] people, and that he has been too long out of direct contact with conditions in Vietnam."[142]

Diem meanwhile began preparing to return to his homeland for the first time in four years. Stanley Karnow, who interviewed Diem in Paris, recalls that he "sounded like a Vietnamese version of Joan of Arc, forecasting that the national army he planned to mobilize 'will inspire the people to flock to us.'"[143] Joan herself would have been confounded by the problems Diem's country faced. A State Department intelligence report noted that the "trends toward governmental disintegration, political anarchy, and military impotence show no sign of being checked." South Vietnam was in ruins. Most bridges had been demolished. Canals, roads, railways, and telephone services were in disrepair. Vast regions of rice land lay uncultivated. The cities were clogged with refugees. Nearly one-quarter of South Vietnamese troops had deserted. As for what remained of the Vietnamese National Army (VNA), the State Department's experts did not mince words: "[The] VNA lacks everything which makes [a] modern army: leadership, morale, training, and combat experience. . . . [C]ombat readiness is practically zero. . . . This presages [a] major disaster."[144]

Bao Dai wrote a check for a million piasters to pay for "spontaneous" demonstrations of support for Diem when he arrived at the Saigon airport, but only about five hundred Vietnamese, mostly Catholics, greeted the new premier.[145] They cannot have been heartened by what they saw. Diem stepped off his plane, paused to glance at the acres of barbed wire the French had strung to protect their aircraft from guerrilla raids, and walked briskly through the crowd without acknowledging the presence of onlookers.[146] He then ducked into the back of a limousine and sped off. None of the South Vietnamese who had gathered along the route from the airport to the Presidential Palace could catch a glimpse of their leader. Colonel Edward Lansdale, the CIA station chief in South Vietnam, remembers "people looking at one another in disappointment. 'Was that *him?*' 'Did you see *him?*' 'He didn't even see *us!*' . . . The 'let down' feeling was something tangible, obvious."[147] Diem's reception was hardly the sort given a returning hero. Denis Warner recalls watching apprehensively as "this squat, strangely youthful-looking figure" rode into Saigon. Warner remarked to a Vietnamese friend, "He seems too much like a priest to drag Vietnam out of this mess." "Not a priest," the Vietnamese replied. "A priest at least learns of the world through the confessional. Diem is a monk living behind stone walls. He knows nothing."[148]

Warner's friend might have added that Diem's ignorance of Vietnamese political realities was exceeded by that of his superpower sponsor. Therein lay the tragedy of what came to be called America's Diem experiment. Had the Eisenhower administration been able to imagine democracy in Asia, had they conceived of the Vietnamese as rational actors capable of choosing their own administrators, this man would never have been in a position to put his notions of government into practice. Diem had no indigenous political base; as Washington knew, even South Vietnam's Catholics were unenthusiastic about their new chief executive. Without U.S. support, Diem would have been hard-pressed to win a province-level election, let alone the premiership. His Catholicism, anticommunism, and friendship with men like Spellman and Mansfield were tremendous political assets in the United States, but they were irrelevant to the vast majority of Vietnamese, those predominantly Buddhist villagers who lived their entire lives within the confines of their hamlets and were less concerned with the abstractions of international geopolitics than with rebuilding their country after eight years of war. Washington's decision to impose Diem upon a people who would not have chosen him as their leader ensured that Vietnam would endure yet another war, longer and more terrible than the first, before the task of reconstruction could begin.

2

"Our System

Demands the

Supreme Being":

America's Third

Great Awakening

Less than a year after the United States inaugurated the atomic age by obliterating Hiroshima, and before the term *cold war* entered the world's political lexicon, General Douglas MacArthur likened America's growing competition with the Soviet Union to the ordeal of Jesus at Gethsemane. MacArthur, head of the U.S. occupation government in Japan, forecast an American victory over the communists because, as he put it, "Christ, even though crucified, nevertheless prevailed."[1] When the USSR exploded an atomic bomb in 1949, the evangelist Billy Graham warned his fellow Americans that communism was "against God, against Christ, against the Bible. . . . [It] is inspired, directed, and motivated by the Devil himself, who has declared war against Almighty God."[2] In the spring of 1954, after the Eighty-third Congress voted to add the words "under God" to the Pledge of Allegiance, Representative Louis Rabaut justified the amendment by declaring, "You may argue from dawn to dusk about differing political, social, and economic systems, but the fundamental issue which is the unbridgeable gap between America and communist Russia is a belief in Almighty God."[3] For the soldier, the preacher, and the politician—as well as for millions of other Americans at midcentury—the conflict with international communism was in essence a holy war.

Such convictions were not unique to the period. Americans have traditionally conceived of their national mission in religious terms. John Winthrop told the band of Puritans he led to New England in 1630 that "the God of Israel is among us. . . . The Lord will make our name a

4. The evangelist Billy Graham preaches to forty thousand persons at the Polo Grounds in New York City. © AP/ WORLDWIDE PHOTOS, 27 October 1957

praise and glory."[4] Abraham Lincoln claimed to "recognize the hand of God" in the Civil War.[5] Both Woodrow Wilson and Franklin Roosevelt asked for God's help in their war messages to Congress.[6] Rarely, however, has the identification of America's cause with God's been made more explicit than during the Eisenhower years. America in the 1950s was, in one historian's phrase, "God's Country," an avowedly Christian superpower engaged in a global contest with an adversary whose chief distinguishing feature was its atheism.[7]

The United States that Ngo Dinh Diem visited from 1950 to 1954 and again in 1957 experienced a remarkable surge of religious interest inextricably bound up with the anxieties and imperatives of the cold war. This religious revival, as much as anything, explains the Eisenhower administration's decision to back Diem as America's vice-regent in Southeast Asia. A Catholic in an overwhelmingly Buddhist country, Diem appeared uniquely qualified to comprehend and implement Secretary of State John Foster Dulles's dictum that "you can no more make a 'deal' with communism to limit itself to certain areas than you can make a 'deal' with Christianity to limit itself to certain areas."[8] Diem, a contemporary noted, saw himself as "directly and personally aided by God, with a mission to fulfill that was inspired by God himself."[9] Such an ideological perspective was neither unfamiliar nor unwelcome to those Americans crafting policy for Vietnam.

"One Nation, Under God"

Had Diem come to the United States in the period between the two World Wars—a span of time labeled "The American Religious Depression" by Robert Handy—he would not have been so warmly received. His solemn devoutness would have been out of place in a nation where churches had difficulty filling their pulpits and poison-penned critics of organized religion like H. L. Mencken and Sinclair Lewis caricatured evangelists, missionaries, and ministers as simpletons and snake oil salesmen. In 1928, the Foreign Missionary Conference of North America reported that only 252 students had applied for foreign missionary work, as compared to 2,700 eight years earlier.[10] A group of New York intellectuals issued a "Humanist Manifesto" in 1933, calling for national repudiation of "religious doctrines and methods which have lost their significance and which are powerless to solve the problem of human living in the twentieth century."[11] One opinion study showed that although 78 percent of the views about traditional Christianity published in 1905 were favorable and only 22 percent were unfavorable, by 1930 the ratio had almost completely reversed, with 67 percent of the opinions published unfavorable.[12]

U.S. involvement in World War II sparked a resurgence of institutional religion, but millions had turned to the churches during World War I as well, only to turn away when the crisis ended. Many members of the American cognoscenti expected a similar decline in religion's fortunes after the defeat of the Axis. Such did not prove to be the case. On the contrary, Americans in the 1950s joined churches in increasing numbers, contributed record amounts to the support of organized religion, and publicly identified themselves with the major religions of their country to an unprecedented degree. *Time* magazine observed in April 1954 that whereas "[t]wenty-five years ago, traditional Christianity seemed to many an American to be rolling up the scroll[,] . . . [t]oday in the U.S. the Christian faith is back in the center of things."[13] Signs of what William O'Neill terms "the religious boom" were so omnipresent that Jacques Maritain, the French neo-Thomist theologian, predicted during a visit to the United States in 1956 that "if a new Christian civilization, a new Christendom, is ever to come about in human history, it is on American soil that it will find its starting point."[14]

"Religiousness," of course, is a slippery concept, but if statistics mean anything, the 1950s were the most "religious" decade of the twentieth century. Whereas previous periods of revivalism had usually affected only lower- and middle-class Protestants, in the 1950s all faiths and classes were influenced: Protestants, Catholics, and Jews, rich and poor, old and young, blacks and whites, suburbanites and city dwellers.[15] Church membership rose twice as fast as the general population.[16] The percentage of Americans officially enrolled in a church or synagogue leaped from 49 percent in 1940 to 55 percent in 1950 to a record 69 percent in 1959.[17] An even larger percentage of Americans identified themselves as church members, 73 percent answering "yes" to the national survey question, "Do you happen at the present time to be an active member of a church or a religious group?"[18] A whopping 99 percent of Americans interviewed by an opinion research firm in 1952 claimed to believe in God.[19]

The reasons for this upsweep in at least the outward manifestations of religious enthusiasm are far from clear. President Eisenhower's pastor, the Reverend Edward Elson, opined that it was a consequence of "the fruits of material progress"—paid vacations, the eight-hour day, and time-saving appliances—which "have provided the leisure, the energy, and the means for a level of human and spiritual values never before reached."[20] Less blithesome analysts cited the arms race and the increasingly soulless jobs that bureaucrats were obliged to perform in "lonely crowd" corporations.[21] Another possible determinant was the desire to belong on the part of suburbanites in an age of economic, social, and geographical mobility. Membership in a church, the sociologist Will Herberg contended, satisfied the need for community, security, and stability.[22] The theologian Reinhold Niebuhr ascribed America's "marked increase of interest in religion" to the fact that "the secular alternatives to historic faiths"—Marxism, fascism, laissez-faire capitalism, and "liberal visions of human perfectibility"—"have been refuted by history." World war, holocaust, atomic destruction, and the division of the globe into two armed camps had, in Niebuhr's view, convinced millions of Americans that "[t]he old symbol of the climax of history consisting of the engagement between Christ and anti-Christ [is] strangely more relevant to our experience than all progressive, secular interpretations."[23] Etiological disputes notwithstanding, the 1950s, especially after the election of Dwight Eisenhower as president in 1952, seemed a high point for the place of religion in the United States.

Religious kitsch saturated American culture. In 1955, millions of Americans listened to a tune entitled "The Man Upstairs," which featured the lyrics:

Have you talked to THE MAN UPSTAIRS?
'Cause he wants to hear from you!
Have you talked to THE MAN UPSTAIRS?
He will always see you through! . . .
Just turn your eyes t'ward heaven,
And say a simple pray'r,
Through clouds of lace you'll see His face
No matter when or where![24]

Other popular songs included "I Believe," "It's No Secret What God Can Do," "I Got Religion," and "Big Fellow in the Sky." In 1954, the Ideal Toy Company responded to what it termed "the resurgence of religious feeling and practice in America today" by marketing a doll with flexible knees that could be made to "kneel in a praying position."[25] Americans seeking religious inspiration in convenient one-minute doses could call Dial-A-Prayer, a venture begun in New York in 1955 that soon spread to every major city in the country. "It caught on like Davy Crockett," Newsweek observed.[26] Dial-A-Prayer's founder predicted that "one day, it will be as much a habit to dial for prayer as to dial for the time."[27]

Such a forecast seemed plausible in a decade in which newspaper syndicates competed for the work of clerical columnists, the best modernist architects vied to design churches and synagogues, and the Jehovah's Witnesses packed more people into Yankee Stadium than Babe Ruth ever did. "Columns could be filled with instances, bizarre or impressive, of this much-publicized 'turn to religion,'" the theologian Paul Hutchinson wrote in 1955. "Once you begin to enumerate them, there seems to be no end."[28] Drive-in churches, modeled after the success of drive-in movies, appeared in the early 1950s.[29] Massive billboards dotted the American landscape urging people to "bring your whole family to church."[30] Many of America's most successful athletes credited their sporting triumphs to the power of prayer. After his team won the National League football championship in 1951, the halfback Gerry Coody revealed, "I was injured and sick. I asked God to strengthen me, and he lifted me up." Heavyweight boxing champion Joe Walcott claimed to read the Bible in training camp and pray between rounds.[31] During a visit to the United States in 1953, the British scholar D. W. Brogan discovered printed forms of "grace" on tablecloths in the dining cars of the New Haven Railroad and informed his European audience that this "is only one sign among many of the degree to which religion is being pushed . . . to the American people."[32]

Nowhere was America's celebration of religion more evident than in the movie industry. Films with religious themes did big business, especially biblical epics like *The Robe, David and Bathsheba,* and *Quo Vadis.* The first CinemaScope extravaganza, Cecil B. DeMille's *The Ten Commandments,* broke box office records in 1956.[33] Tellingly, DeMille urged audiences to view his film as more than a lavish recounting of the story of the Hebrew Exodus. In a personal onscreen prologue, DeMille explained that the "theme" of the movie was "whether men should be ruled by God's law, or by the whims of a dictator like Ramses. Are men the property of the state, or are they free souls under God? This same struggle is still going on today."[34] The United Artists film *Red Planet Mars* (1952) dispensed with analogy and had God side with the United States against the Soviet Union. That movie depicted Russian peasants hearing the voice of God over Voice of America radio and following the Lord's injunction to tear the portraits of Stalin from their walls, reopen their churches, and abolish the Politburo. The film ended with the NATO alliance paying tribute to "a nation finding its soul."[35] Celebrity conversions were widely reported, as if to confirm that the religious reawakening made itself felt even in vice-laden Hollywood. *Modern Screen* magazine ran a series entitled "How the Stars Found Faith," in which Jane Russell proclaimed, "I love God, and when you get to know Him, you find He's a Livin' Doll."[36] Stars who had no need to find faith, having never lost it, touted religion's role in their success. "In show business I'm known as a 'single' act," Eddie Cantor declared in the pages of *Reader's Digest.* "That's not true. I was never alone; my partner was prayer—every step of the way."[37]

Religiosity proved equally adaptable to the small screen, as television shows paused not only for station breaks but also for moments of meditation. A Dallas station went so far as to begin its coverage of a bathing beauty contest with a five-minute prayer.[38] Every Friday afternoon, "Buffalo Bob" exhorted children watching "The Howdy Doody Show" to "worship at the church or synagogue of your choice." The evangelists Billy Graham and Oral Roberts had popular weekly television programs, and the most widely viewed show on television during the mid-1950s was Bishop Fulton Sheen's "Life Is Worth Living," which controlled the Tuesday night prime-time airwaves. From 1952 to 1957, Sheen aired opposite Milton Berle's "Texaco Comedy Hour," regularly drawing a larger audience than the previously invincible Uncle Miltie.[39] Berle took his ratings defeat in good stride; he affectionately referred to Sheen as "Uncle Fultie" and wisecracked, "Heck, we both work for the same boss—Sky Chief."[40]

Books with religious themes were immensely popular. Sales of the Bible reached an all-time record in the 1950s, aided by the publication in 1952 of the Revised Standard Edition, which sold over 26.5 million copies its first year.[41] Nearly half the texts on the nonfiction best-seller list were religious books, among them the Reverend Norman Vincent Peale's *The Power of Positive Thinking,* which sat atop the list for 112 consecutive weeks.[42] Fulton Oursler's fictionalized life of Christ, *The Greatest Story Ever Told,* went through forty-eight printings, and Henry Link's *Return to Religion* went through forty-seven.[43] Bishop Sheen's *Life Is Worth Living,* a collection of transcripts from his TV program dedicated "to our Heavenly Mother who stands behind me at every telecast," was another best-seller.[44] Bookstores even offered such curiosities as *Pray Your Weight Away* and *The Power of Prayer on Plants.*[45]

Virtually every mainstream American magazine, including *Popular Mechanics, Popular Science,* and *Mademoiselle,* ran articles on religion in the 1950s.[46] The two most influential magazine publishers of the decade, DeWitt Wallace and Henry Luce, were children of Protestant ministers, and both saw to it that Sheen, Peale, and other religious figures received favorable publicity in their publications.[47] Luce in particular regularly featured revivalists and theologians in cover stories for *Time, Life,* and *Fortune.* Moreover, he championed America's religious revival as essential to winning the cold war. "Christianity itself is the living and revolutionary force which alone can halt communism," he declared in one editorial. "Enough faith *can* move even the Soviet mountain."[48] Luce believed that America was capable of mustering such a critical mass of religious zeal. "America's faith was never more secure," he noted. "The challenge of communism has deepened and strengthened our churches."[49] *Life* triumphantly proclaimed in its Christmas issue for 1955, "As the Christian era moved toward its 1,956th year, the sights and sounds of an unprecedented revival in religious belief and practice were everywhere in the U.S. Religion was commanding the attention and energies of men as it had not since the days of the country's first devout settlers."[50]

Eisenhower vigorously encouraged the nationwide turn toward religion. According to the Republican National Committee, Eisenhower believed that, as chief executive, he was obliged to serve "not only as the political leader, but as the spiritual leader of our times."[51] Although never much of a churchgoer before he became president, Eisenhower made a show of joining the National Presbyterian Church and attending it often. He became the first president ever to be baptized in the White House.[52] The lead float in his inaugural parade in 1953 was named "God's Float" and consisted of a churchlike building bearing enlarged photographs of scenes of devotion surrounded by mottoes in Gothic script that read "In God We Trust" and "Freedom of Worship."[53] Eisenhower opened his inaugural address with a prayer—the only modern president to do so—and spent the remainder of the speech describing the cold war in starkly religious terms. "We sense with all our faculties that forces of good and evil are massed and armed and opposed as rarely before in history," he declared. He called upon Americans to "give testimony in the sight of the world to our faith" and warned that "the enemies of this faith know no god but force." The struggle with international communism, Eisenhower proclaimed, "is no argument between slightly differing philosophies. This conflict strikes directly at the faith of our fathers. . . . Freedom is pitted against slavery; lightness against the dark."[54]

Throughout his eight years as president, Eisenhower made hundreds of pronouncements on the importance of religion. Sometimes these affirmations verged on the fatuous, most notoriously when Eisenhower declared, "Our government makes no sense unless it is founded upon a deeply felt religious faith, and I don't care what it is."[55] The president defined his terms more carefully—and more militantly—when he told the National Conference of Christians and Jews, "The churches of America are citadels of our faith in individual freedom and human dignity.

5. Billy Graham (right) meets President Eisenhower during one of his many visits to the White House. © AP/WORLDWIDE PHOTOS, 10 May 1957

This faith is the living source of all our spiritual strength. And this strength is our matchless armor in our world-wide struggle against the forces of godless tyranny and oppression."[56] Perhaps the most extreme statement of Eisenhower's religious conception of American identity occurred during a televised address in 1955. "Without God, there could be no American form of government, nor an American way of life," Eisenhower asserted. "Recognition of a Supreme Being is the first, the most basic, expression of Americanism."[57] To judge from the president's speeches, religious faith was not only the bedrock of American life; it was also the indispensable weapon in America's cold war arsenal.

Eisenhower's legacy as spiritual leader went beyond rhetoric. On Flag Day in 1954 he signed legislation that added the words "under God" to the Pledge of Allegiance. A year later, he approved a law adding the phrase "In God We Trust" to American coins and currency. In 1956, as his first term drew to a close, he endorsed a congressional resolution making "In God We Trust" the national motto, replacing "e pluribus unum." He lobbied for and obtained passage of a bill authorizing construction of a prayer room for congressmen near the capitol rotunda.

He began the tradition of prayer breakfasts at the White House and regularly began cabinet meetings by asking for divine assistance. He even considered advocating an amendment to the Constitution that stated, "This nation devoutly recognizes the authority and law of Jesus Christ, Savior and Ruler of Nations, through whom are bestowed the blessings of Almighty God."[58] "What President Eisenhower wants for America," *Reader's Digest* noted, "is a revival of religious faith that will produce a rededication to religious values and conduct. . . . He is determined to use his influence and his office to help make this period a spiritual turning point in America, and thereby to recover the strengths, the values, and the conduct which a vital faith produces in a people."[59]

Some feared that America under Eisenhower was verging on a "Father Knows Best" theocracy. The agnostic Elinor Smith indicted the nation for perverting "our great American concept of the freedom of religion—which I do *not* interpret as meaning 'freedom of religion for everyone but agnostics. You can have any you like, but you gotta pick one.'" Smith contrasted the reputedly "wild and unthinking" America of her youth with the "not-roaring fifties": "Wild [the 1920s] may have been, but there was far more freedom of thought then than we have today. No one questioned agnostics or free thinkers, or used the word 'godless' as a word synonymous with 'evil.' . . . I expect the same courtesy and consideration for my convictions that I give to others. And in 1956 I don't get it."[60]

Smith was attempting to swim up a waterfall. An indication of how completely religiosity permeated American society was the cover story of the same issue of *Harper's* in which Smith launched her broadside. In a piece entitled "Overdue Changes in Our Foreign Policy," George Kennan, the "father of containment," pleaded with Eisenhower for a relaxation of cold war tensions, insisting that while Soviet "objectives have not changed" in the three years since Joseph Stalin's death, there was nonetheless cause for optimism in the Kremlin's adoption of different "means." "[W]ho are we to exalt the ends above the means?" Kennan asked. "As a nation bred in the Christian tradition, we should understand something of the importance of method. . . . This is the task of learning, and of helping others to learn, how man can live in fruitful harmony with the natural environment God gave him to live in."[61] Kennan's appeal to a shared religious ethos—so out of character for this apostle of hardheaded realism—was symptomatic of American popular

6. The Jehovah's Witnesses fill Yankee Stadium for their first international assembly. © Bettmann/ CORBIS, 30 July 1950

culture at the time. When the Reverend George Docherty pronounced in 1954 that "an atheistic American is a contradiction in terms," he did so without fear of Menckenian riposte.[62]

The president took Docherty's truism further. "Our system demands the Supreme Being," Eisenhower insisted in an address to the Daughters of the American Revolution. "There can be no question about the American system being the translation into the political world of a deeply felt religious faith."[63] Eisenhower spoke so often in this vein that when Life published a double year-end issue in December 1955 and chose as its sole subject Christianity, Luce was able to introduce the magazine with words taken from seven of the president's major speeches. Alongside a picture of Eisenhower "praying on the historic battlefield of Gettysburg" ran the excerpt, "Application of Christianity to everyday affairs is the only practical hope of the world. . . . Either man is the creature whom the Psalmists described as 'a little lower than the angels,' or man is a soulless animated machine."[64]

It is tempting to dismiss Eisenhower's rhetoric as Tartuffian, a tool wielded by a politician to mask his true intentions. The president did nothing to counter that interpretation when he delivered an address in

1954 instructing the nation to celebrate Independence Day with "penance and prayer" and then spent his own Fourth of July fishing and playing golf.[65] Michael Hunt, however, makes the compelling argument that

> public rhetoric is not simply a screen, tool, or ornament. It is also, perhaps even primarily, a form of communication, rich in symbols and mythology and closely constrained by certain rules. To be effective, public rhetoric must draw on values and concerns widely shared and easily understood by its audience. A rhetoric that ignores or eschews the language of common discourse on the central problems of the day closes itself off as a matter of course from any sizable audience, limiting its own influence.[66]

Eisenhower repeatedly emphasized the religiosity of the American people because this theme had tremendous explanatory power for the audience he was addressing. Appeals to religion helped reduce complicated problems to manageable proportions and marshal support for government policies. Although Eisenhower himself cannot be characterized as a devout man, his rhetoric is indicative of the climate of opinion during his administration, and the president—a shrewd politician, as even his detractors concede—knew how to exploit prevailing attitudes.

"The High Priest of the Cold War"

If Eisenhower's piety was more strategic than sincere, his chief cabinet officer indulged in no such duplicity. Secretary of State John Foster Dulles was the most unapologetically religious man to superintend America's foreign policy since Woodrow Wilson. Indeed, as Samuel Flagg Bemis observes, "Dulles was the only religious leader, lay or clerical, ever to become secretary of state."[67] Virtually every text dealing with Dulles makes the argument that any understanding of the man and his policies demands consideration of his religious convictions and missionary zeal to extend Christian principles across the globe. Even Townsend Hoopes, the author of an unflattering biography of Dulles, admits that "[t]here is no reason whatsoever to doubt the passionate sincerity" of the secretary's faith; rather, Hoopes argues, that was the weakness in Dulles's diplomacy: his "unshakable convictions of a religious and theological order" that brooked no compromise even at the cost of nuclear annihilation.[68]

Dulles's tendency to interpret international tensions in religious terms frequently exasperated America's allies. Foreign Secretary Anthony Eden of Great Britain dismissed Dulles as "a preacher in the world of politics," and Eden's boss, Prime Minister Winston Churchill, complained that the secretary "preaches like a Methodist Minister, and his bloody text is always the same."[69] India's Jawaharlal Nehru diplomatically told a New York press corps, "I like and respect the American secretary of state, but I must admit that it is difficult to talk to him without God getting in the way."[70] Domestic critics like the standup comedian Mort Sahl and the political cartoonist Herbert Block lampooned Dulles's Bible thumping, but it was no public relations ploy. Roscoe Drummond concludes that Dulles's "political thinking could no more be separated from his religion than a lighted bulb from its electric current. . . . When he related his understanding of God-created man and moral law to policy, he was being his authentic self."[71] Dulles met and corresponded frequently with prominent American churchmen throughout his tenure as secretary of state, and he regularly asked their advice on matters of foreign policy.[72] "No one in the State Department," he once boasted, "knows as much about the Bible as I do."[73]

Unlike Eisenhower, Dulles did not assume the mantle of religiosity only after the Republicans seized the White House. Son of a Presbyterian minister, the future secretary of state grew up in a religious environment, affectionately recalled in a sermon he gave at his father's church in 1953. "To me, this church is richer in memories than any other earthly spot," Dulles reminisced. "Our family life revolved around this church. . . . At times the church services seemed over-long and over-frequent. But through them I was taught of the two great commandments: love of God and love of fellow man."[74] By all accounts, he was a willing pupil. His mother recorded in her diary on his fifth birthday, "Foster . . . is reverential to a striking degree. Whenever he sees his father or mother in an attitude of prayer, he will instantly assume the same attitude."[75] Dulles was a diligent reader of the Bible throughout his childhood and adolescence. His family expected him to enter the ministry. When he elected instead to pursue a career in law, he softened the blow by assuring his parents that he intended to be a "Christian lawyer." As his biographer Ronald Pruessen notes, "in some respects that is what he became."[76]

The key event in Dulles's religious and political maturation occurred in 1937, when, as a successful Wall Street attorney and adviser to the

Republican presidential hopeful Thomas Dewey, he was persuaded to attend a World Conference on Church, Community, and State at Oxford. As Dulles recalled a decade later, "That conference led me to conclude that there was no solution to the great international problems which perplex the world except by bringing to bear upon those problems the force of Christianity. . . . Everything that has happened since then confirms the soundness of that conclusion."[77] Convinced of the inadequacy of traditional balance-of-power diplomacy, Dulles became a tireless advocate for a geopolitics based on faith. His traveling, writing, and speaking on behalf of the Federal Council of Churches consumed a great part of his time, as he kept four or five dozen speaking engagements a year and wrote articles for such prestigious journals as *Foreign Affairs* and the *Department of State Bulletin*.[78] As Mark Toulouse documents, the future secretary of state's aim during the years 1937–45 was to create a successor organization to the League of Nations, a "reformation of the machinery of international relations" that accorded with "Christian principles."[79] Dulles envisioned a new world order in which loyalty to a transcendent God and his moral law would not be eclipsed by loyalties to any state authority. The deification of the state could be checked, Dulles argued, "by some form of spiritual revival which will alter and broaden the concept of what is worthy of devotion and sacrifice."[80]

Appointed chairman of the Federal Council of Churches' Commission on a Just and Durable Peace in 1940, Dulles at first attempted to limit American involvement in the ongoing world war to moral suasion. Once the United States was engaged, he repeatedly insisted that military victory would not be enough: national sovereignty must be made obsolete, and humanity must "recognize the spiritual supremacy of God rather than the state."[81] "I come to you as a layman who, after nearly thirty-five years of international experience, has become convinced that the most practical need of the world today is the spirit of Christ," Dulles told an audience on the eve of Pearl Harbor. "The great trouble with the world today is that there are too few Christians."[82] Richard Goold-Adams notes that while Dulles's motivations for chairing the commission were beyond reproach, "it is an undoubted fact that as a result of this work he did become much more widely known" and "a prominent candidate for high political office."[83] By 1945, Dulles was a recognized authority on foreign affairs, providing counsel to the Truman administration, which courted bipartisan support for its foreign policy.

The scriptural allusions that characterized Dulles's wartime speeches and writings continued to punctuate his postwar geopolitical analyses. His commitment to the universality and interdependence of humankind, however, did not survive the growing tension between the United States and the Soviet Union. Whereas in his "Oxford days" Dulles claimed that national interest motivated Soviet leadership in the foreign arena, by the late 1940s he came to believe that Soviet policy was rooted in the precepts of a secular religion. His book *War or Peace* (1950) asserted, "Soviet communism starts with an atheistic godless premise. Everything else flows from that premise." Dulles contended that the traits he attributed to the men in the Kremlin—insincerity, immorality, brutality—derived from their atheism. Wherever the "simple and elementary religious beliefs" of the West "are widely rejected," he reasoned, "there is both spiritual and social disorder. This fact is illustrated by fascism and communism. These are, in the main, atheistic and antireligious creeds. Communists believe that there is neither God nor moral law. . . . They are free of the moral restraints and compulsions which prevail in a religious society." Westerners and especially Americans "have such high moral standards that they voluntarily refrain from using bad methods to get what they want." Unfortunately, Dulles added, "atheists can hardly be expected to conform to an ideal so high."[84]

In Dulles's view, the only hope of defeating an "evil, repugnant faith" like communism lay in "react[ing] with a faith of our own, a faith that will endure and project us into the world as a great force for righteousness." "If history teaches anything," he declared, "it is that no nation is strong unless its people are imbued with a faith. . . . The impact of the dynamic upon the static . . . will always destroy what it attacks."[85] Dulles frequently used the term *dynamic* when describing the faith he believed America needed to combat the Soviets.[86] Christianity as promoted by Dulles was a hard, muscular creed that placed far greater emphasis on strength and self-denial than on tenderness and forgiveness. "Christians are not negative, supine people," he pronounced in one address.[87] "Religion does not become more popular as it becomes softer and easier," he observed in another.[88] He lectured the general assembly of the National Council of Churches that "dynamism can find proper expression only in moral and spiritual terms, . . . not [in] self-indulgence" and exhorted the readers of *Presbyterian Life* to "have those qualities of self-control, self-restraint, and self-sacrifice . . . necessary to make America's moral force felt."[89]

Dulles believed that the decisive "battle between Christianity and communism" would be fought "in Asia, where the signposts bear Stalin's words: 'The Road to Victory in the West.'"[90] "Asia is the origin of the belief that all men are the creation and concern of a universal God," he reminded the Foreign Policy Association. "There should be no cleavage between the Western and Asian nations."[91] Yet such cleavage did exist. Mainland China had fallen to the forces of atheism, all of Southeast Asia was menaced, and the prospect of the Pacific Ocean becoming a "communist lake" loomed.[92] To prevent such a catastrophe, Dulles argued, America needed to "return to our days of greatness . . . when there was among our people a Christian sense of duty to God and our fellow man." Dulles considered a particular moment of "greatness" especially pertinent to the challenge America faced in the East:

> Among my material possessions, that which I prize most highly is a Japanese colored print which hangs in my library in New York. It portrays my grandfather, John W. Foster, who was a great Christian statesman, negotiating the treaty of Shimonoseki between China and Japan. This print shows him standing at the table with the Chinese delegates . . . and laying down the law to them. . . . [H]e partook of the great . . . qualities of righteousness and justice that all men everywhere were reaching out for, and we were able to supply it because we were a Christian nation.

That neither China nor Japan was a Christian nation at the time Dulles's grandfather laid down the law to them did not matter; "all men everywhere," regardless of religion or cultural background, "were reaching out for" the "qualities" that "great Christian states[men]" possessed. Americans needed to resuscitate those qualities, Dulles contended, and channel them into foreign policy. "Those of us who have the advantage of being Christians," he wrote, "are in a unique position to understand the moral law, to see its relevancy, and to give leadership to the peoples of the world."[93]

This was the man who, in the opinion of most of his contemporaries, crafted America's foreign policy for five of Eisenhower's eight years in office. Soviet premier Nikita Khrushchev went so far as to call the president Dulles's "water boy," and Churchill once remarked that Eisenhower was a "ventriloquist's doll" for his secretary of state.[94] The historiographical revolution termed Eisenhower revisionism has debunked this impression, demonstrating that Eisenhower, far from being in thrall to Dulles, was an astute leader who moved purposefully to achieve his objectives and was not above pushing associates into the line of fire to preserve the image of a "caretaker president."[95] Some revisionists have asserted that Dulles was little more than a point man whom Eisenhower used to palliate the far right while the president "ran the show."[96] This is an instance of the revisionist pendulum swinging too far, replacing Eisenhower the slumbering monarch with Eisenhower the midwestern Machiavelli and thereby denying Dulles proper recognition for the role he played.

Arthur Schlesinger Jr., who has aptly dubbed Dulles "the high priest of the Cold War," strikes the appropriate balance when he concludes that Eisenhower "was the dominant figure in his administration whenever he wanted to be—and he wanted to be more often than it seemed at the time."[97] Certainly, Dulles never enjoyed the freedom to go over the "brink" he so often spoke of approaching without the president's approval. Yet Eisenhower allowed Dulles considerable leeway at several junctures when, for various reasons, he chose not to be the dominant figure. For example, Eisenhower permitted Dulles to shepherd West Germany into NATO in 1954, a diplomatic endeavor fraught with pitfalls that the secretary navigated expertly.[98] More significantly, Eisenhower gave Dulles free rein with regard to America's Vietnam policy during the spring of 1955, the period when the United States made its commitment to the Diem regime.

Given the low estate of Dulles's reputation in the waning years of the cold war—according to a survey of diplomatic historians from 1987, "Dulles ranks among the five worst secretaries of state in America's history"—it is jarring to note how laudatory the American press and public were in their treatment of the man during his lifetime. In 1953, only 4 percent of Americans polled on their "attitudes toward the secretary of state" registered a negative response.[99] When Eisenhower proclaimed in a press conference in 1957 that Dulles was "the greatest secretary of state of the modern era," his judgment was not challenged by any of the assembled journalists.[100] Even in 1965, with the American troop buildup in Vietnam well under way, Henry Luce felt no compulsion to qualify his publishing empire's passionate endorsement of Dulles's conduct of foreign policy a decade earlier. "Dulles has been accused a great deal of being too much the moralist, so forth and so on," Luce observed. "The answer to that is whether either a man's or a country's profoundest convictions have anything to do with politics. If they don't,

7. John Foster Dulles (right) and his son, the future Cardinal
Avery Dulles. © Bettmann/CORBIS, 1 June 1956

why then, it's a very cynical world, and I would say the hell with it."[101]
Luce, like most Americans in the 1950s, shared Dulles's presumption
that Soviet godlessness was as menacing as Soviet H-bombs. As Dulles
pronounced shortly after assuming control of the State Department,
"The terrible things that are happening in some parts of the world are
due to the fact that political and social practices have been separated
from spiritual content. Such conditions repel us. But it is important to
understand what causes these conditions. It is irreligion."[102]

"*Prima Facie* Evidence of Loyalty"

In a deeply religious period, one religion in particular enjoyed an efflo-
rescence in the United States. Thomas McAvoy observes that "the life of
American Catholicism in the years after the war was that of a loosely
formed giant awakening from a sleep, each part of which had grown to
tremendous size and power."[103] America's Catholic population doubled
between 1940 and 1960.[104] During the 1950s, the Catholic share of the

country's population increased from 19 to 23 percent.[105] These demographic changes are probably attributable to the same factors customarily cited in explaining the postwar baby boom: people married younger, high wages enabled more men to serve as sole breadwinners for their families, more women left the labor market to concentrate on raising children, and average family size skyrocketed. Add traditional Catholic injunctions against divorce, abortion, and birth control to this already family-friendly mixture, and it is hardly surprising that Catholic children made up a disproportionate share of the enormous Eisenhower-era birth cohort.[106]

Although Catholics composed by far the largest single community of faith in America in the fifties, their influence was not reducible to numbers. Much of the spectacular economic growth of the decade was concentrated in cities like New York, Philadelphia, Chicago, Detroit, and Pittsburgh—longtime Catholic bastions. By contrast, predominantly Protestant strongholds in the South and Southwest trailed behind the rest of the nation.[107] Postwar upward mobility among Catholics was conspicuous in the medical and legal professions and in big business. A government-sponsored study entitled "Religion and Class Structure" reported in 1953 that "Catholicism has many more middle-class members than popular generalizations have assumed."[108] This economic wherewithal translated into a refurbished and expanded Church infrastructure. Between 1945 and 1965, the number of bishops and archbishops increased by 58 percent, clergy by 52 percent, women religious by 30 percent, and seminarians by 127 percent. One hundred twenty-three new Catholic hospitals, 3,005 new Catholic elementary and high schools, and 94 new Catholic colleges were built. Enrollment in Catholic elementary and secondary schools increased by 3.1 million—more than 120 percent—and in Catholic colleges and universities it increased by a staggering 300 percent, from 92,426 to 384,526.[109] The historian John Ellis observed in 1955 that American Catholics had "the largest and most expensive educational system of any national group in the world."[110] This lavish funding was reflected in perhaps the greatest academic success story of the decade, that of Notre Dame, which went from being an exclusively undergraduate university whose reputation had been made on the football field rather than in the classroom to one of the nation's premier research institutions. Jesuit colleges like Georgetown, Holy Cross, and Fordham likewise gained reputations during the 1950s as fine liberal arts schools.[111]

With strength in numbers, improved schooling, and crescendoing economic power came political clout. The Catholic grip on local political machinery in some states, notably Connecticut, was nearly absolute.[112] By 1960, twelve Catholic senators and ninety-one representatives served in Congress—a representation greater than American Catholics had achieved previously, albeit one in proportion to their numbers.[113] In terms of orientation on the left–right political spectrum, Catholic legislators ranged between two McCarthys, Eugene on the left and Joseph on the right, most tending to cluster near the conservative pole. Even liberal cold war congressmen like John F. Kennedy and Mike Mansfield were spirited in their hawkishness, while Senator Patrick McCarran of Nevada frequently out-McCarthyed McCarthy in his red-hunting exertions and in the Internal Security Act of 1950 that bore his name.

Some Americans were alarmed by what they perceived as political and cultural aggression by Catholics. Martin Marty, professor of history at the University of Chicago, noted with dismay the media's tendency to refer to "our" cardinal and "our" pope.[114] *Christian Century*, a mainstream Protestant journal, ran an eight-part series that asked, "Can Catholicism Win America?" and concluded that, yes, it could.[115] Fears of the Church's growing influence were most graphically articulated by Paul Blanshard, whose screed *American Freedom and Catholic Power* (1949) aimed to expose what Blanshard viewed as a Catholic bloc seeking to impose a Vatican-centered autocracy on the United States. "There is no Catholic plan for America distinct from the Catholic plan for the world," Blanshard declared. "The hierarchy's techniques of promotion vary from country to country, but the master plan is only one plan, and the world-wide strategy is directed from Rome."[116] Evidently quite a few people sympathized with this neonativist angst, for *American Freedom and Catholic Power* sold over one hundred thousand copies.[117]

Blanshard's know-nothingism is at least partially explained by the fact that, as Charles Morris notes, "[b]y the 1950s, the Catholic Church was the country's dominant cultural force. No other institution could match its impact on politics, unions, movies, or even popular kitsch."[118] Books with explicitly Catholic themes like Francis Spellman's *The Foundling* and Thomas Merton's *The Seven Storey Mountain* numbered among the biggest best-sellers of the fifties. Red Foley's song "Our Lady of Fatima" made the Hit Parade in 1950 and was recorded a dozen times throughout the remainder of the decade by artists as diverse as the Ray Charles Singers and Andy Williams.[119] In 1959, the Catholic Press Association reported a record total of over twenty-four million subscribers to 580 Catholic newspapers in the United States. That same year, more than 150 radio stations carried "The Catholic Hour" to an estimated four million listeners.[120] Bishop Fulton Sheen's "Life Is Worth Living" series not only captured the largest television audience of the mid-1950s, with over thirty million viewers per week, but also won every major TV award, many of them several times.[121] Other hugely popular television personalities—Jackie Gleason, Ed Sullivan, and Perry Como, to name but three—made no effort to disguise their identity as Catholics, as they might have in an earlier time; on the contrary, they spoke openly of their devotion to the Church.[122] Depictions of Catholic priests and nuns in the movies were overwhelmingly favorable, in sharp contrast to the brutish interpretations set forth in films from the thirties like *Little Caesar* and *Public Enemy*. Significantly, the Hollywood Catholic priest of the cold war era was a virile figure, prepared to back up his principles with his fists. In the film *On the Waterfront* (1954), Karl Malden's Father Barry flattened a former prizefighter. After viewing this multiple Academy Award–winning movie, Marty noted, "Catholicism tends to dominate the mass media."[123]

As in other spheres of American life, the Church's influence on foreign policy was at its zenith during the early cold war, principally owing to shifting U.S. attitudes toward the Soviet Union. Patrick Allitt has demonstrated that while millions of Americans did an about-face in the late 1940s and early 1950s and went from admiring the Soviets as gallant allies to condemning them as no better than the Nazis, "[f]or American Catholics, . . . zealous anti-communism was nothing new; Catholic schools had been teaching it for the best part of a century, and the wartime alliance with Stalin had not effaced it."[124] During the Hoover and Roosevelt administrations, American Catholics led the fight against U.S. recognition of the Soviet Union.[125] They also protested Roosevelt's closeness to the anticlerical and leftist Mexican regime of the 1930s and supported Francisco Franco in the Spanish Civil War, viewing Franco as the champion of Spain's Catholic Church against the Moscow-backed Republicans.[126] While Adolf Hitler and Benito Mussolini divided up Europe, and Japan carved out an empire on the Chinese mainland, it was common for Catholic spokesmen in the United States to express a preference for fascism over communism as

8. The mesmerizing Bishop Fulton Sheen. © Bettmann/CORBIS, 26 April 1953

the lesser of two evils.[127] Hence, at war's end, when American public opinion turned against Russia, the nation's Catholic population was already fully prepared, and American Catholics benefited from being in the vanguard of the anti-red zeitgeist.

Warmly recalling this watershed moment when national political consensus fell in line with a time-honored Catholic view, Daniel Patrick Moynihan writes, "In the era of security clearances, to be an Irish Catholic became *prima facie* evidence of loyalty. Harvard men were to be checked; Fordham men would do the checking."[128] Catholics became increasingly visible in the late 1940s and 1950s in organizations like the Federal Bureau of Investigation, where J. Edgar Hoover recruited agents who were, in the words of an FBI historian, "young, aggressive, and—not coincidentally—alumni of Catholic colleges, particularly Notre Dame. They were holy terrors."[129] For a group whose patriotism had long been considered suspect because of their alleged devotion to

Rome, these were halcyon days. Catholicism was now synonymous with 100 percent Americanism. David O'Brien observes that "in fighting the red peril, the Catholic could dedicate himself to action which was both Catholic and American. Few would disagree that he was proving his worth as an American, and demonstrating the compatibility of faith and patriotism."[130]

No one demonstrated this compatibility to a greater degree than Cardinal Francis Spellman of New York, the most powerful church prelate of the 1950s. Spellman's influence over Catholic voters made him a man to be courted and feared, and his chancery in New York was justly nicknamed "the powerhouse." Politicians from both parties competed for the opportunity to be photographed in Spellman's presence; these snapshots could mean the difference between a landslide victory and a return to private life. The cardinal's reach extended beyond New York, even beyond the shores of the United States. As military vicar of the American armed forces, he made annual visits to American bases in Europe and the Far East that rivaled Bob Hope's for media attention. Spellman was one of a handful of bishops in the world to enjoy the confidence of Pope Pius XII, and many believed he had an excellent chance of becoming pope himself—although some joked that this would entail a diminution in his authority.[131]

More than any public figure of the day, Spellman embodied the Catholic Church's opposition to communism. He moreover equated this opposition with national loyalty, declaring in 1948 that "it is not alone in defense of my faith that I condemn atheistic communism, but as an American in defense of my country. We stand at a crossroads of civilization, a civilization threatened with the crucifixion of communism."[132] No American, not even Dulles, employed such apocalyptic cold war rhetoric. Spellman's response to the persecution of Catholics behind the Iron Curtain was especially hair-raising. When Archbishop Aloysius Stepinac of Yugoslavia was sentenced to sixteen years' hard labor by the communist regime of Marshal Josip Broz Tito, Spellman lashed out at the "satanic Soviet sycophants . . . who, following the perfidious pattern of communist godlessness, barbarism, and enslavement, [have] . . . sealed the doom of this noble, humane priest as he is subjected to the agonies of a prolonged lynching!"[133] The imprisonment and torture of Cardinal Joseph Mindszenty in Hungary prompted Spellman to mount the pulpit of St. Patrick's Cathedral and ask his parishioners to enlist in the "defense of the rights of God and man against Christ-hating commu-

9. Cardinal Francis Spellman (center) and Pope Pius XII (right). © Bettmann/
CORBIS, 5 November 1950

nists whose allegiance is pledged to Satan!"[134] In the early 1950s, the
Catechetical Guild published a comic book titled "Is This Tomorrow?"
that depicted wild-eyed communists attacking St. Patrick's and nailing
Spellman to the cathedral door.[135]

Other prominent Americans who exhibited the cold war blend of
Catholicism and patriotism were the journalists William F. Buckley and
Brent Bozell, the historian Russell Kirk, and the economist Louis
Budenz. Budenz, the former editor of the *Daily Worker,* joined the
Church in 1945 and wrote a widely read autobiography detailing how he
had acted as a communist and how, as a Catholic, he ought to have
acted.[136] Senator Joseph McCarthy, the most famous red-baiter of his
era, was himself a Catholic and won broad Catholic backing.[137] Donald
Crosby establishes that lay Catholics were less supportive of McCarthy
than the Church leadership; nonetheless, the senator from Wisconsin
consistently enjoyed at least a 10 percent margin of additional support
among Catholics.[138] Few Catholic journals broke publicly with the clerical consensus on McCarthy, and the conservative Catholic Young Turks
Buckley and Bozell cowrote a best-selling defense of McCarthyism,

calling it "a movement around which men of good will and stern morality can close ranks."[139] In the middle of the Army–McCarthy hearings, Cardinal Spellman himself introduced the senator to six thousand whistling, stomping policemen at a communion breakfast in New York.[140]

Catholic influence in early cold war politics was not limited to Hoover's FBI witch-hunts or cheerleading for "Tail Gunner Joe" McCarthy. The State Department and CIA worked closely with the Vatican in 1948 to help defeat the communists in Italy's first postwar elections, while the National Catholic Welfare Conference (NCWC) promoted a letter-writing campaign among Italian Americans to urge their relatives in Italy to vote Christian Democrat. (The post office reported that the volume of mail to Italy doubled prior to the election of the anticommunist Alcide de Gasperi as premier.)[141] Father John Cronin, a seminary professor from Baltimore involved in anticommunist union activities during the 1930s and 1940s, was recruited by the FBI to produce a pamphlet on communism, a million copies of which were distributed through the U.S. Chamber of Commerce. It was Cronin who introduced Richard Nixon to Whittaker Chambers and the Alger Hiss case and who served as a conduit between Nixon and the FBI for a stream of files that ultimately resulted in Hiss's conviction.[142] The State Department coordinated several pro-American campaigns behind the Iron Curtain with the NCWC. With the approval of the Truman administration, various Catholic organizations smuggled paper supplies, printing equipment, and funds to the anticommunist underground in Poland, Hungary, and East Germany.[143]

Several influential non-Catholic intellectuals came to track long-held Catholic views in the late 1940s and 1950s. Chief among these pundits was the most esteemed journalist in America, Walter Lippmann, a man whose previous affiliation with the American Socialist Party and Henry Wallace's Progressives made him a curious brother-in-arms for the likes of Buckley and Budenz. Like other former left-leaning intellectuals in the early years of the cold war, however, Lippmann was disturbed by what he termed "the alarming failure of the Western liberal democracies to cope with the realities of this century." He deplored the indecision he observed in postwar America and concluded that the secular tenets of liberal democracy were insufficient to counter the "mortal challenge" posed by communism.[144] Echoing Dulles, he affirmed that "a civilization must have a *religion*. . . . Communism is a religion of the proletarianized masses."[145] In 1955, the year America made its commitment to the Diem regime, Lippmann published a collection of essays entitled *The Public Philosophy* in which he adopted the identifiably Catholic position that the "decline of the West" could be arrested only by adherence to a "natural law" and "the commandment of God," which was "transcendent."[146] Lippmann's biographer observes that, in the face of perceived communist incursions at home and abroad, the journalist became "strongly drawn to Catholic theology, finding in its hierarchy and sense of order an antidote to a secularism that, in the guise of . . . communism, seemed impervious to moral restraints."[147] Lippmann, along with many of his fellow citizens, gained new appreciation in the 1950s for the righteous combativeness expressed by Catholic Americans like the much-syndicated Father Richard Ginder. "There is only one force in the universe that can destroy communism," Ginder declared in the pages of *Our Sunday Visitor*, "and that is the Catholic Church!"[148]

By a variety of measures, then, the Eisenhower years seemed a triumphal era for Catholicism in the United States. There is a difference, of course, between Blanshard's argument that the Church exercised inordinate control over postwar American life and the more nuanced thesis that a prevailing national consensus simply coincided with time-honored Catholic views, thereby giving the impression of Church influence when in fact largely independent, nonreligious political, economic, and demographic processes were propelling America toward a convergence with the Catholic "line." Whatever the causal relationship between the Church's vitality and that larger phenomenon loosely dubbed "the fifties," Morris does not exaggerate when he asserts, "A team of alien anthropologists would have reported that 1950s America was a Catholic country."[149]

It was in this "Catholic country"—and not in his overwhelmingly Buddhist homeland or the more secular nations of Western Europe—that Ngo Dinh Diem won command of South Vietnam. Diem's Catholic faith stamped him as a mortal enemy of communism who would never betray U.S. cold war objectives by reaching an accommodation with the Viet Minh. As Senator McCarthy proclaimed in 1953, "The fate of the world rests with the clash between the atheism of Moscow and the Christian spirit throughout other parts of the world."[150] To many American policymakers, especially John Foster Dulles, Diem represented Vietnam's Christian spirit, a spirit the vast majority of his fellow

10. The Catholic Youth Organization rallies to protest Cardinal Josef Mindszenty's imprisonment. © Bettmann/CORBIS, 6 February 1949

Vietnamese did not share. The Buddhists, Cao Dai, and Hoa Hao of Southeast Asia appeared too susceptible to the lure of neutralism to serve as dependable allies in the American crusade. Their faiths were stagnant, not dynamic. Therefore, they merited no better than dismissal with the biblical injunction that Dulles frequently secularized when discussing nations that refused to choose sides in the cold war: "Because you are lukewarm, and neither hot nor cold, I will spew you out of my mouth (Revelation 3:16)."[151]

Ironically, midcentury America's ebbing but still powerful tide of *anti*-Catholicism, exemplified by Blanshard's books and the difficulties Kennedy encountered in his presidential campaign, also helped Diem secure U.S. support. Many of the familiar tenets of American Catholic-bashing lost their sting when applied to Vietnam; in fact, they became points in Diem's favor. Catholics, Blanshard and other Americans claimed, were incapable of free thought, having been brainwashed by a repressive Church hierarchy. Their religion programmed them to regard their leader as infallible and obey priests and bishops without question. They were therefore unfit for citizenship in a democracy whose constitution made the separation of church and state absolute.[152]

These were difficult charges for American politicians like Kennedy to rebut, but Diem was not running for office in the United States. While the Democrats' rejection of JFK as vice presidential nominee in 1956 and his subsequent razor-thin margin of victory in the election of 1960 indicated that millions of Americans were still uneasy about the prospect of a Catholic leader for their own country, they had no such qualms where Vietnam was concerned, because few considered the Vietnamese ready for democracy. If the same religion that made Diem anticommunist also made him authoritarian, so much the better; he was even more qualified for the task assigned him by the Eisenhower administration.

In the view of most postwar Americans, the Vietnamese (indeed, Asians in general) were accustomed to serving strong masters. They did not seek the rights and freedoms common to Western societies and were too backward to participate in their own governance. As a 1950 State Department policy planning staff report on Vietnam contended, "the majority of Asians is a peasant [*sic*] steeped in Medieval ignorance, poverty, and localism. . . . They are insensitive to invocations on our part of the bonds of democratic ideology—which do not exist for them —or of the desire of preserving Western civilization."[153] In other words, they were not to be trusted with the responsibilities of self-government, certainly not when their failure to choose Christ and capitalism could cost the United States a major defeat in the cold war. Catholic-bashers like Blanshard might deplore what they considered the Church's "perpetuation of mental childhood" among its devotees, but this was less of a problem in a country in which, as far as Americans were concerned, the people were basically children anyway.[154] Americans' willingness to accept a Catholic leader for South Vietnam at a time when they would have been unlikely to do so at home demonstrated the interlocking, mutually reinforcing nature of their ideological predispositions. Religion and anticommunism, while vital, did not exist independently of the equally significant factor of race.

3

"These People

Aren't Complicated":

America's "Asia" at

Midcentury

In the summer of 1951, two of the premier shapers of public opinion in the United States joined forces to explain Asia to their many loyal readers. Henry Luce, ruler of a multimedia empire that eclipsed all competitors in size, circulation, and profits, published an article by America's most popular "serious" novelist, James Michener. The article, entitled "Blunt Truths about Asia" and given cover-story treatment in Luce's *Life* magazine, appeared at a low point in U.S.–Asian relations: mainland China had fallen to the communists; America's ally France seemed incapable of defeating the Viet Minh; and Chinese intervention in the Korean War had demolished American hopes of unifying Korea under noncommunist rule. Although United Nations forces managed to withstand the Chinese and North Korean onslaught and open a successful drive back to the 38th parallel, they paid a heavy price for restoring the status quo ante bellum.[1] Americans were deeply concerned about events in the Far East, and Luce and Michener could be assured of a large, receptive audience for their primer on Asian "truths."

At the time he published Michener's article, Luce had been the leading press magnate in America for decades, "control[ling] access to millions of minds," in the breathless words of one biographer.[2] Born and raised in China and fascinated by all things Asian, the feudal lord of Time Inc. was a charter member of the "Asia first" school of foreign policy, which contended that the cold war would be won or lost in its Far Eastern theater rather than in Europe.[3] Luce put Nationalist Chinese leader Chiang Kai-shek on *Time*'s cover eight times before the communists seized control of China in 1949 and thereafter relentlessly campaigned for greater U.S. commitment to halting communism's advance through Korea, Vietnam, and the other "dominoes" on the Asian landmass. To promote that agenda, he solicited articles from like-minded public figures such as John Foster Dulles, Madame Chiang Kai-shek, Senator Arthur Vandenberg, and repentant ex-communist Whittaker Chambers.[4] But he never enlisted the services of a more effective propagandist than Michener.

As important as Michener's literary fame was his reputation as America's preeminent authority on Asia. The novelist Pearl Buck had held that distinction during the interwar years, but her leftist political views undercut her popularity in the McCarthy era.[5] Michener, on the other hand, became what one critic aptly called "a phenomenon of magnitude."[6] *Tales of the South Pacific,* which Michener wrote in 1945 while stationed as a naval officer in the New Hebrides, was a runaway best-seller, winning the Pulitzer Prize for fiction in 1947. Two years later, Richard Rodgers and Oscar Hammerstein turned the book into a musical, *South Pacific,* which played to sold-out houses on Broadway, toured nationally and internationally, and won another Pulitzer for drama.[7] During the 1950s, Michener, now writing full-time, produced an exceptional number of novels, short stories, and articles about Asia. Many of the articles appeared in popular magazines like *Reader's Digest* and the *Saturday Review,* and most of the novels, notably *Sayonara* and *The Bridges at Toko-Ri,* became movies.[8] In 1954, *Newsweek* ran a cover story on Michener that credited him with "introduc[ing] the world of the trans-Pacific into almost every American home" at a time when there was great "need . . . for Americans to know their Asiatic enemies and respect their Asiatic friends."[9] If anyone was equipped to tell the American people "blunt truths about Asia," it appeared to be Michener.

Most of Michener's blunt truths were self-evident: that Asia was "a big and imposing continent"; that China was the leading Asian country "in size"; and that Japan's economic boom was largely due to "the dollars America is pumping into the nation." Other truths were provocative but insufficiently explained, as when Michener claimed that religion was "a crucial force" in Asia. "Perhaps more than in any other part of the world," he asserted, "events in Asia are directed by religion." He described the clash between Hindus and Moslems in India and noted that Buddhism was "the principal religion of Burma, Ceylon, Thailand, Indo-china, and Japan." As for Christianity, he conceded that it was "in retreat" but saw in this "a heartbreaking and yet wonderful contradiction." "Even as Christianity is being driven from Red China," he noted, "its power persists as a major influence on the minds of the leaders of Asia. . . . [T]hey acknowledge with astonishing frequency that they owe much of their education, their attitude toward law and toward the world at large to this same alien religion. It is thus an enormously important legacy that the Christian missionaries and Christian teachers have left behind."

Michener's two most crucial points, to judge by the pungency of his prose, concerned Asian ignorance and Asian political immaturity. "ASIA IS A BACKWARD CONTINENT," he pronounced, the words capitalized and rendered in boldface by *Life*. "The great mass of Asians cannot read, have no radios, and have never seen a moving picture. . . . [T]heir knowledge of the world is abysmal." He offered a case in point: "Not long ago, an American journalist, interviewing natives of a village near a major city in India, asked the obvious: 'What do you think of America's intervention in Korea?' The answer was: 'What is Korea?' " Michener's second point was related to the first: "ASIA IS A VAST OLIGARCHY"—again in boldface and capital letters. "Of the six major Asiatic countries," Michener observed, "only Japan has a directly elected parliament." All of "the rest" were "unversed in democracy"; indeed, he insisted, "[t]o talk seriously of general elections in areas where 90% of the electorate cannot read is to mock the very meaning of democracy." Thus, it was unavoidable that "power continues to be held by a tiny minority." Michener hastened to point out that "this minority is neither stupid nor selfish; it may even rule reluctantly—but rule it must."

From Michener's perspective, the fact that most Asian countries were undemocratic should not trouble Americans. These nations were following an "Asia-wide pattern" of evolution, he claimed. After having "overthrown the old order" of Western colonialism, they were progressing—slowly, to be sure—through various levels of governmental sophistication, the highest level at present being oligarchy. Michener asserted that China's "historical experience" had been a textbook example of this national coming of age—until, that is, America made a colossal error:

China . . . set the pattern when it evolved into an oligarchy under Chiang Kai-shek. . . . It was in grappling with this stage of Asia's development that the United States fumbled so badly. We really failed to face the simple facts of life in Asia. This was true in two senses: we failed to recognize that Chiang was an inevitable political fact at this point in Asia's growth . . . and we also failed to realize that his government must inevitably evolve. . . . Had we understood that this evolution, with our help and counsel, would surely follow in due time, we could have lived realistically in the present. Instead, . . . we refused Chiang enough effective support to enable him and China to progress.[10]

Here Michener was reciting a narrative that had become a staple of the Luce publishing empire by the early 1950s. Ever since Mao Tse-tung's communists triumphed in the Chinese Civil War and Chiang's Nationalists were exiled to the island fortress of Formosa, Time Inc. had promoted the theory that Chiang's government would have survived had the United States provided greater aid. According to Luce and other pro-Chiang members of the so-called China Lobby, the Truman administration's insistence that Chiang institute democratic reforms in the midst of a civil war had all but handed mainland China to Mao. Had Truman recognized that Chiang's government was appropriate for China, given its level of political preparedness, then the United States could have turned its entire attention to the problem of winning the civil war. After the communists had been defeated, so the argument ran, America might have nurtured democracy in an evolving China. Instead, U.S. policymakers moralized about Chiang's "dictatorship" while Mao stormed to victory.[11] Michener concurred with this Lucean version of recent history. "To appreciate the greatness of our loss," he lamented, "one has only to visit Formosa. This island today is the bright spot of Asia. The Nationalist government . . . has matured astonishingly. . . . It has established an enlightened commonwealth. . . . *This* might have been China today!"

Michener's main policy prescription "follow[ed] logically" from America's experience with Chiang. "In all of Asia," he submitted, "the first and perhaps the toughest fact that America must accept is that this world is not made in the American image." U.S. policymakers hoping to deal constructively with Asia needed to accept that "it *is* a continent run by oligarchs, and whether or not the idea is congenial to our predispositions, we must deal with them, with all of their prejudices and limitations." Any attempt to impose American-style government upon such "backward" people was bound to fail and result in the forfeiture of still more Asian nations to communism. In Michener's judgment, there was no room for another "egregious error and the irrevocable loss of more friends." If Americans wanted to "help Asia to save itself—and save ourselves in the process," they had to recognize that almost all Asian nations were at a different stage of political refinement than the advanced Western democracies. And time was growing short. "The future of the West in this continent where the white man is so hated is in terrible doubt," Michener averred. "But . . . the cost of failure is too staggering to allow us to proceed with anything less than confidence."[12]

This remarkable article, written by America's foremost interpreter of Asia and disseminated by the twentieth century's most successful American mass communicator, exhibited several features of American anti-Asiatic racism in the early cold war period. First was the assumption that one could speak of a general "Asia" in which one country was much the same as any other, in which Tibet, Burma, Laos, and Vietnam were interchangeable dominoes that America needed to keep from falling. Another was the conviction that Asians were incapable of democratic self-government. Americans who made this assertion often softened it, as Michener did, by claiming that Asians might someday develop the capacity for democracy, but that in their present backward condition the adoption of democratic processes would result in chaos. To his credit, Michener was less disposed than many of his contemporaries to explicitly equate Asians with children, but his use of terms like "evolution" and "mature" in company with the vignette about Indian villagers who had never heard of Korea made the parallel difficult to miss. A third tenet of American racism that grew out of the belief in Asian unfitness for representative government held that minority rule, as exemplified by Chiang's regime, was the most appropriate form of administration in Asian countries. The ruling Asian minority was "neither stupid nor selfish," Michener insisted, and in many instances it "rule[d] reluctantly." Yet "rule it must"; the alternative was anarchy, which would leave Asia's huge population and strategic resources defenseless against the red juggernaut directed from Moscow.

The presumptions showcased in Michener's article worked to Ngo Dinh Diem's advantage as he lobbied to become America's Vietnamese strongman. His unconcealed ambition to govern the "State of Vietnam" as a despot did not alarm U.S. policymakers because they assumed that the Vietnamese, like their counterparts elsewhere in Asia, were still at a primitive level of development and that firm one-man rule was necessary to maintain order. Perhaps the United States, working through

Diem, could gradually introduce the South Vietnamese to the rudiments of advanced civilization, but the day when Diem's country could function as a pluralist democracy was a long way off. Diem also benefited from another precept of American racism that Michener only hinted at, but that other American ministers of information seeking to render a complex world comprehensible stated forthrightly: that it was desirable, if policymakers could contrive to bring it about, for these benighted countries teetering on the brink of communist domination to be governed by a *Christian* autocrat while America went about its task of postcolonial nation building in Asia.

"Getting to Know You"

During the years the Eisenhower administration armed and financed Diem's regime, the American cultural landscape was studded with popular representations of the Far East—in hit movies, highly rated television shows, best-selling books, and mainstream magazines—that reinforced the themes of Michener's "blunt truths" article. The Americans who generated these images would have bridled at the suggestion that their work was racist; indeed, much of it was framed as a denunciation of bigotry. Revelations about Nazi Germany's near-extermination of the Jews of Europe made horrifically clear to Americans in the postwar years where doctrines of racial supremacy could lead, and many of the era's top cultural producers, including playwrights, film directors, novelists, and press lords, stressed the urgent need for tolerance in an increasingly interdependent world. Moreover, the allegedly scientific racism that underlay Social Darwinism and other theories of immutable racial differences between people had lost most of its credibility by the end of World War II. Anthropologists like Franz Boas promoted an alternative explanation for the heterogeneity of the human community, one that identified cultural rather than biological factors, and research in genetics further debunked the notion of an unalterable hierarchy of races with whites in the top position.[13] Michener, Luce, and other cold war liberals never ascribed the conditions they observed in Asia to physiognomy or skin color; on the contrary, they took pains to underscore just how insignificant they considered these attributes to be.[14]

Yet Americans in the early years of the cold war continued to conceive of Asians in racist terms. If they no longer believed that Asian poverty, illiteracy, and despotism were consequences of biological deficiency, they still ranked Asians far below themselves in an imagined pecking order. Their rationale for doing so, however, shifted from racial essentialism to what one historian terms "the more neutral-sounding language of development."[15] Much of that language was drawn, either deliberately or unconsciously, from modernization theory, a formula for understanding processes of global change that had a tremendous impact upon postwar foreign policy. In brief, modernization theory contended that all societies were located along a spectrum between tradition and modernity and that all ascended through various stages of economic and political development. Since modernity was defined in terms of capitalism, industrialization, and democratic government, the United States stood as the most modern society in the world, with Western Europe close behind. Traditional societies, like those in the newly independent nations of Asia, were on the bottom rung of the developmental ladder. They would eventually advance upward, but— and this was the key point for cold war policymakers—they were vulnerable to communist takeover while in their present condition. It was therefore necessary for the United States to move them along the path toward modernization as quickly as possible. This would involve considerable intervention in the affairs of these nations and perhaps the forceful imposition of American institutions upon them, but that was all to the good since America's evolution from backward, class-divided colony to democratic, capitalist superpower provided an ideal model for the underdeveloped world to emulate.[16]

As a number of scholars have demonstrated, modernization theory, while purporting to be an original and scientific means of interpreting global transformation, actually rested upon many of the same assumptions that justified America's Manifest Destiny campaigns against Amerindians and Mexicans in the nineteenth century—and, in fact, that legitimated Western colonialism in general. It portrayed nonwhite peoples as primitive, untutored in the ways of democracy, and incapable of uplifting themselves without the help of a Western mentor. That it explained this portrayal in terms of arrested development rather than of innate racial inferiority did not make the reality of U.S. domination any less galling to the inhabitants of nations like South Vietnam. Furthermore, despite repeated denials of imperialistic intent, the United States exercised the kind of direct military, political, and economic control over these nations that made its relationship to them difficult to distinguish from the most exploitative forms of European colonialism.[17]

General Douglas MacArthur was more comfortable expressing himself in turn-of-the-century "white man's burden" rhetoric than in the clinical language of modernization theory, but he deftly summarized American cold war views of Asians as underdeveloped and immature shortly after President Harry Truman dismissed him as commander of UN forces in Korea. Testifying before the Senate Committees on the Army and on Foreign Relations, MacArthur boasted of his accomplishments in occupied Japan, which had been under his supervision since 1945. MacArthur was confident that the reforms he had forced upon the Japanese would endure because, as he reminded his audience, no people had ever abandoned democracy after experiencing it. When a senator pointed out that Germany had had a democratic government after World War I and later embraced Nazism, MacArthur responded,

> Well, the German problem is a completely and entirely different one from the Japanese problem. The German people were a mature race. If the Anglo-Saxon was, say, forty-five years of age in his development in the sciences, the arts, divinity, culture, the Germans were quite as mature. The Japanese, however, . . . were in a very tuitionary [*sic*] condition. Measured by the standards of modern civilization, they would be like a boy of twelve as compared with our development of forty-five years.

Because the Japanese were children, developmentally speaking, MacArthur believed they were "susceptible to following new models, new ideas. You can implant basic concepts there." These concepts, among them democracy, capitalism, and Christianity, would help the Japanese mature to figurative adulthood, at which point they would be ready for self-government.[18] Naoko Shibusawa persuasively shows how such "metaphors of maturity" enabled policymakers like MacArthur to "naturalize the unequal U.S.–Japan relationship" and rebut any imperialist explanations of America's increasing presence in Asia. Americans could claim they did not intend to deny Japan the rights and privileges of sovereignty forever, as European colonialists did; rather, like a kindly adoptive parent, the United States would allow its children to steer their own course when they grew up.[19]

American cold war policymakers cast other Asians metaphorically as children—notably the Vietnamese, whom Ambassador William Bullitt described to the State Department's Division of Philippine and Southeast Asian Affairs as "attractive and even lovable, but essentially childish."[20] Before the United States displaced France as the principal Western power in Southeast Asia, Secretary of State George Marshall speculated that the "Vietnamese will for [an] indefinite period require . . . enlightened political guidance" from a Western nation "steeped . . . in democratic traditions."[21] Charles Reed, U.S. consul in Saigon in the late 1940s, concurred with his boss, noting that if the French gave the Vietnamese "virtually a free hand" in governing themselves, the results would be "disastrous." Reed doubted whether the Vietnamese were "capable of running an independent state" and pointed to the "fact that the Philippines, after 40-odd years of benevolent tutelage . . . are still not a model of good government." Since policymakers generally regarded America's relations with the Philippines as the embodiment of successful colonial guardianship, this made Vietnamese prospects dismal without what Reed called "Occidental check or control."[22]

The patronizing perception of Asians articulated in State Department correspondence, top secret foreign policy analyses, and testimony before congressional committees was echoed in American popular culture, in what Christina Klein terms "the greatest hits . . . of the postwar fascination with Asia."[23] Most cultural producers did not express themselves as straightforwardly as MacArthur and Bullitt, preferring to promulgate their visions of Asia through cold war allegories set in the distant past or current events disguised as fiction. Yet the "Asia" presented was a consistent construct: an ignorant, heathen place, peopled, figuratively and literally, by children.

Hollywood played a leading role in communicating such images to Americans. Although television had begun to draw audiences away from the silver screen by the mid-1950s, movies remained the most popular form of entertainment in the United States, and technological innovations like Cinerama, CinemaScope, and 3-D kept theaters packed throughout the decade.[24] Many of the highest grossing films of the fifties were set in Asia, among them *The King and I*, *Sayonara*, *The Teahouse of the August Moon*, *The Geisha Boy*, *The Bridge on the River Kwai*, *Island in the Sun*, *South Pacific*, *Love Is a Many-Splendored Thing*, *Don't Go Near the Water*, *Tokyo after Dark*, *The Barbarian and the Geisha*, and *Inn of the Sixth Happiness*. Other box office successes addressed domestic white–Asian relations, usually with the objective of refuting the Soviet charge that America was a racist society: *Japanese War Bride*, *The Crimson Kimono*, *China Gate*, *House of Bamboo*, and *Run of the Arrow* all depicted the United States as making strides toward greater tolerance. American movies had featured Asian characters ever since 1915, when Cecil B. DeMille's *The Cheat* appeared in theaters, but the number of Asian-themed films made and distributed by Americans in the 1950s was unprecedented.[25]

The King and I was a particularly revealing work of fifties Orientalia, both in itself and in terms of the huge audience it attracted. Klein notes without exaggeration that "*The King and I* introduced Southeast Asia . . . into the consciousness of postwar America."[26] As a novel, a musical comedy, and especially a movie, this account of a nineteenth-century Englishwoman who worked as a teacher in the royal court of Siam was perhaps the most enduring representation of the Far East produced by Americans in the cold war. Its origins long antedated that conflict: Anna Leonowens, the real-life British tutor of King Mongkut's children from 1862 to 1867, wrote two popular books about her sojourn in Siam; Margaret Landon, an American missionary's wife stationed in Siam in the years before World War II, then fashioned Leonowens's story into a semifictional biography, *Anna and the King of Siam,* which was published in 1944.[27] The book became a best-seller, a condensed *Reader's Digest* version expanded its readership by millions, and Twentieth Century Fox turned it into a successful movie. Then the musical theater duo of Rodgers and Hammerstein adapted Landon's novel into the form of a stage play, *The King and I,* which opened on Broadway in 1951, the same year Michener's "blunt truths" article appeared in *Life.* Reviews were rhapsodic and audiences enthusiastic. The show ran on Broadway for three years before touring nationally and internationally; an original cast album rose to the number one spot on the charts; and the sheet music sold millions of copies.[28] Even before Fox purchased the film rights, *The King and I* had become a cultural sensation, and the big-screen version only enhanced its stature. At a production cost of $6.5 million, it was the most expensive film of 1956. Almost eighteen million people paid to see the movie in its first year, and it won numerous Academy Awards, among them a Best Actor Oscar for Yul Brynner, who became so identified with the lead role that he continued to play it in touring productions until his death nearly thirty years later.[29]

Brynner was unquestionably a charismatic presence as the king of Siam, but the vision of Asia conveyed by his performance and by the film in general was so ethnocentric as to be cartoonish. A major subplot of Rodgers and Hammerstein's drama, second only to the never-consummated romance between the king and Anna, was Siam's struggle to avoid becoming a British protectorate. This story line was based on historical fact. Siam did maintain its independence from imperial control (the only Southeast Asian country to do so) and historians generally attribute this singular accomplishment to King Mongkut's adroit negotiations with the British.[30] Rodgers and Hammerstein, however, gave the king no credit. In their rendition, Siam's survival was Anna's achievement. The king, outraged that "certain personages" considered him "a barbarian," intended to confirm British impressions of Siamese unrefinement by assaulting Queen Victoria's delegation when it arrived in Bangkok, but Anna persuaded him to offer a banquet instead. Moreover, by offering her suggestions in such a way that the king could pretend they were his own ideas, she managed to do this without causing him to lose face. During the banquet, the king required Anna to instruct him how to eat with a knife and fork, and she prompted him on topics of conversation in which he repeated arguments she had made to him earlier. In this manner he convinced the visiting British of Siam's worthiness to remain a sovereign nation.[31]

This historic diplomatic encounter, as presented to millions of American filmgoers in 1956, resonated with the same racist paternalism that General Mike O'Daniel displayed when testifying before the House Foreign Affairs Committee that same year. O'Daniel, former head of the Military Assistance and Advisory Group in South Vietnam, lectured the assembled legislators that "much can be done" in Vietnam "if we use an indirect approach, which Asians are used to. . . . Quite often, it is necessary to plant the seed of an idea in the mind of an Asian official and subsequently refer to it as 'his,' i.e. the Asian's original project."[32] O'Daniel was at the time serving as chairman of the American Friends of Vietnam (AFV), an organization committed to promoting Ngo Dinh Diem's image in the United States. He frequently ascribed his success in dealing with Diem to such indirect approaches, reminiscing at one point, "Many times I handed Diem . . . an idea of mine on a piece of scratch paper, without any heading or signature, and . . . a week or two later the idea appeared as his own in his own written orders and in the Vietnamese language."[33] According to O'Daniel—and to Rodgers and Hammerstein—this was how one managed an Asian leader: by speaking through him like a ventriloquist and allowing him to believe he was acting independently.

As significant as *The King and I*'s depiction of its main character was the emotional mechanism by which Rodgers and Hammerstein made

11. Yul Brynner and Gertrude Lawrence in the original Broadway production of *The King and I*. © John Springer Collection/corbis, ca. 1951–52

audience members lose their hearts to the Siamese minutes into the film. Deborah Kerr's Anna, just arrived in Siam, threatened to leave because the king refused to honor his promise to provide her with a house outside the palace walls. To entice her to stay, the king ordered his children, her prospective students, to parade before her and overwhelm her with their adorableness. As "The March of the Royal Siamese Children" played in the background, the children entered the room one by one, bowed before Anna, touched their heads to her hands in a gesture of respect, and then prostrated themselves on the floor in orderly rows. After the smallest child entered and endearingly bowed in the wrong direction, Anna was unable to resist sweeping him up into her arms, thus breaking the stately pace of the music and indicating her decision to stay. Hammerstein made plain the effect he wanted this scene to have, noting in his stage directions, "Throughout this procession, Anna has obviously fallen more and more in love with the children. She is deeply touched by their courtesy, their charm, their sweetness."[34] Audiences responded in a similar fashion and probably did not notice that none of the children spoke or was identified by name: they were lovable but interchangeable.

This mix of winsomeness and sameness carried over into the scenes in which Anna instructed the children. *The King and I*'s most popular musical number was "Getting to Know You," set in Anna's classroom and containing the famous lyrics "Getting to know you,/Getting to know all about you." The song ostensibly celebrated the joy of learning about others' cultures, but the learning relationship enacted was almost entirely one-sided. The children mimicked Anna: she showed them how to shake hands, bow, and curtsy, and they emulated her movements. All of the social formalities taught were Western. Moreover, the Siamese found it difficult to master them. Their attempts at shaking hands were clumsy, and Lady Thiang, not one of the king's children but his "head wife," repeatedly bowed rather than curtsied. In the one instance of two-way cultural exchange, a dancer performed a Siamese fan dance complete with a nimble-fingered handling of the fan that suggested a lifetime of practice. Yet Anna easily copied the dancer's moves, manipulating the fan with equal skill. The message conveyed was unmistakable: Anna had nothing to learn from Siam. It was the Siamese who needed to be taught.[35]

The dependence of the Siamese upon Anna was dramatized in especially graphic terms in the film's final scene. Anna, again angrily preparing to leave Siam after the king brutalized his concubine, was entreated to stay by the royal children, one of whom read a speech she had memorized for the occasion. The little girl's loveliness and the earnestness of her delivery deflected attention—at least that of 1950s audiences —from the obsequiousness of her lines, which no American playwright hoping to turn a profit would have dared to put in the mouth of, say, a European princess: "Dear friend and teacher: My goodness gracious! Do not go away! We are in great need of you! We are like one blind. Do not let us fall down in darkness. Continue good and sincere concern for us, and lead us in right road." Anna once again succumbed. She resolved to stay in Siam and rescue her blind Asian students from a descent into darkness. The film concluded with the king's death from a heart attack and the crown prince making his first pronouncement as ruler of Siam: a paraphrase of Abraham Lincoln's Emancipation Proclamation he had learned in Anna's classroom.[36]

The condescension of *The King and I* was almost beyond gauging. Rodgers and Hammerstein rendered the population of Siam and, by implication, that of Asia as children. The king himself, despite his sculpted torso and seemingly innumerable wives and offspring, was a petulant boy, incapable of solving his nation's problems without Anna's direction. "In some ways, he is just as young as you," Anna told her grade-school-age son.[37] This infantilizing of the king was underscored subtly but powerfully with a reprise of "The March of the Royal Siamese Children" in the scene in which the king greeted his British guests.[38] Indeed, the whole movie was a procession of children: needy Asian boys and girls who won the affection of the parental West not through intelligence, nobility, or even separate identities, but by being irresistibly cute and deferential. It was hardly a coincidence that *Deliver Us from Evil*, Tom Dooley's best-selling account of his ministering to Vietnamese refugees, was published in the same year that *The King and I* debuted in movie theaters. Like Rodgers and Hammerstein, Dooley made Asians intelligible by making them children and insisting they would blossom under Western tutelage.[39]

South Pacific, Rodgers and Hammerstein's other blockbuster "Oriental" musical, opened on Broadway two years before *The King and I* but took longer to make the transition to screen. Twentieth Century Fox did not release the film version until 1958. Still, millions of Americans in the early to mid-1950s were able to see the show in touring productions, regional and community theater, and via the new medium of television, which broadcast a Sunday matinee live.[40] What they saw was a narrative that seemed to unequivocally condemn racism. The song "You've Got to Be Carefully Taught," in which the character Lieutenant Joe Cable railed against the prejudice that prevented his engagement to a Vietnamese woman, became something of an anthem for cold war liberals who believed that America's race problem was causing it to lose ground to the communists in the predominantly nonwhite third world.[41] Yet *South Pacific*'s Asian characters were even more simple-minded than those in *The King and I*. The object of Cable's unrequited love, Liat, was virtually mute; since she spoke no English and Cable no Vietnamese, the two had to communicate through hand gestures or with the help of Liat's scheming mother, Bloody Mary. Liat was also passive, yielding to Cable's embrace before learning his name and docilely accepting Mary's verdict that she marry a wealthy French planter instead of the American she loved. Mary, a grotesque caricature, babbled musical-comedy pidgin—"Hey, Lootellan, you damn saxy man!"—and pimped her daughter to Cable from the moment she saw him. Despite the lieutenant's ultimate recognition—and repudiation—of his bigotry, Rodgers and Hammerstein's cross-racial love story did not have a happy ending, as

Cable was killed on a mission. Nonetheless, Liat still benefited from her encounter with the West when Nellie Forbush, a navy nurse and the heroine of *South Pacific*'s other love story, symbolically adopted her in the closing scenes. If Liat could not have a sustained relationship with an American on the equal terms of romantic love, she could at least fill the role of appreciative foster child.[42]

The other Asians whom Americans encountered on the big screen in the 1950s, especially in films that did well at the box office, generally conformed to the stereotypes depicted by Rodgers and Hammerstein. There were a few fear-mongering Yellow Peril movies of the genre so popular during World War II, but these became increasingly infrequent as the Korean War drew to a close. By the time Eisenhower assumed the presidency, Asians were receiving a more benign, if no less racist, treatment from American filmmakers.[43] In almost every instance, they were presented as actual children or as adults who behaved like children. The children were inevitably charming and often afforded the American protagonist an opportunity to display his or her humanitarianism—as in the Jerry Lewis vehicle *The Geisha Boy*, in which Lewis, a magician on a Far Eastern tour, was captivated by a Japanese boy and, after the requisite visual gags, adopted the child.[44] Americans also adopted Asian children in two of the most popular films about the Korean War, *Steel Helmet* and *Battle Hymn*, and the movie *Three Stripes in the Sun* portrayed an American serviceman saving an entire Japanese orphanage from starvation.[45] Adult Asians tended to fall into two groups, both childlike. Usually, they were meek and respectful, like Lady Thiang in *The King and I* and Katsumi in *Sayonara*. They could also be irrational and histrionic, but those whom filmmakers wished to show in a positive light displayed a willingness to improve themselves by emulating Western codes of conduct. Brynner's career-defining role was an example of this specimen of salvageable Asian, as was the character Hana-Ogi in *Sayonara*, who sacrificed her position as the most celebrated performer in a cloisterlike Japanese theatrical troupe to marry an American pilot and move to Texas. Hana-Ogi's servile line "I am not allowed to love, but I will love you—if that is your desire" was featured prominently in advertisements for the film.[46] If playing a less-sympathetic role, the adult Asian's puerility undercut his or her character's potential for evil. Asian villains like *South Pacific*'s Bloody Mary and Ichiro in *The Geisha Boy*, for example, were more ludicrous than threatening.

There were rare exceptions to these kinds of cinematic portraiture.

12. Jerry Lewis and his Japanese ward in *The Geisha Boy.* © John Springer Collection/CORBIS, ca. 1958

Marlon Brando's performance as Sakini in *Teahouse of the August Moon* defied easy categorization. It was certainly racist, if for no other reason than that Brando, a white American actor, played a Japanese interpreter by resorting to the same cosmetology that Shirley MacLaine used in *My Geisha*: canary-yellow makeup, shiny black wig, and latex eye treatments to create epicanthic folds. Yet Sakini, as played by Brando, was a complex figure, more intelligent than the film's Western characters.[47] And audiences could not laugh off Sessue Hayakawa in *The Bridge on the River Kwai*. Hayakawa exuded genuine menace as Colonel Saito, commander of a World War II Japanese prison camp. But Brando's standing as the most popular film star of the decade gave him unique freedom to defy artistic convention, and *The Bridge on the River Kwai* was a British, not an American, production. In addition, one of the most memorable scenes in *The Bridge on the River Kwai* involved Alec

Guinness's Colonel Nicholson manipulating Saito by employing tactics identical to those demonstrated by Anna in *The King and I* and endorsed by O'Daniel before the House Foreign Affairs Committee. Nicholson, an engineer, gave his proposals for constructing the bridge as if they were thoughts he assumed were Saito's, and the Asian was thereby able to save face by celebrating Nicholson's ideas as his own.[48]

Television offered a somewhat different portrayal of Asians, although the representation was equally unflattering. As a rule, TV shows made in the 1950s took place in an all-white world, performers like Ricky Ricardo, Sidney Poitier, and Ossie Davis being notable anomalies. In the midfifties, however, film companies sold or leased to the major networks the broadcast rights to thousands of pre-1948 movies.[49] Many of these films, especially those made during World War II, depicted Japanese as bloodthirsty savages and Chinese as loyal allies, a racist dichotomy that reversed itself to a degree in the early cold war years.[50] The Fu Manchu and Charlie Chan serials of the 1920s and 1930s were given a second life on the small screen, where they generally played as camp. Neither Boris Karloff's Fu nor Warner Oland's Chan retained much capacity to impress TV viewers, and the broadness of their characterizations likely reinforced the comic book image many Americans had of the Far East.[51] And Asians almost never appeared live on American television in the fifties, which made an episode of the series *The Big Picture* noteworthy.

The Big Picture was a regular feature on ABC for thirteen years. Essentially a propaganda instrument sponsored by the U.S. Army to build support for America's costly cold war commitments, it presented documentary films depicting the army in action and live studio interviews with military figures who explained the latest weaponry, training, and maneuvers. The series garnered high ratings throughout the fifties despite its often deadly pace, and in 1951 viewers' interest was doubtless piqued by the announcement that one program would feature "a special interview with a captured Chinese communist soldier." Colonel William Quinn, a series regular, conducted the interview. His guest, identified as "Hong Yi," sat sullenly behind a desk, clad in a heavy gray jacket and cap, and barked out responses to Quinn's questions in broken English:

Quinn: Are you a communist?
Hong: Me good communist, yes.

Quinn: Well, why?

Hong: Reason for communist is because they give me lots of promise for my family.

Quinn: Who promises you all this?

Hong: Oh—big man.

Quinn: Big man, huh?

Hong: Big man.

Quinn: . . . Why do you stupidly stay in your foxholes and trenches when you can see the American infantry coming?

Hong: Commissar tell us to stay there.

Quinn: Who's he?

Hong: He big man.

Quinn: A big man. What is he, in your battalion?

Hong: No—he big, big, big, *big* man!

Quinn: Oh, I see. So he makes you stay in your foxhole. Suppose you *don't* stay in your foxhole. What'll happen to you?

Hong: Me no stay in, he chop my neck off.

Quinn: Well, you finally made a little sense there.

After some further banter, Quinn turned to face the camera and said, "Well, there you are, ladies and gentlemen. The commie logic goes on and on." Then, his face brightening, he declared, "Now I'd like to introduce the star of our communist soldier plot, if you will—Sergeant Kim of the United States Army!" The interviewee removed his cap, smiled, and shook Quinn's hand. When Quinn thanked him for "taking such a poor part," Sergeant Kim replied that "it was a pleasure to be of service." Quinn then assured viewers that despite the sergeant's "very convincing" performance, he was really a loyal American, born in Honolulu, and that the cast and crew of *The Big Picture* hoped he did not "have to take this kind of a part any more." The image dissolved and the credits rolled.[52]

In a few minutes of prime-time TV, *The Big Picture* managed to spotlight almost all of the most fateful premises of American views of Asia at the time the United States began its descent into Vietnam. "Hong Yi" was a child, emotionally and intellectually. He believed whatever his communist masters told him, as a child believes in Santa Claus. He made life-or-death decisions not after mature deliberation, but out of fear of a "big man's" wrath. He was predisposed to defer to authority, provided it was backed up by force. Even after revealing his true identity as Sergeant Kim, he was still the familiar Asian of American imaginations: respectful, agreeable, eager to "be of service" to his superiors, even if that meant being humiliated on national television. Viewing this program during the most anxious days of the Korean War, Americans might easily have concluded that neither the free world's South Korean allies nor its North Korean and Chinese enemies were mature enough for democratic institutions. The former were good Asians and the latter bad, but benevolent authoritarianism was clearly the best political system for both.

"One Shouldn't Fight a War with Children"

The decade's best-selling works of fiction and nonfiction did not offer American readers any subtler rendering of the Far East. If anything, the portrayal of Asians in popular books was more malignant than in movies and television because the authors' reputations for expertise lent their words tremendous authority. Readers of James Michener's *The Voice of Asia*, which Random House published in 1951 to ecstatic reviews, knew that Michener was the nation's foremost Asia specialist and that he had logged more than twenty-one thousand miles doing research for the book.[53] Hence, they were inclined to trust him when he declared, "We must support the oligarchs" in Asia. "Why does Asia prefer oligarchs?" Michener asked. "Why have there been no general elections? For one simple reason. Up to 90 percent of the people are illiterate, and people who cannot read cannot rule. Since they are illiterate, they cannot understand words like democracy, elect, judiciary, or parliament. And modern democratic life depends upon such terms."[54] This seemed impeccable logic; that it led to the U.S. underwriting of dictators like Ngo Dinh Diem was, readers could assume, a necessary consequence of Asian political realities.

Two books deserve special consideration for helping to form the set of assumptions through which Americans understood Asia in the 1950s. *The Quiet American* and *The Ugly American* were exceptional texts not only because of the controversy they engendered but because they dealt specifically with Vietnam at a time when American knowledge of that country was almost nonexistent.[55] Scholarship on both books has become a cottage industry.[56] Scenes and sentences from both have achieved the status of literary cliché, in particular the world-weary remark of *The Quiet American*'s narrator: "I never knew a man who had better motivations for all the trouble he caused."[57] For present purposes, the debate over which book was "right" in terms of its representation of U.S. involvement in Vietnam is less important than the fact that both texts depicted the Vietnamese in similar fashion and that this depiction was hardly empowering.

Graham Greene wrote *The Quiet American* after five years living in and reporting about Vietnam. Although an introductory note asserted that "this is a story and not a piece of history," the book described actual events, like the fall of Dien Bien Phu, which give it a journalistic quality.[58] Greene's plot was essentially a love triangle. His two protagonists, the aging British reporter Thomas Fowler and the young American CIA officer Alden Pyle, vied for the affections of a Vietnamese woman, Phuong, who was Fowler's mistress. Pyle, the quiet American of the book's title, arrived in Vietnam intent on encouraging a native "third force" that was neither colonialist nor communist. He fell in love with Phuong at first sight; after some hesitation, she accepted his marriage proposal and left Fowler. While in Saigon, Pyle became convinced that a renegade South Vietnamese general was America's best hope for third-force leadership and accordingly supplied him with plastique, which the general used to set off bombs in Saigon's public square. Partly out of disgust with Pyle's complicity in this terrorist act and partly as a means to recover Phuong, Fowler betrayed Pyle to the Viet Minh, who stabbed him and cast his body into a canal.

A brief synopsis can only hint at the richness of Greene's novel—possibly his finest—and the degree to which *The Quiet American* became, in the words of one historian, "a basic text for the antiwar movement" of the 1960s and 1970s.[59] For many Americans opposed to the Vietnam War, Greene had been a prophet, predicting the course of the conflict at a time when America's presence in Vietnam was far below the half-million troops it would eventually involve.[60] Yet Greene's prescience did not prevent him from describing the Vietnamese in terms that even Michener might have found patronizing. Phuong, almost the only Vietnamese who spoke in *The Quiet American*, was childlike and naïve—"wonderfully ignorant," according to Fowler's first-person narration. "If Hitler had come into the conversation," Fowler noted, "she would have interrupted to ask who he was." Fowler, whose wife remained in England and refused to grant him a divorce, admitted that he loved Phuong because she was so submissive: "She always told me what I wanted to hear, like a coolie answering questions." When he commanded her to kiss him, "she did at once what I had asked, . . . just as she would have made love if I had asked her to, straight away, peeling off her trousers without question." Given such unquestioning devotion, Fowler did not mind that Phuong thought the Statue of Liberty was in London.[61]

Indeed, while Greene's sympathies were clearly with Fowler in the tug-of-war over Phuong, neither the British nor the American suitor treated the object of their love as though she were an adult capable of complex feelings and mature judgment. In the novel's most famous scene, Pyle and Fowler, on their way back to Saigon after witnessing a Cao Dai ceremony, ran out of gas; they spotted a guard tower in which they took refuge from the omnipresent Viet Minh, sharing the space uneasily with two terrified Vietnamese soldiers. To pass the time, Fowler and Pyle discussed politics, religion, and sex; during this sleepless night they learned to know each other. When Pyle insisted that the Vietnamese wanted to "think for themselves," Fowler replied, "Thought's a luxury. Do you think the peasant sits and thinks of God and democracy when he sits in his mud hut at night?" Fowler warned Pyle not to expect love from the Vietnamese: "It isn't in their nature. You'll find that out. It's a cliché to call them children—but there's one thing which is childish. They love you in return for kindness, security, the presents you give them." After the two men returned to Saigon, Pyle concluded that Phuong was in fact "a child" who needed to be rescued from the degradation she suffered as a married man's "comfortable lay." The showdown between the two men, during which Fowler decided to lure Pyle into the communists' trap, featured a heated exchange over who understood the Vietnamese better:

> "You talk like a European, Thomas. These people aren't complicated."
> "Is that what you've learned in a few months? You'll be calling them childlike next."
> "Well, in a way."
> "Find me an uncomplicated child, Pyle."[62]

Readers entranced by Greene's dialogue might miss the fact that Fowler, while arguing for the complexity of the Vietnamese, still tacitly accepted that they were children. Greene emphasized that point elsewhere in *The Quiet American*. He summed up one of Fowler's native informants with a few memorable images: "the sunken cheeks, the baby wrists, the arms of a small girl." When Pyle disarmed a Vietnamese soldier in the guard tower, Fowler noted that the soldier "slumped against the wall and shut his eyes, as though like a child he believed himself invisible in the dark." After Viet Minh guerrillas shelled the tower, wounding one of the soldiers, Fowler heard his cries from the safety of a nearby rice paddy. "It wasn't like a man weeping," he observed. "It was like a child who is frightened of the dark and yet afraid to scream.... One shouldn't fight a war with children."[63]

Several scholars have noted that Greene, while deploring American intervention in Asia, was hardly a champion of Vietnamese independence. Rather, he accepted the central premise of colonialism: that certain peoples, given their level of political development, were not prepared for full sovereignty and required the leadership and protection of a civilized great power.[64] Greene believed that France had honorably fulfilled that parental role in Vietnam. His portrayal of French colonialism was positive, even romantic, as when he had Fowler lecture Pyle: "[T]he French are dying here every day. . . . I'd rather be an exploiter who fights for what he exploits, and dies with it."[65] *The Quiet American* never suggested that there was any rational basis for Vietnamese demands for independent nationhood; it just made the case that America, on the verge of inheriting France's colony, was not handling the task of imperial protector very skillfully. Whereas the French had brought order and enlightenment to the ignorant mass of Vietnamese, Greene implied, Americans like Pyle brought only mayhem.

Not surprisingly, critical response to Greene's novel in the United States differed markedly from notices elsewhere. *The Quiet American* earned glowing reviews from Europe's most finicky aestheticians (even Evelyn Waugh deemed it "masterly") but many Americans were scandalized by Greene's representation of their national character. *Newsweek* took uncommon offense, speculating that Greene's anti-Americanism derived from his having been "temporarily denied a visa to the United States" because of his prior membership in the Communist Party. A subsequent *Newsweek* piece titled "When Greene Is Red" accused Greene of aiding the USSR and cited as proof the fact that his novel received "a chorus of acclaim from Soviet journals and newspapers." A. J. Liebling marveled in the *New Yorker* at Greene's "implacable hatred of milk shakes, deodorant, and everything else American."[66]

Greene's American detractors got their revenge when Oscar-winning producer-director Joseph Mankiewicz bought the movie rights to *The Quiet American* and altered the story line almost beyond recognition.[67]

Mankiewicz was a member of the American Friends of Vietnam, which did much to shape the prism through which Americans at midcentury understood Vietnamese politics. The organization rarely exercised its power more effectively than in Mankiewicz's adaptation of *The Quiet American*. Before shooting the film on location in Saigon, Mankiewicz assured AFV Chairman O'Daniel that he intended to "completely change the anti-American attitude" of Greene's book, a task that even the U.S. ambassador to South Vietnam, Frederick Reinhardt, considered impossible.[68] "If [the book] were to be edited into a state of complete unobjectionableness," Reinhardt advised the AFV's executive committee, "there might be nothing left but the title and the scenery."[69]

Yet Mankiewicz succeeded, turning Pyle into a hero and Fowler into a communist stooge. The film cleared Pyle of any connection to the Saigon square bombing, gave him many of the memorable lines that Greene put in Fowler's mouth, and underscored his nobility with a singular casting choice: while Mankiewicz wanted Montgomery Clift to play Pyle, O'Daniel persuaded him to offer the role to Audie Murphy instead.[70] Murphy, the most-decorated GI of World War II—Harry Truman called him the finest American soldier since George Washington—had served under O'Daniel in Europe and joined the AFV at O'Daniel's request.[71] His limited acting talent did not trouble Mankiewicz, who noted that Murphy was "the perfect symbol of what I want to say."[72] In case the star's symbolism did not speak loudly enough, Mankiewicz wrote a monologue for Pyle in which he reminisced about his years at Princeton, noting that he had met a "prominent Vietnamese living in exile in New Jersey. . . . If all goes well, if Vietnam becomes an independent republic, this man will be its leader." The allusion to Diem's stay at the Maryknoll Seminary would have been clear to many viewers when the film debuted in 1958, as Diem had recently made a tour of the United States featuring a high-profile "homecoming" to Maryknoll.[73] In a twist worthy of Pirandello, Colonel Edward Lansdale, on whom the character of Pyle was allegedly based, assisted Mankiewicz in rewriting Pyle's dialogue.[74] The AFV was so pleased with the results that it hosted the film's premiere at Washington's Playhouse Theater.[75] Greene, appalled, raged in a letter to *Le Monde*, "Far was it from my mind, when I wrote *The Quiet American*, that the book would become a source of spiritual profit to one of the most corrupt governments in Southeast Asia."[76]

Ironically, Eugene Burdick's and William Lederer's *The Ugly Ameri-*

can, which many reviewers interpreted as a rebuttal to Greene's novel, offered an even more scathing denunciation of U.S. policy in the Far East. That accounted for much of its impact. As John Hellmann notes, the book "provid[ed] the American public with a purgative ritual of self-criticism" at a time when Americans were increasingly fearful that the United States had become too soft, materialistic, and corrupt to compete with the discipline and single-mindedness of communism.[77] By both confirming these fears and offering a blueprint for national regeneration, *The Ugly American* became one of the most popular books in U.S. history, remaining on the best-seller list for seventy-eight weeks and ultimately selling over five million copies. President Eisenhower read it and appointed a committee to investigate America's foreign aid program. Secretary of State John Foster Dulles, Vice President Richard Nixon, and Senator William Fulbright cited it in speeches. Few books have had greater influence on American popular and elite opinion.[78]

Burdick and Lederer appeared to be well qualified to evaluate America's efforts to halt the spread of communism in Asia. Burdick, a professor of political science at the University of California, Berkeley, had served in the Pacific during World War II and written widely on Asian affairs. Lederer had also served in Asia and remained there after the war as one of the navy's Asia specialists. In addition, he was special assistant to the commander of the Pacific fleet from 1950 to 1958, which gave him access to the most up-to-date information on political and military developments throughout Asia. Shortly before *The Ugly American* appeared in bookstores, Lederer became a full-time Asia correspondent for *Reader's Digest*.[79]

While *The Ugly American* was set in the fictionalized Southeast Asian country of Sarkhan, readers had little difficulty recognizing that its real-life model was Vietnam. Apart from Lederer's and Burdick's opening tip-off that "[t]his book is written as fiction, but it is based on fact," the authors threw out two none-too-subtle hints when they noted that Sarkhan was "a small country out toward Burma and Thailand" that had "border difficulty with the communist country to the north."[80] Indeed, Lederer and Burdick initially wrote *The Ugly American* as nonfiction. The manuscript accepted for publication included real names, dates, and places as it detailed the blunders of State Department bureaucrats in a number of Southeast Asian nations, notably Vietnam. But days before the book was scheduled to go to press, Lederer and Burdick withdrew the galleys. According to Lederer, his friend Michener read the final draft and warned him, "People don't emotionally commit to a nonfiction book the way they do to fiction."[81] Michener advised the authors that if they wanted to provoke nationwide outrage over the incompetence of U.S. foreign service personnel, they should rewrite the book as a novel, with melodramatic anecdotes that would catch the attention of Middle America. Lederer and Burdick burned their manuscript, secluded themselves in a hotel room with dictating machines and an army of stenographers, and emerged six days later with the book that, in the words of one historian, "led to . . . a national soul-searching."[82]

Structured as a series of loosely interrelated story lines, *The Ugly American* made the case that communism in Asia could be combated only by counterinsurgents who understood "the Asian personality and the way it play[s] politics." For Lederer and Burdick, the fact that America provided more material aid to the third world than the communists was not enough; Russia and China still bested the West in the field of symbolism, which was all-important in "the Asian mind." The communists were masters of localized opinion manipulation, bamboozling hapless Asians through stratagems like pasting hammer-and-sickles on U.S. aid packages.[83] What America needed, according to Lederer and Burdick, were fewer grandiose programs of economic development that never reached the people and more anticommunist agents capable of beating the reds at their own game. To dramatize this point, *The Ugly American* alternated between horror stories about arrogant, ill-informed bad Americans clustered in their embassy enclaves and instructional how-to accounts of those few committed good Americans who were unafraid to get their hands dirty winning hearts and minds.

Although the book's cast of characters was large, three figures stood out for their ability to cultivate personal relationships with the Sarkhanese. One was Edwin Hillandale, an Air Force colonel who was almost certainly modeled after Edward Lansdale, Ngo Dinh Diem's top American adviser.[84] Another was Homer Atkins, an inventor, engineer, and self-made millionaire brought to Sarkhan to supervise the building of military roads and dams. The third was his wife, Emma. All three accomplished what, in Lederer's and Burdick's view, America's culturally illiterate diplomats, military leaders, secret service agents, and public information officers failed even to attempt: they learned about Asia and taught Asians to appreciate the basic goodness of America by integrating themselves into an Asian community. Yet the episodes in which these exemplary characters won Asian friendship fairly pulsed with the racist condescension evident elsewhere in Eisenhower-era popular culture. Despite Lederer's and Burdick's attempt to portray Hillandale and the Atkinses as ideal ambassadors who transcended the boundaries of race and nationality, all three protagonists treated the Asians they encountered as children—and not very bright ones at that.

Hillandale was *The Ugly American*'s central hero. His biggest triumph—the operation that earned him his posting to Sarkhan—took place during the Philippine elections of 1953 in which American-backed Ramon Magsaysay defeated the communist opposition. As narrated by Lederer and Burdick, Hillandale motorcycled, alone and unarmed, into a "province north of Manila" where communist propagandists "had persuaded the populace that the wretched Americans were rich, bloated snobs [who] . . . couldn't possibly understand the problems and troubles of the Filipino." Hillandale took out his harmonica and played "Filipino tunes in a loud and merry way," drawing a crowd of "about two hundred people" who soon joined him in a sing-along. Having overcome the natives' apprehension, Hillandale showed them his empty pockets to demonstrate he was as poor as they were, thereby initiating an argument among them over who could invite him to lunch. The colonel resolved this quarrel by insisting that they eat en masse. "After a while," Lederer and Burdick wrote, "no one in that area believed any more that all Americans were rich and bloated snobs," and "ninety-five percent of the inhabitants of the province voted for President Magsaysay and his pro-American platform."[85] Lederer and Burdick may not have intended this vignette to call forth images of the pied piper leading children, but American readers could be forgiven if they made that connection.

In *The Ugly American*'s other parable centering on Hillandale, the colonel came close to achieving an even greater public relations coup. Soon after arriving in Sarkhan's capital, Hillandale noticed "the large number of signs advertising palmistry and astrology establishments." He concluded that "occult science" was "held in high regard by the Asians" and decided to use this angle to persuade the Sarkhanese prime minister to send his army on maneuvers that would be interpreted as pro-American by the communists. Through "a little discreet questioning," Hillandale learned official secrets that he pretended to read off the prime minister's palm during a state dinner. According to Lederer and Burdick, after this dissembling, "the prime minister was gazing up" at Hillandale "with obvious awe." The colonel had brilliantly exploited native superstitions and was now in control of Sarkhan's military forces.

Unfortunately, a foolish chargé d'affaires blew Hillandale's chance to further manipulate the prime minister by mishandling arrangements for another palm-reading session—precisely the kind of bureaucratic blunder Lederer and Burdick abhorred. They seemed less troubled by Hillandale's dishonesty.[86]

The Ugly American's two other heroes, Homer and Emma Atkins, were not as cunning as Hillandale but similarly unable to interact with the Sarkhanese on equal terms. Homer, the eponymous "ugly American" whose physical unattractiveness masked his inner decency, took up residence in the village of Chang 'dong to witness firsthand the conditions under which the natives lived. His observations convinced him that costly highways and dams would be less useful to people at such a primitive stage of development than a low-cost project like a water pump. Homer then enlisted the help of a local man whom the villagers called Jeepo because of his skill in fixing jeeps. Working together, Homer and Jeepo designed a pump that made use of part of a bicycle. The two men became business partners, recruited villagers as workers and sales representatives, and introduced Sarkhan to the wonders of small-scale free-enterprise capitalism. Lederer and Burdick repeatedly emphasized the novelty of Homer's relationship with Jeepo: the residents of Chang 'dong, they noted, "had never heard of a binding legal document between a white man and a Sarkhanese"; Homer's haggling with Jeepo over the terms of their contract "caused the Sarkhanese workmen a great deal of pleasure. . . . [It was] the only time that the Sarkhanese had ever seen one of their own kind arguing fairly and honestly, and with a chance of success, against a white man." But the pretense of equality was betrayed by the two men's manner of address: Homer continued to call his business partner "Jeepo," never bothering to learn his real name, while Jeepo and the other villagers always addressed Homer as "Mr. Atkins." Moreover, the process of inventing the pump involved Jeepo doing the manual labor and Homer the brainstorming; although Jeepo made the final adjustment that allowed someone to operate the pump without dismantling the bike, all of the preceding innovation had come from Homer, much of it spoon-fed to the Sarkhanese.[87]

Lederer's and Burdick's paternalistic perception of Asians revealed itself in especially hideous form in the tale of Emma Atkins, the "ugly American" 's wife, who made an even greater contribution than Homer to improving the quality of life in Chang 'dong. After two weeks of living among the villagers, Emma "asked an unanswerable question," inquiring why all the elderly residents of Chang 'dong "walked with a perpetual stoop." The Sarkhanese could answer only that "old people become bent. . . . That's the natural thing which happens to older people." While the natives "accepted their backaches as their fate," Emma did some detective work. She noticed that older villagers were "inevitably" given the task of sweeping out their homes, and that they used brooms made of palm fronds with short handles. Emma began searching the countryside for "a substitute for the short broom handle," found some tall reeds, transplanted them to the village, fashioned them into a long-handled broom, and began sweeping out her house with it. The natives all copied her new broom, observing that "your way of sweeping is a more powerful way." After Homer completed his work in Chang 'dong, the Atkinses returned to the United States where, four years later, Emma received a letter from the headman of the village:

> Wife of the engineer,
>
> I am writing you to thank you for a thing you did for the old people of Chang 'dong. For many centuries, longer than any man can remember, we have always had old people with bent backs in this village. . . . But, wife of the engineer, you have changed all that. . . . For four years, ever since you have left, we have been using the long reeds for broom handles. You will be happy to know that today there are few bent backs in the village.

The headman concluded by informing Emma that the villagers had built a shrine in her memory. She was officially a saint in Chang 'dong.[88] American readers no doubt found this deeply moving, but it would have been difficult for them to conclude, on the basis of Emma's triumph, that the peoples of Southeast Asia were capable of creating and preserving an independent, democratic state. If spinal disfigurement that had afflicted the Sarkhanese "for many centuries" could be cured by adopting a long-handled broom—and if the Sarkhanese required an American housewife to figure this out for them—then they were a long way from being ready for self-government. In their benighted condition, they needed a protector to teach them the skills to survive on their own. America's task, according to Lederer and Burdick, was to assume that protective role before the communists did, a point they pounded home in their "factual epilogue." Moscow and Beijing, they insisted, were "better at public relations than is the free world." Communist representatives in Asian countries learned the local language and culture and lived the way the natives did. While Americans huddled in their officers' clubs, the communists were out in the villages winning converts to their cause. Tellingly, *The Ugly American* credited only one free world institution with having understood the communists' tactics and used them in defense of liberty: the Catholic Church. "Like the Russians," Lederer and Burdick noted, "but unlike ourselves, the Church realizes that its work in Asia cannot be done without close communication with Asians."[89]

Other popular books presented fifties America with comparable belittling images of the Far East. Michener's fiction and nonfiction outsold all competing texts, except for *The World of Suzie Wong*, a semiautobiographical novel by Richard Mason that largely identified postwar Hong Kong with an illiterate, orphaned Chinese prostitute rescued from the hopelessness of her situation by a British painter.[90] (The painter became an American in the film version.)[91] *The Bridges at Toko-Ri*, Michener's novel promoting the official reasons for U.S. involvement in Korea, included few Asian characters, the only one identified by name being Kimiko, a Japanese woman who betrayed her navy lover with the childlike excuse, "While Mike at sea, I lose my heart to Essex man. Essex not at sea."[92] Michener's *Sayonara* purported to show how love between American servicemen and Japanese women could overcome prejudice, but the terms in which Michener had the character Joe Kelly express affection for his Japanese bride were more suggestive of a colonial master coping with a dull-witted servant than a union of adults: "I told her if she ever giggled again, . . . I'd break her arm off at the wrist"; "Until Katsumi met me, she was a real moron"; "Honest to God, Ace, it's easier to train a dog."[93]

More portentous in its implications for U.S. foreign policy was *Return to Paradise*, a combination of short stories and what Michener called "jammed-crammed essays containing all I knew" about the South Pacific.[94] The book enjoyed the standard success of a Michener text, becoming a top ten best seller, a Book of the Month Club selection, and the basis for two movies.[95] In it, Michener took his readers on a long pilgrimage through Guadalcanal, Tahiti, Fiji, Australia, and other locales, and then extracted some lessons in an epilogue titled "What I Learned." From Michener's perspective, the most significant fact about people in the South Pacific was how anxious they were to submit to U.S. hegemony:

13. James A. Michener (right) tours the front lines of the cold war in Asia. © CORBIS, undated

I was not on a single island but what someone with good sense and responsible years approached me with this direct question: "Did the American government send you out here to report on whether or not we want America to take over this island? Let me tell you, my friend, we dream of nothing else. When will America adopt us?" ... I can honestly say that never was this vital question asked—"When will America take over?"—without awakening in me a tremendous appreciation of my native land.[96]

This was a seductive picture for Americans, on several counts. First, Asia—or its Southern Pacific region—was presented as an orphan child needing to be adopted; such imagery personalized U.S.–Asian relations and cast them in almost irresistibly sentimental terms. Second, Asia was *asking* to be adopted, virtually pleading for the privilege. Americans could therefore claim that their intervention was not imperialistic, but rather an act of generosity, done at the request of Asians themselves. Finally, there was the ever-present concern, unvoiced by Michener but pervasive in the Eisenhower years, that if America did not adopt these children, the Soviet Union would, and the global balance of power would tip permanently against the United States. "For the Atlantic democracies to leave the Asian infant unattended would be suicide," the liberal magazine *New Leader* editorialized in 1954. "Because it is plain that whoever rocks the Asian cradle will rule the world."[97]

"Freedom, My Friend, Is a Very *Relative* Thing"

Americans learned by the mid-1950s that a specific kind of Asian leader was best suited to help them rock that all-important cradle. Broadly speaking, he (it was always a man) welcomed American aid, was committed to modernization, and intended to transform his country along democratic lines. At the same time, he recognized the unfamiliarity of his people with democracy and therefore delayed implementation of measures like universal suffrage until he believed the masses were ready. If he seemed dictatorial at times, that was because his nation's existence was threatened by an evil empire; wartime conditions, after all, required peremptory, occasionally repressive governance. What was important was that he was *trying*, struggling toward civilized maturity, and he was wise enough to realize that he needed guidance from a more advanced superpower. In sum, he was much like the king of Siam as envisioned by Rodgers and Hammerstein—with one notable exception. Whereas *The King and I*'s main character was a Buddhist, America's ideal Asian ally was a Christian.

No less legendary a figure than Douglas MacArthur repeatedly stressed the importance of Christian leadership in the East. Shortly after assuming his duties as supreme commander of occupied Japan, MacArthur made an appeal to Protestant and Catholic missionaries, inviting them to fill Japan's "spiritual vacuum" and warning, "if you do not fill it with Christianity, it will be filled with communism." MacArthur insisted that "Japan cannot be a democracy without Christianity," vowed to "absorb missionaries as fast as the church can send them," and claimed that it was his "duty as a Soldier of God to . . . revive religion in Japan." Many Japanese politicians, who remained in office at MacArthur's leave, reinforced the supreme commander's views. Prime Minister Prince Higashikuni informed a delegation of American missionaries two weeks after Japan's surrender, "We need a new standard of ethics, like that of Jesus Christ. Buddhism can never teach us to forgive our enemies, nor can Shintoism. If Japan is to be revived, we need Jesus

Christ as the basis of our national life." When a Christian socialist won the Japanese premiership in 1947, MacArthur issued a press release triumphantly noting that "three great Oriental countries now have men that embrace the Christian faith at the head of their governments: Chiang Kai-shek in China, Manuel Roxas in the Philippines, and Tetsu Katayama in Japan."[98]

Generalissimo Chiang Kai-shek, the "Christian general," towered above Roxas, Katayama, and other Asian allies in terms of the exposure he received in the U.S. media. Americans reaching middle age during the Eisenhower years had grown up following Chiang's exploits; they read about them in magazines like *Time* and *Life*, viewed them in docudramas like *The March of Time* and *Why We Fight*, and heard them extolled by the nation's most powerful statesmen. Millions of Americans had developed a deep emotional attachment to the generalissimo—and to his wife, the Wellesley-educated, Methodist "missimo" — as Chiang's Nationalist Chinese fought alongside the United States in World War II. American devotion to Chiang intensified in the early postwar years, when the Nationalists and communists battled for control of China. Although Chiang's defeat and flight to Formosa tarnished his image, he was still widely beloved in cold war America.[99] Indeed, some pundits attributed the election of the Republican Eisenhower in 1952, after twenty years of Democratic rule, to the "Who lost China?" debate that convulsed American politics after the communists won the Chinese Civil War.[100]

Many Americans first became aware of Chiang in 1931, when he converted from Buddhism to Christianity. *Time* magazine ran a major feature on the event, calling Chiang "as much a conqueror as Constantine I, the Roman general who espoused Christianity when convinced by the Sign of the Cross he would conquer . . . Rome." According to *Time*, Chiang made his decision for "no apparent reason, except sincere conviction." After informing a priest in Shanghai that "I feel the need of a God such as Jesus Christ," Chiang was "sprinkled with baptismal drops." Taking this step "required the highest moral courage," *Time* noted. "The bulk of the Chinese rabble scarcely had a religion. . . . In certain interior provinces there have even been killings, recently, of Chinese Christian missionaries by their pagan brothers." Yet "the most exalted man in China" publicly embraced Christianity.[101]

This gesture made a searing impression upon Henry Luce, the missionary's son who had lived in China until his teens. Luce's media empire trumpeted Chiang's virtues to Americans throughout the Depression, World War II, and the cold war. Typical was a *Time* cover story in 1936 that rationalized the generalissimo's failure to respond to Japanese military provocations by noting that he was practicing a "policy of always turning the Christian other cheek." The same article praised Chiang for "ramm[ing] some rudiments of Christian conduct and morality" into China's soldiers and called him "unquestionably the greatest man in the Far East." When Chiang was briefly kidnapped by a rival warlord weeks after appearing on *Time*'s cover, the magazine noted that he "insisted upon reading the Bible during most of his 13 days' captivity." In late 1938, with the Japanese assault on China proceeding at full force, *Life* praised Chiang for his "remarkable courage and resolution" and pointed out that he was "a converted Methodist who has now found solace in the examples of tribulation in the Christian Bible." The Japanese attack on Pearl Harbor in 1941 made the United States and China allies, eliciting even more strident advocacy for Chiang from the Luce publications. *Life* featured Chiang on its cover and hailed him as "an Old Testament Christian." The correspondent Theodore White assured readers that the generalissimo's much-advertised conversion was not done "for the sake of publicity. . . . A man of Chiang's iron will does not easily doff or don a creed."[102]

Chiang's conversion may not have been a publicity stunt, but he recognized its propaganda value in the United States and was not reluctant to remind Americans of it. His Good Friday message in 1937, published as a cover story for *Christian Century*, began with the assertion, "I have been a follower of Jesus for nearly ten years and make a daily practice of reading the scriptures." Chiang credited his "religious faith" with helping him endure attacks from both Japanese invaders and communist insurgents. The title of another of Chiang's sermons, "Why I Believe in Jesus," graced the cover of the *Christian Century* a year later. On this occasion, Chiang noted a "striking resemblance" between conditions in contemporary China and "the situation in Jesus's day." As had been the case two thousand years earlier, a "spiritual depression" afflicted China that required Christlike solutions. Chiang was confident that, like Jesus, he would bring about a "new birth" in his homeland. "Let us hold Jesus as the goal for human living," he proclaimed. "Let us keep the mind of Jesus as our mind, the life of Jesus as our life. Let us bravely go with him to the cross."[103] Although the generalissimo was ostensibly speaking to his fellow Chinese, most of whom, of course, were non-Christian, his true audience was in America, a fact made manifest when Luce's *March of Time* newsreel series broadcast Chiang's speech in theaters throughout the United States.[104]

A few American journalists dared to criticize the Christian general as World War II gave way to the cold war and Chiang proved unable to translate billions of dollars in U.S. aid into victory over the Chinese communists. Brooks Atkinson, Thoburn Wiant, and an apostate Theodore White warned of Chiang's increasingly brutal efforts to stamp out dissent.[105] When the generalissimo fled mainland China with his remaining forces in 1949, the Truman administration attempted to dissociate itself from the disaster by issuing a white paper that laid the blame for the Nationalists' defeat at Chiang's door.[106] But millions of Americans refused to accept this verdict. Representative Walter Judd, a former medical missionary in China, spoke for many Chiang loyalists when he ridiculed the notion that "Chiang's government wasn't good enough for us to support." It may not have been perfect, he insisted, but it was better than communism, and Washington had been unrealistic to expect anything different given conditions in Asia. "We don't demand reforms from our enemies, but our friends, they've got to have democracy, they've got to have full civil rights—right away," Judd scoffed. "We haven't got them in our country in 175 years, but they've got to in Korea or China or South Vietnam—at once. . . . The people of Asia have a little difficulty understanding that."[107] Judd came nearer the root of the matter when he declared, "Chiang Kai-shek, instead of being a heathen, barbarian war lord, was a Christian."[108]

Judd's was a difficult argument for Americans to dismiss. Luce essentially restated it when, in April 1955, around the time that Ngo Dinh Diem crushed his rivals to assume absolute command of South Vietnam, Chiang made a record tenth appearance on the cover of *Time*. The magazine's rationale was similar to the defense Diem's supporters would mount later on: it admitted that Chiang had made many "errors over the years," that "he thought in moral, not social terms," and that he "exhorted and scolded his people like a Savonarola, when the times called for vigorous reforms." These defects were real—but they were beside the point. What mattered was that Chiang had grasped a "big truth" before any other world leader, namely, that "the world's primary and implacable enemy was and is the communist conspiracy directed from Moscow." *Time* portrayed Chiang as a "very spiritual person," a "saintly man" who "tries to find the answer not only in himself, but in the God he serves." It was Chiang's "unshakeable determination" to oppose atheistic communism, *Time* contended, that gave him "sureness" and "tranquility . . . in a time of confused issues and uncertain men."[109] Chiang, in brief, was a Christian, and as such he was an indispensable ally against the red Antichrist poised to engulf Asia.

Second only to Chiang in reputation among Americans during the cold war years was Syngman Rhee, the venerable leader of South Korea whom U.S. Ambassador James Cromwell described as "a great Messiah sent by Providence to save the Korean people from stumbling into the foul pit of that medieval military despotism that calls itself communism." Like Chiang, Rhee had converted from Buddhism to Christianity —under circumstances which *Reader's Digest* almost certainly exaggerated in an adoring 1953 profile. This "great Christian leader," the *Digest* reported, had campaigned for "reform" of the "backward absolute monarchy of Korea" in the first decade of the twentieth century. His reward had been seven years' imprisonment, during which "his fingers were twisted and crushed in vices, bamboo spikes were driven into his legs, and the soles of his feet were beaten to a bloody pulp." That persecution led him to Christ. "When I was put in jail and tortured, I thought my life had reached its end," Rhee told the *Digest*. "For the first time, I prayed. A missionary had sent me a Bible. Fellow prisoners held it and turned the pages for me because my fingers were so crushed that I could not use them. I read the Bible, and I have read it the rest of my life." A biography of Rhee published in 1955 contended that the South Korean president "picture[d] himself as an instrument which must be always ready and willing to be used as God's will might direct."[110]

Rhee's American admirers acknowledged that South Korea was every bit as autocratic as Chiang's regime in Formosa but contended this was unavoidable given the circumstances. Rhee had "accomplished a Herculean task," insisted the *Washington Sunday Star.* "For armchair experts in safe lands to criticize him for not being able overnight to establish a full-orbed democracy, under conditions prevailing, is sheer folly. . . . [H]e has not a drop of dictatorial blood in his veins." Quite the contrary, the *Star* maintained, "He is an inspiring Christian." General James Van Fleet, commander of the U.S. Eighth Army in Korea, went further, claiming that Rhee "stands out" among "the outstanding statesmen of the many countries of the world." Even though "the people of Korea are not well educated," Van Fleet noted in a *Life* article, "President Rhee has made an untutored and disorganized nation into one of the world's strongest bastions against communist aggression." Van Fleet claimed that those critics who wanted Rhee to institute governmental reform while "the Korean people were being bombarded by communist propaganda" did not understand that doing so would be "ruinous to Korean freedom." Luce's other leading publication, *Time* magazine, agreed. *Time* likened Rhee to George Washington and observed that if "his people have not yet heard of a Korean Thomas Jefferson, it is because the political climate of Korea . . . is against the free development of such a typically democratic figure." The magazine respectfully quoted a Korean journalist who raged, "Freedom of speech, freedom of the press, freedom of this, freedom of that. Here in Korea now, such questions are idiotic. Freedom, my friend, is a very *relative* thing. Now we have a little—more than the communists, but still not much. But we have enough to start with. Meantime, don't push us too hard, don't ask for too much too soon."[111]

The third member of what Michael Hunt calls "the Luce pantheon of great Asian leaders" was Ramon Magsaysay, a Catholic military officer famed for his suppression of the communist Hukbalahap rebellion in the Philippines.[112] Magsaysay won the presidency of that country in 1953 with lavish U.S. support and the collaboration of Edward Lansdale, who was posted to Saigon shortly thereafter with orders to apply the lessons of the Magsaysay triumph to Diem's problems.[113] Although *Time* hailed Magsaysay as the "Eisenhower of the Pacific," he did little to reform the Philippines's corrupt political machinery or improve the lot of its people.[114] His most attractive characteristic, from the perspective of his superpower backers, was virulent anticommunism; the American media often referred to him as a "Huk-fighter" or "Huk-killer."[115] Several hagiographic books about Magsaysay were published in the United States from the mid- to late 1950s, among them *Crusade in Asia*, *Philippine Freedom*, and *The Philippine Answer to Communism*.[116] In *The Magsaysay Story*, the Pulitzer Prize–winning journalist Carlos Romulo described the Philippine president as someone who regularly "invoked God. He quoted from the Bible. . . . He was an evangelist in khaki who refused to be silenced."[117]

The Eisenhower administration wholeheartedly endorsed Luce's pantheon, which by 1955 would come to include Diem. Secretary of State Dulles was especially sensitive to criticism of America's Christian soldiers in Asia. At a state dinner with Dulles, Ambassador George Allen made the mistake of faulting Chiang and Rhee for their refusal to allow free elections. The two leaders, Allen understated, were "not exactly paragons of the democratic process." Dulles shot back, "Well, I'll tell you this. No matter what you may say about the President of Korea and the President of Nationalist China, those two gentlemen are the equivalent of the founders of the Church. . . . They have been steadfast and have upheld the faith in a manner that puts them in the category of the leaders of the early Church."[118] Eisenhower, though normally less prone to rhetorical overkill than Dulles, toasted Rhee during the latter's visit to Washington in 1954 by thanking him for giving Americans an opportunity "to venerate those qualities that we call ennobling, that we believe are somewhat Godlike in their quality."[119]

Commitment to representative government was not, apparently, among the qualities Eisenhower venerated in Rhee, at least insofar as it related to conditions in South Korea—or in South Vietnam, where Diem was at that moment laying the foundation for a dictatorship. As Eisenhower wrote to Prime Minister Winston Churchill midway through his first term, "In a number of areas, people are not yet ready for self-rule, and any attempt to make them now responsible for their own governing would be to condemn them to . . . communist domination."[120] One of those areas, Eisenhower believed, was Asia. Nothing the president or any other American encountered in U.S. popular culture—nothing read, heard, or seen on page, stage, or screen—challenged that assumption. It is impossible to know how much of the fifties' extraordinary proliferation of American representations of Asia received Eisenhower's personal attention, although he was very fond of Rodgers and Hammerstein's musicals and almost certainly saw *South Pacific* and *The King and I*.[121] But unless Eisenhower took the time to track down obscure academic monographs, an unlikely venture for this most unscholarly of presidents, he could scarcely have avoided seeing in Asia what his culture prepared him to see.[122]

Michener, one of the most influential producers of that culture, was at the height of his celebrity in 1954, when *Newsweek* saluted him as "the man who makes Asia real to us."[123] Fittingly, this tribute appeared the same year that Diem returned to Vietnam as America's handpicked choice to hold the line against communist penetration. The vision of Asia that Michener presented to Americans in the postwar era seemed suited to a leader with Diem's qualities. Since Western notions of the dignity of the individual were alien to Asians, the Diem regime's contempt for civil liberties was no cause for concern. Since Asians knew

14. Two of America's Christian soldiers in Asia: South Korea's Syngman Rhee (left) and South Vietnam's Ngo Dinh Diem. © Hulton-Deutsch Collection/CORBIS, ca. 1958

nothing of democratic processes, it made no difference that Saigon's government lacked popular legitimacy. Besides, the Vietnamese were not ready to make mature decisions like determining who was best qualified to lead them. Politically underdeveloped and essentially child-like, they were wards of the United States and its proxy, Diem, who would teach them to think and act like democratic, capitalist, Christian adults. Like most Asians, they would require a long period of supervision before they would be ready for self-government, especially since the task of democratizing South Vietnam demanded less immediate attention than that of preserving the country from communism. But prescribed the proper combination of paternal solicitude and tough-minded counterinsurgency, they would someday be ready to take on the responsibilities of modern nationhood. "Sooner or later, the people of Asia will govern themselves," Michener predicted in 1951. "I don't know when the transfer of authority will take place. . . . But it will take place. . . . Let us work on the assumption that the present uneducated masses of Asia will one day become both educated and competent."[124]

Michener continued publishing well into his nineties. In one of his final works, a memoir titled *The World Is My Home* (1992), he came close to admitting there were dimensions of the postwar environment in Asia and especially in Vietnam he had either neglected or under-emphasized in the years when he had been America's foremost popular teacher of the East. Specifically, he regretted his portrayal of the Viet-namese woman Bloody Mary in *Tales of the South Pacific*, the book that won him the Pulitzer Prize. If anything, Michener's literary rendering was more farcical than the racist burlesque created by Rodgers and Hammerstein. "She was, I judge, about fifty-five," he had written in that early novel. "She was not more than five feet tall, weighed about 110 pounds, had few teeth and those funereally black, . . . and had thin ravines running out from the corners of her mouth. These ravines, about four on each side, were usually filled with betel juice, which made her look as though her mouth had been gashed by a rusty razor. Her name, Bloody Mary, was well given."[125]

Yet Michener revealed in his memoir that the real Bloody Mary's nickname derived not from her chewing of betel nuts but from her "outspoken . . . advocacy of Tonkinese rights" and "strong resistance to exploitation." Bloody Mary, whom Michener met on a French planta-tion in the New Hebrides, told him that "when the war ended, she would go to Tonkin, the area that would later be known as North Vietnam." Michener recalled, "I got the strong impression that when she got there she intended to oppose French colonialism." He claimed he often thought of her "in later years, when American troops were fighting their fruitless battles in Vietnam, and I wondered if our leaders realized that the enemy they were fighting consisted of millions of determined people like Bloody Mary." Michener could not blame those leaders if they failed to appreciate the depths of Vietnamese national-ism. "[E]ven I was deficient in my understanding," he conceded mag-nanimously, "for when I wrote about her in *Tales of the South Pacific* I depicted her not as a potential revolutionary but as a Tonkinese woman with a pretty daughter to care for."[126] Like others who sought to explain Asia to postwar America, Michener simplified and ultimately trivialized his subject, fashioning a complex, explosive state of affairs into an easily comprehensible one complete with template for U.S. policy. The flaws in his vision would become apparent long before the communists uni-fied Vietnam and a much-maligned Bloody Mary had the last laugh.

4

"Christ Crucified
in Indo-China":
Tom Dooley and the
North Vietnamese
Refugees

Shortly before collaborating with Eugene Burdick to write *The Ugly American*, a novel that at least four historians have dubbed "the *Uncle Tom's Cabin* of the Cold War,"[1] William Lederer offered a preview of that book's themes in "They'll Remember the *Bayfield*," published in the March 1955 issue of *Reader's Digest*. A first-person narrative of Lederer's journey with two thousand North Vietnamese exiles aboard the USS *Bayfield* en route from Haiphong to Saigon, the article hewed closely to *Digest* editor DeWitt Wallace's philosophy of selling cold war internationalism by wrapping its tenets in human interest stories.[2] Lederer was less interested in the details of Vietnam's postarmistice political situation than in personalizing a far-off rescue operation for American readers. Consequently, he did not refer to the Geneva Conference or to the accords reached at the conference, which mandated refugee resettlement in North and South Vietnam. In fact, he did not mention Ho Chi Minh or the defeated French. The *Bayfield* piece was aimed at the heart rather than the mind, as Lederer exploited Eisenhower-era religiosity and racism to wring tears from his audience, thereby contributing to a genre of reportage that shaped Americans' perspective on events in Vietnam and made the U.S. commitment to South Vietnamese Premier Ngo Dinh Diem increasingly irresistible.

Although Lederer laid on his message with a trowel, the *Digest* prefaced his story with a note that drove the point home further. "When the reds took over North Vietnam last year," an anonymous editor declared, "a half million refugees fled southward from their homeland. Most of

them were Catholics. They sacrificed their homes and all their possessions for one precious thing: the right to worship in the religion of their
choice." Then Lederer spun his tale of hardship and heroism. The refugees picked up at Haiphong by the *Bayfield*, he reported, had "melted
into one pathetic mass of perspiration, scabies, and sores. . . . If it were
not for the priests, they never would have pulled through." Lederer
furnished the exiles with an italicized internal monologue as they
waited, "with the eyes of a cornered fox," for the U.S. ship to dock: "*Will
the communist propaganda prove true? Will we all die on this sea trip?
Will the Americans cut our hands off, as the communists said? Already we
have suffered, O Lord. . . .*" He described "one of the first passengers to
reach the deck of this American ship, . . . an eight-year-old girl with her
three-year-old brother strapped to her back. Mud was caked on her legs
and arms. The only clean part of her was the path made by tears rolling
down her cheeks." Deeply moved, the American sailors sprang into
action, "picking up heavy bundles, supporting the aged, carrying kids,
comforting the people with smiles and acts of kindness."

Communication was difficult at first aboard the *Bayfield*, Lederer
recalled, given that few refugees spoke English and no sailors spoke
Vietnamese. But "Lieut. Francis J. Fitzpatrick, usnr, a chaplain from St.
Joseph, Mo.," found a solution. Father Fitzpatrick "spoke fluent Latin.
So did the Vietnamese priests. They jibber-jabbered like crazy with
Fitzpatrick in this so-called 'dead language.' " When Fitzpatrick asked a
refugee priest why the Vietnamese were fleeing their homes, the response was unequivocal: "Because the communists are burning our
churches and won't let us worship Christ."

Much of Lederer's article recounted how he hoodwinked the refugees into believing he could communicate directly with Washington. A
delegation of Vietnamese elders approached him with the request that
they be allowed to name their new village in South Vietnam after the
ship that carried them to freedom. "But we must have permission from
American authorities," they insisted. Lederer assured them that his
wristwatch was "a Dick Tracy wrist radio like they've seen in the funny
papers" and proceeded to carry on a "make-believe radio-telephone
conversation" with President Dwight Eisenhower in which he received
official authorization. "The old men's eyes popped," Lederer remembered. "They laughed like boys at a circus." Before the refugees disem-
barked, Lederer handed them a phony telegram from Eisenhower proclaiming, "The United States is honored that you desire to name your

next town after the *Bayfield*. Authority is hereby granted. . . . With courageous people such as you, the town will be a monument to free people all over the world." The Vietnamese were overcome. "It will have cool, broad streets," they promised, "quiet churches, and schools for everyone. . . . It will be Bayfield, USA, South Vietnam. Good-bye, sir. God bless you!"[3]

The paternalism of this portrayal anticipated scenes in *The Ugly American* in which U.S. counterinsurgency experts persuaded the Sark-hanese to follow American directives by feigning supernatural powers of palmistry.[4] As Renny Christopher observes, "Here we have the spectacle not only of the Asian as childlike and simple, but also of the American cheating in order to pursue 'higher' ends. . . . It is like a gigantic wink at American readers, enlisting them in scorn for the gullible Asians."[5] In a vignette redolent of the attitude Christopher identifies, Lederer had the same mud-caked little girl who first approached the *Bayfield* respond to a spray of white delousing powder by exclaiming to her mother, "Mama, the big American is a priest! First he blessed me, and then *he baptized me an American!*"[6]

In the mid-1950s, *Reader's Digest* was the most widely read magazine in the world.[7] For many readers, especially in America, Lederer's racist potpourri *cum* travelogue was their introduction to a mysterious place called Vietnam. Indeed, if any one image dominated Americans' understanding of Vietnam during the Eisenhower era, it was that of the Catholic refugee: starving, tortured, and devout, with an inflexible claim on America's conscience. From the conclusion of the Geneva Conference in 1954 until well after John F. Kennedy's inauguration in 1961, Americans who tried to follow Vietnamese politics were bombarded with maudlin and macabre refugee narratives of betrayal, suffering, and salvation in a country that few Americans would have been able to locate on a map at the onset of the 1950s but that had become the testing ground of U.S. cold war credibility by the time the following decade dawned.

Passage to Freedom

It is unlikely that any delegate to the Geneva Conference envisioned that article 14(d) of the Geneva Accords would generate more controversy than the rest of that unwieldy package of trade-offs combined. As conference participants recognized, the accords held the potential for disaster in virtually every clause. Chief among their defects were the fixing of the provisional boundary between North and South Vietnam along the 17th parallel rather than the 13th, which Viet Minh military success warranted, and the scheduling of all-Vietnam elections and reunification for July 1956, two years after the conference's adjournment, as opposed to a briefer delay that would have minimized the crystallizing of separate southern and northern national identities. In addition, the International Control Commission charged with implementing the accords was powerless, the accords failed to specify whether France or the Bao Dai regime was responsible for civil administration in the South, and neither the United States nor the newly minted State of Vietnam signed the accords, thereby leaving both free to assert they were not bound by any decisions taken at Geneva.[8] "Of all of the important peace-making documents of our time," Anthony Short observes, "none was so badly drafted and curiously drawn as the so-called 'Geneva Settlement' of 1954. . . . [It] was open to almost undreamt-of possibilities for avoidance if not evasion."[9]

Article 14(d) did not appear to present possibilities for avoidance or evasion. It represented a slight modification of one of seven "nonnegotiable" conditions set forth by President Eisenhower and British prime minister Winston Churchill in June 1954. The sixth of the so-called Seven Points demanded that any armistice settlement "provide for the peaceful and humane transfer . . . of those people desiring to be moved from one zone to another of Vietnam."[10] No delegate at Geneva challenged or even discussed this provision. Little attention was given to the logistics of population resettlement because most assumed it would be a minor matter. The French commander in Indochina, General Paul Ely, believed that no more than thirty thousand landlords and businessmen would voluntarily move south.[11] French prime minister Pierre Mendès-France declared that the French Expeditionary Corps (FEC) would take responsibility for the transport of all North Vietnamese and planned to provide for up to fifty thousand displaced persons.[12]

The authorities, however, vastly underestimated the enormity of their task. When the Geneva Accords came into force on 21 July 1954, a mass exodus from the northern provinces near Hanoi had already begun. The French navy and air force attempted to move the refugees to Saigon, but as news of the relocation option spread, thousands of fugitives descended upon Hanoi and the port of Haiphong. Riots broke out as refugees fought over shelter, food, medicine, and places on the ships and planes leaving for South Vietnam.[13] General Ely urgently requested U.S. surface transport for up to one hundred thousand refugees a month above what the French could carry.[14] The Defense Department ordered the navy to mobilize a task force. Day after day, until the free movement period prescribed by the accords elapsed in May 1955, French and U.S. ships departed as fast as the refugees could be loaded aboard, making over five hundred trips in three hundred days. All told, roughly one million Vietnamese moved from north to south in what the U.S. Navy called Operation Passage to Freedom.[15]

The exodus drastically altered the religious balance of Vietnam. Entire northern Catholic provinces packed up and relocated below the 17th parallel. In the North, the number of Catholics declined from 1,133,000 to 457,000, while the number in the South increased from 461,000 to 1,137,000. By 1956, the diocese of Saigon had more practicing Catholics than Paris or Rome.[16] This huge demographic shift elicited an outpouring of generosity from private Catholic voluntary agencies, especially in the United States. The National Catholic Welfare Conference (NCWC) and Catholic Relief Services (CRS) contributed over $35 million and sent hundreds of workers to Vietnam to distribute food, clothing, medicines, and other supplies. Prominent American churchmen like New York's Monsignor Joseph Harnett, an associate of Cardinal Spellman, spent over a year in Saigon and the surrounding countryside, supervising the establishment of orphanages, hospitals, schools, and churches.[17] Harnett submitted impassioned reports to NCWC headquarters in which he praised the refugees as "the finest group of Catholic people I have ever met in all my life" and called their flight "a religious migration if there ever was one."[18] So ubiquitous were representatives of Catholic organizations in Passage to Freedom that one historian describes the movement as "primarily a Catholic operation."[19]

The tidal wave of humanity flooding south in 1954–55 has been portrayed as a movement in which refugees "voted with their feet," a characterization that on the surface seems persuasive.[20] Anthony Bouscaren, Diem's biographer, notes, "The fact that all the movement was from north to south pretty well demonstrated how the people . . . felt about the communist Viet Minh."[21] Matters were not that simple, however. The Politburo in Hanoi instructed many cadres and military personnel to stay in the South to drum up support for the Viet Minh cause in anticipation of the all-Vietnam elections to be held in 1956. According to one province-level communist leader who later defected, Ho Chi

15. American sailors help a Vietnamese woman and her infant
disembark during the Passage to Freedom exodus of 1954–55.
© Bettmann/CORBIS, 8 October 1954

Minh wanted only those Viet Minh who had "incurred the enmity of
the people" to move north; the rest were ordered to remain.[22] More
important, as the CIA veteran Chester Cooper understates, "the vast
movement of Catholics to South Vietnam was not spontaneous."[23] On
the contrary, the United States promoted the exodus through one of the
most audacious propaganda campaigns in the history of covert action.
At the pinnacle of this operation was Colonel Edward Lansdale, a legend in the annals of cold war cloak-and-dagger exploits who has been
celebrated and damned, respectively, in two of the most popular novels
ever written about Vietnam—*The Ugly American* and *The Quiet American*—and likened to pop culture icons as diverse as Lawrence of Arabia,
James Bond, and Oliver North.[24] In 1954, Lansdale's assignment was to
plan and implement a campaign of subversion north of the 17th paral-

lel. As he recalled, "U.S. officials wanted to make sure that as many persons as possible, particularly the strongly anti-communist Catholics, relocated in the South."[25]

Lansdale and his team employed a number of devices to persuade northerners to move, from pouring sugar in the tanks of the Viet Minh trucks to hiring Vietnamese soothsayers to predict a famine in the Red River Delta. South Vietnamese agents helped spread the word that those going south would be well cared for under a government supported by American aid. Forged documents purportedly issued by the Viet Minh warned of an impending government seizure of all private property. Lansdale proudly recalled, "The day following distribution of these leaflets, refugee registration tripled."[26] Perhaps the most effective rumor spread by Lansdale's agents was that the United States intended to launch an atomic attack on the North after Passage to Freedom concluded. Hundreds of thousands of copies of a handbill were distributed showing an aerial view of Hanoi with three circles of nuclear destruction superimposed upon it.[27]

Lansdale's most inspired appeals were to North Vietnamese Catholics. Soldiers of the South Vietnamese army, shipped north and dressed as civilians, distributed fliers advertising that "Christ Has Gone to the South" and "The Virgin Mary Has Departed from the North." Psychological warfare teams pasted enormous posters in Hanoi and Haiphong depicting communists closing a cathedral and forcing the congregation to pray under a picture of Ho Chi Minh; the caption read, "Make your choice."[28] The Central Evacuation Committee in Haiphong, which was financed by the United States, issued thousands of circulars like the following:

> Dear Catholic brothers and sisters, hundreds of gigantic airplanes are waiting to transport you gratis to Saigon. In the South the cost of living is three times less, you will receive twelve piastres a day and in addition you will be given fertile rice fields and other means of livelihood. By remaining in the North you will experience famine and will *damn your souls.* Set out now, brothers and sisters! Hurry so as not to miss the opportunity. To miss it would be like burying yourselves alive with your own hands.[29]

Unsurprisingly—in light of such ballyhoo and the more-tangible factor of the United States laying out about $89 for each refugee in a country with an $85 per capita income—many North Vietnamese were persuaded to relocate south.[30]

Passage to Freedom was the largest civilian evacuation in history. Given that Vietnam was a country in which most citizens rarely ventured beyond the boundaries of their villages, the consequences were profound. Families were divided, some permanently. The North lost skilled workers who might have aided in resuscitating the Democratic Republic's economy after eight years of war. The South gained a mass of people but lacked the facilities to feed, house, and employ them. The exodus also had significant repercussions in the United States. As the authors of *The Pentagon Papers* note, "the refugees engaged the sympathies of the American people as few developments in Vietnam have before or since, and solidly underwrote the U.S. decision for unstinting support of Diem."[31]

American press coverage of Passage to Freedom emphasized three themes: the devoutness of the Catholic refugees, the suffering they endured in making their pilgrimage, and the perfidiousness of the Viet Minh, who employed every obstructionist tactic from bureaucratic stonewalling to murder to stem the exodus. While the most lurid write-ups appeared in the American Catholic press, secular magazines and newspapers like *Look* and the *New York Times* also portrayed the flight from Ho to Diem as a modern-day miracle pageant. Thus, the *Times* quoted a fleeing but defiant bishop to the effect that "any Catholic in this country betrays his faith if he is not a soldier. . . . To compromise with communism is treachery. You must fight. It is the only Christian solution." *Newsweek* detailed Cardinal Spellman's ministering to a crowd of exiles freshly arrived from Haiphong: "Accompanied by Premier Ngo Dinh Diem of South Vietnam, the Cardinal blessed the aged, the newly born, the seasick, the dirty, the pathetically ragged refugees from communist North Vietnam. One wretched woman, carrying her child, thrust a broken image of the Virgin Mary into Cardinal Spellman's hands. He blessed that, too." Henry Luce's *March of Time* newsreel series showed a group of refugee children making the sign of the cross on board a navy carrier while commentator Ed Herlihy proclaimed, "Civilization could but pause to admire the righteous will that drives men away from bondage to the freedom of religion." Leo Cherne, later a founding member of the American Friends of Vietnam, wrote a feature story for *Look* that displayed a large color photograph of refugees kneeling in prayer on the deck of an American ship. The caption read, "Battered and shunted about by war, they are too weary to resist the reds without us." Cherne warned readers that "if elections were held

today, the overwhelming number of Vietnamese would vote communist. . . . What can we do?" Cherne answered: "There is an army of
400,000 Catholic Vietnamese ready and anxious to convince their
countrymen that they must choose freedom."[32]

The notion of a Catholic army waiting to be mobilized against the
Viet Minh, so representative of John Foster Dulles's brand of "dynamic"
Christianity, found its way into a number of reports. In its coverage of
the French evacuation of the North Vietnamese province of Nam Dinh,
Time observed, "There was courage here: a bunch of Catholic teen-agers
strapped grenades to their belts and vowed they would start a guerrilla
war against the communists. . . . The cathedral enclosure includes an
army barracks. Adjoining the priests' quarters is a factory for making
grenades, mortar bombs, and grenade throwers." *Life* ran a full-page
photograph of armed Catholic teenagers in the Red River Delta with the
legend "Last Line of Defense." Under the headline "Catholics Form
Backbone of Resistance to Viet Minh," the *Washington Sunday-Star*
correspondent Earl Voss reported, "The core of anti-communist resistance among Vietnamese is the Catholic population. . . . Monasteries
have been converted into basic training camps, troop quarters, supply
centers, and ammunition dumps. . . . People who have spent Christmas
with Catholic Vietnamese say that each soldier makes his own tiny
manger and worships at it in his foxhole or dugout."[33] One would never
gather from reading these accounts that Catholics made up only a small
percentage of anticommunist Vietnamese, and that the Viet Minh considered the virulently anticommunist Hoa Hao and Cao Dai a greater
threat than any monastery-turned-barracks.[34]

The excesses of *Newsweek* and *Life* were trifling compared to the
treatment accorded Passage to Freedom in the American Catholic press.
The St. Paul *Catholic Bulletin* called the exodus "one of the biggest
stories—simply as news—in human history. . . . Some refugees drowned.
Some were killed or kidnapped by the communists. But the 800,000
flowed on in a tidal wave of heroic devotion to the right of human beings
to worship their Creator." *Jubilee* waxed ecstatic as it described the
welcome Diem's government extended to the refugees. "The scene was
Biblical," the correspondent Fred Sparks proclaimed. "I saw the Church
here . . . playing an important fighting role not duplicated since the
Crusades." *Catholic Digest* ran a photostory called "Vietnam's Flight to
Freedom" that described images of huddled Vietnamese in a series of
captions: "They leave behind their homes, their land, and their wealth, to

keep a lasting treasure—faith"; "Courage such as this makes saints of men"; "Premier Ngo Dinh Diem, Vietnam's leader in this dangerous hour, kneels with the refugees at Mass"; and, in one composition, the drawn, sobbing face of a nun with the word "SUFFERING" blazoned beneath it. The *Ave Maria* noted that "traditionally, those who have suffered much before the world in the confession of their Faith have been given the title of Confessor. It would seem that at the present time, the Church is being given hundreds of thousands of candidates for that title in the land of Viet Nam."[35]

Passage to Freedom received daily front-page coverage in all of America's 111 diocesan newspapers.[36] The most prolific chronicler of the operation was Patrick O'Connor, a priest stationed in Hanoi by the National Catholic Welfare Conference. O'Connor's dispatches for the conference's news service were syndicated to Catholic papers across the United States, reaching millions of Americans, and were published in many secular papers as well.[37] Like other journalists, O'Connor wrote rousing tributes to Diem and the North Vietnamese exiles, but his reports were especially notable for their accounts of communist atrocities against fleeing Catholics. In a typical bulletin, O'Connor accused the Viet Minh of "grabbing infants from their mothers' arms to prevent families from leaving. Many an infant has been badly disfigured in such a grotesque 'tug-of-war.'" He asserted that "Viet Minh prisons are a graveyard for thousands of priests and nuns who have been tortured to death" and that "most refugees died of drowning when they tried to escape to the sea, while others were machine-gunned to death on the beaches." O'Connor's magnum opus was his final report from the North Vietnamese capital, "Goodbye to Hanoi: Neck-Deep in Tears," in which he hammered home the tragedy that had befallen a "once Godly" city:

> Goodbye to Hanoi, . . . to the city pavements where I have seen men go down on both knees to kiss the Bishop's ring in public. . . . Goodbye to . . . the hallowed gray cathedral, to all of the churches, none of which I have ever seen without worshippers. Goodbye to the schools I have seen thronged with Vietnamese youth, learning from Catholic Brothers and Sisters, schools I later saw crowded with refugees who left everything for their faith. Goodbye to Hanoi, where young men who craved independence and reform listened to Karl Marx and not to Christ. . . . Goodbye to Hanoi, where prayer will not cease and grace will not be wanting. Goodbye, Hanoi![38]

The overall effect of the secular and Catholic media's coverage of Passage to Freedom was to render the Vietnamese civil war in American eyes not as a battle between communists and noncommunists, but as a battle between communists and *Catholics*. The *Progressive*'s Far Eastern correspondent, O. Edmund Clubb, contributed to this misperception with an article that set up "Divided Vietnam" as a showdown between "in the North, the communist Ho Chi Minh" and "in the South, the Catholic Ngo Dinh Diem."[39] Huge domains of Vietnamese culture were omitted, and Clubb's readers were left with the impression that political parties and constituencies in Vietnam were parallel to those in Italy. According to Cardinal Spellman's biographer, by the close of Passage to Freedom, "many Americans came to believe that Vietnam was a predominantly Catholic country."[40]

The archival record does not evince a more sophisticated understanding of the Vietnamese situation on the part of the U.S. State Department. Randolph Kidder, chargé d'affaires at the American embassy in Saigon, sent Secretary of State Dulles a report in December 1954 that rationalized the overrepresentation of Catholics in South Vietnamese refugee camps by concluding, "Lack of religious freedom means more to them than to the average non-Christian." Furthermore, Kidder reasoned, "Catholics have been coming out in much greater numbers so far [because] they can confide in each other and make joint plans with the assurance that their fellow Catholic will not be a Viet Minh agent"— as though members of the Cao Dai and Hoa Hao enjoyed no such assurance. Kidder did, however, qualify his argument by listing the "three reasons given by refugees" for making their escape from the North—"excessive taxation, excessive corvées, and lack of religious freedom"—and acknowledging that "the first two, at least, weigh heavily on non-Christians also."[41] On other occasions, embassy personnel sent the White House secondhand reports of the Viet Minh torturing children, machine-gunning elderly refugees, blowing up churches, and burying people alive.[42] The U.S. consul in Hanoi, Thomas Corcoran, was a lonely dissenting voice, asserting that most of the NCWC's reports of communist atrocities were "false." The consul noted he did not "know where the American bishops get their information," but observed that "many priests . . . believe almost anything they are told."[43]

Corcoran erred in restricting this gullibility to men of the cloth. The brief, dazzling career of Tom Dooley would demonstrate that Ameri-

16. A refugee girl, newly relocated in South Vietnam. © Bettmann/
CORBIS, 26 August 1954

cans from all walks of life were capable of believing almost anything
they were told about Vietnam.

"A National Hero and a National Hazard"

When Thomas A. Dooley died of cancer on 18 January 1961, one day
after his thirty-fourth birthday, a Gallup poll ranked him third among
the "Most Esteemed Men" in the world, after Dwight Eisenhower and
the pope. A typically effusive editorial tribute to the famed "jungle
doctor of Asia" proclaimed, "Tom Dooley is survived by his mother,
two brothers, and three billion members of the human race who are
infinitely richer for his example."[44] The historian Daniel Boorstin saluted Dooley as a throwback to a heroic age when accomplishment
rather than celebrity was the measure of an individual.[45] Monsignor

George Gottwald, who delivered the eulogy at the pontifical requiem mass for Dooley, compared him to Christ, declaiming,

[T]he greatest life that was ever lived was thirty-three years. Dr. Dooley was thirty-four. . . . It should be a tremendous joy to his family, especially to his mother—a mother like the Mother of Jesus Christ—who keeps these things in her mind . . . and who, like the Mother of Jesus Christ, standing at the foot of the Cross, was proud of Her Son, even though it was a horrible death, because, as Mary looked back, She saw Her Son completely dedicated to God.[46]

Bitingly cold fifteen-degree weather did not prevent thousands of mourners from lining the route in St. Louis as Dooley's coffin was carried to Cavalry Cemetery. Eisenhower sent a public telegram to Dooley's mother in which he declared, "There are few if any men who have equaled Tom Dooley's exhibition of courage, self-sacrifice, faith in his God, and readiness to serve his fellow man."[47] Congress awarded Dooley the Medal of Honor, newly inaugurated President Kennedy gave him the Medal of Freedom, and a popular groundswell built to have the doctor canonized.[48] In all, the nationwide paroxysm of grief that greeted news of Dooley's demise was a fitting response to the death of the man whom many Americans had come to regard as a saint.

Within a decade, however, Dooley was forgotten. His books, which sold millions of copies during his lifetime, disappeared from stores and gathered dust on library shelves. Hollywood studios had plans to make a film of his life, but nothing came of them. Two biographies of Dooley, one written by his mother and the other by his assistant, sold poorly.[49] Campaigns to promote the cause of Dooley's sanctity in the Catholic Church fizzled.[50] The maxim about all glory being fleeting is applicable to the whole of modern American culture, but rarely more poignantly than to the case of Tom Dooley.

There are several reasons for Dooley's plunge from what one biographer terms "celebrity sainthood" to obscurity.[51] First of all, he left no lasting monument to his life's work. The Medical International Cooperation Organization (MEDICO) that he founded proved dependent on his charisma for money and collapsed shortly after his passing.[52] Then there was Dooley's homosexuality, never completely hidden but a matter of public record only after his death. One of Dooley's classmates at St. Louis University recalls being informed by a professor that "homosexuality is something that only happens in hell," an indication of how gay men and women were viewed by most Americans in the 1950s, to say nothing of the conservative Catholic circles from which Dooley drew his staunchest support.[53] The post-obit revelation that this cherubic figure was not only gay but promiscuously so no doubt contributed to his erasure from collective memory.

But probably the most significant reason for Americans' amnesia with regard to Dooley was the Vietnam War. In an article written for the Catholic magazine *Critic* in 1969, Nicholas von Hoffman blamed Dooley's "ethnocentric fusion of piety and patriotism" for helping to create "a climate of public misunderstanding that made the war in Vietnam possible." Dooley, von Hoffman charged, "contributed to the malformation of our knowledge and moral judgments about Southeast Asia" by depicting the region's complex conflicts in simple terms of good versus evil. Such "muddled, primitive political thinking" had led to a war that ravaged America's spirit and squandered the moral capital the United States had accumulated by defeating the fascists in World War II. Von Hoffman predicted that "eight years hence, Tom Dooley may appear so bizarre, . . . so much a defunct social type, that no one will make the effort to remember him."[54]

Von Hoffman's forecast proved accurate. None of the major histories of the Vietnam War published from the late 1970s through the early 1990s mentioned Dooley's name.[55] Nothing of substance was written about Dooley for almost twenty years, while the overall field of Vietnam War scholarship grew vast.[56] Yet interest in Dooley revived with the publication of several journalistic and scholarly works, notably Diana Shaw's article "The Temptation of Tom Dooley" (1991), Randy Shilts's monograph *Conduct Unbecoming* (1993), and James Fisher's biography *Dr. America* (1997). These works differ in tone and reliability, but neither Shilts nor Shaw would dispute Fisher's conclusion that "no American played a larger role [than Dooley] in announcing the arrival of South Vietnam as a new ally whose fate was decisively bound to that of the United States. Dooley's enormously popular 1956 account of his work in Vietnam, *Deliver Us from Evil*, quite literally located Vietnam on the new world map for millions of Americans."[57]

That Tom Dooley, who remained almost comically ignorant of conditions in Southeast Asia his entire life, could have had such an impact reveals much about America in the Eisenhower years. Dooley's influence is inexplicable unless placed in the context of religious revivalism and anti-Asian prejudice in the 1950s: these overlapping ideologies provide the key to his career. In a different era, Dooley would have been, as von Hoffman noted, "too preposterous a figure for youth to identify with."[58] But in the mid- to late 1950s, he was, to cite the *Chicago Sun-Times*, "a combination of Tom Swift, Frank Merriwell, the Rover Boys, and Jack Armstrong the All-American Boy leavened with a dash of Albert Schweitzer and a touch of Bishop Sheen!"[59] Dooley's fleeting renown furnishes the historian with an exquisite case in point of the man and the hour meeting in perfect conjunction.

In his indistinct but ardent religiosity, Dooley typified the American "civil religion" that Will Herberg examined in his best-selling *Protestant-Catholic-Jew*, a religion of the "American Way of Life" that stood above the three large historic communities of faith in the United States. Never did Dooley present his Catholicism as incompatible with the other organized churches of "the West." As far as he was concerned, the historic expressions of Judaism and Christianity had been integrated into a single entity: religion. The only relevant distinction was between atheistic communism and what Dooley termed "freedom" or "democracy," a condition inextricably bound up with religious ardor. Dooley underscored this point in his speeches and interviews, telling a reporter in 1956, "We Americans have got to take communism down from the clouds and rub our noses in it. It's alive! It's devouring mankind in big gulps! We don't have time left for talk. Our only answer is God! . . . There can be no compromise, no concessions, no co-existence with godlessness."[60] In a speech that same year in St. Louis, he lectured his audience, "Mothers, teach your children about God! . . . We don't need soldiers and sailors that are merely tough. We need soldiers and sailors that believe in God. If you mothers will teach your children the truths of your religion, . . . they will know the true meaning of words like 'freedom' and 'liberty.' "[61]

This passionate inexactitude meshed with the brand of religiosity that Eisenhower promulgated. "One might say," the theologian William Miller remarked in 1953, "that President Eisenhower, like many Americans, is a very fervent believer in a very vague religion."[62] Eisenhower would not have contested that assertion; indeed, he insisted in a television address, "I am the most intensely religious man I know, but that does not mean I adhere to any sect."[63] Dooley never challenged this all-inclusive religiosity or the presumption that belief in God was the cardinal distinction between "our" way of life and "theirs." He did not oppose the guiding principles of U.S. foreign policy on religious grounds, as sixties-era Catholics like the Berrigan brothers would. In this regard, Dooley worked within the system; he was safe.

Dooley made the Vietnamese seem safe as well. His books, articles, and speeches presented the Catholic refugees of Passage to Freedom as typical Vietnamese: deeply religious, anticommunist, ready to welcome American business interests. Although he never credited the Vietnamese or Laotians to whom he ministered with anything approaching American intellectual ability—in none of his works were Asians given agency or independent thought—he portrayed them in such benign terms as to elicit his readers' sympathy and indulgence. One recognizes in this depiction an essential dichotomy of American racism addressed by Renny Christopher: when Asians "are good, they are passive and malleable, and when bad they are sinister, powerful devils."[64]

Vietnamese malleability was a constant theme in Dooley's writings and public addresses. In 1957, Dooley exhorted a group of his supporters, "Let Americans always gently and inexorably help to mold free men for Asia. From the clay of contradictions and the chunky confusion of custom can come Asians of fire and flame, capable of doing a magnificent job for the right!"[65] The imagery was significant; from Dooley's perspective, if a Vietnamese chose communism over freedom, it was because a communist ceramicist molded the clay of that Asian's mind before American hands had the opportunity to shape it differently. The possibility that the Vietnamese's choice was one of individual volition was not entertained. Moreover, Dooley did not even accord the Vietnamese the dignity of a separate national identity, using instead the broadest possible term, "Asian." Dooley, considered an expert on "the Orient" by millions of Americans, thereby obviated the possibility of there being any variation within the region of Asia. Despite his reputation for having a keen understanding of "the Oriental mind" (itself a meaningless expression), he never deviated from the prevailing cold war view of Asia as a playing field for the United States and the USSR in which all Asians—Vietnamese, Cambodians, Laotians, Thai, Chinese, Burmese—were either on one side or the other.[66]

In his conceptual fusion of patriotism and religion and his belief that Asians became communists because they were brainwashed by evil people, Dooley was a product of his time. But he was more than that, and the unique strengths and defects of his personality profoundly influenced the most important alliance entered into by the United States in the 1950s. While no one person can be blamed for America's

Vietnam commitment, a repentant William Lederer was correct when in 1991 he observed of his former protégé, "He was a national hero and a national hazard. It was his mammoth ego, his need for recognition, that helped get us into that mess over there."[67] How Dooley managed to accomplish this feat is an illuminating chapter of the early cold war.

"Bac Sy My"

Nothing in Dooley's life prior to Passage to Freedom gave the barest hint that he was destined for celebrity sainthood. The journalist Robert Allen was more incisive than he realized when he noted in 1958, "Listening to Tom Dooley talk, you might easily get the impression that he was born at the age of twenty-eight aboard the USS *Montague* in Vietnam's Haiphong Bay."[68] Dooley's reluctance to discuss anything other than the diplomatic-medical mission that became his life's work in 1954 was more than a display of single-minded devotion to a calling. Rather, he recognized that his youth hardly mirrored the ideal of red-blooded American boyhood that he and his publicists created and that 1950s popular culture required of its heroes. Dooley was still young when he treated his first Vietnamese refugee—far too young to be termed a "failure"—but his early adulthood seemed to presage a life of modest achievement.

Born into one of St. Louis's most prominent families, Dooley enjoyed a childhood untouched by the Depression. His grandfather had made a fortune by designing the first all-steel boxcar prior to America's entry into World War I, and by 1935 the family's assets were such that Dooley's father could afford to employ a cook, a maid, and a houseman. "I was a rich man's son," Dooley later admitted, almost shamefacedly.[69] He was also, biographer Fisher notes, more interested in achieving recognition as "one of the most popular beaus in St. Louis society" than in academics or athletics.[70] A teacher counseled the sixteen-year-old Dooley, "Think, if you would only harness that energy, all the good you could do."[71] Dooley proved incapable of exercising such discipline as an undergraduate at Notre Dame, and he floundered even more after family connections gained him admission to St. Louis University School of Medicine. A miserable student, he probably would have been expelled if the dean had not been a family friend and willing to press the administration board to let him stay. Nonetheless, before the class of 1952 graduated, the board informed Dooley he would have to repeat his senior year. He complied, but the faculty determined at the end of this second go-round that he was still too immature to begin a residency. Fed up, Dooley joined the military and secured admission to the Navy Medical Corps. After a year's internship, he was transferred to the U.S. Naval Hospital in Yokosuka, Japan. It was there he had the opportunity to volunteer to serve aboard the USS *Montague*, which was under orders to move Vietnamese refugees from Haiphong to South Vietnam under the Geneva Accords. Chafing at the discipline of a military hospital, he applied to take part in Passage to Freedom. His ability to speak French counted considerably in his being approved for the assignment.[72]

Dooley wrote to his mother almost every day of the eleven months he served in Passage to Freedom, and she saved every letter, thereby compiling what Fisher considers "the best surviving firsthand account of the opening chapter in America's long, slow descent into the Vietnam quagmire."[73] This identification of Dooley with America is not over-drawn, for he became in effect the prism through which millions of Americans got their first glimpses of Vietnam. The manner in which he interpreted events in that country therefore had consequences far be-yond his own experience. When, for example, he observed in January 1955 that "these Vietnamese are a grateful people, in spite of being Oriental," he was more than simply betraying his own ignorance of Asians;[74] he was sounding a theme around which he would structure several best-selling books and upon which he and other propagandists would persuade Americans of South Vietnam's importance. The notion that the Vietnamese were "superior" Asians, "Oriental" in their back-wardness and obtuseness but uniquely appreciative of American in-struction—a presumption that the American Friends of Vietnam would exploit in the late 1950s—had its origin in Dooley's government-issue typewriter.

In later years, Dooley described his first encounter with the North Vietnamese refugees as "the white light of revelation," but the version he relayed to his mother at the time was less momentous.[75] His initial reaction appears to have been queasiness, an understandable response given his unpreparedness for the scene that awaited him in Baie d'Along, the harbor thirty miles south of Haiphong where the *Montague* picked up refugees for transport to Saigon. "All the pictures and descriptions in the world cannot give you the true account, the stench, the fatigue, the swollen bellies, the nausea, the filth, and the magot-ridden [*sic*] wounds that these people have," he wrote. "Eighty per cent are very old men and women, and the rest are infants, all swollen with malnutrition and starvation, and literally dozens without limbs." At first, Dooley was less concerned with easing the refugees' suffering than with the health hazard they posed. "They will live deep in the holds of the ship," he reported. "[W]e *must* keep them off our decks. Even with the delousing that we do with them as they come up the ladder, they are ladened [*sic*] with disease." Dooley admitted that "it is much like animals in a cage that we have to treat them"; he added, however, in the earliest hint of the Manichean motif that would evolve into *Deliver Us from Evil,* "they don't seem to mind, because they do realize that we are carrying them from slavery to a free world."[76]

This "slavery versus freedom" story line, while ever-present in Dooley's letters, did not rise above the level of subplot for the first month of his service. His greatest initial hostility was reserved not for the Viet Minh, but for the departing French, to whom he referred as "the most frustrating people in the world."[77] Dooley was outraged by French "coldness" toward American sailors and complained that the French were obstructing the rescue operation through inattention to duty. "The French are suppose to furnish interpreters, but they usually flub the dub," he wrote. "Also, the French are supposed to handle the delousing on the beach. . . . They have not done this either. The French said they would supply interpretors [*sic*] on each vessel for the complete operation, round trip. They have, but they are Vietnamese officers who can interpret from Vietnamein to French, but no further. BIG HELP!!!"[78]

Ironically, it was the incapacity of the French to supply interpreters that led to Dooley's first promotion in Passage to Freedom. He was initially instructed to remain on board ship to supervise the construction of the *Montague*'s medical facilities, but his language skills made him valuable to the line officers responsible for the evacuation. Not only was he fluent in French, but he quickly acquired a working knowledge of Vietnamese. "I can say about twenty stock expressions," he informed his mother, "and the words for 'don't urinate on the ground, use the toilet.' "[79] After only one voyage from Baie d'Along to Saigon, Dooley was reassigned to a special task force centered in Haiphong.[80] The unit's official purpose was epidemiological research, but this proved less of a priority than the medical needs of the refugees.[81] Captain Julius Amberson, Dooley's immediate superior, submitted a report on camp conditions, declaring, "As we entered Haiphong, we found every available vacant lot, parks, schools, vacated buildings—packed with refugees. . . . They were living in the most squalid conditions. . . . Wormy feces were common and carelessly scattered about. . . . Strong odors permeated the air."[82] Faced with the prospect of an epidemic of either cholera or bubonic plague, Dooley and his fellow medical officers plunged into a campaign to screen and treat all of the Haiphong refugees before they boarded the transport vessels.[83]

It was a titanic project, and it represented the first time Dooley was able to "harness that energy," as he had been advised to do years before. While his deserved reputation as a self-promoter makes it obligatory for the historian to treat all aspects of the Dooley legend with circumspection, he does appear to have undergone something of a spiritual conversion during his months in Haiphong. No date may be said to mark the epiphanic moment, but the tone of Dooley's letters home gradually shifted. The refugees became, in his eyes, progressively nobler, while his irritation with the French gave way to anticommunist bellicosity. In one letter, he projected his own transformation onto the "white hats" to whom he lectured on board ships docking in Baie d'Along: "Previously, many of the sailors were angered with the refugees. They smell bad, have poor toilet habits (anywhere at any time)[,] have awful-looking diseases. . . . I try to let these boys know that they are really a fine and noble people. . . . They have to run and hide and travel under darkness. . . . They have heard Vietminh born rumors that they will be gassed and tortured by the Americans. So they come to us frightened and like children."[84]

Dooley made several attempts to write a narrative of his experiences. A manuscript titled "Passage to Freedom" was filed among the reports he prepared in late 1954. It was a much coarser piece of work than *Deliver Us from Evil,* which had to run the gauntlet of editors at *Reader's Digest* and the publishing firm of Farrar, Straus, and Cudahy. The atrocity stories that later became a staple of Dooley's writing were absent, as was any attempt to make himself the center of activity. But his emphasis on the religious motivation for the exodus was as intense as it would be in his published texts. For Dooley, Passage to Freedom was not about relocating constituents to support the Diem government. It was a moral drama as uncomplicated by fine distinctions as the contest between Heaven and Hell. "One of the largest Exodus known to history is occurring now in Indo China," Dooley wrote. "The people . . . are abandoning all they have to escape the rule and the whip of the red-run Viet Minh." Dooley recalled asking one of the refugees why the average age of the men fleeing south was only seventeen: "He replied, 'There are no twenty-year-old men in Indo China who are Christians. They have been killed in eight years of war, or captured and sent to China. Better they had been killed.'" Dooley considered this combativeness testimony to "the truly great tradition that the race of Annamites possess" despite "that familiar Oriental complacency and belief in tomorrow caring for itself." The account of the refugees boarding the cargo ship demonstrated Dooley's eye for the heart-tugging detail, as he described "a six-year-old child carrying a three-year-old on his back. Like the motto for Father Flanagan's Boy's Town: 'He ain't heavy, he's my brother.'" The North Vietnamese priests aboard ship in Haiphong harbor, Dooley wrote, "would offer Mass in the various holds. It is poignant to hear these people, plagued by so many years of war, singing their praises to God." Possibly as a means of endearing himself to his superiors, Dooley closed with a tribute to "the defiant Prime Minister Ngo Dinh Diem."[85]

Despite the obtrusive religiosity of his report, Dooley never seems to have learned much about Vietnam's various religions. He did not mention the Cao Dai or the Hoa Hao in the hundreds of letters he wrote to his mother, and his statements regarding Buddhism were typical of the views espoused by Americans at the time. In late November 1954, he wrote of an "amazing" development that piqued his interest in Southeast Asia's predominant faith. "[T]he Buddists are beginning to leave Tonkin," he reported, "which is considered extraordinary, as theirs is a religion of resignation, and if Budda has sent the curse of communism to them, they must bow their heads and endure." Unable to reconcile his understanding of Buddhism with such initiative, Dooley asked his mother to contact a professor friend and "ask her to give you the name of some good books that she used in her course on the Comparative Religions of the Orient. . . . I should like to understand more about these religions. So if you could send to me some books on these, Buddism, Coptism, Taoism, Shintoism, and Confuciusianism, I would appreciate it."[86] Agnes Dooley mailed the texts her son requested, and she sent several books on Catholic philosophy as well. Tom responded, "I can see you puzzled and concerned for fear I might become an apostate and join the local order of Buddist bonzes. Have no fear."[87]

More dismaying than any incipient Bohemianism in Dooley's religious beliefs were the accounts of Viet Minh atrocities he began sending home in late November 1954. The first of these began on an appropriately dramatic note, as Dooley declared, "Mother[,] I have seen things here that I didn't believe humans capable of doing." He detailed how a Vietnamese priest brought him to see a colleague who had been conveyed south from Haiphong: "Eleven kids . . . pushed him on a raft while they swam kicking softly so that the Viet Minh would not stop them." Two nights earlier, Dooley was informed, "the priest had been in his village church . . . and the Vietminh soldiers came in to tell him that he had been preaching lies to his people about the vietmin. . . . The only anser the old priest would say was that he was teaching of God." The priest paid for his audacity:

> They took this old priest and hung him from a beam overhead in the mission by his feet. They stripped him naked. Then they beat him with short bamboo rods, with the emphasis of the beating on his genitals. Into his head they stuck thorns (so he could be like the Christ of whom he spoke)[,] and then into his ears they rammed chop sticks. . . . [W]hen I saw him there was hardly a square inch of flesh that was not swollen and purple, and often split. . . . Being left hanging feet up all night, the vessels in his eyes ruptured, leaving him nearly blind. . . . He was a mass of hemotomata, black and blue, and purple and bruised all over. His scalp, where the children had removed the thorns, was just a mass of matted blood, and his ear drums were both punctured. . . . He was in tremendous pain, from the beating, and from the hideous condition of his groin.[88]

This letter points up a delicate issue in Dooley scholarship. One of the first treatments of the doctor based upon archival research was Shaw's "The Temptation of Tom Dooley," which claimed that "[n]one of Dooley's correspondence, official or personal, describes the atrocities that, in his book [*Deliver Us from Evil*], he attributed to the communists. There are no corroborating accounts . . . in anything Dooley wrote during the [naval] operation."[89] That assertion is untrue. In fact, Dooley provided a number of corroborating accounts of Viet Minh atrocities in his letters home and in the lectures he delivered to U.S. sailors newly arrived in Haiphong. Every atrocity described in *Deliver Us from Evil* was prefigured in Dooley's papers from Passage to Freedom. Of course, this ought not to be taken as proof that the atrocities Dooley described actually occurred. Several credible sources have rejected his claims. Lederer, Dooley's mentor and the man who prevailed upon *Reader's Digest* to publish *Deliver Us from Evil*, admitted years later that the "atrocities [Dooley] described in his books either never took place or were committed by the French. I traveled all over the country and never saw anything like them."[90] Norman Baker, who served as a corpsman under Dooley's command in Vietnam—and whom Dooley lauded in *Deliver Us from Evil* as "a fine sailor, a good American, my constant companion, my helping hand, and my friend"[91]—declared in 1991, "If I'd found a priest hanging by his heels with nails hammered into his head, I'd have the whole camp hearing about it. If those atrocities had occurred, human nature would make you talk about it at the time." Dooley, Baker testified, never said a word.[92]

Dooley may have fabricated or exaggerated the atrocities he claimed to have witnessed in Vietnam. If he did create his Indochinese Grand Guignol out of whole cloth, however, he did not do so months after the fact to make his book more sensational. His atrocity stories grew out of the same period of immersion in the refugee drama that forged much of the Dooley mystique. From September 1954 until May of the following year, Dooley drove himself so mercilessly that he lost 60 of his 180 pounds, nearly died of malarial fever, acquired four types of intestinal worms, and suffered so acutely from sleep deprivation that he frequently hallucinated.[93] One can only speculate as to what aspect of Passage to Freedom engaged Dooley so much more forcibly than anything in his previous twenty-eight years. Wounded pride seems to have played some part. "Please keep as many people informed of my whereabouts and doings as possible," he wrote to his mother in early 1955. "One of the reasons I am trying so very[,] very hard to be more than average is to shove it in the faces of all those doctors in St. Louis and in the Medical School."[94] Yet something more than ego was at work. Dooley's growing empathy for the refugees was unmistakable. His letters conveyed a more authentic identification with their suffering than did his subsequent published works. "When I take care of these Viets, mother, I feel like packing them all up in my suitcase and sending them to Thomas Dunn Memorial [Hospital]," he observed in one dispatch. "These kids are so cute and sweet and honest, and they all try to help each other so."[95] Having never experienced anything like the hero-worship the refugees showered upon him, Dooley was moved by such devotion. "Every street urchin in town knows me because I take care of so many," he wrote. "I am the 'Bac Sy My,' or the 'good American Doctor.' . . . They love me."[96]

More significant, perhaps, than fondness for the refugees or desire to rehabilitate his image in St. Louis circles was Dooley's growing conviction that he played a pivotal role in the struggle between Christendom and communism. One has to be careful in distinguishing between rhetoric and belief, especially when dealing with so mercurial a figure as Dooley, but the terms in which he cast Passage to Freedom in his private correspondence (as opposed to books and lectures) suggest that careerism and sentimentality cannot entirely account for his accomplishments while stationed in Haiphong. As he tried to explain to his mother in one of many accounts of tortured priests—this one "so miserably beaten that . . . I vomited and vomited until my guts turned upside down"—the drama being played out in Vietnam "wasn't just medical, it was something sort of the soul and heart, and very nature of man."[97]

Whatever his motivation, Tom Dooley, who had shunned responsibility his entire life, suddenly could not get enough of it. He was put in charge of a network of clinics that treated up to five hundred people a day. He regularly performed major surgery. He lobbied American pharmaceutical companies for cases of antibiotics. Thanks in large part to his vigilance, not a single epidemic broke out in Haiphong or on the ships leaving for Saigon. By late October 1954, Dooley's commodore was receiving requests from ship commanders in the bay that " 'the officer so eloquent in the history of the political situation' be sent . . . to talk to the men and officers." "So," Dooley wrote, "I get a free chow on the ship, and a talk."[98] Before long, these talks evolved from informal question-and-answer sessions in the mess hall to ceremonious affairs on deck with "a podium and loud speakers rigged for it, just like a SENATOR." Self-conscious about speaking before so large an audience, Dooley worked from a "sort of stock [script] in the beginning, . . . but I have done it so often now that I don't need anything."[99]

The "sort of stock" playbook was entitled "Treatment for Terror," and its impact on an audience was spectacular. Norton Stevens, a naval intelligence officer working in Haiphong at the time, recalled in 1992 that Dooley succeeded in eliciting sobs from the most "grizzled old bosuns."[100] "Tonight, I want to tell you of the sheer terror and horror, as I saw it in everyday life," Dooley would begin, and then describe the atrocities he had witnessed, from "a screaming seven-year-old child who had chopsticks jammed into both ears because he was caught by the communists listening to a catechism class" to "old women who had very meticulously had both their collar bones broken, making their shoulders slump forward on their chest and collapsing their lungs." The account of the battered priest that Dooley had first related to his mother was embellished with even grislier detail: "I tried to drain out the fluid and the pus that I thought was in his scrotum, but it was all congealed, clotted blood." With his listeners thunderstruck at the crimes recounted, Dooley switched gears. The theme now was religion: "Through my camp there passed 600,000 stinking, filthy people who taught me the true, fine nobility of a militant Christianity, . . . who taught me what it means to be a Christian." Dooley recalled how a small refugee craft, lashed together in haste and launched into the South China Sea amid a hail of Viet Minh bullets, "pulled up to the stern of the American ship and hoisted their flag. . . . Sewed to the top of a broken spar, they pulled up the golden-crowned flag of the pontifical Pope of Rome. . . . Under communism, they had been ordered not to believe in Jesus Christ. Under communism, there were to be no internal manifestations of religion, and all external manifestations were destroyed. This is the reason they left." This was also the reason, Dooley concluded, his voice cracking, "that with this monster of communism—with this ogre, . . . there can be no concessions, there can be no compromise, and BY GOD, there can be no peaceful coexistence. Thank you." Sustained applause and cheers followed.[101]

Inevitably, the American press began to notice Dooley. Journalists visited the northern refugee camp and composed stories about this selfless, idealistic, and, conveniently, very attractive young doctor who ministered to thousands of Vietnamese as the deadline for the communist takeover of Haiphong drew nearer. "The correspondents are beginning to be interested in Indo China, I think," Dooley observed in January 1955. "RKA, Pathe, and all the others were photographing our work."[102] Three months later, he marveled, "*Time* and *Life* and *Look* all have correspondents and photographers here."[103] The most important reporter to cross paths with Dooley was William Lederer, who visited Haiphong looking for human interest stories to drum up support for Passage to Freedom. After listening to Dooley speak to an audience of spellbound sailors, Lederer took the doctor aside and informed him that he had a "helluva book" on his hands.[104]

Dooley was one of the last Americans to leave Haiphong as that city passed under Viet Minh control. After being debriefed by Saigon embassy personnel at the home of General Mike O'Daniel, head of the

Military Assistance and Advisory Group (MAAG), Dooley encountered a red-faced O'Daniel, who shouted at him, "Where the hell have you been? I've been hunting all over town for you for two hours!" Premier Diem, it appeared, had learned of the doctor's arrival. As Dooley gleefully reported, "The president of ALL INDO CHINA requested that I come to his palace at 1200 so that he could decorate me for what I had done." Diem was not yet president of South Vietnam, much less all Indochina, but that hardly detracted from the splendor of the occasion, as Dooley, "without even a chance to change my shirt," was ushered into the cabinet room of the Norodom Palace, where, before a crowd of dignitaries, Diem presented him with a medal bearing the inscription "Officier de l'Ordre National de Viet Nam," the highest honor South Vietnam could give to a foreigner.[105] Diem praised Dooley for "the outstanding work you have done for the past ten months in the refugee camps of Northern Viet Nam." Dooley's "medicine and knowledge," the premier declared, had "shown the people of the Tonkin rice fields the true goodness and spirit of help and cooperation that America is showing in Viet Nam and in all the countries of the world."[106]

Dooley was awestruck. "A raft of newspaper reporters covered it," he told his mother. "After the usual delay of several weeks[,] the pictures should be arriving in American papers, so keep your eyes out for it." He could not resist adding, "Well, mother dear, it is a long time since I flunked my senior year. He [possibly the dean of the medical school] didn't think I was adequate[,] yet the president of Indo China thinks I am!"[107] Dooley returned from his decoration by Diem at the palace to what he described as a "hero's welcome" in Yokosuka, but it did not take his superiors long to recognize that their hero was in no condition to resume his medical duties.[108] Commander Charles Mann of the Medical Service Corps ordered the toil-worn doctor to take two weeks' leave. Perhaps feeling that Dooley needed something to occupy his mind, Mann also ordered him to write out a manuscript about everything that had happened in Vietnam.[109] Although Dooley had already tried to chronicle Passage to Freedom in his free time, idle moments had been few in the maelstrom of Haiphong; now, with nothing to distract him, he labored feverishly. "I spent all last night and all today working on the book," he wrote his mother in early June. "Doesn't that sound formidable? But that is just what it is, a book."[110]

It would prove to be considerably more than that.

"Vietnam Could Not
Have a Better Spokesman"

Having admired Lederer's "They'll Remember the *Bayfield*" in *Reader's Digest*, Dooley contacted Lederer for assistance in composing and marketing his story.[111] He showed the journalist the first draft of what he intended to title either "Exodus from Agony" or "Bamboo and Blood."[112] Lederer was impressed. After thrashing out a second, third, and fourth draft in a series of marathon meetings with Dooley, the future coauthor of *The Ugly American* accompanied him when he debriefed Admiral Felix Stump, the commander-in-chief of the Pacific Fleet. Dooley's book was quickly cleared by Stump and the navy censors. Then Lederer made arrangements to introduce Dooley to DeWitt Wallace of *Reader's Digest*.[113] Accustomed to looking to Lederer for tips on promising material, Wallace invited Dooley to a working luncheon at his San Francisco office. There were half a dozen senior editors present, one of whom recalled years later that "Dooley began his rapid-fire recital that day even before he sat down at the luncheon table. Two hours later, his listeners were still spellbound. . . . The *Digest* editors recognized at once that Tom Dooley was a singularly colorful personality with a great story." Not only did the *Digest* agree to run Dooley's book as an abridged text, but Wallace also introduced the doctor to Roger Straus of the publishing firm Farrar, Straus, and Cudahy, who committed on the spot to publishing the full-length version.[114]

Deliver Us from Evil: The Story of Viet Nam's Flight to Freedom became the great early best-seller on Vietnam. Nothing until *The Pentagon Papers* fifteen years later received comparable readership or interest. The book went through twenty printings in English and was translated into more languages than any text save the Bible.[115] The fact that Dooley's book sold so well in its full-length, hardcover version is doubly impressive given that its publication by Farrar, Straus, and Cudahy coincided with the appearance of the condensed rendition in the *Digest* for April 1956, which was not really much of an abridgment. The *Digest*'s editors allowed *Deliver Us from Evil* more pages than they had for any book since 1922. Apart from juxtaposing a few scenes and excising a chapter on Dooley's return to the States, they reproduced the text in full.[116] Any reader who wanted the substance of the book could get it for 50¢, yet almost a million paid $3.50 for the clothbound version.[117] It was a publishing bonanza. DeWitt Wallace trumpeted in a note to Dooley, "It is no news to you that the condensation of your book . . . was read by the largest magazine audience in the United States. But I know you will be gratified to learn that, in addition, this excellent piece was reprinted in fourteen of our international editions. Thus you have reached millions of other readers in many lands."[118]

As literature, *Deliver Us from Evil* was a brilliant work of cold war propaganda in which the communist enemy was irredeemably evil and the Americans and their South Vietnamese allies were virtue incarnate. Racist, lacking in subtlety, and barren of even a sketchy awareness of the complexities of Vietnamese history and politics, the book nonetheless retains a capacity to affect the reader on a visceral level that gives some hint of how powerful its impact must have been in 1956. Dooley's description of a Vietnamese teenager whose legs were pounded by Viet Minh with their rifle butts—"the feet and ankles felt like moist bags of marbles"—still provokes a shudder. His alleged quotation from a communist radio broadcast is, if invented, inspired humbug and, if authentic, a masterpiece of observed detail: "This is an American. His head is a blockhouse. His beard is barbed wire. His eyes are bombs. His teeth are dum-dum bullets. His two arms are guns and from his nose flames shoot out. . . . His forehead is a nest of artillery and his body is an airfield. His fingers are bayonets, his feet tanks."[119]

More than *The Ugly American*, *Deliver Us from Evil* deserves designation as the *Uncle Tom's Cabin* of the cold war, not only because of the wide audience it attracted, but also because in contrast to Lederer and Burdick, who proposed a strategy to combat communism in the East, Dooley wrote with pure emotion. He shuttled back and forth between almost pornographic descriptions of Viet Minh atrocities and tear-jerking vignettes of suffering Vietnamese (usually children) bonding with their American benefactors. Readers were whipsawed from moral outrage to lachrymosity at dizzying speed and never afforded the opportunity to question Dooley's fidelity to facts.

The unifying theme of *Deliver Us from Evil*, around which Dooley constructed his typology of communist brutality and Catholic suffering, was his transformation from spoiled playboy to servant of the poor, the sick, and the oppressed of Southeast Asia. "I had never before borne real responsibility or authority," Dooley recalled. "But now I had to provide shelter and food, sanitation and some human solace to a flood of humanity, undernourished, exhausted, bewildered, and pitifully frightened." Dooley admitted that he signed on to Passage to Freedom because it "sounded like a lark," that he "knew nothing about Indo-China other than the fact that it was south of China and east of India," and that "for me, tropical medicine had been a drowsy course at St. Louis University Medical School." By the conclusion of his labors, however, "I had been taught to believe in and do believe in God's love, His goodness, His mercy. . . . [The refugees] were no longer a mass of mere wretchedness. . . . They had become my suffering brothers."[120]

Again and again, Dooley emphasized the religious significance of Passage to Freedom. He conceded that the Viet Minh were popular, even among Vietnamese Catholics, after defeating the French. He acknowledged that most Vietnamese had viewed Americans with mistrust when the evacuation from Haiphong began, both as a consequence of communist propaganda and because of America's identification with France. None of the refugees were motivated to relocate below the 17th parallel out of affection for the United States, Dooley insisted, or because they found the oppressive taxes and forced labor of Viet Minh–style Marxism unendurable. They fled by the hundreds of thousands, he contended, for one reason: "The Viet Minh suppressed their religion. The Viet Minh closed their churches. The Viet Minh put priests and ministers into the fields to work, or killed them. All outward manifestations of religion were destroyed. Because of this, and not because of anything we did, they decided that it would even be worth the risk of contact with the Americans in order to gain what they knew was religious freedom in the South under Ngo Dinh Diem."[121]

The most famous chapter of Deliver Us from Evil was titled "Communist Re-education," and it was here that Dooley took up the issue of Viet Minh atrocities. "The purpose of this book is not to sicken anyone," he assured his readers, "or to dwell upon the horror of Oriental tortures. . . . But . . . justice demands that some of the atrocities we learned of in Haiphong be put on the record." The first entry on the record was an account of how the Viet Minh cut off the tongue of a religious instructor whom they accused of preaching "heresy." "He could not scream," Dooley remembered. "Blood ran down his throat. When the soldiers let him loose, he fell to the ground vomiting blood; the scent of blood was all over the courtyard." Next was the story of the battered priest, which Dooley first related in a letter to his mother in November 1954. This time, the stylistic touches were more cringe-inducing: "His body was a mass of blackened flesh from the shoulders to the knees. The belly was hard and distended and the scrotum swollen to the size of a football."[122] The only follow-up report on the priest's progress in Dooley's personal correspondence stated, "Reference that horribly beaten priest: yes, he recovered very well due to a fortitude that only these Orientals seem able to demonstrate."[123] In *Deliver Us from Evil*, the dénouement packed a greater dramatic wallop: "One day, when I went to treat him, he had disappeared. Father Lopez told me that he had gone back to that world of silence behind the Bamboo Curtain. This means he had gone back to his torturers. I wonder what they have done to him now."[124]

The highlight of the "Communist Re-education" chapter, and the story most frequently cited in reviews of Dooley's book, involved a priest whom Dooley encountered in the living quarters of the Philippine Catholic Mission in Haiphong. "His head was matted with pus and there were eight large pus-filled swellings around his temples and forehead," Dooley recalled. "Even before I asked what had happened, I knew the answer. This particular priest had also been punished for teaching 'treason.' His sentence was a communist version of the Crown of Thorns, once forced on the Saviour of Whom he preached. Eight nails had been driven into his head, three across the forehead, two in the back of the skull, and three across the dome. The nails were large enough to embed themselves in the skull bone." Lest readers miss the point, Dooley marveled, "So many [atrocities] seemed to have religious significance. More and more, I was learning that these punishments were linked to man's belief in God."[125]

Almost all of the Vietnamese who appeared in *Deliver Us from Evil*, and the only ones with whom readers were invited to sympathize, were elderly priests and nuns and little children. Their chief virtues, that is, the traits that won Dooley and, by extension, America to their cause, were passive: capacity to absorb pain, readiness to obey American instructions, gratitude for American aid. "This patient race is not robust," Dooley noted. "Many are frail and susceptible to a variety of diseases. Yet their faith . . . was strong enough to provide the nourishment they needed in this time of stress." The only Vietnamese who seemed to possess individual initiative was Premier Diem. The rest were, if not actually children, childlike—small, immature, credulous, and weak. It was impossible to envision Dooley's Vietnamese developing a modern technological or economic infrastructure without American tutelage. None of the refugees in *Deliver Us from Evil* ever came up with an original or constructive idea. They seemed incapable of solving problems on their own or of proposing alternative solutions to the ones the Americans set forth. Their greatest accomplishment, rarely realized, was the imperfect emulation of American methods. A group of shoeshine boys in Haiphong whom Dooley befriended considered it an honor that their studied aping of his manner earned them the nickname "little Dooleys."[126]

On only one occasion was a Vietnamese allowed to challenge Dooley, and even then the conflict ended with the refugee prostrate with shame at having questioned American expertise. "One day a woman brought me a baby whose body was covered with ulcers," Dooley wrote. "Yaws and ulcers respond miraculously to penicillin, and this looked like a routine case. I gave the infant a shot in the buttocks and told the mother to bring it [*sic*] back the next day." The baby had an "angry-looking, though quite harmless" reaction to the medication, breaking out in hives, and the mother reacted hysterically: "She handed her baby to a bystander, grabbed a stout stick, and called up a dozen sympathizers. When [Norman] Baker rescued me at last, I had broken ribs, black eyes, and miscellaneous bruises." The baby's hives as well as the ulcers disappeared by the next day, and when Dooley returned "alone and unarmed" to the mother's tent, her reaction was predictable: "She burst into tears and fell at my feet, begging forgiveness." Dooley acknowledged that he experienced some trepidation at the prospect of going back to the area where he had been beaten the previous day but insisted it was necessary that he return. "[R]emembering the importance of 'face' in the Orient," he noted, "we were always careful to take up where we left off." He was likewise careful to "always wear [his] collar insignia and . . . Navy hat" while treating patients because, he informed the reader, "symbols mean a lot in the Orient." Elsewhere in *Deliver Us from Evil*, he thanked a colleague for affording him "insight into the Oriental mind."[127]

The Viet Minh, who before Dooley arrived in Haiphong had defeated a French army funded with billions of dollars in American aid, were not permitted to have the soldierly qualities of bravery and resourcefulness. Their only warlike actions were war crimes committed against old people and children. Their triumph in the Franco–Viet Minh war was ascribed to a "sellout" at the Geneva Conference. "I hope the men who made the deal at the lovely Geneva lakeside are happy with the results," Dooley sniffed. Dooley's history of America's involvement in Vietnam began with the navy mission to aid the refugees, not with the billions funneled into the French war effort between 1950 and 1954. "We had come late to Viet Nam," he observed, "but we had come. . . . We had come with ships to take them to freedom, with medical aid to heal their ills and bind up their wounds, with large supplies of life-saving drugs freely donated by American firms merely on my say-so."[128] The power relationship was clear: Dooley, acting on behalf of the United States, was the savior and knight-errant; the Vietnamese were his supplicants. The book ranked among the most condescending depictions of Asians in twentieth-century literature, and it was received with nearly unanimous critical acclaim.

The New Yorker lauded Deliver Us from Evil as "a moving poem of the human spirit victorious." The Washington Post proclaimed, "All Americans can be proud of what Dooley has accomplished." Peggy Durdin, who had previously written in the New York Times about how Saigon seemed doomed, began to shift her stance after reading Dooley's story, praising it as "a compelling account in very human and personal terms of one of the epic migrations from communist rule." William Hogan of the San Francisco Chronicle called it "a profoundly moving book that is also one of the best accounts of the Indochina situation I have seen." Edwin Stanton, former U.S. ambassador to Thailand, raved in the New York Herald Tribune, "Dooley has written a moving story which radiates his deep religious faith and yet is tinged with wit and humor. . . . It is a magnificent achievement."[129]

These were among the more subdued responses. The San Diego Union gushed that "Dooley overcame communist-inspired hate, saved thousands of lives, and made the word 'American' almost a holy one, instead of a curse." The Helena Register saluted Dooley as "a great American" and expressed hope that "the writing of this man gets wide circulation." America's Book-Log agreed: "This is a moving tale that is recommended to all who are proud to be Americans." Other critics were similarly acclamatory: "This book is by turns terrible, eye-opening, and heart-warming"; "His story strikes with an impact that will bring tears to the eyes of the sourest reader"; "Despite the horror and tragedy that fill its pages, it rings with hope—hope for a world that knows ordinary Thomas Dooleys who become extraordinary heroes." Response to the book was enthusiastic even when the reviewer seemed confused as to where Dooley's heroism had been enacted, as in the case of one critic who hailed his "ministering to Indonesian refugees" and another who wrote, "[W]hen you are as low as a snake's tail for no reason, just think of these poor blessed people in Viet Naw in South America and what they suffered to simply exist."[130]

Reviews in the American Catholic press focused less on Dooley's gallantry than on the biblical drama of suffering and salvation played out in Passage to Freedom. Father James Murphy, writing for the *American Ecclesiastical Review*, noted that *Deliver Us from Evil* offered "an eyewitness account of the terrible struggle raging between communism and Christianity. . . . [T]he author paints a portrait of Christ crucified in Indo-China." The Carmelite journal *Spiritual Life* credited Dooley with "shock[ing] us into the reality of the application of the doctrine of the Mystical Body as we learn of the Christlike ministrations of American sailors to the persecuted Vietnamese." Other sectarian reviews were less erudite, but no less effusive. "By all means, read this book!" instructed the *Catholic Review Service*. "Dooley gives a sermon which will stick like the gummy rice of the Vietnamese." The *Catholic Free Press* exclaimed, "Would that there were more Tom Dooleys!" Dooley's personal papers indicate that his "favorite review" was composed by Mark Heath for the Catholic journal *Torch*. "This book will storm your heart and hold you spellbound in the reading," wrote Heath. "This is a book of Christ. This war in Viet Nam is His Passion, this suffering His; this blood is shed in His name. And all this love and this labor and dedicated skill are the compassion of His Sacred Heart."[131]

Enthusiasm for Dooley's book spilled over onto the floor of the Senate, where Mike Mansfield endorsed *Deliver Us from Evil* in the *Congressional Record*. "If the United States had abroad more ambassadors like Thomas A. Dooley," Mansfield declared, "I think it not only would be better off, but it would be better understood in the countries which are underdeveloped."[132] Henry Cabot Lodge, ambassador to the United Nations and future ambassador to South Vietnam, likewise asserted, "One feels that if there were an unlimited number of Dr. Dooleys, this country would have practically no foreign relations problems."[133] Dooley received letters of praise from such figures as President Eisenhower, Chief Justice Earl Warren, Eleanor Roosevelt, and, unsurprisingly, Cardinal Spellman.[134] Ngo Dinh Diem, fresh off his electoral triumph over Bao Dai for the presidency of South Vietnam, wrote from Saigon to "express . . . gratitude for the wonderful service you have

rendered Vietnam with the substance of this book."[135] South Vietnamese ambassador Tran Van Chuong added his voice to the chorus: "I
am sure that Vietnam could not have a better spokesman."[136]

The southern half of Vietnam could scarcely have had a more ener-
getic spokesman than "Dr. Tom" in the months after his return to the
United States. In January 1956 Dooley began a book-promoting lecture
tour cosponsored by the navy and Charles Pfizer and Company, the
pharmaceutical giant that had supplied him with medicines for his
refugees. As Agnes Dooley recalls, "He talked to medical societies, so-
rorities, high schools, grade schools, Rotarians, press clubs, Chambers
of Commerce, U.S. Navy stations, and religious groups of all faiths. He
gave TV interviews, radio interviews, and press interviews. . . . Everywhere he traveled, he told the story of his 'Passage to Freedom.' "[137] By
the time the tour concluded in June, Dooley had gone to eighty-six
engagements in seventy-four cities. At least three-fourths of his addresses were broadcast. He proved especially popular on college cam-
puses, where, his assistant Teresa Gallagher remembers, "the cheering
could only be compared to the kind of rapturous cheering the Beatles
aroused."[138] One of Dooley's aides during this cross-country circuit
recalled him complaining that his constant speech making had caused
him to develop blisters on his tongue.[139] "How many times have I told
that story?" mused Dooley at tour's end. "I told it whenever and wherever I could find Americans willing to listen."[140]

Quite a few Americans were willing. When Dooley spoke at the U.S.
Naval Station at Columbus in early May, the commanding officer noted
in his introduction that the doctor had already "reached more than
500,000 persons with his speeches."[141] Response to the addresses was
invariably positive, often panegyric. In a typical tribute, the Reverend
James Norton, vice president of Notre Dame, wrote to the surgeon
general of the navy, "Dr. Thomas A. Dooley addressed an audience of
over two thousand in the Navy Drill Hall on the campus on the evening
of Friday, April 13, 1956. For approximately one hour, he held the audience spellbound as he told his story. He had them laughing and
crying as he described his experiences in Viet Nam. I have heard nothing but the greatest praise from priests, lay faculty, and students."[142] A
less prestigious source of adulation—although more representative of
the average audience member at a Dooley speech—was Suzi Leslie, a
junior at the Immaculate Heart High School. "I wish to inadequately
express the appreciation and honor I felt for having heard you speak,"

Suzi effervesced. "I did not believe that such tremendous faith and love of humanity could exist in one man."[143]

Like his writing, Dooley's speeches were overpoweringly emotional, piling image upon horrifying image until his listeners were virtually bludgeoned into supporting his cause. "What do you do for children who have had chopsticks driven into their ears?" he asked one audience. "Or for old women whose collarbones have been shattered by rifle butts? Or for kids whose ears have been torn off with pincers? How do you treat a priest who has had nails driven into his skull to make a travesty of the Crown of Thorns?"[144] American ignorance of Vietnam ensured that no one noticed when Dooley got his facts wrong. "My story is a story of Viet Nam, a country just a few miles wide and fewer miles long," he proclaimed in a Chicago address, reversing the true geography of Vietnam, which is longer than it is wide. In another speech, he claimed that the "tragedy in Vietnam was partly . . . of America's making, because we failed to completely crush the Chinese armies in Korea to the point where they could never have moved down . . . to Southeast Asia, and taken over."[145] How could America's failure to crush the Chinese armies in Korea between 1950 and 1953 be responsible for a Vietnamese civil war that began in 1946?

During his tour Dooley made his first appearance on the Gallup Poll's list of "Ten Most Admired Men," debuting at number seven. He was also voted one of the "Ten Outstanding Men of 1956" by the Junior Chamber of Commerce,[146] an award that, as Dooley wrote to his mother, made him feel "like the small village priest who has just been informed he made Cardinal."[147] Unfortunately for Dooley, by the time the Jaycees announced their selection he would have had a better chance of making cardinal than of achieving his goal of surgeon generalship of the navy. In January 1956, just as Dooley's nationwide tour got under way, the chief of naval personnel initiated an investigation of the doctor's alleged homosexuality. By the time he finished touring in July, the youngest naval officer ever to receive the Legion of Merit had been dishonorably discharged—albeit without the public humiliation that normally accompanies such a dismissal. The navy could not afford to make a spectacle of Dooley, having already decorated him and endorsed his book.[148]

While this was a disappointment for Dooley, his career as a celebrity saint was far from over. Quite the contrary: he would become more famous and beloved in the remaining five years of his life, during which time, in addition to founding MEDICO and publishing two more best-selling books, he made weekly radio broadcasts from Laos and undertook several fund-raising tours of the United States that powerfully shaped Americans' perceptions of Asia in general and Vietnam in particular. If *The Ugly American* was, as many have claimed, the *Uncle Tom's Cabin* of the cold war, then Dooley's broadcasts, titled "That Free Men May Live," were the Fireside Chats of America's early involvement in Vietnam.

"You Are Just Like Jesus"

Dooley's immediate reaction to his discharge was not to begin planning for a return to Asia. As he admitted in 1956, with perhaps more candor than he intended, "Two years ago, I swore I would never go back to that filthy, stinking place."[149] Despite the navy's treatment of him, he saw no reason to drop out of the public eye; however mortifying the circumstances of his resignation, they remained top secret. Young, handsome, and adored, he suffered no dearth of attractive options in his native land. A position as a St. Louis "society doctor" was his for the asking, he commanded over one thousand dollars per lecture, and Kirk Douglas had recently purchased the movie rights to *Deliver Us from Evil*.[150]

The doctor's new future was the contrivance of the American Friends of Vietnam and its parent organization, the International Rescue Committee (IRC). The AFV, as detailed in chapter 6, was probably the most effective publicist for the Diem regime in the United States, while the IRC's record of aiding refugees from fascist and communist countries had earned it a venerable reputation by the mid-1950s. Leo Cherne, the IRC chairman and a member of the AFV, recognized Dooley's value as a spokesman who could guarantee generous donations and media exposure for any humanitarian venture. Cherne therefore asked Dooley to establish a mission in Laos under IRC auspices.[151] Judging from Dooley's correspondence, at the time this offer was made he did not know how to spell the name of the country where he would spend most of the rest of his life; he continually misspelled it "Loas" in letters to friends and family members.[152] That cosmetic defect in his knowledge was easily remedied. The deeper aspects of his racism proved more resistant, as indicated by an interview he had with the journalist Mike Wallace before his departure for Southeast Asia. "I don't want you standing on some immaculate American pedestal reaching down to pull up the poor dirty Asian," Dooley remarked in explaining his philosophy

17. Tom Dooley (right) and Kirk Douglas. © Bettmann/CORBIS, 17 April 1956

of treatment. "You take off your nice white suit, understand? You get off the pedestal and you get down in the mud with them, knee-deep in the mud with them. Then you push."[153] This can-do presumption would characterize much of the program that Dooley christened Operation Laos. His official announcement, called "Plans for the Medical Mission," asserted, "We want to be on the offensive for America. . . . If America as a nation ignores the Asian's physical needs, . . . we justify the communists' characterization of our religion as an 'opiate of the peoples.'"[154]

Shortly after Dooley arrived in Laos and set up his clinic, he began making weekly tape recordings and shipping them to St. Louis. There, by prior arrangement, they were played by KMOX, the midwestern flagship of the CBS network with a range covering over twenty states.[155] Millions of Americans listened to the doctor every week as he ruminated on Laotian political issues, the difficulties of operating a hospital in the jungle, the impossibility of coexistence with communism, and, most often, the Asian character and how to manage it. Dooley's program ran for almost five years. It was one of the most effective propaganda campaigns of the cold war.

The radio series' lack of technical polish worked to its advantage. Dooley's tapes were scratchy, the jungle noises in the background sometimes drowned out his voice, and he was occasionally interrupted by a patient needing treatment. "That Free Men May Live" reeked of "authenticity." As Rex Davis, the KMOX announcer who introduced Dooley every week, noted before one broadcast, "Tom is in a very primitive country. The only way he can tape record these messages is on portable equipment, the current supplied by a gasoline generator. Then, after he has recorded them, there is the job of getting them through, by one means or another, to a place where they can be put aboard a plane and sent winging their way to us."[156] The process of transporting Dooley's soliloquies from the border of Red China to the living rooms of Middle America seemed to confirm two things: first, the sheer backwardness of Southeast Asia; second, that Dooley's position as the man on the spot afforded him a privileged vantage point from which to relate the truth of what was occurring there.

One "truth" Dooley emphasized over and over was Asian passivity, a trait he often attributed to religion. "I have found out how to think like a little Asian villager," he announced in one broadcast. "The people here wallow in superstitions and metaphysical beliefs, in sorcery, in witchcraft, and necromancy. . . . They are philosophically resigned to fate. They become apathetic in the face of severe crisis. This has political implications."[157] Dooley frequently ascribed communist inroads in the Laotian government to such submissiveness. He conceded that this attitude might lead Americans to conclude that "Asians . . . are indolent and lazy by nature, or that they aren't worth saving or even helping because they will not take the initiative and help themselves." The doctor did not rebut that conclusion but entreated his audience to "stop criticizing, condemning, and complaining about the Asians. Let us try fervently to understand them, and you will soon come to love them, as I do."[158]

In compliance with his sponsors' wishes (and, most likely, with his own convictions) Dooley made a point of stressing that "Vietnam, with Ngo Dinh Diem at the helm, has no queasy moments like in Laos. It has a firm, solid leadership that is the best in Asia. . . . Diem has . . . thrown traditional Asian caution to the four winds by saying, matter-of-factly, that there just isn't any room in this day and age for neutrality. . . . It's refreshing to hear that kind of diplomacy in 1957, straight from the shoulder, curt, distinct, and honest. Bravo, President Diem! We need more like you in Asia!"[159] After a coup toppled Prime Minister Phoui Sananikone of Laos in 1960, Dooley noted, "It is amazing that a few men could overthrow a government which has been supported by a tremendously generous flow of American dollars." "However," he added, "Vietnam has simply been magnificent."[160]

Dooley never connected Diem's rejection of "traditional Asian caution" with his Catholicism, but he did make numerous critical statements about Buddhism, the predominant faith in Southeast Asia, in his KMOX broadcasts. Describing a frustrating encounter in Bangkok, Dooley lamented the inability of "these young Thai doctors" to comprehend "their duty to other people." He noted, "There just isn't this sense of sociology among the people of Asia. . . . [I]n Asia, because of their Buddhism and because of the way they've been brought up, they do not have that much of a sense of duty to anybody else."[161] On another occasion, Dooley recalled how a Lao man "desperately sick with blazing fever" refused to accept treatment. "He said that he was a 'high Buddhist' and could not take any medicines," Dooley grumbled. "I asked why he called on me. He said that he 'just wanted my opinion on his malady.' . . . I said I understood—which, believe me, I did not!"[162]

As for the other faiths of the Lao people, Dooley's contempt was undisguised. "I feel like writing to the Pope and requesting his permission to burn some of these witches at the stake," he fumed in a 1957 broadcast.[163] Dooley often complained he was obliged to "split fees" with Lao "witch doctors" so that they could save face.[164] On one broadcast, he turned the microphone over to "the oldest witch doctor in the village here" and asked him to "please chase away the evil spirit from the house of Tom Dooley." Shortly after the "witch doctor" began his incantation, Dooley seized the microphone from him, chuckling, "Well, I think I had better interrupt the old gentleman now, because if I don't he will probably go on for about forty-five minutes, and I don't think you, KMOX, or Tom Dooley could stand that."[165] Dooley was more indulgent when he broadcast from a Catholic orphanage in Saigon, standing patiently aside while a young Vietnamese stammered his way through "Silent Night" and exclaiming at song's end, "When you see kids like this, one thinks that Christmas ought to last all year long—and all our life long!"[166]

These derisive views pervaded Dooley's fund-raising tours in the United States, during which he made such statements as "The pious phrases of democracy do not translate well into Asian tongues."[167] "I've learned how to get along with and handle and put up with difficult people like witch doctors, because, well, you see, I was educated by the Jesuits," he wisecracked in a 1959 address to the John Carroll Society. "We can work together because . . . all faiths agree upon the fact that the brotherhood of man exists as certainly as does the fatherhood of God." None of the society's members pointed out that certain faiths—Buddhism, for instance—do not posit a father figure or Supreme Being in their credenda.[168] The *New York Times* published an article by Dooley in 1958 that recycled the imagery of his interview with Mike Wallace: "We have seen that it is much better—although sometimes more messy—to get off that pedestal, stand knee-deep in the stench of some parts of Asia, and attempt to urge and lift the Asian up a bit."[169] Dooley's conception of himself as a medical messiah raising primitive Asians to a level of semicivilization frequently verged on megalomania. As he informed *Redbook* magazine, "Without me, my people have black magic, necromancy, sorcery, witchcraft, baboon's blood. . . . Without me, they have nothing but wretchedness."[170] Dooley acknowledged in a guest editorial for the *Journal of American Medicine* that "one assumes god-likeness in a village when he eradicates yaws. . . . Hundreds of medieval —no, earlier than medieval—customs still command the Orient."[171]

The America of the 1950s did not find anything unseemly about such observations. Mansfield assured Dooley, "You are a credit to our country. . . . As long as the United States has Tom Dooleys doing the kind of work that you do . . . the Republic will be in good and safe hands."[172] Mansfield's colleague Hubert Humphrey declared on the Senate floor, "[I]t is to be hoped millions of Americans endorse and support Doctor Dooley with all their hearts."[173] In 1959, at the height of Dooley's fame, his office in New York was receiving over five thousand fan letters a day.[174] These messages lay bare with especial vividness the religious ethos of the Eisenhower era: "To my mind, your work is the one and only way to be a Christian"; "May you go over the top in your appeal for help—I'm sure you will because we Americans believe in God and his wonders to perform"; "My heart bursts with joy to see a fine Catholic man steeped in the teachings of the Mother Church"; "I saw and heard you, and all I have to say to you is just three little words: GOD BLESS YOU"; "May all of life's greatest blessings be yours—that American flag belongs in your home more than any one's I know!"[175] A third-grader expressed the sentiment many of her more reserved elders felt when she wrote to Dooley, "You are just like Jesus."[176]

The greatest tribute Dooley received during what may be termed the Laotian phase of his career was in Lederer's and Burdick's *The Ugly American*, the most influential and widely discussed novel published in the 1950s about America's relations with Asia. It is an article of faith among historians of the Vietnam War that Colonel Hillandale in *The Ugly American* was modeled on Edward Lansdale.[177] With the exception of James Fisher, however, scholars have been slow to recognize another character as based on a real-life model: Father John Finian, a hero nearly equal in Lederer's and Burdick's eyes to Hillandale, was Tom Dooley, although with a few years and a clerical collar added on.[178] In the first "how to combat communism" parable in *The Ugly American*, Finian learned the language and customs of Burma and then recruited supporters to act as an anticommunist cadre in the region. At one point, Finian tested the mettle of a man named U Tien by posing deliberately provocative questions. When Finian ventured that "good Burmans [*sic*] could be good communists as well as good Catholics," U Tien at first equivocated because, Lederer and Burdick informed readers, "Asians dislike saying anything that is unpleasant. Intuitively, they say what they think their listener wants to hear." Ultimately, U Tien overcame his native sycophancy and declared, "I think it would not be possible to be a good communist and a good Catholic. . . . [I]f one is right, then the other cannot be. That is the best I can put it. I am sorry." U Tien had nothing to apologize for—he had passed Finian's test with flying colors, and he performed even more admirably in a subsequent meeting when he lectured counterinsurgency recruits: "The communists have made all worship impossible except the worship of Stalin, Lenin, Mao. . . . I too am a Catholic, but I do not require that all of us be Catholics. The thing we want is a country where any man can worship any god he wishes."[179]

Lederer and Burdick dropped the pose of fiction in a 1959 *Life* article entitled "Salute to Deeds of Non-Ugly Americans" that praised Dooley as "a doctor of democracy . . . who was ready to do a needed job in a foreign land for nothing more than prayerful thanks."[180] Fortunately for Dooley's reputation, the journalists did not have access to his letters home from Laos, which, even allowing for the human tendency to express unattractive sentiments under stressful conditions, were note-

18. Tom Dooley and Lao patient. © Bettmann/CORBIS, undated

worthy for the scorn he displayed toward his patients. In one letter he referred to them as "slant eyes," and in another seethed, "Sometimes I feel like I will give you this whole country for ten cents."[181] When Agnes Dooley complained to her son about "having to learn to cut you out of my life," he angrily shot back, "Why in hell do you choose to cut? Because I am working in Laos longer than originally intended? . . . I assure you, mother, were it not for my 'mislead and misdirected' sense of duty, I'd get the hell out of this stinking hole!"[182]

Reports from Laos that Dooley's doctors had discovered a cancerous lymph gland in his body prompted a torrent of publicity in the United States, typified by an editorial that wailed, "We can't afford to lose such a splendid American! We pray he wins his greatest fight against cancer, as he has beaten the communists on their own ground."[183] Dooley returned to America and parlayed his cancer treatment into a public relations event, inviting CBS News to film his operation at New York's Sloane Kettering Medical Center. The resulting documentary, "Biography of a Cancer," won several awards and attracted a mammoth viewing audience. The doctor appeared on "The Tonight Show," "What's My Line?," "The Jack Paar Show," and an ABC News documentary entitled "The Splendid American."[184] Wherever he spoke, overflow audiences spilled into the streets. Dooley received thousands of letters of support and condolence every day. People who did not know how to reach him addressed their correspondence to "Doctor Tom Dooley, Saint Patrick's Cathedral, New York City."[185] In one letter that reflected Dooley's unique fusion of fifties religiosity and foreign policy, a woman wrote, "When I read of your suffering, I think of how close you are to God. Please help me to come closer to God through the people of Vietnam."[186]

According to Randy Shilts, Dooley "claimed to know two things about his future" from an early age: "that he was meant to accomplish some great task in his lifetime, and that he would die young."[187] Given that no man in Dooley's family for two generations had lived past the age of forty-six, the latter prediction did not require abnormal prescience. Dooley chose his own epitaph in the closing pages of *Deliver Us from Evil*, where he wrote, "If apologies are due for some of my erratic ways, then I ask you to remember that

> *The woods are lovely, dark and deep,*
> *But I have promises to keep,*
> *And miles to go before I sleep.*"[188]

This snippet from Robert Frost's "Stopping by Woods on a Snowy Evening" became permanently associated with Dooley's life and work. Two biographies of Dooley are titled *Promises to Keep* and *Before I Sleep*; Shilts ends *Conduct Unbecoming* with a lengthier excerpt from Frost's poem; and Fisher titles the closing chapter of his biography "And miles to go. . . ."[189] The overexposed verse was most vigorously pressed into service during Dooley's funeral, at which Monsignor George Gottwald proclaimed,

> Lovely are the woods, very lovely, very attractive! Then, like a sword cutting through a soul, comes a decision in his mind—yes, but I have promises to keep!

> . . . *I have miles to go!* The miles, Dr. Dooley, are finished.
> *I have promises to keep!* The promises, Dr. Dooley, are fulfilled.
> *Lovely are the woods, dark and deep!* May you enjoy them throughout Eternity.[190]

Dooley seems to have grown less enamored of these lines in his final months, perhaps feeling that Frost had not caught the essence of the

MEDICO errand in the wilderness, or possibly because he was sick of encountering the same poem in every newspaper and magazine treatment of him. In any event, shortly after learning that his cancer was malignant, he attempted to compose his own poetic testimonial to what his mission in Vietnam and Laos had signified. The result, titled "Listen to the Agony of Asia," was broadcast on Dooley's radio program seven months before his death. In part, it read,

> Listen to the agony of Asia;
> I, who am strong,
> With health and love and laughter in my soul,
> I see a throng
> Of stunted children reared in wrong,
> And wish to make them whole.
> Listen to the agony of Asia;
> But know full well
> That not until I share their bitter cry,
> Their pain and hell,
> Can God within my spirit dwell
> And bring America's blessings nigh![191]

Given the poor grammar and forced rhymes, it is not surprising that only one newspaper printed "Listen to the Agony of Asia" in a posthumous tribute.[192] Artistic flaws notwithstanding, the poem gave a truer picture of Dooley's conception of his role as jungle doctor than did Frost's verse, although the picture was less flattering. "Asia" was identified with "a throng of stunted children"; Dooley was the "strong" American savior "with health and love and laughter in [his] soul," who came to know God by dispensing "America's blessings" to those "reared in wrong" in the "pain and hell" of the East. As a foundation on which to base future U.S.–Southeast Asian relations, this portrayal was considerably more primitive—and more dangerous—than the folk medicine Dooley fought against in Laos.

"Listen to the Agony of Asia," like all of Dooley's writings, throbbed with the cultural narcissism identified by Edward Said in works by European and American authors. Said could be describing *Deliver Us from Evil* when he observes, "The book invariably locates the source of all significant action and life in the West, whose representatives seem at liberty to visit their fantasies and philanthropies upon a mind-deadened Third World. Without the West, the outlying regions of the world have no life, history, or culture to speak of, no independence or integrity worth representing."[193] That was Dooley's frame of reference in epitome. From his persistent use of the reductive terms "Asia" and "Asians," implying a unitary racial character transcending differences of culture and personality; to his unshakable belief in the superiority of American ideas and practices; to his inability to countenance the possibility that some Asians might not want to serve as passive building blocks for America's New Israel, Dooley contributed immeasurably to the creation of those false impressions that drew the United States into Vietnam. Dooley, of course, did not cause the Vietnam War, but he did contribute greatly to the body of information that was available when the war began to break out, and more than any other American he helped move Vietnam to the forefront of public concern. Gilbert Jonas, Ngo Dinh Diem's official publicist in the United States, recalled in 1993 that Dooley "could get the American people on a popular level to have some sense of an obligation to Vietnam. He was the first character in America who could do this, . . . and he did it better than anybody else."[194]

In light of the outcome of America's experiment in nation building in Southeast Asia, Dooley may be said to have penned a more fitting epitaph in an earlier section of *Deliver Us from Evil*, well before he apologized for his "erratic ways" and cited Frost. While Dooley chose to insert this passage in chapter 3 of his book, DeWitt Wallace recognized its dramatic effectiveness and saw to it that the *Reader's Digest* version of the text began with Dooley reminiscing: "One night last spring I lay sleepless and sweltering in the dying city of Haiphong, North Vietnam, asking myself the question that has taunted so many young Americans caught in faraway places: 'What in hell am *I* doing here?' "[195]

In coming years, over two million young American soldiers in faraway South Vietnam would find themselves taunted by that same question.

5

"The Sects and the
Gangs Mean to Get Rid
of the Saint": "Lightning
Joe" Collins and the
Battle for Saigon

After two months in South Vietnam, the American envoy General J. Lawton "Lightning Joe" Collins momentarily allowed his self-command to lapse. His official reports to Washington and even his private correspondence had thus far been models of decorum, but a letter from his friend Alfred Gruenther set Collins off. Gruenther, the supreme allied commander in Europe, compared the frustration of managing the squabbling NATO allies to running a six-ring circus. Collins responded,

> When you think you are running a six—or perhaps fourteen—ring circus, just give a thought to our minor show down here. . . . We have five separate armies; until recently an open clash between the chief of staff and the premier; gambling houses and worse, all operated with the tacit, if not open, approval of the chief of state; two religious sects with their own private domains; a pope; an active underground Viet Minh; a Foreign Expeditionary Force; and an absent emperor who still remains the only legal source of power in the state. Fit all of this to a good musical score and you would have a smash hit on Broadway or the Champs Élyseés!

Collins signed off with the complaint that Gruenther had failed to include a promised "bottle of medicine" with his New Year's greetings from the Continent. "I'm making no accusations," Collins joked, but speculated that one of Gruenther's aides had "consumed it en route," thereby depriving Collins of a needed stiff drink after his daily imbroglio with South Vietnamese premier Ngo Dinh Diem.[1]

Collins's missive captured in a few splenetic lines the clash of cultures that occurred when America attempted to create a nation in the former French Indochina. The Eisenhower administration's most fateful foreign policy venture could scarcely have been undertaken in an environment at a greater remove, both culturally and geographically, from the United States. In his ignorance of and derogative attitude toward the Vietnamese, Collins was typical of the generation of American policymakers who set their country on a course of intervention on the Asian mainland that would culminate years later in failure and disgrace.

Yet Collins displayed a capacity to transcend, if only partially, the framework of preconceptions that distorted policymakers' understanding of events and compelled men like Secretary of State John Foster Dulles and Senator Mike Mansfield to invest so heavily in the Diem regime. Specifically, Collins did not assume that Diem's Catholicism ipso facto established his moral or cognitive superiority to his non-Christian political opponents. Although a Catholic himself, Collins correctly identified Diem's religious militance as tending to undermine indigenous support for his government. Furthermore, while Collins was no more prepared than the departing French to make the Vietnamese equal partners with the West in charting their national destiny, he did not accept Diem's policy of one-man rule as natural and necessary in Asia. Rather, he urged Diem to institute a more representative government that the citizenry would have some reason to defend against communist encroachment.

The Collins mission, as it was called, marked a crucial juncture in the history of U.S. foreign policy.[2] For over six months in 1954–55, the general furnished Washington with dozens of reports arguing for Diem's replacement by another South Vietnamese: a Buddhist, a coalition builder, a practical politician with experience in Vietnamese affairs. The Battle for Saigon of late April 1955 seemed to vindicate all of Collins's recommendations. As Collins predicted, Diem proved incapable of uniting noncommunist elements in his country. Indeed, he accomplished just the reverse: his despotic, creedbound policies so alienated the most powerful of those elements as to trigger what amounted to a civil war within a civil war. The firefight that gutted South Vietnam's capital city exacted a horrific price in lives lost and property damaged and was irrelevant to America's goal of containing communism in Southeast Asia. From Collins's perspective, there was little good to be said and much to deplore about Diem's shootout with his political opponents.

But Collins's views were not shared by the Eisenhower administration, which seized upon the fighting in the spring of 1955 as a reason to overrule its ambassador's verdict that the Diem experiment had to be dissolved. Diem's victory in the Battle for Saigon was less important for what it revealed about his popularity in Vietnam than for the manner in which it was interpreted in the United States. American policymakers and the American media misconstrued what was in fact a complex tragedy for which each combatant deserved a share of blame as a clear-cut case of virtue against corruption. Despite Collins's insistence that Diem was more tyrannical and less sophisticated politically than the worst of his rivals, statesmen like Dulles and Mansfield persisted in viewing the premier as an island of lawfulness and piety assailed by cultists whose bizarre religious practices made them scarcely less odious than the Viet Minh. Keywords like "Christian," "sect," and "nationalist" evoked a particular set of associations in American minds and commanded a particular responsive action—even though those terms meant something different in the context of South Vietnam's infighting.

Collins's heroic but unsuccessful campaign to steer U.S. foreign policy away from the costliest fiasco in its history suggests some answers to a question that, at one time or another, bedevils all students of the Vietnam War: Why did Washington ignore the counsel of the persons assigned to give it? That Collins, who was not only a celebrated statesman but a close friend of President Eisenhower, failed to blast through his superiors' cognitive rigidity is a testament to the power of ideological mind-lock, of policymakers' remarkable resistance to any challenge of their fundamental racial and religious beliefs. Rather than rethink its official construction of Vietnam and detach itself from a losing proposition, the Eisenhower administration chose to disregard the information it had sent Collins to obtain. By the conclusion of the Battle for Saigon, Washington was more firmly committed to the Diem experiment than ever. It was Collins, not Diem, whom Eisenhower replaced.

"Special Representative"

Lightning Joe Collins became a participant in the crafting of U.S. policy toward Vietnam in late October 1954. The general was in Oklahoma City preparing to give a luncheon talk to a local civic group when, as he recalls, "one of President Eisenhower's aides" called to inform him "in guarded words" that the president intended to send him on a special mission "to a country where 'Iron Mike' was located." Collins recognized this as a reference to General John "Iron Mike" O'Daniel, who headed the U.S. Military Assistance and Advisory Group (MAAG) in South Vietnam.[3]

That young country was in desperate straits. Little more than a piece of real estate south of the 17th parallel, the Republic of Vietnam lacked almost totally the sense of "imagined community" that Benedict Anderson deems essential to nationhood.[4] The region was a hornets' nest of dueling ethnic, religious, economic, and political groups. Over one hundred thousand Viet Minh soldiers controlled one-third of the territory, including most of the border with Cambodia. One million Chinese were concentrated in Cholon, a suburb of Saigon, where they exerted disproportionate financial leverage despite their pariah status. Seven hundred thousand Khmer, or ethnic Cambodians, held sway over three large southern provinces on the outskirts of Saigon. More than forty tribes of Montagnard hunters and foragers controlled the Central Highlands. Two million members of the Cao Dai religious group dominated much of the northwestern Mekong River delta, while the Hoa Hao, a smaller but still powerful religious denomination, ruled over the area southwest of Saigon. Other influential religious groups were the Buddhist monks and, bringing up the rear in sheer numbers, the Roman Catholics.[5]

Another group, the Binh Xuyen, was not religious and its membership never exceeded forty thousand, but it wielded as much power as any organized group in South Vietnam. Essentially the Vietnamese Mafia, the Binh Xuyen was based in Cholon. Its leader, Le Van "Bay" Vien, presided over a dominion of vice that included the Hall of Mirrors, reputedly the world's largest brothel; the Grande Monde, a gambling complex that occupied several city blocks; and an opium factory that refined a high-grade product for distribution throughout Indochina.[6] In an outrageously venal maneuver, Vietnamese emperor Bao Dai transferred control of the Vietnamese Sureté, the national police, to the Binh Xuyen in mid-1954. The emperor received about $1.25 million in bribes and kickbacks from Vien in exchange for allowing the Binh Xuyen to run its many gambling casinos, houses of prostitution, and drug factories without fear of reprisal.[7] As *Newsweek* editorialized, Saigon, long acclaimed as the "Pearl of the Orient," had become, in the last year of the Franco-Viet Minh War, "the world's most sinful city. . . . Entire blocks of opium dens, gambling mills, and brothels cater to every purse and taste. And it is all legal!" *Newsweek*'s appalled reaction was typical of the American press. The famed journalist Joseph Alsop called the South Vietnamese capital "an obscene basket of eels." Homer Bigart of the *New York Herald Tribune* wisecracked that "making Saigon a sinless city would be like trying to convert the Augean Stables into a dairy bar."[8]

Sitting atop the basket of eels was Diem, a man who, according to reports from most on-site observers, was so ill-equipped for the task confronting him as to guarantee his nation's absorption by the communists in short order. Donald Heath, America's ambassador to South Vietnam, informed Washington only weeks after the launching of the Diem experiment that the premier was "scarcely capable of influencing people, making friends, or undertaking determined action." As a consequence of Diem's "positive gift for alienating even those who wish to assist him," Heath observed, the "number of his supporters has dwindled away."[9] Robert McClintock, U.S. ambassador to Cambodia, concurred, calling Diem a "messiah without a message."[10] These sentiments were echoed by French officials, who to a man were offended by Diem's Francophobia and exasperated by the premier's substitution of sermonizing for statesmanship. Guy LaChambre, French minister for the Associated States of French Indochina, spoke for many of his colleagues when he predicted that Diem's policies would lead "courageously, virtuously, and rapidly to complete collapse."[11]

That collapse nearly occurred less than three months after the Geneva Conference that provisionally divided Vietnam. General Nguyen Van Hinh, chief of staff of the Vietnamese National Army (VNA), began a series of public attacks against Diem, proclaiming that South Vietnam needed a "strong and popular" leader like himself and bragging about the coup he was preparing.[12] At one point, Hinh sent tanks to surround Diem's headquarters. While Diem remained unflappable, nine members of his government resigned, and Bao Dai recommended that Diem resign as well.[13] Heath warned Dulles that because of Diem's "intrinsic faults," the United States should "look for a relief pitcher and get him warming up in the bullpen."[14] Malcolm Macdonald, Britain's commissioner general for Southeast Asia, was more direct, emerging from his first conference with Diem to announce flatly, "He's the worst prime minister I have ever seen."[15]

When Eisenhower complained to Dulles about the unvarying tenor of panic in reports from South Vietnam, the secretary suggested that

Washington send a high-ranking general to Saigon to serve as the president's personal envoy. Dulles observed that the "official would have to be one of considerable prestige" and "be given very broad authority." Eisenhower decided that General Collins would be "best qualified" for such an assignment.[16] Collins had been Eisenhower's most skilled corps commander in World War II, acquiring the nickname "Lightning Joe" for his bold, decisive leadership. He had also displayed notable diplomatic skill in his relations with the prickly British general Bernard Montgomery during the Battle of the Bulge. Following the war, Collins rose to become army chief of staff and then the U.S. representative on the NATO Military Committee and Standing Group.[17] Although not given to flattery, Eisenhower wrote Collins in 1948, "I would feel remiss if I did not set down for the record, in black and white, my personal testimonial to a great soldier and leader of men. . . . [Y]our service in peace was as peerless as your conduct of battle."[18] The president would have been hard-pressed to find anyone better suited to assess America's prospects in Vietnam.

Held in Secretary Dulles's office, the meeting at which Collins received his orders was brief and straightforward. Dulles conceded that the "chance for success" of the general's mission was only "one in ten," but that the "importance of checking the spread of communism in Southeast Asia" made the effort worthwhile.[19] The secretary informed Collins that he would be allowed a good deal of latitude in implementing policy and that he had been chosen for this assignment because of his "thorough knowledge of the problems of the Far East," presumably a reference to Collins's service in the Pacific theater during the early years of World War II. With what turned out to be undue optimism, Dulles told Collins his mission would last from sixty to ninety days.[20] A White House press release described Collins as "Special United States Representative in Vietnam with the personal rank of ambassador," and Eisenhower's official directive granted him nearly carte blanche "to direct, utilize, and control all the agencies and resources of the United States Government" in South Vietnam.[21]

A special State Department conference convened to bring Collins up to speed on conditions in Saigon. Collins's notes from this meeting suggest a preoccupation with religion either on his part or, more likely, on the part of his tutors. Listening to reports from area specialists, the general jotted down profiles of the leading personalities in South Vietnamese politics:

19. General J. Lawton "Lightning Joe" Collins. © CORBIS, ca. 1940s

- *Chief of State is Bao Dai* . . . apparently sufficiently able but without necessary "messiah" urge to provide true leadership for Viet-Nam. . . .

- *Bay Vien* is the head of a sect which claims some religious affiliation but actually is apparently pretty irreligious. . . .

- *Diem (pronounced Ziem), present Prime Minister.* . . . Very nationalistic, patriotic, and of a high moral character. . . . He is a Catholic and his brother is a Bishop. . . .

- *Cao Dai.* . . . This is a religious sect with a "pope" all its own. . . . [T]here is a dissident branch of this movement which may or may not have the blessing of the "pope."

Collins concluded with a generalization one suspects he would not have applied to East Germans, Poles, or Yugoslavs: "Diem is faced by an apathetic people, ill-informed and caring little who rules them, whether they are free or enslaved."[22]

The briefing book prepared for Collins by State Department analysts reinforced his preconceptions of Vietnamese passivity. "The Cochin-Chinese are a cheerful, *dolce far niente* people who are easily led and in fact prefer to have their decisions made for them," the book asserted. "They do not go hungry and they never get cold." In fact, Vietnam was the site of the greatest World War II–era famine in Asia—over two million Vietnamese starved to death, presumably after going hungry a long while—but Collins had no reason to doubt the accuracy of the report. He was likewise inclined to accept the department's explanation of why Ho Chi Minh and his ruling clique were better able to compel loyalty and sacrifice than the free world's representatives in the South: "The administrators of the Viet Minh regime are dedicated men imbued either by the spirit of nationalism or of communism or a combination of both. They are possessed by what the French call a *mystique,* which is almost completely lacking in Free Vietnam with the exception of the Catholic Church." It is unclear why the State Department felt that only Catholic South Vietnamese could counter the North's "spirit"; most members of the Viet Minh were Buddhist, and this did not preclude their being "possessed by a *mystique.*"[23]

Collins's briefing book also contained a copy of Mansfield's recent "Report on Indochina," in which the Senate's Asia expert praised Diem for his "intense nationalism and equally intense incorruptibility." In a singular choice of attributes, Mansfield synopsized Diem for his colleagues as "a bachelor, an intellectual, and a Catholic." The senator concluded that since the "visible alternatives to Diem" were "not promising," there was only one course of action to adopt: "In the event the Diem government falls, . . . I believe that the United States should consider an immediate suspension of all aid to Vietnam."[24] Mansfield's recommendation had been construed in both Vietnam and France as official American policy.[25] Dulles advised Collins before his departure for Saigon that the senator's report deserved "serious consideration."[26]

Within a week of receiving his assignment, Collins was in South Vietnam, declaring at his first press conference, "I am here to give every possible aid to the government of Ngo Dinh Diem and to his government only."[27] Yet the Collins mission did not get off to a promising start. General Paul Ely, commander of the French forces in Indochina, took the occasion of his first meeting with Collins to express "regret" that his "directive called so explicitly for support of Diem." Ely considered Diem a "losing game" and noted that the Diem-Hinh feud had paralyzed civil-military relations at a juncture when the Viet Minh might invade South Vietnam any day. Taken aback, Collins insisted it was Washington's position that Diem must "be given every possible chance to succeed."[28] Collins met Diem three days later at the palace and tried repeatedly to focus his attention on such matters as cabinet reorganization and American training of the VNA. Diem, however, wished to speak only about "the insubordinate attitude of General Hinh," insisting that Hinh was "utterly untrustworthy" and that the "only solution" was his "departure from Vietnam." Collins managed to inject a few of his thoughts on governmental restructuring but he informed Dulles afterward, "I am not sure [Diem] grasped all the implications of the presentation."[29]

Collins then attended a military briefing by Diem's nemesis, Hinh, and found him a far cry from the headstrong traitor depicted by the premier. Instructions prepared by State Department specialists and given to Collins on the eve of his departure for Saigon stated unambiguously, "We do not recommend Hinh as a reliable long-term asset."[30] Collins, however, judged Hinh's presentation "exceptionally able" and recommended that "every possible effort . . . be made to preserve and put to use in Vietnam the talents which, in my judgment, Hinh possesses."[31] Washington did not respond to this suggestion, but an apparently coerced imperial order from Bao Dai summoning Hinh to France indicated that the Eisenhower administration wanted Diem's adversary out of the picture. On 19 November, Hinh left for Paris, never to return.[32] He blamed his banishment on the United States and on Senator Mansfield in particular, calling Mansfield's "Report on Indochina," with its recommendation that Congress discontinue aid if Diem were deposed, "pure slander."[33]

With the Hinh crisis resolved, Collins proceeded to address the military aspect of his mission. The French had made an informal request in mid-1954 that the MAAG begin training the VNA, and one of Collins's primary errands in Saigon was accordingly to help organize an effective military force.[34] Collins and Ely collaborated on a proposal for a smaller but better-trained and better-equipped VNA.[35] They drew up their reorganization proposal in less than a week, and the State Department promptly approved it.[36]

Tellingly, Collins did not consult with Diem or any other high-ranking South Vietnamese while overhauling the VNA. As he informed Dulles in early January 1955, "It was never my intention that our memo of understanding itself would be submitted to [the] Vietnamese government. . . . Our intention was that [the] memo would be [a] strictly bilateral agreement between us, and as such need not be shown to [the] Vietnam government." Still, the ambassador did not want to appear to be presenting Diem with a "*fait accompli* in [the] form of [a] prior U.S.-French agreement," since this might offend "Vietnamese sensibilities." Collins therefore suggested that the "agreed program of U.S. and French support for reorganization and training of [the] Vietnamese forces should come from Diem himself in [a] manner designed to enable him to get credit for enlisting French and U.S. aid in strengthening Vietnam Armed Forces." In other words, Diem's job was to give his imprimatur to a plan designed by his great-power supporters. For all of the Eisenhower administration's professed anticolonialism, Collins felt no qualms about westerners taking charge of South Vietnam's government and dictating terms to its chief of state.[37]

Similarly, when Collins and Ely met at the Commissariat General to map out the State of Vietnam's educational system, no Vietnamese were invited, as though this was a subject that did not concern them. Ely began by noting that the Vietnamese needed "to avoid [the] danger of hyper-nationalism, with [the] consequence of relying too strongly on [their] own personnel and of returning to traditionalistic education and culture." He believed such turning inward would result in "neutralism, which would be highly undesirable." In Ely's opinion, France and the United States should "aid Vietnam to develop a system of national education which will be open to Occidental influence." Toward this end, he recommended that South Vietnam "retain [the] French language and culture, since [the] Vietnamese language and culture offer little chance to fulfill a modern nation's requirements." Collins concurred, stressing the need for Western-sponsored "educational activities." It was "urgent," he said, that "assistance be given in training youths against communism through organizations such as Boy and Girl Scouts, Catholic Youth, [and] Boys Clubs."[38] While these were abstract speculations rather than detailed proposals, the fact that Collins could engage in such a dialogue—voicing sentiments anathema to Vietnamese nationalists like Diem—indicated his hauteur toward the people he had been sent to assist.

"We Are About to Have a Religious War Here"

Before the end of his first month in Saigon, Collins concluded that Diem himself presented the "chief problem" in creating a stable regime with political appeal.[39] He was especially troubled by Diem's exclusion of non-Catholics from his government and tried to persuade him to appoint prominent Cao Dai, Hoa Hao, and Buddhist South Vietnamese to cabinet posts. Collins did not hold disciples of these faiths in higher regard than most Americans; in his memoirs he refers to the Cao Dai and Hoa Hao as "pseudo-religious sects that . . . appealed to the peasants with a veneer of Buddhism and a protective paternalism comparable to that of New York's Tammany Hall."[40] Nonetheless, Collins recognized that Cao Dai and Hoa Hao leaders had popular support and administrative skill. In addition, they were unquestionably anticommunist and, in Collins's judgment, "the strongest anti-Viet Minh element" in the country.[41] The historian Ellen Hammer notes that "One of the few political certainties in southern Viet Nam in 1954 and 1955 was that no Viet Minh elements were active in regions controlled by the Cao Dai and the Hoa Hao; there were not many other areas of southern Viet Nam of which this could have been said."[42]

Furthermore, the Cao Dai and Hoa Hao were not sects in the sense of being splinter groups on the fringes of Vietnamese society. Rather, they were among the best-organized mass movements in the nation, and the only ones with roots in the peasantry deep enough to rival communist influence. By describing the Cao Dai and Hoa Hao as sects, American policymakers minimized both their political force and, perhaps more important, their nationalism. Collins in particular betrayed his ignorance of Vietnamese history and culture when he dismissed the groups as "devoid of any sense of national conscience."[43] In fact, the Cao Dai and Hoa Hao had a long tradition of anticolonial struggle. Established in the early twentieth century, they almost immediately took on anti-French overtones, subverting imperial supervision in areas under their influence and providing a home for many Vietnamese nationalists. Japan's promises of independence induced several Cao Dai and Hoa Hao leaders to form armies to fight against France in World War II, but their intense anticommunism prevented any partnership with the

Viet Minh, especially after communist guerrillas assassinated the Hoa Hao's founder in 1947. Cao Dai and Hoa Hao claims of anticommunist patriotism were just as valid as those of the Catholics. Moreover, they could (and did) point out that their faiths were indigenously Vietnamese, while Catholicism was an alien religion introduced by the French. The designation "sect" more properly applied to the Catholics than to the Cao Dai and Hoa Hao; indeed, Bernard Fall, Graham Greene, and others reporting on Vietnam during this period often referred to Vietnamese Catholics as a sect.[44] Diem's installation as premier and the Passage to Freedom exodus of 1954–55 increased the Catholic presence in Saigon, but the Cao Dai and Hoa Hao controlled much larger areas of South Vietnam's countryside and attracted millions more adherents.[45]

These realities were precisely what Diem found threatening about the two groups, and they explain why he refused to bring their leaders into his cabinet. He did not want to share prerogative with men who might oppose him. He intended to run South Vietnam as an autocracy, not as a coalition government, and Collins, who had a different recipe for nation building, grew progressively more concerned about the premier's centralization of power. "None of his subordinates is delegated sufficient authority to work," Collins complained shortly after Hinh's departure. "Diem wishes to do everything himself."[46] This resulted in Diem's working as long as twenty hours a day, immersing himself in minutiae: divorces, passport applications, and promotions and reassignments of military commanders and civil servants all required his personal approval. Meanwhile, as a National Intelligence Estimate noted, "The political situation in Vietnam south of the 17th parallel is one of almost total paralysis."[47] Collins considered this intolerable. Diem, he insisted, had to bring "strong leaders" into his cabinet to provide the administrative skills he lacked.[48]

In casting about for such a strong leader, Collins fixed upon the former defense minister, Doctor Phan Huy Quat, who made an even more favorable impression upon Collins than Hinh. From their first meeting, Collins considered Quat "the ablest Vietnamese" in Saigon.[49] His anticommunist credentials were impeccable, and he had considerable experience in government, having held several cabinet posts before Bao Dai eased him out of office to make way for a royal flunky. Adding to Quat's political viability was the fact that, unlike Diem, he was an adherent of the majority Buddhist faith.[50] Collins reasoned that Quat would be the ideal choice for defense minister. The doctor was a "first rate man," Collins told Diem; his appointment to this vital post would relieve the premier of much of his workload and persuade his American sponsors that the government of South Vietnam was acquiring a more democratic cast.[51] Yet Diem, worried that Quat would use the defense ministry and its close association with the armed forces to seize the premiership, repeatedly failed to follow through on promises to appoint him. Collins's reports to Washington grew testy: "Diem is authoritarian in spirit and arbitrary"; "Diem's objective is to surround himself with lackeys"; "At present, I am highly dubious of Diem's ability to succeed"; "My initial impression of his weaknesses has worsened rather than improved."[52]

Dispatches like these alarmed the State Department. Undersecretary of State Walter Robertson and Kenneth Young, director of Philippine and Southeast Asian affairs (PSA), paid a call on Senator Mansfield and confronted him with Collins's cables. Mansfield agreed that Quat was "an able man" but reminded Robertson and Young that the United States wanted to preserve the appearance of South Vietnamese autonomy; it would look like neocolonialism if America told the premier of a sovereign nation whom to accept into his cabinet. Mansfield moreover stated that "the most remarkable aspect of Diem was, unlike most Vietnamese, he really was honest, incorruptible, and devout."[53] Dulles followed Mansfield's lead, admonishing Collins not to give the impression that the "U.S. and French [are] ganging up on Diem." The "initiative" had to come from the premier, Dulles noted, "on internal matters such as specific ministers."[54]

Diem finally exercised that initiative. In a letter dictated to one of his American mentors, Wesley Fishel, he informed Collins that he had decided it would not be in the national interest to bring Quat into the cabinet.[55] Collins, disgusted, fired off a blistering report to Dulles in which he asserted that "acceptance of the status quo . . . is simply postponing [the] evil day of reckoning as to when, if ever, Diem will assert [the] type of leadership that can unify this country." Collins recommended that the administration "[s]upport [the] establishment of another government" and identified Quat as the politician best qualified to head it. "Quat is able, forceful, and resourceful," the ambassador wrote. "If given [the] chance he may succeed where Diem failed."[56] In a subsequent cable, Collins was even more emphatic, informing Dulles that Diem's decision not to appoint Quat defense minister was the "final development that convinces me that Diem does not have [the] capacity to unify [the] divided factions in Vietnam, and that unless some such action is taken, . . . this country will be lost to communism."[57]

This was as unequivocal a vote of no confidence as the historian could expect to find in diplomatic correspondence. Allies have been abandoned for far less. For stridency of tone, Collins's cables recalled the final reports of the "China Hands" prior to the Truman administration's disowning of Chiang Kai-shek, and none of America's spokesmen at the Chungking embassy had possessed the authority granted Collins by Eisenhower. Given the confidence the president had in his World War II comrade-in-arms, Lightning Joe had every reason to believe his recommendations would become U.S. policy.

Collins must have been shocked, therefore, by Washington's reaction. First came a scolding from Mansfield, dictated to Undersecretary of State Robertson and sent to the embassies in Paris and Saigon. The senator continued to stand by Diem, questioned whether Quat was "essential to [the] development of an independent, stable, non-communist Vietnam," and demanded that Collins "cut through personality squabbles."[58] Then Dulles weighed in, objecting to Collins's pessimism and arguing that, although there were "many complex and difficult factors confronting Free Viet Nam," this was "no reason [to] admit defeat." Dulles acknowledged that the pace of government consolidation "may not please us" but reminded Collins that "major changes" in Vietnam came "more slowly than in [the] West." "Under present circumstances," Dulles declared, "we have no choice but to continue our . . . support of Diem. There [is] no other suitable leader known to us."[59] Washington apparently considered the Diem premiership sacrosanct, and Collins would have to try to save South Vietnam with its current administration intact.

Stymied in his efforts to broaden Diem's cabinet or lend it a more interdenominational aspect, Collins urged Diem to at least make some public statement in favor of the separation of church and state and call a moratorium on all visits to Saigon by prominent Catholic cardinals and bishops. Collins observed that when men like Australia's Cardinal Norman Gilroy arrived in the capital to offer their support to the refugees from the North, the streets of the city were hung with banners reading "Long Live the Catholic Church" in French, Latin, and Vietnamese. This could not fail to alienate Buddhists, Cao Dai, and Hoa Hao from the government, as their faiths received no such state-supported pag-

20. General J. Lawton Collins (holding hat) tours a refugee camp in Hanoi. Visible over his right shoulder is his guide, Tom Dooley. Courtesy of Thomas A. Dooley Collection, Pius XII Memorial Library, Saint Louis University Archives

eantry.[60] Diem not only declined to heed Collins's advice to downplay his regime's religious affiliation but extended an invitation to Cardinal Spellman to visit South Vietnam. Spellman accepted. It had been over a year since his last televised tour of Korean battlefields, and he was eager to bring the Bible to the red-menaced Orient once again. The cardinal sent the Saigon embassy a note announcing his intention to stop by in early 1955.[61]

Embassy chargé Randolph Kidder warned Collins that "a visit to Vietnam by Cardinal Spellman at this time is not desirable. This visit can be expected to emphasize further the prevailing impression that Diem is the American protégé and, moreover, the American Catholic protégé." Kidder worried that "the Viet Minh may seize the opportunity to draw a fictitious connection between the visit of an American Catholic Cardinal to Vietnam and the fact that Diem is, himself, a Catholic." On the other hand, the chargé acknowledged that Spellman had placed the embassy in a delicate position. Did Collins want to tell one of

America's most beloved churchmen he was not welcome in Saigon? Kidder noted that "Spellman, in informing you of his visit, . . . did exactly that; he informed you but did not seek counsel or suggestions as to the advisability of his visit at this time."[62] Collins decided not to interfere with the cardinal's stopover but asked MAAG commander O'Daniel to "see what can be done . . . to keep [the] reception orderly."[63]

As news of Spellman's visit spread through Saigon, Quat arranged a meeting with Paul Sturm, Collins's adviser on Vietnamese politics, to "talk about the trend of thinking in Saigon circles." Quat revealed that there was "a commonly held view . . . that Diem's policy has taken a definite new turn in recent weeks, and that this turn is sanctioned by the U.S." According to the doctor, many Saigonese believed that Diem was bent on "creat[ing] a new 'Catholic sect' . . . designed to neutralize already existing sects in Vietnam." Quat listed a number of recent developments that tended to confirm this view, from Diem's formation of a "National Guard [that] is [an] all-Catholic (i.e., sectarian) army" to his dispatch of all-Catholic "army units" to Central Vietnam "with the intention of developing a feudal Catholic stronghold." Quat further noted that "Cardinal Spellman's forthcoming visit is taken to indicate both Church and U.S. approval of Diem's policies."[64] Hoa Hao and Cao Dai representatives voiced similar complaints. A Hoa Hao handbill accused Diem of "secretly setting up an assassination corps recruited among the Catholics" for the purpose of "break[ing] down any group other than the Catholic in order to turn Viet Nam into a Catholic land."[65] General Tran Van Soai of the Hoa Hao claimed VNA troops, acting on Diem's orders, were "desecrating Hoa Hao places of worship."[66] General Nguyen Thanh Phuong of the Cao Dai told Collins Diem was "constructing a Catholic militia" by "replacing elements of National Army battalions . . . with Catholics responsive to the prime minister's direction."[67] Diem made no effort to counteract the charges of sectarianism. Indeed, he seemed oblivious to them, assuring Collins through Fishel that "there is no religious conflict in Free Vietnam." Diem blamed "political opponents" for "stress[ing] his Catholicism in dealings with foreign diplomats and journalists" in order to exploit the fact that "religious questions are of considerable moment in Western affairs."[68]

The complaints of Diem's political opponents received further corroboration when Spellman arrived in January 1955. As Monsignor Joseph Harnett, head of the National Catholic Relief Services in Vietnam, reported to his stateside supervisors, "Vietnam has never seen anything quite like the visit of Cardinal Spellman to this country."[69] The cardinal was received at the airport with military honors by the vna. He met privately with Diem at the palace, emerging to announce he was making a gift of $50,000 for the Catholic refugees in the name of the Knights of the Holy Sepulcher. When Spellman celebrated mass at the cathedral of Saigon later that day, he congratulated "the people of Viet-Nam" on "the defense of their faith against a godless ideology." The next morning, Spellman flew by helicopter to visit refugee resettlement areas. According to the *Catholic Universe-Bulletin,* he "was nearly mobbed by enthusiastic Catholics" at every stop, and the mass he held at the Shrine of Our Lady in Dongha was "jammed by 20,000 faithful." Diem hosted a sumptuous dinner for the cardinal when he returned to Saigon, toasting Spellman as "the foremost friend of Vietnam." An outdoor mass that evening drew fifty thousand people, and another crowd of ten thousand was on hand to see the prelate off as he departed for Manila the following afternoon.[70] One can surmise the reaction of Saigon's non-Catholic majority to this spectacle. American policymakers ought not to have been surprised when, three months later, a Binh Xuyen spokesman hissed at an embassy official, "We are about to have a religious war here. All we ever hear is Catholic-Spellman, Catholic-Spellman, Catholic-Spellman, and we are sick of it."[71]

Although Collins deplored the way in which Spellman's visit was handled by the Diem regime, he maintained a buoyant tone when he returned to Washington in late January 1955 to brief the National Security Council (nsc). He dutifully listed Diem's "disadvantages"—"his lack of executive experience, . . . his lack of 'know how' in selling himself to his people, his narrowness of view, and his great stubbornness"—and confessed that the "least successful aspect of my mission has been my failure thus far to induce Diem to broaden his government by including other able, experienced leaders." Nevertheless, Collins assured his listeners that there was "at least a 50-50 chance of saving South Vietnam from the communists."[72] Since Dulles had initially rated Collins's chances of success at one in ten, the fifty-fifty figure seemed to signify miraculous progress. Dulles was so encouraged that he proposed making Collins permanent ambassador to South Vietnam, an offer Collins declined.[73] He did agree to stay on in Saigon for another two months, however, and Eisenhower sent Diem a letter hailing the fact that "General Collins's presence in your country has strengthened the will and the ability of the Vietnamese people to resist communist efforts to subjugate them."[74] Before leaving Washington, Collins appeared on NBC's *Meet the Press* and reported that "President Diem . . . has made genuine progress."[75]

"Buddhist Passivity Could Be Helpful to Communism"

Indices of Diem's progress remained conjectural. He had done little since assuming office to develop a base of popular support among non-Catholic Vietnamese. His government conspicuously favored the Catholic refugees from the North: a disproportionate share of U.S. aid went to the refugees; northern Catholics held privileged positions in the army and the state bureaucracy; and refugee villages were founded in regions that were deforested by the VNA and then used for cultivation— all but ensuring that the displaced persons would never assimilate into the native southern population. The Catholic Church, unlike the Buddhist Church, enjoyed special rights to acquire and own property. Diem even continued the French colonial policy of legally defining Catholicism as a "religion," while Buddhists were designated members of an "association." These ordinances had the effect of exacerbating differences between South Vietnamese at a time when Collins would have liked to see Diem building bridges among the anticommunist elements in his country.[76]

South Vietnam's Buddhists, Cao Dai, and Hoa Hao who had access to the American press would have found their leader's disdain for their faiths echoed by every mainstream newspaper and magazine. To the degree that America's fourth estate paid any attention at all to non-Catholic Vietnamese, it held them in derision. The Hoa Hao, *Time* informed its readers, was "a rowdy sect of dissident Buddhists" whose founder "was sent to a lunatic asylum." The *New York Times* reported that the Cao Dai believed in "a sort of Ouija board spirituality." *U.S. News and World Report* dismissed the Hoa Hao as "a pseudo-religious sect which follows a perverted form of Buddhism," while the Cao Dai "worships a fantastic assortment of 'gods' ranging from Buddha and Confucius to Victor Hugo and Charlie Chaplin." *Commentary's* Peter Schmid found a certain "beauty" in many "Cao Dai ideas," insofar as that sect "has sedulously copied the Catholic Church"; otherwise, he sniffed, "it is hard to overlook the absurdities that have crept into this religion." Patrick O'Connor, principal chronicler of the North Vietnamese refugees' Passage to Freedom, rendered the harshest verdict: the Cao Dai and Hoa Hao, he insisted, "are impelled by no religious sentiment. It is notorious that they are simply 'on the make' opportunists out for their own material interests. . . . They are united only in their opposition to President Ngo Dinh Diem, whose virtue and increasing prestige they fear. . . . They are capitalizing on hare-brained offshoots of Buddhism and Ouija boards."[77]

It was in its treatment of Buddhism that the American media made its greatest contribution to ensuring that no South Vietnamese other than the militantly Catholic Diem would receive U.S. support. Vietnam's predominant religion was invariably identified with passivity, unindustriousness, and moral relativism, hardly desirable qualities in an ally when one is waging a crusade. In a pronounced instance of this caricature, Life's series "The World's Great Religions" followed up its first installment on Hinduism with a review of Buddhism, which hit the newsstands on 7 March 1955, just as Collins was endeavoring to persuade Diem to widen his appeal in South Vietnam beyond the constituency of a million Catholic émigrés. A questionable piece of scholarship even by the standards of the Luce publishing empire, this issue of Life, particularly its epilogue, titled "Gentle Religion Faces Communist Threat," is nonetheless an invaluable primary source. "Most intelligent Asians agree that Buddhism and communism are basically incompatible and opposed," the anonymous author observed. "To Buddhists man is not primarily an economic creature. His purpose is spiritual. . . . Like all great religions, Buddhism postulates a life of the spirit that transcends the human span. . . . It preaches self-discipline, not discipline from without." Thus far, the basic tenets of Buddhism, by way of Henry Luce, could have been scripted by John Foster Dulles. But there was a sting in the tail: "Its avoidance of force and coercion makes Buddhism one of the world's most gentle religions and may be a weakness in its defense against communism. . . . [It] could make Buddhists reluctant fighters against conquest by belligerent outsiders. . . . The question is whether the practical moral vigor of Buddhism goes deep enough. . . . Buddhist passivity could be helpful to communism." This commentary ran beneath a photograph of the Dalai Lama bowing to Mao Tse-tung and presenting him with a "ceremonial sash."[78]

Mistrust of Buddhism as too passive to serve America's cold war purposes was expressed elsewhere in the media also, nowhere more explicitly than in *National Review,* in which the columnist Frank Meyer defended international anticommunism as a "holy war." "If to fight for this civilization in the belief that we do God's will is blasphemous," Meyer inveighed, "then not the Western but the Buddhist view of things of this world is true: they are but shadows to which no man should give a moment's allegiance. But this the West has always denied. Its Christian vision has seen this sentient world as reflecting and embodying . . . issues of transcendent significance." The *New York Times* observed in the days following partition of Vietnam at Geneva, "The communists will have advantages not reflected by comparative figures. The Viet Minh rebels will have under their control the Northern Vietnamese, who are more tough and vigorous than the Southern Vietnamese and the easygoing Buddhists of Laos and Cambodia." The *Atlantic* agreed, noting that "partly because of their passive Buddhist philosophy, the Cambodians . . . are an easygoing people; the peasants would put up with their lot a long time without revolting."[79] One wonders what aspects of Laotian and Cambodian history, which in the decade prior to Geneva had witnessed insurgencies against first the Japanese and then the French, induced the pundits at the *Times* and the *Atlantic* to ascribe a quality like "easygoing" to these people.

The American Catholic press devoted several articles in the mid-1950s to Buddhism, usually with the objective of demonstrating its vast inferiority to Christianity. *Our Sunday Visitor* presented the instructional tale of "Yoshi Tekisui of the Obaku branch of Zen Buddhism," who in 1954 became "the first Buddhist priest from Japan to embrace Christianity." Tekisui was said to have received medical treatment at the Immaculate Heart of Mary Mission in Himeji, where he engaged a certain Father Spae in theological debate. Impressed by Spae's "sincere belief" in the tenets of Catholicism, Tekisui allegedly lamented, "That's my trouble, Father. I wish I were sure of what I teach. I have doubts, but as yet I have found no substitute for Buddhism." Spae invited Tekisui to "attend a course of Catechism lectures," and "after six months, Tekisui and his wife were baptized Pius and Pia on Ascension Day." *Our Sunday Visitor* spelled out the moral of this story: "The fact is—and we say it charitably—that no non-Catholic can be absolutely certain of the truth of his religion. It is too easy to prove that it did not originate with Christ. . . . Catholics are *certain* they are in the right." In their saturation coverage of Passage to Freedom, a number of Catholic newspapers spotlighted the story of Ky My Nguyen, a Buddhist teenager from North

Vietnam who converted to Catholicism while in Diem's relocation camps. The photogenic Nguyen's face was featured under such headlines as "Buddhism to the Faith" and "From Buddha to Christ." Her conversion was judged especially significant because, as the *Catholic Herald-Citizen* observed, "Missionaries tell us that it is far more difficult to win converts to Christianity from Buddhism than from any other non-Christian religion. . . . For this reason the Holy Father bids us pray . . . for 'Christians in Buddhist lands.' "[80]

Americans seeking a more scholarly analysis of Buddhism than that offered in the popular press found few texts to consult. At the time of Diem's installation as premier, the most recently published study in English was Henri de Lubac's *Aspects of Buddhism,* which did not present this ancient and complex faith in a flattering light. De Lubac contended that "Buddhism lacks the only possible foundation: God. . . . All the insufficiency—all the falsity, in fact—of the Buddhist religion comes in the final analysis from this." For a Buddhist, according to de Lubac, "there is no ontological solidity deriving from a Creator. . . . He is nothing but a mass of component parts . . . unable to see beyond popular animism to the face of God." Consequently, de Lubac concluded, "Buddhism looks upon existence as a dream. . . . [T]he universe tends to be regarded as nothing more than one vast illusion. Such an attitude would be a remarkable betrayal of Christianity, annihilating its very substance." Buddhism's "amorphous mysticism of the Void," de Lubac noted, "always has a powerful attraction for a certain type of mind. It is one form of the danger which comes to us from India."[81]

De Lubac's seeming non sequitur about India, an overwhelmingly Hindu country with a minuscule Buddhist population, was representative of the sort of undifferentiated modes of thought Harold Isaacs discovered while researching *Scratches on Our Minds.* This classic social science text, briefly addressed in chapter 1 above, examined what Isaacs termed the "ideas, notions, and images . . . Americans have in their heads" about China, India, and Asia in general. Isaacs found that many of the men and women he interviewed did not draw sharp distinctions between such putatively "Eastern" faiths as Taoism, Hinduism, and Confucianism; these tended to be lumped together into a "blurred largeness," as in the case of the man who observed of the "undifferentiated crush of humanity" in Asia, "They are heathen, people with other gods." Those interviewees who did discriminate between "Eastern" religions had little good to say about any of them. A journalist dismissed

21. Binh Xuyen chieftain Le Van "Bay" Vien (left) and Cao Dai
Pope Pham Cong Tac. © Bettmann/CORBIS, 22 April 1955

Confucianism as little more than a "code of manners" and noted that
the Chinese "never produced great ideas, that is, emotional religious
works. . . . They have no grasp of the Christian concept of humanitarianism." A Catholic priest agreed: "The Chinese is not spiritual in out-
look. . . . They . . . have no yen for religion, just for empty forms." A
"large majority of . . . interviewees" condemned Hinduism, often in
extreme terms. One subject called it "a debased, hopeless sort of religion; a complicated, alien mess; mystic nonsense, stupid taboos; horrible practices in a clutter of cultural dead weight." Another concluded
that Hindus suffered from "a diseased state of mind in which any
possibility of constructive action is vitiated. . . . There is a basic insecurity in their religion, which is no damn good at all, and they must realize
it. So they discuss! There would be more to talk about with a Hindu on
a desert isle than with a Catholic!"[82]

The similarity between such remarks and the treatment accorded Cao Daism, Hoa Haoism, and Buddhism in the American media is striking. Collins did not realize how much he furthered Diem's cause when, at the conclusion of a cable to Dulles detailing the premier's faults, he conceded, "Diem does have a certain spiritual quality which could be built into a valuable asset in combating the phony but insidious religion of communism."[83]

"With Great Regret, but with Firm Conviction"

In early March 1955, Diem set in motion a chain of events that would climax weeks later in the Battle for Saigon. He refused to renew the Binh Xuyen's license for their gambling enterprises and announced that the French policy of subsidizing the Cao Dai and Hoa Hao as anti-Viet Minh allies would be terminated. At the same time, he purchased the loyalty of Cao Dai and Hoa Hao generals with millions of American dollars.[84] Binh Xuyen leader Bay Vien retaliated by forming a "United Front" with several Cao Dai and Hoa Hao commanders and demanding governmental reform.[85] Collins, by his reckoning, met "almost continuously" with Diem, representatives of the front, cabinet ministers, and French officials "in order to prevent violent action."[86]

Collins's efforts seemed to have gone for naught when, on 21 March, Vien issued an ultimatum insisting that Diem "undertake *within five days* [a] complete re-organization of the cabinet and its replacement by a new cabinet acceptable to the United Front National Forces."[87] Diem refused to budge. He told Collins that if Vien, "having gone so far as to make demands . . . in [the] form of [a] classical 'ultimatum,'" fomented any acts of civil disobedience, he would break up the demonstrations with VNA troops. Collins attributed Diem's intransigence to "Oriental psychology," which "cannot allow [such] demonstrations to be 'successful.'"[88] But when the Binh Xuyen positioned mortars around the presidential palace, Collins concluded it was time to bring about a détente. He received grudging permission from Diem to meet with dissident generals Trinh Minh Thé and Nguyen Thanh Phuong and try to entice them into the government.[89]

The summit conference ended in disarray minutes after it began. Neither Thé nor Phuong seemed interested in reconciling with Diem; rather, they were spoiling for a fight. Collins drew upon long-standing

American notions about Asian immaturity to explain his failure as pacificator. "This conversation left me with a sense of unreality which marks so many situations here," he cabled Washington. "Discussing this problem with these generals was like trying to reason with two stubborn four-year-old children. They were either lying very ineptly or they are alarmingly stupid considering the influence and power they wield. . . . Trying to determine from them exactly what they wanted was absolutely futile." It was clear, however, what Thé and Phuong did not want: a continuation of Diem's policies of one-man rule and religious persecution. Phuong charged that "Diem . . . pits religion—Catholic—against religion, sect against sect." He repeated the allegation that Diem was in the process of organizing a "Catholic party designed to establish a family dictatorship."[90]

After the United Front's five-day deadline passed without incident, Diem became bolder, revoking Bao Dai's grant of police powers to the Binh Xuyen. He ordered the VNA to seize the headquarters of the Saigon police, a heavily fortified building in one of the most densely populated areas of the city. General Ely, fearing a bloodbath, persuaded Diem to suspend his order, but not before units of the VNA partially occupied the periphery of the compound. Bay Vien then ordered an assault on VNA headquarters by over two hundred Binh Xuyen troops. For three hours into the early morning of 30 March, the VNA and Binh Xuyen clashed. The hostilities were inconclusive, but both sides suffered heavy casualties. Moreover, many innocent bystanders were killed and scores injured in the crossfire that raked Saigon's busiest streets. Ely managed to broker a temporary cease-fire, and Bao Dai cabled Diem to demand his resignation.[91]

A frustrated Collins sided with the emperor. From his perspective, Diem's feud with the Binh Xuyen was a distraction that prevented the VNA from concentrating on the real threat posed by North Vietnam. Even if Diem succeeded in driving Bay Vien and his followers out of Saigon, the gangsters would only switch their allegiance from the West to Ho Chi Minh. America would hardly profit from such an outcome. Collins believed that Diem's principal objective should be to rally noncommunist Vietnamese to the government's side, yet Diem was pursuing a course of action that generated disunion rather than cohesiveness. The seemingly pointless carnage of 30 March 1955 convinced Lightning Joe that if Diem remained premier, South Vietnam would be lost. Collins told Washington that it was "essential" to consider "alternatives to

[the] Diem government." Again he identified a regime led by Quat as the most promising alternative and recommended former foreign minister Tran Van Do for premier if, for whatever reason, Quat was unacceptable to Washington. Should the administration determine that neither Quat nor Do was viable, then the best course of action would be for "Bao Dai to return and assume [the] presidency over a new government." In other words, any arrangement was preferable to Diem's staying in office.[92]

This report caused consternation in Washington. An anxious Dulles woke Eisenhower shortly after midnight and read Collins's cable over the phone. Eisenhower remarked that he did "not see that we can do much except to tell [Collins] not to give up on Diem because we bet on him heavily." Dulles advised the president to sound out Senator Mansfield before replying to Collins. "Mansfield is devoted to Diem," Dulles noted and reminded Eisenhower that the senator "has been out there and . . . is most familiar with the situation." Eisenhower asked whether a consultation with Mansfield was necessary. Dulles affirmed that it was. He did "not mean to be controlled by Mansfield's judgment," he said, "but just to get his views." Dulles ascribed Mansfield's affection for Diem to the fact that "both are Catholics." Eisenhower pointed out, "Collins is a Catholic, too."[93]

That Dulles felt the need to deny being controlled by the judgment of a first-term senator from Montana was an indication of the influence Mansfield wielded as Washington's Indochina expert. In his biography of Mansfield, Gregory Olson concludes that "there may never have been another time in the nation's history when the opinion of one member of Congress was given so much credence."[94] While Mansfield later complained that Dulles "leaned a bit too heavily on me in the matter of Diem," he was not reticent about expressing his views when the secretary met with him hours after speaking to Eisenhower.[95] Mansfield, after reviewing Collins's cables, conceded Diem's failings but insisted that the alternatives proposed by Collins were "worse than keeping Diem in office." "If Diem quit or were overthrown," Mansfield predicted, "there would very likely be civil war . . . and, as a result . . . Ho Chi Minh would be able to walk in and take the country without any difficulty." Mansfield refused to lend his support to the abandonment of his friend and coreligionist. He threatened to withhold congressional appropriations for South Vietnam if the United States collaborated in Diem's ouster.[96] With Mansfield's admonition fresh in his mind, Dulles cabled Saigon that "re alternatives to Diem, we do not think that [a] switch would be desirable or practicable at [the] present time."[97]

When Collins put down the secretary's cable to survey the situation in Saigon, he saw the army he had hoped to train for battle against the communists deployed against a gangster mob. In some cases, VNA troops and Binh Xuyen thugs bivouacked in fortified encampments on opposite sidewalks of boulevards and streets.[98] Collins could also see, displayed at newsstands throughout the city, the 4 April edition of *Time* magazine, which featured Diem on its cover. Colonel Edward Lansdale, head of the covert Saigon Military Mission, recalls that the magazine "made a striking background to the soldiers' sandbagged forts."[99] The artist's rendering of Diem showed him staring determinedly forward while a red scythe tore the flag of Free Vietnam in half in the background.

With the exception of its championing of Chiang Kai-shek in the 1940s, the Luce empire never took up the cudgels for an American ally more zealously than in this issue of *Time*. The feature article, titled "The Beleaguered Man," portrayed Diem as "a resilient, deeply religious Vietnamese nationalist who is burdened with the terrible but challenging task of leading the 10.5 million people of South Viet Nam from the brink of communism into their long-sought state of sovereign independence." *Time* offered an account of the Hinh crisis that was exceptionally flattering to Diem, gave the premier credit for a number of reforms that existed only on paper, and depicted the Diem-Collins feud as good-natured. The greatest cause of friction between the two men, according to *Time,* was Collins's "rough language," to which the saintly premier objected. Overall, however, Collins and Diem had forged "a partnership that shows progress and promises more." *Time* allowed that Diem had his share of eccentricities—"considering someone he dislikes, he will sometimes spit across the room and snarl, 'dirty type!' "—but otherwise lauded him as a paragon of "nationalist purity" whose "achievements are encouraging."[100]

Luce's opinion samplers would not have received this appraisal had they consulted Collins, who bombarded the State Department in early April with cables demanding an end to the Diem experiment.[101] Unfortunately, Collins had to compete for Washington's attention, as Red China's shelling of the islands of Quemoy and Matsu in the Formosa Straits generated a war scare that left policymakers with little time to assess the intrigues of Saigon politics.[102] Dulles, who was microman-

22. Ngo Dinh Diem's countenance first graces the cover of *Time* magazine on the eve of the Battle for Saigon. © Time Life Pictures/Getty Images

aging the Vietnam crisis while Eisenhower devoted his attention to Quemoy-Matsu, found Collins's dispatches insubordinate, given that the administration had made clear Diem's remaining in office was non-negotiable.[103] As Dulles observed in response to a reporter's question about Indochina, "There are some problems there that can't be dealt with adequately by the people on the ground, although General Ely and General Collins . . . have settled most of the problems. But there always are a few that . . . need to be dealt with at the higher level."[104] Diem's status was one of those problems. Dulles refused to consider any schemes for replacing him and demanded that Collins ratify whatever move the premier felt was necessary to wrest control of the Sureté from the Binh Xuyen. He also ordered Collins to meet with Ely to make certain the French understood Washington's position.[105]

Collins's conference with Ely proved a fateful discussion. Ely insisted upon meeting with no staff present. He told Collins that Diem could be preserved only at enormous cost, "and if he is saved, we shall have spared for Vietnam the worst prime minister it ever had." The French general ridiculed American notions of Diem as a nationalist leader, pointing out that the premier had no popular support and was "more of a puppet than any of his predecessors." In Ely's opinion, "it was in [the] interest of Vietnam and [the] free world that Diem not be saved." When Collins asked whether Ely would support a Quat or Do premiership, Ely replied he was "prepared to accept anyone but Diem." He did not expect Collins to respond to his recommendations immediately but felt obliged to point out that this was his "final judgment."[106]

It was Collins's as well. "As you know, I have been doing everything in my power to assist Diem in accordance with my original directive," Collins wrote Dulles at 11:00 P.M. on 7 April. "I must say now that my judgment is that Diem does not have the capacity to achieve the necessary unity of purpose and action from his people which is essential to prevent this country from falling under communist control. I say this with great regret, but with firm conviction." Collins stressed that he did not feel, nor had he ever felt, that Diem was "indispensable" to the formation of a viable anticommunist government in South Vietnam. "I believe that Tran Van Do or Dr. Quat could form and successfully head such a government," he declared, and closed on an almost condolatory note: "I fully appreciate the gravity of the recommendations I have made. I need not tell you with what a heavy heart I file this message."[107]

At first, Collins's cable seemed to have the intended impact on Dulles and Eisenhower. The secretary met with the president twice over the weekend of 8–9 April to discuss Collins's verdict.[108] While no record of these meetings is available, their substance can be inferred from Dulles's subsequent telephone conversation with his brother, CIA director Allen Dulles. John Foster reported that "the boss" had decided to "go along with" his special representative's recommendation for a new South Vietnamese premier. He complained that despite the State Department's having sent "2-3 strong messages" urging Collins to stick with Diem a bit longer, "these have not shaken him. . . . [I]t looks like the rug is coming out from under the fellow in Southeast Asia."[109]

Yet the secretary was in no hurry to yank the rug and held off on responding to Collins until he had the opportunity to discuss the general's conclusions with Mansfield. If Congress's leading authority on Asia refused to moderate his pro-Diem stance, then Collins would have to be reminded of the likely Senate reaction to Diem's removal.[110] Dulles sent Kenneth Young, the State Department's director of Philippine and

Southeast Asian affairs, to get Mansfield's views. The senator did not equivocate. "The U.S. should stick to its guns in continuing to support Diem," he advised. Mansfield was unimpressed with Collins's recommended alternatives to a Diem premiership. "Ngo Dinh Diem and Ho Chi Minh are the only two national leaders in Viet-Nam," he claimed. "To eliminate Diem will leave the field to Ho." Mansfield threatened to urge Congress to withhold appropriations for Vietnam if the United States abandoned Diem and to go public with his disagreement with the administration. "We have nothing to be ashamed of in supporting Diem in the past or in the future," he declared.[111]

Dulles relayed Mansfield's objections to Collins, who responded that any attempt to equate Ho and Diem in terms of popularity was wishful thinking. "I have tried to convey to [the] Department how slender [the] basis of Diem's support now is," Collins wrote. "If U.S. support is withdrawn, Diem would be hard pressed to muster any allies. . . . Few nationalists outside his family and immediate entourage would lift a finger in Diem's support." The great imperative at present, Collins maintained, was to "*persuade Diem to resign, or if he refuses, have Bao Dai relieve him.*" In a transparent indication of his lack of confidence in Vietnamese capacity for self-government, Collins suggested that if, as expected, Diem had difficulty "bow[ing] out gracefully," the U.S. embassy could "draft a statement for him."[112] Dulles attempted to slow Collins's momentum by making an explicitly racist appeal: "I feel that as with most Orientals Diem must be highly suspicious of what is going on around him and that this suspicion exaggerates his natural disposition to be secretive and untrustful. If he ever really felt that [the] French and ourselves were solidly behind him, might he not really broaden his government?"[113] Collins replied in the negative, using Dulles's own racist preconceptions to shore up the case for Diem's removal. "We are not dealing here with fully rational, educated, unbiased Westerners," Collins declared. "The prime minister of this country must know how to direct and handle men who are highly venal, and who have not yet learned to subordinate their selfish interests for the good of their new and unstable country. Diem cannot make these mental adjustments, and has no knack for the solution of these problems. Do and Quat do."[114]

This ought to have decided matters. And, for a time, it appeared to have done so. What transpired in Washington in the wake of Collins's cable is obscure, but a partial account of the transformations undergone by Eisenhower's instructions to his special representative can be assembled from the documentary record. As he prepared for an afternoon conference with the president on 11 April, Dulles drafted a cable to Collins authorizing him to "acquiesce in plans for [Diem's] replacement." Dulles presented the draft to Eisenhower over lunch. The president made some cosmetic revisions but approved the decision to remove Diem from power.[115] Several hours later, Dulles phoned Undersecretary of State Walter Robertson to ask about "reaction from Mansfield." Robertson replied that he had not spoken to the senator yet, but that he had conferred with PSA Director Young. Dulles told Robertson there would be "a meeting at 5 to go over" Eisenhower's instructions to Collins. Robertson promised to see to it that Mansfield attended.[116] After speaking with Robertson, Dulles met with French ambassador Maurice Couve de Murville and warned him that "Senator Mansfield, who was very influential in these matters, felt strongly that Diem should be backed to the limit."[117] Dulles then made a long-distance call to Senator Walter George, who was vacationing in Vienna. George, a close friend of Mansfield and a member of the Senate Foreign Relations Committee, was bound to be displeased by the administration's decision to oust Diem. Dulles told George that "we may have to make some changes" in Vietnam, but that he was "extremely reluctant to do so." He assured George that he was "talking with Mansfield" about proposed shifts in U.S. policy.[118]

There is no known record of the meeting that occurred at 5:00 P.M. that day, but its participants must have included Dulles, Robertson, Young, and, almost certainly, Mansfield. Young apparently tabled an alternate draft of a cable to Collins that postponed a final decision on his recommendations. While willing to go along with Collins "in principle," Young advised, "we should not discard Diem so abruptly and completely" before examining "several intermediary combinations" that might facilitate a more gradual shift from one premiership to another.[119] Later that evening, a tidied-up version of Young's cable was dispatched to Saigon. It is unclear whether Dulles consulted with Eisenhower about delaying authorization for Diem's removal. What *is* clear is that Collins received instructions not to jettison the premier, as the president had earlier decided, but to devise "an intermediate solution which would not kick Diem completely out of the picture or keep him in his present status with full powers." Dulles wanted a "transitional arrangement" that would "retain Diem in some general capacity as chairman of a new council . . . while delegating detailed administration of the program to Quat or Do." Collins's many reports chronicling Diem's refusal to delegate authority were ignored.[120] Shortly after the meeting at which the telegram ordering Collins to cashier Diem was scrapped in favor of Young's "intermediate solution," Dulles delivered an after-dinner speech titled "Principles in Foreign Policy" to a crowd of State Department officials. Among other things, the secretary reminded his audience that "our policies must be dependably embraced by our own people, who are essentially religious" and that "the great deeds of history were wrought primarily by men with deep conviction and dynamic faith."[121]

"This Fellow Is Impossible"

Collins did not hear Dulles's speech, and his judgment would not have been altered if he had. After receiving the Young/Dulles cable, Collins reminded the State Department that the "present tenuous truce may explode at any moment. . . . Therefore, I believe action should be initiated with minimum delay."[122] This was not hyperbole. The day Collins responded to the administration's plan for a "transitional arrangement," Diem again rattled his saber, warning Collins that he intended to violate the truce between his government and the Binh Xuyen by having the VNA occupy police headquarters in Saigon. Collins managed to persuade Diem to stay his hand, but this was a temporary respite. As long as South Vietnam retained its present leadership, the nation would never be far from civil war.[123] "Even Diem's own men believe he is incapable of governing," Ely remarked to Collins. "[The a]rmy does not support him. . . . [The] intellectuals are against him. . . . [The] sects are unanimously against him. . . . Diem remains in power only by U.S. intervention." Ely contended that Diem's utter dependence upon American aid "stigmatized [him] as [the] most thoroughgoing puppet yet to govern Vietnam."[124]

When Eisenhower expressed "confusion" at the obvious difference of opinion between his envoy in the field and his advisers at home, Dulles recommended that Collins be summoned to Washington to defend his policy prescriptions. Perhaps, Dulles ventured, Collins would become more tractable if he experienced firsthand the sentiment behind Diem within the administration. The president agreed that an in-person report was warranted.[125] Dulles cabled Collins that the State Department could not "give any effective U.S. commitment to a program for replacing Diem without your personally going over the program with us here in Washington." He suggested that Collins use upcoming congressional hearings on "appropriation[s] for Vietnam" as the pretext for his recall.[126]

In his final conference with Diem prior to departing from Saigon, Collins gave the premier one last chance to reform his government. The report of this meeting is painful to read. After Collins again emphasized the necessity of forming a coalition cabinet, Diem rejected all the men who would give substance to any power-sharing arrangement, insisting that cabinet ministers should be "neutral men . . . *having [the] same political concepts as himself.*" Collins's bleak parting words were a clear indication of what he intended to recommend when he returned to the United States. "I said that . . . I had done my best to help," Collins reported. "I admired his accomplishments and his character, but not his method of working, and only regretted that I had not been able to do more for him and his country." Collins closed with the verdict, "I see no, repeat *no* alternative to the early replacement of Diem."[127]

Lightning Joe arrived in Washington to face a hostile audience. His most formidable adversary at his initial debriefing was PSA Director Young, whose 11 April draft cable had furnished the administration with a rationale for evading Eisenhower's earlier decision to abandon Diem. Young subjected Collins to strident questioning, but the general stood his ground, affirming that "no solution in Vietnam is possible as long as Diem remains in office." Still reluctant to abandon Diem outright, Young inquired whether he "could be kept on the scene in some new role, such as . . . giving special attention to the refugees, most of whom are Catholics." Collins deemed this an impossibility. By the close of the meeting, Collins had so successfully set the tone of debate that Young and his aides were reduced to haggling over questions like "What should we say to Diem, if anything, before we decide on assenting to some new arrangement?"[128]

Collins won this round. More significant than his bulldozing of any debriefing panel, however, was an encounter with Eisenhower that same day. When the debriefers took an afternoon break, the president invited his special representative to lunch with him at the White House. Disdaining pleasantries, Collins launched into a lecture that was delivered at such velocity that Dillon Anderson, Eisenhower's special assistant and the man who composed a memorandum of this meeting, had difficulty keeping up:

General Collins said that the state of affairs in Saigon had reached the point where, in his opinion, the continuation of the present government under Diem was no longer supportable; that Diem had lost his cabinet ministers one by one; . . . that—to give an example of his lack of administrative capability—he is presently signing personally all visas for entry into and exit from the country; that he is completely intractable, unwilling to accept suggestions, and using such poor judgment, as General Collins sees it, in his efforts to maintain the government, that his government will inevitably fall.

Collins concluded that "the net of it is, . . . this fellow is impossible." When Eisenhower asked for a plan that might save South Vietnam from "chaos and communism," Collins replied that the only plan he considered "workable" was that "Quat should be built up and encouraged to take over. . . . Quat is the best man on the scene now."[129] Young later told the journalist Robert Shaplen that after Collins's lunch with the president, the State Department staff "seemed to be confronted by a *fait accompli*. . . . It appeared to be a presidential decision that Diem had to go."[130] Eisenhower, however, did not make that decision final just yet. He emphasized difficulties with Congress and public opinion and advised Collins to take his views to the foreign policy specialists and persuade them. He wanted Collins to meet with Dulles when the secretary returned from a week's vacation at Lake Ontario and made a point of insisting that "Mansfield . . . be asked in." For now, he would reserve judgment, and policymakers would have to hope that the brittle peace in Saigon held for a few more days.[131]

This was a risky prospect. The number of violent incidents between the Binh Xuyen and the VNA escalated sharply in Collins's absence. Hours after the general left South Vietnam for Washington, VNA headquarters came under Binh Xuyen attack.[132] The *New York Times* observed that "casual violence and casual acceptance of death" had become the norm in Saigon: "Reports of clashes between the Army and the rebels come in every day."[133] If the city was not yet in a state of civil war, it was not far removed. Chargé Kidder, in command of the U.S. embassy while Collins was in Washington, doubted whether Diem could long be prevented from unleashing his soldiers. "Diem has made it plain he wishes to resort to physical force," Kidder cabled. "VNA troops are resorting to kidnapping of Binh Xuyen and have been acting in [a] provocative manner."[134]

As the goading continued on both sides in Saigon, Collins strove to enlist State, Defense, and CIA officials in his campaign to oust Diem. He was partly successful. Struve Hensel, assistant secretary of defense for international security affairs and previously a Diem supporter, reported to Undersecretary Robertson after meeting with Collins, "I feel that in the past we have made a mistake in building the [South Vietnamese] government upon one man."[135] Eisenhower, although still leery about siding with Collins against Dulles, appeared to use his weekly meeting with Republican legislative leaders to soften the impact on Congress of an impending about-face in Vietnam. The president told the assembled legislators that "General Collins . . . was discouraged over the future of Diem, the man we had backed to bring order to that country." Eisenhower even dropped the name of Diem's likely successor, Phan Huy Quat, and cut short any debate by remarking that he "considered General Collins to be a very good man who could . . . handle the situation out there if anyone could."[136]

Collins had made some headway, but he failed to persuade Diem's supporters in Congress, including the all-important Senator Mansfield. After addressing the House Foreign Affairs and Senate Foreign Relations Committees, Collins met privately with Mansfield and insisted that Diem "did not have executive ability." Collins assured the senator there was a "chance to rescue the situation" in Vietnam, but that this required an "able premier," one of the "modern-minded men like Quat who could sit around the table with any of us, talk our language." Diem, Collins declared, was "so completely uncompromising, acetic [sic] and monastic that he cannot deal with realities."[137] The memorandum of this meeting does not record Mansfield's reaction, but Francis Valeo, the senator's aide, waited in the hallway while Mansfield conferred with Collins and recalls Mansfield remarking afterward, "Collins really doesn't know much."[138]

Dulles returned from his vacation to find Diem's base of support in Washington substantially eroded. He met with Collins over lunch, and while no record of their meeting exists, Young believed that it marked the turning point in Dulles's acceptance of Collins's recommendations. As Young reported to Undersecretary Robertson, "The basic shift in our approach was taken at a long luncheon meeting with the secretary. . . . [Collins] reiterated even more vigorously and firmly his view . . . that Diem must be replaced."[139] Over the next two days, Collins, Dulles, and the staffs of the Far Eastern and Philippine and Southeast Asian offices worked out two cables to be dispatched simultaneously to Paris and Saigon. The telegrams directed French and American envoys to inform Diem that "as a result of his inability to create a broadly-based coalition government, . . . their governments are no longer in positions to prevent his removal from office." They also identified Phan Huy Quat and Tran Van Do as the new South Vietnamese premier and second-in-command. Dulles got away with inserting the proviso that "[a]n effort must be made to find some important and useful role for Diem in order to utilize his . . . good qualities." Nonetheless, Collins had the final say. "[I]f Diem refuses," the message went on, "the program should nevertheless be carried out anyway."[140]

"The Black Hand, the Pirate, the Mercenary, and the Witch Doctor"

Historians are divided as to whether Diem instigated the Battle for Saigon to save his premiership. He certainly had the most to lose from prolongation of the status quo and may have elected to take a now-or-never leap in the dark.[141] Regardless of whether Bay Vien's gangsters or government troops fired the first shot, Dulles received word shortly after ordering Diem's removal that the isolated skirmishes that had characterized the Binh Xuyen-VNA "truce" had given way to a full-scale battle.[142] Saigon was in a state of frenzy by the morning of 28 April. Shelling transformed a square mile of the city into a free-fire zone, house-to-house combat drove thousands of residents into the streets, and artillery and mortars obliterated the poor districts, killing five hundred civilians and leaving twenty thousand homeless.[143] Dulles cabled the embassies in Paris and Saigon to disregard his previous telegrams "until further instructions."[144]

News of the fighting galvanized Diem's advocates in Washington. "There is far too much loose talk indicating that our government's policy is no longer in full support of Premier Diem," Senator Hubert Humphrey declared. "This must stop. Premier Diem is the best hope that we have in South Vietnam."[145] Senate Majority Leader Lyndon Johnson proclaimed, probably for the first time, that "Premier Diem is the Churchill of Asia."[146] Through Representative Edna Kelly, members of the House Foreign Affairs Committee registered their opposition to the administration's withdrawing support from Diem. One member called for the replacement of Special Representative Collins.[147] Mansfield delivered an address in support of the embattled South Vietnamese premier. The senator had initially scheduled the speech for Monday, 2 May, but, perhaps prompted by a press leak of the administration's plotting against Diem, he released the text on Friday, 29 April.[148] The speech called for "an end to all but humanitarian aid" to South Vietnam if Diem were overthrown. Mansfield asserted that the "showdown in Saigon" was "between two sets of forces. The one, personified by Diem, stands for a decent and honest government. . . . The opponents of the Diem government have power, but it is a power built largely on corruption. . . . It is the power of the Black Hand, the pirate, the mercenary, and the witch doctor."[149] After reading a transcript of Mansfield's speech, Dulles cabled the embassies in Saigon and Paris that "American opinion is increasingly opposed to removal of Diem. . . . Senator Mansfield's statement is clear evidence of this position."[150] PSA Director Young warned Undersecretary Robertson that "there are going to be real difficulties on the Hill if Diem is forced out."[151]

Mansfield's choice of words was revealing. The term "witch doctor" seemed to imply that the religious groups were rebelling against Diem's government alongside the Binh Xuyen. This was not the case; neither the Cao Dai nor the Hoa Hao joined Bay Vien in his attempt to topple the premier. Diem's use of millions of U.S. dollars to bribe generals like Trinh Minh Thé paid dividends, as the Cao Dai and Hoa Hao either remained neutral or joined the VNA.[152] Yet Mansfield lumped the Cao Dai and Hoa Hao together with a secular, criminal gang as "opponents of the Diem government," a misinterpretation he reinforced in a speech delivered weeks later. Recalling events surrounding the Battle for Saigon, the senator remarked, "Diem was opposed, not only by the communists, but by a fantastic assortment of gangsters, racketeers, ex-river pirates, and witch doctors of strange religious sects."[153]

Dulles portrayed the battle in a similar fashion while addressing the Washington Council of Governors. "There is, of course, going on now in Vietnam a very complicated struggle between different forces," he observed. "You have got the legal government which is headed by Ngo Dinh Diem, . . . a man of high moral character and stature, . . . and then you have the sects. Sometimes the Binh Xuyen are called a sect. I never will dignify that group by the name of sect, because it is nothing but a bunch of Al Capone sects. Then [there are] the other two sects, the Cao Dai and Hoa Hao, who do have a certain religious basis for their existence." Dulles had difficulty explaining what that basis was. "Cao Dai, I think, is supposed to be a group which is going to make the religion that is going to end all religions," he ventured. "In other words, all the religions of the world are going to be brought together and unified through the Cao Dai." He did not attempt to explain Hoa Haoism, other than noting it had "some natural cultural basis." In any event, Dulles declared, "I think the struggle that is going on was inevitable. . . . [S]ooner or later there had to be a test of strength between the national government and these dissident forces."[154] From Dulles's perspective, the Cao Dai and Hoa Hao were behaving no differently than the "Al Capone sect."

The American press echoed Washington's simplistic construal of conditions in South Vietnam. The Battle for Saigon became, in the hands of Luce and other cold war propagandists, a morality play in which Diem squared off against what *Time* described as "an exotic consortium of religious fanatics, feudal warlords, uniformed hood-lums, and racket bosses." "Indo-Chinese gangsters sell protection to governments," *U.S. News and World Report* announced. "They run the police. . . . They pose as 'popes' and make religion a racket." The magazine explained that Diem, "the defiant, honest little premier," was standing virtually alone against "an unholy alliance . . . between these gangsters, racketeers, soldiers of fortune, and religious fanatics." Max Lerner of the *New York Post* likened Diem to "a calendar saint" and observed that "the sects and the gangs mean to get rid of the saint." The *New York Times* demanded "an end to . . . pseudo-religious sects whose chief function is the maintaining of private armies." *Commonweal* asked, "Who are the main protagonists in strife-torn South Vietnam?" and answered, "On one side, there is . . . a gang of river pirates with lucrative brothel and gambling concessions[;] . . . [t]he Cao Dai, a religio-military sect with its own 'pope' who resides near a gingerbread cathedral[;] . . . [and] the Hoa Hao, another religio-military group who call themselves 'reformed Buddhists.' " Confronting these "enemies of the Vietnamese people," the reporter Howard Simpson detailed, was "Premier Ngo Dinh Diem, an intrepid native leader who . . . is univer-sally recognized as patriotic and incorrupt." The *Christian Century* sim-ilarly set up the conflict in South Vietnam as between "the semifeudal, war-lord regimes of the Hoa Hao and of the Cao Dai" and "Diem, a man of integrity, courage, and wisdom." The *Century* excoriated the "degenerate Buddhist gangsters who staged a revolt in Saigon."[155]

Life, as always, was guilty of the grossest puffery. Luce's weekly edi-torial trumpeted,

23. A dead RVN soldier and his comrades during the Battle
for Saigon in 1955. © Bettmann/CORBIS, 8 May 1955

Every son, daughter, and even distant admirer of the American Revolution should be overjoyed and learn to shout, if not to pronounce,
'Hurrah for Ngo Dinh Diem!' . . . Diem's task, which is just beginning, looks more complicated than George Washington's. He has not
one enemy but several: the communists, the French, the Binh Xuyen
gangsters, the sects, and probably others lurking in the rice fields, to
say nothing of the backwardness of his own people. . . . But Diem's
political assets . . . are just what his country needs. . . . He is a Roman
Catholic and a simon-pure Vietnamese nationalist, thus doubly
proof against communist force. . . . Diem's growing strength immensely simplifies the task of U.S. diplomacy in Saigon. That task is,
or should be, simply to back Diem to the hilt.[156]

Calvin Trillin once explained to an audience of students born long after
World War II that the decade of the 1950s was "the era when *Life* . . . had

the cultural impact of all three television networks rolled into one."[157] In the spring of 1955, this media colossus stated in no uncertain terms what American policy toward Diem ought to be, and press organs across the country concurred. Ambassador Douglas Dillon advised the State Department that "Diem may . . . believe from articles in [the] U.S. press that he has unqualified U.S. support for whatever he does."[158]

"Diem Is Not Only Incapable but Mad"

Collins arrived back in South Vietnam on 2 May, the same day the *Boston Herald* ran a front-page headline that read, "U.S. Friend Wins Saigon Fight."[159] The general had remarked to reporters prior to leaving Washington that he intended to "pick up where I left off" and commented, "It's rather difficult to see exactly what the situation there is when you're on the other side of the world."[160] What Collins saw upon his return was the VNA conducting mopping-up operations. "Victory was costly to [the] civil population of the city," Chargé Kidder understated.[161] In fact, Saigon suffered worse damage in terms of lives lost and property destroyed during Diem's assertion of his authority than it would during the Tet Offensive in 1968 or the communist takeover in 1975. A *Time-Life* correspondent observed, "The scene as we drove along the bullet-torn Boulevard Gallieni . . . might have been Madrid 1936, Manila 1942, Paris 1944, Seoul 1951."[162] Diem, riding the wave of victory, proclaimed to his troops, "Your courage has written a glorious page. Free Viet Nam is immortal! Righteous nationalism will triumph!"[163] A pro-Diem coalition thrown together by Diem's brother Nhu and calling itself the "revolutionary committee" agitated for extreme measures: deposal of Bao Dai, reconstitution of the government, and immediate withdrawal of the FEC from South Vietnam.[164] Although Diem never confirmed the committee's legality or endorsed its program, he did ask Kidder if "he could expect full and immediate U.S. support should he depose Bao Dai and form [a] new government."[165]

When Collins returned to the Saigon embassy, he found a message from Dulles awaiting him. "Events in [the] past few days have put [the] Vietnamese situation in a broader and different perspective than when you were here," the secretary declared. "In [the] U.S. and [the] world at large Diem rightly or wrongly is becoming [a] symbol of Vietnamese nationalism struggling against . . . corrupt backward elements." The administration had decided to shelve indefinitely any plans drawn up during Collins's visit. Nonetheless, Dulles assured Collins, "I recognize that in such a fast-moving situation there may develop factors of which we are unaware here. I will be looking forward to your analyses."[166] Dulles would not have many more to look forward to. Collins's mission had stretched on for half a year, and he had made clear during his week in Washington that he wanted to return to his NATO assignment.[167] Indeed, the nomination of Frederick Reinhardt as ambassador to South Vietnam was confirmed by the Senate as early as 20 April 1955. The only reason he had not been flown to Saigon immediately was Dulles's reluctance to have a changing of the guard before Diem resolved his quarrel with the Binh Xuyen.[168] Now that the premier had met the rebel challenge, Dulles recommended to Eisenhower that "we should let Collins come back and send over our regular ambassador."[169] The White House issued a press release announcing Collins's relief and replacement by Reinhardt.[170]

Collins plodded through the remainder of his mission, convinced that nothing he recommended would be translated into policy. Perhaps as a gesture to posterity, he composed a trenchant ten-page cable outlining the challenge the United States still faced in Vietnam. While conceding that Diem's position had been "strengthened by recent events," he wrote, "I still feel . . . this will not change Diem's basic incapacity to manage the affairs of Govt. His present success may even make it harder for us to persuade him to take competent men into [his] Govt., to decentralize authority to his ministers, and to establish sound procedures for the implementation of reform programs." If Diem did not demonstrate improvement in his administrative skills, Collins recommended, "we should either withdraw our support from Vietnam, because our money will be wasted, or we should take such steps as can legitimately be taken to secure an effective new premier."[171]

Washington had never heeded these warnings in the past and was not likely to do so in the wake of Diem's triumph. Dulles's attention shifted from Saigon to an upcoming NATO conference in Paris, where the issue of Indochina was certain to dominate the West's agenda. Many State Department officers believed that the Franco-American partnership had become a liability and wanted to put greater distance between France and the United States. PSA Director Young counseled Dulles not to allow America "to be mixed up with the French as powers trying to suppress nationalism." Washington should especially avoid appearing to side with Bao Dai in his rivalry with Diem, Young advised, since the emperor was too identified with French colonialism to be of any use to the free world.[172] Eisenhower agreed, instructing Dulles not to meet with Bao Dai while he was in France.[173]

Young need not have worried about the French pressuring Washington for more intimate Franco-American collaboration. Premier Edgar Faure began the American-British-French trilateral talks with an astonishing proposal. "What would you say if we were to retire entirely from Indochina and call back the FEC as soon as possible[?]" Faure asked. Dulles, blindsided, replied that a decision of such consequence should not be made hastily and added that "Vietnam was not worth a quarrel between France and the U.S." Faure would not be put off. There was already a quarrel between France and the United States, he insisted, and it centered on Ngo Dinh Diem:

> [N]ow it is time to speak frankly, Faure said. . . . France is convinced that Diem is leading to catastrophe. Diem took advantage of Collins's absence to effect a "coup de force" which won primary victory, but which has not contributed to any lasting solution. . . . Diem is impossible, and there is no chance for him to succeed or improve the situation. . . . Diem is not only incapable but mad. . . . Diem is a bad choice, impossible solution, with no chance to succeed and no chance to improve the situation. Without him, some solution might be possible, but with him there is none.

Although no one recognized it at the time, Faure's diatribe signaled a milestone in the history of U.S. foreign policy. It was at the Paris Conference of 1955 that Vietnam became America's war. Until the spring of that year, the Eisenhower administration had been able to profess either that France retained primary responsibility for the security of South Vietnam or that Washington and Paris shared the burden equally. The Battle for Saigon, however, dispelled any such illusions. Now Washington would have to weigh its commitment to the Diem experiment against its interest in keeping the French in Southeast Asia.

Dulles acknowledged the "grave problem" with which Faure had confronted him and remarked that he would like to "think about it overnight." Faure obligingly did not press for an immediate answer.[174] Dulles cabled the White House that Faure "was not bluffing." If the French bid was sincere, Dulles observed, and Faure was willing to force the issue, then the administration—unless it changed its position on Diem—would have to assume unilateral responsibility for South Vietnam. Was the retention of the premier worth such a risk?[175] Collins predictably chimed in from Saigon with an emphatic no. He reminded Dulles of the importance of the FEC for the defense and internal security of South Vietnam. French officers like Ely provided essential staff for training and organizing the VNA, Collins noted, and since the Geneva Accords forbade the introduction of new American personnel into Indochina, the United States would not be able to replace France in this capacity in the event the FEC were withdrawn. It was far better, the general declared, to sacrifice Diem than the FEC.[176]

Once again, Collins found himself swimming against the tide. The State Department was eager to accept the French offer. Robert Hoey, officer in charge of Indochinese affairs, drafted the department's official response to Dulles's request for guidance, but it was cleared by the Far Eastern and European offices, the policy planning staff, and Acting Secretary of State Herbert Hoover Jr. Hoey informed Dulles that "withdrawal [of the] FEC would have politically desirable effects [on the] local situation [in] Vietnam."[177] General C. H. Bonesteel, the Defense Department's spokesman on the NSC's planning board, waxed ecstatic over Faure's proposal. "A move of this sort would clearly disengage us from the taint of colonialism," Bonesteel observed. Departure of the FEC would serve to reinforce America's image as champion of "independence and legitimate national aspirations." It would have beneficial effects on anticommunist movements "throughout Asia." Rather than continuing to connive with France in its efforts to hold on to an Asian empire, the general concluded, "we should be happy to see the French leave."[178] Eisenhower left it to Dulles and his advisers to weigh the merits of Faure's bid.[179]

Dulles never explicitly accepted the French proposal, but he did not reject it either. Over the course of the remaining ministerial talks, Faure agreed to soften his characterization of impending FEC withdrawal from "as soon as possible" to the more benign-sounding "progressive reduction" and indicated that he was aware of the destabilizing effects that a French retreat would have on the political climate in Saigon.[180] Dulles likewise adopted a conciliatory tone, acknowledging that Diem "was by no means a perfect head of government." Nonetheless, Dulles restated America's determination not to support any other South Vietnamese leader. He moreover all but announced that Washington was prepared to go it alone in Indochina. "If [the] French withdrew[,] the U.S. would continue to support [the] anti-communist nationalist Govt.

in Vietnam," Dulles declared. "Diem is not a person to whom one can dictate. . . . He has [a] mind and will of his own, and [the] fact that he has survived proves he has virtues not easily replaced."[181] If the threat of withdrawal had been designed to test the strength of the American commitment to Diem, then the French knew where Washington stood.

Both Dulles and Faure endeavored to preserve the veneer of Franco-American unity when they faced an international press corps at the close of the Paris talks. Dulles described the outcome of the conference as "a kind of gentleman's agreement that was as yet neither formal nor precise." Faure said more or less the same thing. While he admitted there was "no contract, no written commitment or accord" on Indochina, he nonetheless felt that the two allies had agreed to a "temporary" acceptance of the status quo. He hastened to point out, however, that "France entered into no agreement about the Expeditionary Corps and remains free to do as she likes."[182] The London *Times* saw through the charade, commenting that "it is now clear that no agreement as such exists; all that was arrived at, in practice, . . . was an agreement not to disagree, and even that was of a somewhat tenuous nature."[183]

The conference generated no bilateral statement of any kind—only what Dulles termed "a scheme of parallel but unagreed instructions" to French and American representatives in Saigon.[184] Still, ensuing events make plain the significance of what had occurred. Almost all French troops left Indochina before the year was out. After Ely's departure in June, the French high command was dissolved. When in July the North Vietnamese government invited the South to consult on preparations for all-Vietnam elections, as stipulated by the Geneva Accords, Diem refused, and the United States supported him. Three months later, a rigged referendum deposed Bao Dai as chief of state and conferred the presidency of South Vietnam upon Diem. Washington applauded the result.[185]

The Paris Conference of 1955 was noteworthy for another reason. It was there that Dulles, almost casually, rendered the entire purpose of the Collins mission null and void. When Faure pointed out that despite the best efforts of Collins and Ely, Diem had failed to make any strides toward broadening his cabinet, Dulles responded, "In that part of the world there was no such thing as a 'coalition' government, but one-man governments." The secretary attested that "he did not know of another Oriental government where Western standards of coalition apply and [that were] not headed by [a] strong individual." "We would like to see

Diem's government strengthened," Dulles assured Faure. "We are not confident that the government is necessarily strengthened by enlarging it in the sense of bringing in political opponents on the theory that a coalition government can function."[186] Dulles thus rationalized away Diem's greatest shortcomings: lack of a popular political base and dictatorial ambitions. In case Dulles had not been sufficiently foursquare with Faure, he made the point even more forcefully during the first NSC meeting after his return from Paris. "[A] coalition government as understood in the West was virtually impossible in that part of the world," Dulles insisted. "In the Orient it was necessary to work through a single head of government rather than through a coalition in which various personal interests had to be submerged in a common loyalty." To illustrate what he meant, Dulles cited "Singman [sic] Rhee in Korea and Ho Chi Minh in Indochina itself."[187]

It would be difficult to conceive of two politicians more dissimilar in philosophy and tactics than Rhee and Ho, and Dulles's conflation of them under the heading "Orient" revealed two hallmarks of American racism. First was the homogenization of as many as a dozen Asian countries as if they had no individuality, a notion that gave birth to the domino theory and enabled it to become an article of faith. Second was the conviction that democratic self-government by Asians was not something on which to base U.S. policy; in the view of Dulles and other American statesmen, Asians were predisposed to submit to "a strong individual"—a Mao, a Chiang, a Kim Il-Sung—and the goal in cold war geopolitics was to ensure that more of these Asian strongmen allied with the free world than with the communists.

From Diem's perspective, such attitudes were a blessing. They gave him the freedom to consolidate his rule without remonstrance from Washington. This he proceeded to do before the last Binh Xuyen soldier was driven from Saigon. As Collins feared, Diem's victory over his domestic rivals made him even more intent on hoarding power. He did assemble a cabinet, but, as Kidder noted, it "appears to be made up largely of . . . men not prominent in political life. It is apparent that these would be men who would agree with Diem's policies."[188] South Vietnamese ambassador Tran Van Chuong formed a similar impression of the "persons Diem had in mind." "None of them . . . would effectively take charge of his department but would simply refer all decisions to Diem," Chuong observed to PSA Director Young. "Therefore, Diem, if he appointed such a cabinet, would be 'alone' and still keeping to his practice of one-man rule."[189] Collins reported that the "[n]ew cabinet represents a true broadening of [the] government only in [a] numerical sense. [The m]ost common reaction in Saigon to date has been 'who are they?' "[190]

Dulles was not concerned with who the new ministers were. They were the men Diem wanted, and that was enough. In his instructions to the incoming ambassador, Reinhardt, Dulles made plain he was in South Vietnam to assist, not criticize. "You will continue to give complete, loyal, and sincere support to the government of President Diem," the secretary ordered, "and you should deal with it as the independent and sovereign government which we believe it is and should be. The U.S. has no right and no desire to dictate the composition of the government of an independent and sovereign state."[191] Reinhardt obeyed. In his first statement upon deplaning in Saigon, he announced, "I came here under instructions to carry out United States policy in support of the legal government under Premier Ngo Dinh Diem."[192]

Meanwhile, Collins, as he recalls, "made the rounds of receptions, luncheons, and dinners that mark the departure of officials from any post." It was not a pleasant social whirl, as "uncertainty as to what my departure might signify to future French, American, and Vietnamese cooperation lent an air of tension to these parties."[193] There were no scenes, however, and on the evening of 14 May Collins and the staff he had brought with him six and a half months earlier left by military air transport for home. In his last communication prior to the special representative's return to the United States, Dulles papered over the unfulfilled expectations of the Collins mission with flattery so insincere it must have stuck in Collins's craw. "I want to tell you again of my appreciation of your magnificent service in Vietnam," Dulles wrote. "Your achievement, in the face of the most trying circumstances imaginable, fully deserves the high commendation which it has universally received, publicly and privately. Your country is, once again, greatly in your debt."[194]

To a degree, the secretary was right. Collins had done his best to reverse the course of American policy. But policymakers in Washington rejected the evidence Collins furnished and persisted in their support of an autocracy for which allegiance increasingly had to be won by outsiders. In this regard, the Collins mission was a prolegomenon, in miniature, to the cataclysm that would engulf Vietnam and the United States in the 1960s and 1970s.

6

"This God-Fearing
Anti-Communist":
The Vietnam Lobby
and the Selling of
Ngo Dinh Diem

When heads of state came to Washington in the Eisenhower years, their
first encounter with the president took place at the White House. Eisenhower did not make a habit of welcoming visitors at Washington National
Airport, primarily because he considered the gesture time-consuming
and also because aides worried about security. In the first five years of his
administration, Eisenhower violated greeting protocol only once, when
King Ibn Saud demanded that the president come to Washington National.[1] But the welcoming ceremonies that greeted the Saudi Arabian
monarch did not match those provided by the White House on 8 May
1957.[2] Clearly, President Ngo Dinh Diem of South Vietnam was someone
special. As the *New York Times* editorialized on the day of his arrival,
"President Diem . . . is a substantial partner in a going enterprise on
behalf of free men in his country and in ours. We honor him and make
him doubly welcome on that account."[3] Washington was rolling out its
red carpet for the "Miracle Man" of Southeast Asia.

Diem flew in from Honolulu on Eisenhower's personal plane, the
Columbine III, a silver Constellation with the presidential seal blazoned
on its sides. It touched down at 12:00 and taxied up to the terminal
ramp, where Eisenhower, Secretary of State John Foster Dulles, and
Joint Chiefs of Staff Chairman Nathan Twining stood perspiring in the
muggy afternoon heat. When the plane doors opened, Diem emerged
to the sound of a twenty-one-gun salute. Andrew Tully of the *Washington News* informed his readers that Diem's "air of modest solemnity
was far more impressive than any grinning, arm-waving performance

could have been." Diem had unwisely dispensed with his customary white sharkskin attire and was wearing a dark, double-breasted suit that accentuated his plumpness. One reporter remarked to Tully "not unkindly" that "Diem looks like a fat little teddy bear." Tully conceded that he did.[4]

After Diem trotted down the runway steps, Eisenhower escorted him past the honor guard to the speakers' platform. Eisenhower spoke first, extolling Diem's "patriotism" and noting, "You have brought to your great task of organizing your country the greatest of courage, the greatest of statesmanship—qualities that have aroused our admiration and make us indeed glad to welcome you." Diem then read his remarks in a high-pitched cadence replete with misplaced emphases that betrayed his lack of fluency in English. He thanked Eisenhower for "your kind words about me" but insisted it was "mostly the courage of the Vietnamese people, your own faith in my country, and unselfish American aid which has accomplished a miracle in Vietnam."[5] The audience was silent for a moment, unsure of whether Diem had finished. When he confirmed that he had by stepping away from the microphone, they burst into applause. The district commissioner presented Diem with the key to the city, prompting photographers to shout "Hold up the key! Hold up the key!" Eisenhower joked, "They're very dictatorial, these boys." A member of Diem's entourage translated Eisenhower's comment for Diem, who laughed.[6] Following the photo session, the two presidents stepped into an open-air limousine and were driven to Blair House, where Diem would rest before addressing both Houses of Congress. Over fifty thousand district and federal government employees, given the afternoon off to witness Diem's arrival, lined the reception route. "Today," the journalist Russell Baker noted, "only the best was good enough."[7]

Diem's 1957 visit to the United States marked the zenith of his popularity—in America, if not in Vietnam. After defeating the Binh Xuyen in the spring of 1955, Diem might have settled into one of those shallow notches in the American imagination reserved for other Eisenhower-era Asian allies like Thailand's Phibun Songhram. Instead, he became something of a folk hero in the United States. From the conclusion of the Battle for Saigon until the coup attempt five years later that nearly toppled his government, Diem was treated with unconditional positive regard by the Eisenhower administration and the American media. One of the most important factors in keeping his image unmarred in Ameri-

24. U.S. President Dwight Eisenhower (right) chats with South Vietnamese President Ngo Dinh Diem at Washington National Airport. © AP/WORLDWIDE PHOTOS, 8 May 1957

can eyes was a private group of elite opinion-makers known as the Vietnam Lobby that exploited to great effect prevailing religious and racial presumptions. Diem, they claimed, was a Catholic and therefore an archenemy of communism, but he was also thoroughly Vietnamese, with a native's appreciation of how much democratic reform his country could absorb. According to lobbyists like the publisher Henry Luce and the philanthropist Joseph Buttinger, Diem's refusal to permit multiparty elections in South Vietnam reflected his understanding that any attempt to grant illiterate, superstitious, and frankly childish peasants a voice in their government would only invite communist takeover. Circumstances required that he wield absolute authority until his people were mature enough to conduct their own affairs. Yet he was not a dictator. His devotion to God and freedom compelled him to govern in accordance with the terms of a constitution, champion capitalist values, and encourage, as far as possible, given wartime conditions and Vietnamese backwardness, the enjoyment of civil liberties. It was America's immense good fortune that this man of destiny emerged from exile to frustrate the communists without resorting to unnecessary repression and that he now promised to shepherd his primitive nation into the modern era on a Christian, pro-Western basis. The Vietnam Lobby's depiction of Diem as a holy warrior and South Vietnam as a nation of political neophytes reinforced those mainstays of American ideology that undergirded Washington's Vietnam policy and bound America ever more tightly and calamitously to the Diem regime.

"Miracle Man"

After J. Lawton Collins left Saigon in May 1955 to resume his NATO post, no major American policymaker raised a voice in opposition to Diem for the remainder of the Eisenhower years. In a televised address heralding Diem's victory over the Binh Xuyen, Secretary of State Dulles apprised viewers, "I am very much impressed by Prime Minister Diem. He is a true patriot and dedicated to independence and to the enjoyment by his people of political and religious freedoms."[8] Assistant Secretary of State for Far Eastern Affairs Walter Robertson observed in 1956, "Asia has given us in President Diem another great figure, and the entire Free World has become the richer for his example of determination and moral fortitude."[9] During Diem's visit to Washington, Eisenhower declared that the South Vietnamese president was "an example for people everywhere who hate tyranny and love freedom."[10] Two years later, Undersecretary of State Chester Bowles assured members of the Vietnamese-American Association, "This miracle of Vietnam . . . did not occur of itself. . . . It took form through faith [and] dynamic leadership."[11]

Such praise was amplified in the American press. Conservative Catholic journals groped for superlatives to describe Diem's accomplishments. The Brooklyn *Tablet,* the Catholic newspaper with the largest circulation in the United States, called Diem "one of the persons to whom the whole world is indebted." The *Catholic Universe Bulletin* hailed Diem for "fighting courageously and successfully against our common enemy, atheistic communism." *National Review* ran a cover story titled "The Amazing Mr. Diem," in which Freda Utley gushed, "President Diem . . . is that rare phenomenon, an intellectual with faith and a man of action with moral as well as physical courage. No one who meets him can fail to be impressed by the depth and strength of his Catholic faith and his hatred of tyranny."[12]

More significant than the encomiums of rightist Catholics was the support Diem received from mainstream publications. *Time-Life-Fortune* publisher Luce was an outspoken advocate, rhapsodizing, "President Ngo Dinh Diem is one of the great statesmen of Asia and of the world. . . . In honoring him we pay tribute to the eternal values which all free men everywhere are prepared to defend with their lives."[13] It was a *Life* headline that tagged Diem "The Tough Miracle Man of Vietnam," and the word "miracle" became indelibly associated with Diem's name. Ernest Lindley, *Newsweek*'s Washington pundit, affirmed, "Ngo Dinh Diem is living proof of what is often called a miracle, . . . proof of what an authentic patriot . . . can accomplish." The *New York Herald Tribune* extolled the "Miracle-Maker from Asia—Diem of South Vietnam." William Randolph Hearst Jr., writing for the *New York Journal-American,* posed the rhetorical question, "How did the miracle of South Viet Nam happen? . . . The story is largely written in the ascetic personality of Ngo Dinh Diem." The *New York Times* "salute[d] President Ngo Dinh Diem" for carrying out a "five-year miracle" in South Vietnam. Edward R. Murrow, whose capacity to see through cold war smokescreens was immortalized in his TV evisceration of Joe McCarthy, bought into the miracle of Diem's achievement. In a radio interview in 1956, Murrow asserted, "Diem . . . has made so much progress in the past six months that some people use the overworked word 'miracle' in describing improvements in South Vietnam."[14]

Even when that overworked word was not used, the heroic narrative remained the same: if not for Diem, twelve million South Vietnamese would have been consigned to communist slavery. The *Saturday Evening Post* designated South Vietnam "the bright spot in Asia" and proclaimed, "Two years ago at Geneva, South Vietnam was virtually sold down the river to the communists. Today, the spunky little Asian country is back on its own feet, thanks to a mandarin in a sharkskin suit who's upsetting the red timetable." *U.S. News and World Report* presented a photograph of Diem surrounded by a cheering mob; alongside the photo ran the caption: "Ngo Dinh Diem, South Vietnam's president, has sought and gained popular support. The success of Diem's leadership has surprised the skeptics and aroused the anger of the communists." *Time* credited the "dynamic President Diem" with bringing "to South Vietnam a peace and stability few would have dared predict when his country was dismembered at Geneva." *Reader's Digest* christened Diem the "Biggest Little Man in Asia." "In the midst of the dark storms that threaten the East," the correspondent O. K. Armstrong noted, "Diem stands like a beacon of light, showing the way to free people."[15]

Scholarly publications proved no less susceptible to the miracle legend. The prestigious journal *Foreign Affairs* asserted, "History may yet judge Diem as one of the great figures of twentieth century Asia." The author William Henderson claimed that prior to Diem's assumption of the premiership, South Vietnam "seemed certain to sink into the abyss of bloody internecine strife ending in complete collapse." Yet a mere two years later, "South Vietnam is very much in business. . . . In short, a wholly unexpected political miracle has taken place in South Vietnam. . . . [T]he principal credit should be given to President Ngo Dinh Diem." The *Foreign Policy Bulletin* was equally uncritical, applauding Diem's "shrewd sense of timing, . . . stubborn patriotism and honesty." Guy Pauker assured the *Bulletin*'s readers that Diem was well on the way to "transform[ing] South Vietnam into one of the Free World's great successes in Asia." Francis Corley, writing for *Thought,* concluded that South Vietnam "has made noteworthy progress" and extolled "the high personal integrity, the strong devotion to his people and his land that characterize Viet-Nam's president." Ellen Hammer toured South Vietnam in 1957 and reported in *Pacific Affairs,* "[T]he first and most lasting impression received is one of substantial achievement. . . . [T]here is every reason to believe that unity, when it comes, will be established on nationalist and not on communist terms."[16]

The liberal press was most lavish in its praise, a development that seems counterintuitive given Diem's conservatism and religious zealotry. These traits were more than offset, however, by his uprightness and apparent independence. Whereas Asian allies like Bao Dai and Chiang Kai-shek had, either through corruption or sloth, earned the label of puppet, Diem appeared immune to such obloquy. Self-denying in his lifestyle, he did not visibly profit from the aid America funneled into his regime. Furthermore, his determination to steer his own course, even if that meant initiating war with the Binh Xuyen against the wishes of Eisenhower's special representative, seemed to demonstrate his freedom from superpower coercion. The phrases "nobody's puppet" and "nobody's pawn" recurred frequently in the stories run on Diem in the American media.[17] If Diem were no puppet, it followed that the United States was not practicing neocolonialism by supporting him, and cold war liberals like Senator Mike Mansfield and Supreme Court Justice William O. Douglas could be secure in their own righteousness and confident that America would not repeat France's failure in Vietnam. The Miracle Man's appeal to the messianic liberalism of the early cold war—as distinguished from the more jaded liberalism of post-Vietnam America—ensured that, in James Fisher's words, "Diem was lionized . . . as a beacon of non-communist Left internationalism in the 1950s."[18]

"Lionized" is not an excessive term. The *New York Post,* then America's leading newspaper of liberal opinion, called Diem "an incorruptible nationalist" and predicted that, with American help, South Vietnam "could be transformed, by Asian standards, into a little paradise." The *Reporter,* a magazine whose articles reflected liberal concerns about social reform and civil rights, hailed America's commitment to Diem as a wholesome departure from past errors. "[P]erhaps because it is tired of backing unsavory characters to fight communism," the correspondent Gouverneur Paulding observed, "the U.S. is backing idealistic little Mr. Diem. . . . [W]e certainly felt good when we learned that . . . the experiment of backing an honest man is being tried." *Commonweal,* a progressive Catholic journal that frequently condemned the McCarthyite agenda of most of the U.S. Catholic media, echoed that sector's acclamation of Diem, referring to him as "the surprisingly honest, sincere little man in the palace."[19]

The most remarkable aspect of this media enshrinement, apart from its sheer volume, was the fact that none of it was a consequence of any programs initiated by Diem as leader of the Republic of Vietnam. On the contrary, Diem moved swiftly after consolidating power to transform his country into a police state structurally indistinguishable from the most oppressive dictatorships on either side of the Iron Curtain. A Vatican diplomat visiting Saigon in late 1955 remarked to Diem's brother Ngo Dinh Nhu that South Vietnam could become a "communist country overnight" if Diem "just changed the flags."[20] The extent to which the machinery of government became the president's psyche writ large was reminiscent of Stalinist cults of personality, a parallel underscored by a council of Vietnamese elders in their plea to Diem in June 1956 for greater political freedom. "You have imitated dictator such as Hitler, Staline, Peron, and compelled the people to worship and blindly obey your orders," the elders complained. "Due to your mistakes, our fatherland is drowned into grave troubles."[21] Although the American embassy counselor Daniel Anderson assured the State Department the elders were "sincerely anti-communist," Diem threw them in jail.[22]

Diem's rule by terror began in the wake of his defeat of the Binh

Xuyen and did not abate until he was overthrown more than eight years later. For all his protests against Viet Minh violations of the Geneva Accords during the northern refugees' Passage to Freedom, he displayed no compunctions about transgressing the Geneva provision against political reprisal. Rather, he launched a crusade against "subversives" in South Vietnam, organizing an "Anti-Communist Denunciation Campaign" in which his government's Department of Information and Youth dragooned peasants into mass meetings and pressured them to inform against Viet Minh members and sympathizers. Thousands of innocent people were either jailed or placed under house arrest. Executions were frequent.[23] In early 1956, Diem determined that the campaign was not rigorous enough and expanded the scope of government repression. His Ordinance No. 6, issued in January, legalized the use of concentration camps to hold anyone suspected of being a threat to "the defense of the state and public order." Squads of police invaded the hamlets outside Saigon, where they apprehended alleged communists, forced confessions out of many through torture, and spirited them off to Diem's camps.[24]

Although such measures did succeed in reducing the number of Viet Minh in South Vietnam, they created more rivals for Diem than they eliminated. Guerrilla uprisings in the countryside were common well before the establishment of the National Liberation Front in 1960, as Diem seemed determined to drive a wedge between his people and their government. He pounded that wedge ever deeper with decrees in June and August 1956. First, he appointed chiefs for South Vietnam's 41 provinces and personally selected all administrators for the nation's 246 districts. Then he abolished the ancient tradition of elected village chiefs in favor of installing his own men, eliminating with a stroke of the pen the limited autonomy that villages had enjoyed even under the worst years of French colonial rule.[25] Most of the village chiefs Diem selected were recently arrived northern Catholics, men without roots below the 17th parallel who had no conception of the particular social and economic problems of the heavily Buddhist rural South.[26]

Nothing demonstrated Diem's disinterest in democratic processes more vividly than the plebiscite in October 1955 in which South Vietnamese voters replaced the centuries-old monarchy with a republic. Diem would have preferred to bypass the electorate and consign his fate to his American sponsors, but Bao Dai forced the premier's hand. After a year of vexation from his subordinate, the emperor issued a royal pronouncement "put[ting] an end to the mission I have entrusted to Diem." Bao Dai justified his decision by asserting that "dictatorship ought to be ended."[27] This put Diem in a ticklish position, for technically Bao Dai remained the source of all authority in Vietnam. It was one thing for Diem to disregard imperial requests to resign; it was another for him to continue to assert executive power after the emperor had publicly dismissed him. But Secretary of State Dulles had recently hinted during his weekly press conference that America would welcome an overhaul in South Vietnam's form of government. While Dulles was careful not to appear to be encouraging a coup, he did remark that "[t]here is always the possibility of changing the status of a country. France no longer has a king."[28] Diem could be certain that the United States would at least not act to prevent a referendum.

What made the ensuing showcase vote so absurd is that Diem would have defeated Bao Dai in a fair election. The emperor's prestige was at an all-time low after the Battle for Saigon. Even Edward Lansdale, Diem's most tenacious American supporter in South Vietnam and a man who rarely dodged an opportunity for engaging in skullduggery, told the premier not to rig the election. "All you need is a fairly large majority," Lansdale advised his friend. "I don't want to read that you have won by 99.9 per cent. I would know that it's rigged then."[29] Diem did not listen. Of the six million people who voted, 98.2 percent cast their ballots for Diem. The premier received two hundred thousand more votes in Saigon than there were registered voters in that city.[30] Diem's preelection agitprop would have made Kim Il-Sung blush. Typical government slogans on posters read, "Being aware of vicious Bao Dai's preference for gambling, girls, wine, milk, and butter, those who vote for him will betray their country and despoil the people!"; "Bao Dai—Master Keeper of Gambling Dens and Brothels!"; "Welcome Ngo Dinh Diem, the Savior of the People—to kill communists, depose the king, and struggle against colonialists is a citizen's duty in Vietnam!"[31] Unable to restrain his instinct for going for the jugular, Lansdale pitched into this charade by designing the ballots to sway the electorate: those for Diem were red, which traditionally signified good luck, while those for Bao Dai were green, the color of misfortune.[32] Although he deemed the referendum a "resounding success for the Diem government," U.S. Ambassador Frederick Reinhardt conceded that the "results

25. Posters announcing Diem's overwhelming victory over
Emperor Bao Dai in the plebiscite of 1955. © Bettmann/
CORBIS, 2 November 1955

do not prove that Diem commands even majority support in South
Vietnam."[33] Embassy Counselor Anderson was more direct, calling
Diem's election "a travesty of democratic procedures."[34]

Diem followed up his victory with the adoption of a constitution. In
future years, much would be made in the American press of South
Vietnam's constitutional form of government, which was typically set in
pleasing contrast to communist dictatorships.[35] No in-depth examina-
tion of the South Vietnamese constitution was ever undertaken in the
1950s, and hence the American people never learned what manner of
constitution governed Diem's country, only that his government was
constitutional. That term, however, is elastic. The constitution of the
Republic of Vietnam allowed Diem to issue laws by decree and to
change existing laws. He was free to appoint or dismiss all military
officers and civilian officials without the concurrence of the legislature.

Article 44 gave Diem the right to rule by emergency and implied that he might declare an emergency whenever he wished. Article 98 delegated "[f]urther extraordinary powers"; if he deemed it necessary, Diem could "suspend temporarily the exercise of liberties of movement and of residence, of opinion and of the press, of meetings and of associations, of syndical liberties and the right to strike." The most remarkable passage in this document was an addendum, probably composed by Diem himself, explaining the "Spirit of the Constitution." South Vietnam's constitution was founded, it asserted, on a "rule . . . whose essence is symbolized intimately by two of the world's greatest religious moralities: The Golden Rule of Christ and the Silver Rule of Confucius. . . . Our people is ready to receive all currents of progress with a view to perfecting before the Almighty its mission." There was to be no separation of church and state in the Republic of Vietnam.[36]

Having adopted a constitution, Diem proceeded to ignore it. The treatment accorded Phan Quang Dan shortly after Diem's American tour provided a graphic illustration of the president's disdain for civil liberties. Dan, a Saigon physician, managed to win election to the national assembly on a reform platform despite Diem's sending eight thousand soldiers in plain clothes to vote for the government candidate. Irritated, Diem refused to allow Dan to be seated in the assembly, and when Dan protested, Diem ordered him imprisoned and tortured.[37] In May 1959, Diem passed a law that, as the journalist Wilfred Burchett notes, "Hitler would have been proud to have fathered." Law 10/59 targeted anyone who "commits or intends to commit crimes with the aim of . . . infringing upon the security of the state" and set up military courts that traveled from district to district with mobile guillotines. Those accused of actual or "intended" offenses were given twenty-four hours to assemble a legal defense, an impossibility for most poor peasants, and denied the right to examine evidence or call witnesses.[38]

To these violations of democratic principles were added Diem's sanctimony and religious bigotry. An antivice campaign launched in late 1955 aimed to purge the country of opium smoking, alcoholism, prostitution, dancing, adultery, blue movies, horse racing, fortune telling, divorce, beauty contests, and even sentimental songs. The use of contraceptives was banned, and a legislative attempt to prohibit women from wearing falsies failed only because questions about enforcement procedures proved embarrassing. Public bonfires of such "wicked" materials as playing cards and phonograph records were common.[39] Diem staffed his administration almost exclusively with Catholics and saw to it that Catholic villages received the bulk of U.S. aid. His favoritism was so flagrant that, in central Vietnam, thousands of people converted to Catholicism in order to avoid being forcibly uprooted and replaced by Catholic refugees from the North.[40]

Diem's repression was thus hardly new when correspondents like David Halberstam and Neil Sheehan began reporting on it from Saigon in the early 1960s or when U.S. Ambassador to South Vietnam Henry Cabot Lodge called for Diem's scalp in 1963. There is a flawed narrative of the Diem era that achieved virtual hegemony among Americans concerned with Vietnam in the mid-1960s. It asserted that Diem had been a progressive reformer for many years, but that he somehow changed and turned tyrannical. Former undersecretary of state Chester Bowles recited this stock version in an interview given to the *Boston Globe* in 1971. "At first," Bowles averred, "Diem demonstrated a heartening degree of courage and understanding. . . . [B]ut gradually, like most recipients of American military aid in the underdeveloped world, he slipped under the control of . . . right-wing elements who were determined at any cost of blood and suffering to maintain the political status quo."[41] In truth, Diem himself was the most right-wing element in South Vietnam, and he required no prompting from entrenched interests to subject his people to blood and suffering.

Furthermore, Diem did not, having gulled the Eisenhower administration into thinking him a man of the people, "gradually" adopt the harsh mode of governance for which America would abandon him. Such an interpretation gives Diem too much credit for cunning and lets American policymakers off the hook. Less than a year after Diem won the presidency by besting Bao Dai, the Saigon embassy furnished Washington with an analysis titled "President Diem's Political Philosophy" that characterized Diem as a "despot" who believed that "the more reprehensible aspects of authoritarianism" were "essential means" for fulfilling "the destiny and mission of the Vietnamese nation." The dispatch went on to observe that "the fundamental concepts of Western democracy" were "alien to Diem."[42] Thematically, there was little difference between Lodge's cables and those sent by Collins almost a decade earlier. One can imagine the latter nodding in sympathetic approval at Lodge's plaint that Diem "has scant apprehension of what it is to appeal to public opinion and really no interest in any opinion other than his own. . . . [W]e must face the possibility that Diem himself cannot be preserved."[43] Lodge, however, issued his reports in 1963, a time when no American politician or journalist was still using the word miracle to describe Diem and his regime.

"Get American Public Opinion on Our Side"

Lodge had an added advantage in that the most powerful pro-Diem organization in the United States had largely imploded by the early 1960s and was thus unable to discredit his alarums as effectively as it had those of Collins and others during the Eisenhower years. This controversial alliance of journalists, politicians, and other consensus-builders was officially titled the American Friends of Vietnam (AFV) but better known as the Vietnam Lobby, a pejorative term coined by Robert Scheer and Warren Hinkle in an exposé written for *Ramparts* magazine in 1965.[44] *Ramparts* accused AFV stalwarts like Cardinal Spellman, Joseph Buttinger, Tom Dooley, and Mike Mansfield of generating "a massive pro-Diem lobbying campaign that had a great deal to do with getting the U.S. into the Vietnam War." According to Scheer and Hinkle, the AFV "maneuvered the Eisenhower administration and the American press into supporting the rootless, unpopular, and hopeless regime of a despot."[45]

Several authorities have questioned the *Ramparts* thesis. George Herring acknowledges that the AFV represented a unique case of "liberals and conservatives join[ing] hands . . . to lobby the U.S. government to support the Diem government." But Herring believes the Eisenhower administration was "[a]lready deeply committed to South Vietnam" by the start of 1955 and hence "needed no urging from private lobby groups."[46] Joseph Morgan, the author of the most detailed study of the AFV, likewise dismisses Scheer and Hinkle's findings. Morgan's *The Vietnam Lobby* depicts an organization hobbled from the outset by financial difficulties (the AFV did not acquire tax-exempt status until the 1970s) and torn apart by internecine squabbles. "Although able to reach a wide and often sympathetic audience," Morgan concludes, "the American Friends of Vietnam exerted, at the most, a marginal influence over America's Vietnam policy. Its activity on behalf of the RVN [Republic of Vietnam] in the 1950s was largely superfluous because Washington had committed itself to anti-communist governments in Vietnam since 1950."[47]

Morgan's argument suffers from a conceptual confusion. There was a difference between justifying an anticommunist South Vietnam and justifying Diem. While it is true that the United States was committed to preventing further communist encroachments in Asia after the outbreak of the Korean War, such a policy by no means entailed a commitment to a devout Catholic in a Buddhist society, much less to a self-advertised autocrat. David Anderson correctly notes that, in backing Diem, "America became the guarantor not only of an independent South Vietnam, but also of a particular Vietnamese leader."[48] Although the AFV did not generate single-handedly the anticommunist imperative of the early cold war years, it did influence which anticommunist surrogate the United States elected to underwrite in South Vietnam, and it played a crucial role in ensuring that the Diem experiment lasted as long as it did. In this regard the much-disdained *Ramparts* thesis is nearer the mark than Morgan's conclusions allow.

Tellingly, Buttinger, the founder of the AFV, attempted to dissociate himself from responsibility for America's Vietnam debacle by setting forth Morgan's argument thirty years before Morgan articulated it. In 1967, Buttinger blasted *Ramparts* for presenting a "politically misleading" picture of the AFV's efforts. "The facts as reported are on the whole correct," Buttinger admitted, "but the basic assumption of the article is absurd, for it attempts to prove that the Vietnam Lobby was responsible for U.S. involvement in Vietnam. This involvement had long been decided upon, and no one in Washington at any time considered abandoning South Vietnam." Buttinger then dug his own grave by arguing, "The question is whether South Vietnam's survival was helped or hindered by Diem's policies. . . . *Whether to support or drop Diem, not whether to defend or abandon South Vietnam, was the issue.* I still believe that without Diem, South Vietnam would very likely have been lost to the communists."[49]

Buttinger first met Diem in Saigon in late 1954 while serving as field representative for the International Rescue Committee (IRC), a group organized in the 1930s to assist in the escape and resettlement of intellectuals from Nazi Germany and later from Soviet-occupied areas. Leo Cherne, chairman of the IRC, had previously visited South Vietnam to investigate the possibility of his organization contributing to Passage to Freedom; he determined that the IRC should inaugurate refugee assistance programs at once and was encouraged in this venture by Harold Stassen, head of the Eisenhower administration's overseas aid program.[50] As Cherne recalled, "I figured this job would be right down Joe

Buttinger's alley."[51] Buttinger's qualifications were impressive. A former member of the Austrian underground during World War II, he had helped thousands of people flee the Third Reich, and later served as the IRC's director of refugee relief in postwar Europe.[52] His fluency in French promised to serve him well in dealings both with departing colonialists like General Paul Ely and with Diem, who spoke no English. Most important, in Cherne's view, was Buttinger's Catholicism. As Cherne explained to the IRC's board of directors after returning from South Vietnam, the "head of a U.S. mission to investigate the problem of the refugees" should be "a member of the Catholic faith, because more than eighty percent of the refugees who come into Saigon are Catholics."[53] Cherne also felt that Diem, whom he found "Lincoln-esque" but "inaccessible," might be more inclined to trust a Catholic representative.[54] In a letter announcing "the beginning of our program of assistance," Cherne informed Diem that Buttinger's "effective opposition to communism was previously paralleled by his own struggle as an Austrian Catholic against fascist penetration of his former homeland."[55]

Buttinger was reluctant to accept the Saigon assignment, protesting that he had no experience in Asia, but eventually complied with Cherne's wishes.[56] He arrived in South Vietnam a few weeks before Special Representative Collins and spent almost three months organizing the IRC's assistance programs to refugee camps. As Cherne had hoped they would, Buttinger and Diem became friends. Buttinger's first encounter with the premier was unexceptional (he noted in his diary that Diem was "soft" and "short, as they all are"), but the association between the two men gradually developed into a comradeship of considerable depth.[57] After a month in Saigon, Buttinger was writing Cherne that "Diem is the man on whom the best people . . . have pinned their political hopes. If he does not succeed, nobody will."[58]

Diem's detractors attempted to recruit Buttinger to their side. Ambassador Collins made no secret of his being "fed up" with the premier.[59] Representatives of the Dai Viet Party presented Buttinger with a "long list of grievances," denouncing Diem's authoritarianism, nepotism, and pro-Catholic bias. "His Catholicism could be forgiven," they noted, "if it did not make him a political sectarian, [but] Diem favors the Catholics politically." Buttinger dismissed the charge of "authoritarion [sic] tendencies" by concluding that Diem had no other choice than to establish a "temporary dictatorship" to "clear up the mess left to him.

... We need a strong man at the head." Of all the Dai Viet's complaints against Diem, Buttinger informed Cherne, "the only point . . . that I would take rather seriously is the danger coming from his strong attachment to his Church."[60]

Overall, Buttinger found Diem "a man of extraordinary strength, courage, and political ability" and was dismayed by press reports, notably those by the American journalist Joseph Alsop, that portrayed him as inept.[61] "Pure nonsense what they write about President Diem," Buttinger scribbled in his diary after reading one of Alsop's dispatches.[62] He drafted numerous rebuttals to Alsop and other anti-Diem journalists, which he planned to publish stateside.[63] But he worried that this might not be enough, warning IRC headquarters, "it would be a tragedy if, through a misapprehension of the relative balance of forces on the side of freedom and slavery in Vietnam, American policy should be distorted and discount the strength of the government of Premier Diem."[64] Someone whom Buttinger identified in his diary only as an "American officer" advised him, "You must help get American public opinion on our side. Create a committee of friends of Vietnam."[65] This Buttinger resolved to do. Prior to returning to the United States, he sent Diem an emotional letter in which he called his stay in Vietnam "one of the most fascinating and happy periods of my life" and pledged, "I will spare neither time nor energy. . . . I will speak of the hard-working men and women who have come from the North, . . . hoping for security and freedom; of the many courageous priests who guided these people in their heartbreaking migration." Above all, Buttinger promised, "when I speak of the Vietnamese people, I will . . . speak of their president—of his courage, his wisdom, and his devotion—whose leadership has given hope to so many, in his own country and in the whole democratic world."[66]

Upon returning to America, Buttinger became, in his words, "a one-man lobby for Diem."[67] He engaged the publicist Harold Oram, whose Madison Avenue firm provided fund-raising services for the IRC, to "act as a public relations representative in organizing a group to be known as the 'American Friends of Vietnam.'"[68] The "objective" of the AFV, as Oram understood it, was "to see that opinion leaders, government officials, and legislators of the United States are . . . favorably disposed toward such measures as may be necessary to maintain the freedom of Vietnam."[69] Oram's firm began receiving a three-thousand-dollar monthly retainer to burnish Diem's image in the United States.[70] Oram introduced Buttinger to Cardinal Spellman, who, Buttinger recalled, helped him conduct "a vigorous private campaign in Washington in support of Diem at the Department of State and with many prominent senators."[71] One legislator whom Buttinger impressed was Representative Walter Judd, who already shared Buttinger's high opinion of Diem and who persuaded officials at the State Department to allow Buttinger to present his case to the director of the Office of Philippine and Southeast Asian Affairs (PSA), Kenneth Young.[72] Buttinger advised Young that U.S. "support of the Diem government" was "the best hope of saving South Vietnam for the Free World." Young passed Buttinger's views on to Secretary of State Dulles.[73] Buttinger also inaugurated a correspondence with CIA Director Allen Dulles that would continue for five years.[74]

Through Oram's good offices, Buttinger gained an audience with the editors of the *New York Times, New York Herald Tribune, Newsweek, Time,* and *Life.* As Buttinger recalled in a letter to Senator Mansfield, "Without exaggeration, I can say that this campaign was successful beyond my expectations. The *Times, Tribune, Newsweek,* etc., after the meetings . . . came out strongly in support of Diem."[75] Indeed, the *Times* ran a piece praising Diem's "character and determination" the day after its representatives spoke to Buttinger and published a guest editorial by Buttinger the day after that.[76] Buttinger also published articles in the *New Leader, Reporter,* and *New Republic* in which he asserted, among other things, that "Premier Ngo Dinh Diem is a wholly dedicated and incorruptible man. . . . In terms of energy and ability, he is the equal of anyone to be found in Asia today."[77] Oram's associate David Martin congratulated Buttinger in early 1955 for "almost singlehanded[ly] . . . chang[ing] the climate of American public opinion on the subject of Vietnam in the course of a month."[78]

How did one man, or one lobby, manage to obtain such results? The AFV's chronic penury and internal friction would seemingly have precluded the outfit's ever becoming an effective pressure group. But Buttinger and his associates had a number of advantages. First, and most important, was the fact that many of America's press lords were AFV members, among them Whitelaw Reid, editor and publisher of the *New York Herald Tribune*; Malcolm Muir, publisher of *Newsweek*; Walter Annenberg, head of the *Philadelphia Inquirer;* William Randolph Hearst Jr. of the *New York Journal-American*; and, foremost among titans, Time Inc.'s Henry Luce.[79] With such media giants in its ranks, the AFV was able to generate a tremendous amount of pro-Diem propaganda in U.S. newspapers and magazines and ensure that, almost without exception, the shortcomings of the Diem regime would not be scrutinized by the American press.[80]

In addition, the leading figures in the AFV—Buttinger, Cherne, Oram, and the diplomat Angier Biddle Duke—had spent many years working for the IRC, the largest nonsectarian refugee organization in the world. The IRC gained international renown in the 1930s and 1940s for saving European Jews from Hitler's tyranny, and its anticommunist credentials were certified in the 1950s with well-publicized fund-raising drives to rescue East German and Hungarian victims of Soviet repression. An IRC résumé conferred enormous moral authority upon its possessor and tended to place that individual beyond suspicion of legally questionable activity. Moreover, even if such suspicion were piqued, there was little chance of harassment by the U.S. Justice Department, as Oram pointed out in an interview with the historian William Brownell. "Even by 1962, there were only four lawyers to oversee the Foreign Agents Registration Act for the entire United States," Oram recalled. Hence, no one raised the issue of conflict of interest when Oram's firm received money from Diem's government while Oram continued to serve on the board of directors of the AFV. More important than lack of legal oversight was the vacuum of Vietnam expertise in the United States at the time of the AFV's emergence. Cherne remarked to Brownell that the AFV had "a clear field of fire. . . . There was no alternate body of information on Vietnam."[81]

James Fisher notes that the crazy-quilt pluralism of the AFV's membership also worked in the group's favor, serving to distinguish it from other one-issue lobbies whose rosters featured only hard-line conservatives or liberal/leftists. The national committee of the AFV, Fisher observes, "comprised perhaps the most ecumenical coalition of opinion-makers ever witnessed," including the Democrats Mike Mansfield and a young senator from Massachusetts, John F. Kennedy, the Republicans Walter Judd and Clement Zablocki, the conservative publishers Henry Luce and William Randolph Hearst, the liberal academics Samuel Eliot Morison and Arthur Schlesinger Jr., the war heroes Audie Murphy and Mike O'Daniel, the Oscar-winning director Joseph Mankiewicz, the author and "celebrity saint" Tom Dooley, and even Norman Thomas, the president of the American Socialist Party.[82] Securing Thomas's membership was a coup for Buttinger, who courted Thomas until he finally submitted, with the proviso that "my interest in Viet-Nam does not extend to automatic endorsement of American participation in war to that end."[83] Thomas recalled Buttinger explaining that "it was desirable to include socialists so that [the AFV] would not seem to be a partisan group."[84]

Buttinger's decision to make the AFV's membership base "as wide as possible" paid dividends in the first years of the group's activities.[85] While conservative cold warriors and AFV loyalists like Representative Edna Kelly and the multimillionaire Marshall Field Jr. could be expected to inveigh full-throatedly against the Geneva Conference's stipulation for nationwide elections in Vietnam in 1956, Thomas's signature on a letter arguing that Diem was justified in refusing to permit the scheduled elections was doubly effective; if the socialist leader believed that holding a single election in both parts of Vietnam could "only be regarded as an imperialist endeavor contrary to the will of the South Vietnamese people," then, it appeared, the AFV was not merely spouting a party line.[86] Although unable to project an image of sufficient disinterestedness to win tax exemption, the AFV always received a more respectful hearing in the highest echelons of government than most pressure groups. When William Donovan, an early chairman of the AFV, wrote to President Eisenhower to protest communist Chinese premier Chou En-lai's call for compliance with the Geneva Accords, Eisenhower responded personally within two days, assuring Donovan that he "completely agreed" with the chairman's position and that he would "instantly" take up the matter of Chou's "impertinence" with the State Department. "As you know," the president wrote, "I consider that President Diem is the most potent force we have in South Viet Nam to halt the arrogant march of communism."[87]

"Iron Mike"

Many glittering names adorned the AFV's letterhead. At the first meeting of the group's executive committee in late 1955, Oram proudly reported that over eighty "distinguished Americans" had already joined, including almost one-third of the membership of the House Foreign Affairs Committee. But the AFV was after bigger game. While Donovan was listed as honorary chairman, and while his status as former director of the Office of Strategic Services was a feather in the AFV's cap, the founding members unanimously resolved that "General John W. O'Daniel be invited to serve as chairman of the American Friends of Vietnam."[88]

"Iron Mike" O'Daniel's name would confer a luster upon the organization that few living military figures other than Eisenhower or MacArthur could match. By the time he assumed the mantle of AFV chairman in 1956, O'Daniel had been a soldier for four decades, enlisting in World War I at age twenty-two and winning the Distinguished Service Cross, the Croix de Guerre, and the Purple Heart before his first year in combat was over. In World War II, he commanded the Third Infantry Division in its march from the Italian beachhead to Hitler's headquarters in Berchtesgarden, picking up another Croix de Guerre, two Distinguished Service Medals, and the Legion of Honor along the way. From 1948 to 1950, he served as the U.S. military attaché in Moscow, where he demonstrated his skills as an anticommunist propagandist with a series of articles published in several magazines. By the close of the Korean War, he had risen to command all army forces in the Pacific.[89]

O'Daniel spent his final months of military service as the head of the MAAG in South Vietnam. Assuming the post in the spring of 1954, he supervised the transition of the national army's training and supply from French to American hands. It was during this last leg of his brilliant career that O'Daniel began exhibiting erratic behavior. His record for sound counsel with regard to Vietnam had never been good: sent on an inspection tour of the front lines of the Franco–Viet Minh War in March 1954, O'Daniel reported back to Washington that "the French are in no danger of suffering a major military reverse."[90] Less than a month later, Dien Bien Phu fell. While in charge of the MAAG in Saigon, O'Daniel clashed with U.S. Ambassador Donald Heath, who complained to Secretary of State Dulles in late 1954 that the general repeatedly acted "in direct contravention of my instructions."[91] In another cable, Heath reported,

> O'Daniel . . . is always immediately ready with a tactical or strategic solution to every problem, and every one I personally have heard him make has been neither realistic nor sound. Some of them have been downright foolish. . . . O'Daniel's military estimates and judgment for this war in Indochina are not only defective but bad. That is the feeling of his staff, one of whom said to an attaché that he thought the general was getting "senile."[92]

Senescent or not, O'Daniel demonstrated one quality as MAAG commander that made him attractive to the AFV: after Lansdale, he was Diem's most devoted American supporter in South Vietnam. Although under instructions to observe the "strictest neutrality" during the Battle for Saigon, O'Daniel was seen by the journalist Robert Shaplen driving alongside a government battalion heading into combat and shouting, "Give 'em hell, boys!"[93] O'Daniel is also alleged to have slammed a Hoa Hao general against a wall, thundering, "I hear you are against Diem! If you don't support him, we will cut off all your American aid. You won't be able to live. If you don't support Diem, we'll smash your faces!"[94] Throughout the turbulent months of March and April 1955, O'Daniel objected to Special Representative Collins's suggestions that Diem be replaced, and after Diem crushed the Binh Xuyen rebels, Iron Mike became an even more tenacious partisan of the premier. "We need people who are willing to continue to 'shoot the works' and make it 'all or none,'" he advised Oram. "That's the way I feel about Diem."[95]

Oram recognized that O'Daniel's reputation as a war hero, flair for public relations, and devotion to Diem made him the ideal candidate for AFV chairman. Shortly after O'Daniel's return from Vietnam, Oram telephoned the general and asked him to attend a reception in his honor hosted by the AFV.[96] Angier Biddle Duke also contacted O'Daniel, declaring that his acceptance of the chairmanship "would serve to emphasize to the American people the strategic importance of Viet Nam in our foreign relations."[97] Although O'Daniel attended the reception, he remained ambivalent about the chairmanship until Eisenhower's deputy assistant assured him that the AFV was "sound in every respect."[98] After this endorsement, O'Daniel wrote the AFV, "I am now in a position to assume the role of chairman which you have so kindly asked me to accept. I will do everything in my power to assist in attaining the objectives set forth by the American Friends of Vietnam."[99] Iron Mike never tackled any assignment with greater initiative.

Most studies of the AFV focus on the brains of the group: the liberal intellectuals like Cherne, Buttinger, and Wesley Fishel. Yet O'Daniel was equally if not more important. If Tom Dooley represented the Catholic refugees from North Vietnam, O'Daniel represented Diem—and he did so more indefatigably than either Lansdale or Buttinger, both of whom gave up on their Miracle Man by 1960. In that year, O'Daniel published a picture book "for young readers" in which he called Diem Vietnam's "greatest leader," a "great hero to his people," and "the father of his country, as Washington became the father of ours."[100] When Diem was assassinated in 1963, O'Daniel was the only member of the AFV who refused to sign a letter of congratulations to the generals who carried out the coup; instead, he resigned from the organization in protest at such "betrayal."[101] The AFV's pleas for contributions, letters to the editor, and articles in a slew of journals originated, for the most part, from the desks of Buttinger, Cherne, or Fishel, but the name affixed to many of them was O'Daniel's and Iron Mike wrote much of his own material as well. His contribution to the Miracle Man myth deserves closer scrutiny.

O'Daniel considered himself, and was considered by others, an expert on Southeast Asian affairs.[102] The AFV played up the general's expertise. Shortly after he assumed the chairmanship, a poster announcing a series of three O'Daniel lectures proclaimed, "General O'Daniel has made many friends for America in Indochina. . . . By his keen understanding of the Oriental mind, General O'Daniel has been able to convince the Vietnamese of our good faith."[103] Yet O'Daniel's "understanding of the Oriental mind" was typical of that of many policymakers of his generation. More than any member of the Vietnam Lobby, save perhaps Dooley, O'Daniel incarnated the paternalistic side of American attitudes toward Asia. On hundreds of occasions, in his private correspondence, speeches, books, and articles, Iron Mike referred to Asians in general and the Vietnamese in particular in terms normally reserved for naughty children or, at best, sullen adolescents, who had to be nurtured, cajoled, and, if need be, tricked into doing what their American benefactors knew was best for them. "You are all, no doubt, well aware of the suspicions that are inherent with Orientals, of the importance of creating suitable climates before anything can be done," O'Daniel lectured a group of businessmen planning to invest in South Vietnam in 1957. "They must be made to appear, at least, as the leaders and directors of their national destiny, although there are few who know anything of government operations or how to conduct them."[104] America needed to be patient in its tutelage of these people, O'Daniel cautioned, or the Soviets would take America's place. "It must be remembered that the Russian is Oriental in his thinking and that the outstanding characteristic of the Oriental is patience," the AFV chairman observed. "Orientals think in terms of ten years and one hundred years. . . . We are an impatient people."[105]

O'Daniel's strategy for luring Asians away from the communist bloc primarily involved stroking their egos and deluding them into believing the American agenda was, in fact, their own. He assured Assistant

Secretary of State Robertson in 1956 that "the Vietnamese will do most anything we want them to do if it can be 'their' idea."[106] He stressed the same point in a 1957 article in which he reminisced of his MAAG days in Saigon: "I tried to impress upon the Vietnamese that this is *your* Army, *you* decide from what we show *you* of our methods which things *you* want to adopt for *your* own. . . . Understanding the Native and his problems and being sympathetic with their customs is *so* important. Patience is a *must* for one working in the Orient."[107]

Like many of Diem's American supporters, O'Daniel repeatedly referred to the political immaturity of the South Vietnamese as justification for their president's antidemocratic policies. On one occasion, he upbraided the editors of the *Chicago Sun-Times* for criticizing Diem's restriction of civil liberties. "In an Asian society such as Vietnam's," the AFV chairman observed, "real democracy requires generations in which it can evolve."[108] O'Daniel was willing to be patient. "Diem knows his own people and what they respond to," he averred in 1958. "Democracy as we know it has to be a growing thing. Diem wants to get things done and he feels justified in cracking the whip. If he opened the doors to democracy as we know it, the communists would go all out and step in."[109] Moreover, as O'Daniel reminded his AFV colleagues, democracy required a sophisticated citizenry. "[M]any of the old and honored cultures of Asia do not easily fit into the framework of a modern society," he reasoned. "The educational systems in which many Asians study were designed to turn out colonial clerks rather than people who could think for themselves."[110] If this were not reason enough for Diem's policies, there was also the fact that South Vietnam was at war. "When waging war, you have to be ruthless," O'Daniel insisted. "In a shooting war, men die and little is said about the loss of one or two individuals. But now there is a hue and cry from a few who accuse Diem of being totalitarian. He has to be that way for a while longer, I think."[111]

O'Daniel received a golden opportunity to instruct American policymakers on the subtleties of "the Orient" in March 1956, when he was invited to address the House Foreign Affairs Committee. At issue was the amount of U.S. funding Diem's government was to receive in the coming year, but O'Daniel transformed the proceedings into a seminar on cultural relations. "In our affairs with the Vietnamese, we should bear in mind their sensitivity and not embarrass them by publicly or openly seeming to direct them or tell them in what manner they appear to be deficient," the general lectured. "Much can be done if we use an indirect approach, which Asians are used to. . . . Quite often it is necessary to plant the seed of an idea in the mind of an Asian official and subsequently refer to it as 'his,' i.e. the Asian's original project." When Chairman Zablocki asked O'Daniel to comment on allegations that Diem had "established a dictatorship," O'Daniel dismissed such reports as "communist propaganda," assuring the committee that Diem had personally told him "on several occasions that in his efforts to decentralize authority in the government, he had been forced to take back much authority into his own hands." This was not authoritarianism, O'Daniel stressed, merely pragmatism: "Diem is so far ahead of most of his government in ability and drive that it was understandable that he exercised more authority than a comparable Western head of state." With regard to the charge that Diem had put people in jail "without just cause," O'Daniel remarked that he "could only speculate that these were Viet Minh agents." He doubted that their jailing "was evidence of a dictatorship." Several legislators hastened to "voice their hearty approval of jailing communist agents." Representative Judd put in a "request for even more rigid rule," going on to assert that he had "visited many Asian countries," and he was "unaware of another American official who was held in such great esteem and affection as was O'Daniel in Vietnam." Other congressmen agreed that "we could use more Americans of O'Daniel's character and ability."

It was a compelling performance. Robert Hoey, the State Department's officer in charge of Vietnam-Cambodia-Laos affairs, alerted his superiors that the "committee was ready to take O'Daniel's word without question."[112] Eisenhower shared the legislators' credulity, informing Secretary of State Dulles that O'Daniel had supplied "a very refreshing account of conditions in Indochina, of American prestige there, and of the progress being made by Diem." Eisenhower suggested that the White House "ask O'Daniel to talk to the Foreign Relations and Foreign Affairs Committees" during future congressional aid hearings.[113] For the remainder of the decade, if a member of Congress wanted to sound the depths of Asia, one of the first experts he or she consulted was Iron Mike. A grateful Diem thanked O'Daniel in 1957 for "the magnificent contribution you are making to further close relations between the United States and South Vietnam. . . . Your intimate knowledge of my country and its problems . . . have indeed stood us in good stead."[114]

"The Keystone in the Arch, the Finger in the Dike"

Except for Diem's tour of the United States in 1957, the AFV's greatest propaganda masterstroke was a conference titled "America's Stake in Vietnam" held at the Willard Hotel in Washington in June 1956. Planning for this symposium began at an executive committee meeting in February of that year, and the following month the committee agreed that "a Washington conference would be desirable in terms of educating the American public on current Vietnamese situations." Buttinger volunteered to set a "top-level" agenda.[115] Over the next few weeks, according to his reports, he courted "representatives from leading national civic, public, veterans, and foreign-affairs organizations; . . . representatives from all branches of the government having contact with Vietnam; representatives of the diplomatic corps in Washington; [and] the press."[116]

The response was overwhelmingly positive. State Department officer Paul Kattenburg met with AFV coordinator Gilbert Jonas to advise him that the department looked "quite favorably" upon the conference and would permit Walter Robertson to be a featured speaker.[117] Robertson was eager to participate, calling the conference "an excellent opportunity to focus public attention on the excellent progress the Republic of Vietnam has been making."[118] Equally keen to speak at the conference was Senator Kennedy, who was contacted at the eleventh hour when his more prominent colleague Mike Mansfield became indisposed.[119] The late substitute Kennedy would deliver the conference's most oft-quoted address.

The purpose of "America's Stake in Vietnam," according to the AFV's press release, was "to focus American attention on the nature of the current threat posed by communist demands for holding all-Vietnamese elections."[120] This seemed a timely concern, given that less than a month after the conference was held, Saigon and Hanoi were to confer under the Geneva Accords to arrange unification. No U.S. policymaker gave Diem a chance against Ho Chi Minh in a nationwide election. Diem, however, had declared he had no intention of abiding by the accords, and Ambassador Reinhardt counseled Secretary of State Dulles that it was "unwise . . . to focus attention" on the election issue. Reinhardt urged the State Department to persuade the AFV to "concentrate instead on means of expanding U.S.–Vietnamese relationships."[121] Young met privately with O'Daniel and convinced the general that the focus of the conference should be changed.[122]

Lack of a unifying theme did not prevent "America's Stake in Vietnam" from being a public relations tour de force. The Willard Hotel had rarely seen a more star-studded panel. Luminaries from a variety of professions and organizations lent their voices to Diem's cause: from the military, O'Daniel; from academe, Professor Hans Morgenthau of the University of Chicago; from the Catholic Church, Monsignor Joseph Harnett; from the medical profession, Doctor Tom Dooley; from Capitol Hill, Senator Kennedy; and from the State Department, Assistant Secretary Robertson. The roughly two hundred people who attended the conference came from an equally broad spectrum: representatives of business firms, church groups, and labor and educational associations rubbed shoulders with academics, diplomats, and military officers.

O'Daniel's welcome sounded the note that would echo throughout the conference. "From the very beginning, first as premier and then as president of South Vietnam," the general declared, "Ngo Dinh Diem has shown great courage and determination. . . . This conference has been called to emphasize the progress made by President Diem and his people, progress which inspires admiration and respect."[123] Kennedy then praised Diem in extravagant terms, citing his "amazing success in meeting firmly and with determination the major political and economic crises which had heretofore continually plagued Vietnam." The senator strung together a sequence of metaphors that would become famous, appearing in most treatments of the Vietnam War: "Vietnam represents the cornerstone of the Free World in Southeast Asia, the keystone in the arch, the finger in the dike." In an expression of staggering paternalism, Kennedy asserted, "If we are not the parents of little Vietnam, then surely we are the godparents. We presided at its birth, we gave assistance to its life, we have helped to shape its future. . . . This is our offspring. We cannot abandon it."[124] Assistant Secretary Robertson also lauded Diem's accomplishments. "The free world owes President Diem a debt of gratitude," Robertson declared. "In him, his country has found a truly worthy leader." There was "no more dramatic example" of Diem's "moral fortitude," Robertson attested, than his "battle against the parasitic politico-religious sects in the spring of 1955."[125] Cherne followed Robertson with an account of the economic situation in South Vietnam and concluded by extolling Diem in florid language. "Diem has succeeded beyond the expectations of the most optimistic," Cherne asserted. "There is an opportunity to create in South Vietnam . . . a showcase of freedom. All in Asia who hunger for dignity may look therein and find their lesson."[126]

The morning session was drawing to a close, and the audience's growling stomachs and flagging attention might have discouraged the next speaker. Tom Dooley, however, had played to tougher houses. "What I have to say isn't very pretty," the jungle doctor said in unwitting understatement. "I will tell you something about the refugees of Indochina. . . . I want to tell you a little of the wretchedness and misery of these refugees, the hideous atrocities we witnessed in our camps every single day." He spoke of Vietnamese children whose eardrums had been ruptured because they overheard the phrase "give us this day our daily bread" and of an old man whom the communists had stripped naked, tortured, and hung upside down by his ankles to die. "He looked at me and said: 'My crime? I am a Catholic priest.'" Next came the story of a boy who had attempted to accompany the refugees on the Passage to Freedom, but who had been caught by the Viet Minh. "Because that boy might grow, might stand tall, might be a soldier and fight against this godlessness, they punished him. They formed a circle around him and with the butts of their rifles they crushed his feet on the road surface. . . . The next day his knee, his hip, and his thigh were matted, bloated, and crepitant with gangrene, and he died." Such fiendish maltreatment of people who wanted nothing more than to "openly worship Jesus Christ," Dooley contended, was typical of communism, "an evil, driving, malicious ogre which . . . has succeeded in conquering half of all mankind."[127] Almost sheepishly, Monsignor Harnett assumed the stage after Dooley and pointed out, "Vietnam is not a Catholic country, despite some notions prevailing to that effect." Harnett's report on refugee resettlement, tamer than Dooley's, noted that "the Catholic priests had a large voice in the eventual decision that was taken in many northern villages" to resettle below the 17th parallel but also stressed that "the Buddhist monks undoubtedly had a large voice in the villages that were Buddhist." He even conceded that some "mistakes were made" in resettling the refugees and that perhaps a greater effort ought to have been made to mingle Catholics and Buddhists in newly erected southern villages. Like every other speaker, however, he concluded with an emotional tribute to America's ally. "The Vietnamese are a great and dignified people," Harnett stated. "They are animated by a love of God."[128]

The conference's afternoon session was notable for an address by Representative Judd, who figuratively seized the audience by the shirt collar with a harangue against "defeatism" in America's Asia policy. Judd claimed that Ambassador Collins "kept ringing home about the impending demise of the young republic. . . . They [Collins and his staff] came home, wrung their hands, and thought matters were hopeless. While they were out of the country, fortunately, Diem went in and cleaned things up." With an approving glance at O'Daniel, Judd added, "General O'Daniel egged Diem on, as I understand, all the way." If Judd scorned State Department naysayers like Collins, his contempt for those "academics" who wanted Diem to install "a perfect democracy in the middle of a civil war" knew no bounds. He explained that requiring the citizens of "Free Vietnam" to participate in elections was "like asking a baby in diapers to pole vault. It takes time to do that." Judd understood that Americans wanted to see results quickly in South Vietnam: "This is because we are enthusiasts. We are doers. But there is such a thing as the imperialism of efficiency. A Burman [sic] once said to me: 'You Americans are so aggressively friendly.' . . . They need what a boy needs when he comes and says: 'See what I have done.' You can say: 'What an amateurish job that is. Let me show you how to do it right.' What you do is kill your boy! You should say: 'Wonderful. How can we work together to get along?' " If American policymakers exercised such parental discretion with the Vietnamese, Judd declared, "please God, we can pull through."[129]

Before the conference adjourned, a beaming O'Daniel read the gathering a telegram from Eisenhower that commended the AFV for "aid[ing] the American public to achieve a better understanding of the Republic of Vietnam, an ally of the Free World, and of the problems it faces as a newly independent nation."[130] The president's description of South Vietnam as an independent nation was doubtless strategic. In thirty days, according to the Geneva Accords, discussions were to begin between representatives of the governments in North and South Vietnam to determine procedures for conducting nationwide elections. By referring to Diem's domain as an independent nation, rather than the provisional political entity that the accords said it was, Eisenhower tipped the administration's hand. Clearly, America intended to back Diem in his refusal to subject himself to a popularity contest with Ho Chi Minh for overall Vietnamese sovereignty. Secretary of State Dulles also sent a telegram wishing the AFV "every success."[131] O'Daniel later told a member of the White House staff that the telegrams from the president and his chief cabinet officer "gave the meeting the prestige that was needed."[132]

This prestige was enhanced by subsequent reaction to the Washington conference. *Pacific Affairs* reviewed a truncated transcript of "America's Stake in Vietnam" put out by the AFV and judged it "penetrating and discerning . . . brilliant. . . . This symposium . . . may be recommended to any serious student of Vietnam."[133] Kennedy's address was included in *Vital Speeches of the Day* for 1956.[134] At the conclusion of a speech in praise of Diem on the Senate floor, Mansfield was granted permission to insert Robertson's contribution to the conference into the Congressional Record.[135] Before it celebrated its first anniversary, the AFV had to be counted among the elite political lobbies in America.

Having projected the image of Diem's nation as a vital U.S. interest, the AFV took the logical next step of attempting to persuade American businessmen to invest in the fledgling republic. Oram called for "a shift in program emphasis" from political to economic matters, arguing that South Vietnam needed to develop an industrial infrastructure and skilled workforce comparable to those of other economically vibrant Asian nations like Japan.[136] Toward this end, O'Daniel persuaded Diem to release a statement affirming, "I am opposed to nationalization and to any form of economic discrimination." The AFV mass-mailed copies of this pronouncement to American newspapers and prominent businessmen.[137] O'Daniel then invited "leading American economic experts" to a conference titled "Economic Needs of Vietnam." He announced that South Vietnam offered a friendly business environment for foreign firms and that Diem's "historic decision" to welcome American investors "stands in brilliant contrast to that of other nations of Asia, where private capital, especially from the United States, is viewed with alarm and mistrust."[138]

About forty people, including technical experts, journalists, academics, and government officials, met on 15 March 1957 to formulate a development strategy for South Vietnam. They produced little of substance, apart from the recommendation that Diem employ the services of a private company to survey investment possibilities. For the most part, the conference played up O'Daniel's proposition that the Vietnamese were unique among Asians in terms of their congeniality to business interests and embrace of a distinctly Western, not to say American, work ethic. Buttinger informed the participants that in contrast to the "inertia" that characterized much of Asia, "the Vietnamese think of themselves as frustrated Japanese geniuses" who "could have outdone" Japan economically had they not been "prevented by those who imported the Western techniques" into Vietnam "from exploiting and using them." One of the most remarkable features of Diem's country, Buttinger contended, was "the quality and the character of the labor force. . . . The Vietnamese has not only a very highly developed memory and great manual skill; . . . he also has a great tradition of disciplined work." O'Daniel dismissed concerns that South Vietnam's "culture . . . will not support continuing economic growth." He pointed out that Vietnamese Buddhism was "the 'greater vehicle' Buddhism and not the 'lesser vehicle.' . . . I think that making money is not despised in Vietnam. . . . [M]y impression is that this Buddhism doesn't interfere with the acquisitive impulse."[139]

South Vietnam's distinctly non-Asian love of free enterprise was a constant theme in AFV propaganda. It was picked up occasionally by the American media, as when the reporter Joseph Lash of the *New York Post* informed his readers that the "South Vietnamese are so industrious that they are called the 'Prussians' of Indochina."[140] Diem recognized the value of this issue and frequently belabored it. "Aside from the Japanese," he lectured Robert MacAlister, a member of the IRC, in 1956, "our people are the only people in this part of the world who are willing to work to live—eager to work. . . . They are industrious."[141] South Vietnamese Ambassador Tran Van Chuong made a similar case when he visited New York City at the behest of the AFV. With Buttinger translating his remarks, Chuong told an audience at the posh River Club that South Vietnam's workforce was "cooperative, intelligent, and active. They have the gentleness of the Thai and the Indonesians, with the dynamism of the Chinese!"[142] No one asked whether Chuong was referring to the Nationalist or communist Chinese, and it is unlikely that the ambassador dealt in such fine distinctions. His capacity to reduce three countries, the combined populations of which made up almost half the people on earth, to one-word stereotypes in a single sentence was a breathtaking feat of oversimplification.

"Diem's Godfather"

Perhaps the most potent item of pro-Diem propaganda to come out of this heady time was an article by Senator Mansfield in *Harper's* for

January 1956. Titled "Reprieve in Viet Nam," the piece was such a glowing homage to the South Vietnamese president that the AFV printed up one hundred thousand copies for "distribution among actual or potential members."[143] Mansfield echoed O'Daniel's views on Asian incapacity for self-government, musing: "In some respects, leadership as a molder rather than an expresser of the social forces in a country is more significant in Asia than in the West. The shock of independence has left these countries in a very amorphous state. They are nations turning on a kind of gigantic potter's wheel. The fingers which shape them before the clay hardens will have much to do with their ultimate forms."[144] Mansfield's analogy was telling: to him, the Vietnamese were clay, equally pliable in the hands of Soviet or American potters. Dooley, as noted earlier, used similar figurative language when he urged backers of his mission to Laos to "gently and inexorably help to mold free men for Asia . . . [f]rom the clay of contradictions and the chunky confusion of custom."[145] Would these men have employed the same imagery in describing a European nation, or so casually excused a Western leader's restriction of civil liberties as an indication of that leader's need to be a "molder rather than an expresser of the social forces"? One suspects not, but yet again Diem had found an American policymaker willing to defend his despotic practices as appropriate in the East. "If Viet Nam has not set in the communist mold," Mansfield declared, "it is due in large part to Ngo Dinh Diem."

Mansfield observed that Diem had "unique training" to "steer his country between colonialism and communism and toward freedom." He had been "educated in the democratic and humanistic precepts of the West" and therefore "understood the pitfalls of both colonialism and communism"—unlike, one presumes, those millions of Asians untutored in such precepts. The senator recounted Diem's battle with his domestic enemies, "mystical, weird, quasi-religious sects," and commended Diem for standing his ground against the "web of corruption and decadence" that had flourished for so long in an atmosphere of "Eastern passivity" and "inertia." Mansfield glossed over any "irregularities" in Diem's electoral triumph over Bao Dai, calling the premier's 98.2 percent of the vote "a reflection of [the voters'] search for a leader who would respond to their needs." The article concluded with the prediction that "Diem's star is likely to remain in the ascendancy and that of Ho Chi Minh to fade, because Diem is following a course which more closely meets the needs and aspirations of the Vietnamese people."[146]

The senator from Montana was probably Diem's most important advocate in the United States during the 1950s. Joseph Alsop noted in 1966, "I've always thought the deciding factor [in securing American support for Diem] was Mike Mansfield. Everyone has forgotten that Mansfield was a great friend of Diem, on account of the Church."[147] While O'Daniel and Buttinger were more prolific in their output of pro-Diem pieces, Mansfield was in a better position to influence American foreign policy: his chairmanship of the Senate Foreign Relations Committee and reputation as an expert on Asia made him an invaluable ally. Contemporaries recognized Mansfield's contribution to the underwriting of American sponsorship of Diem. The editors at *Harper's* called Mansfield "the chief architect of United States policy in Southeast Asia" and "Diem's godfather, . . . largely responsible for keeping Diem's government afloat."[148] The *Economist* concurred, describing South Vietnam in late 1955 as Mansfield's "creation" and noting that "the prime minister of southern Vietnam, Mr. Ngo Dinh Diem, would not have survived the successive crises of the past year without American support, and this support has largely been based on the senator's recommendation."[149] Appreciative of Mansfield's value as a partisan, Diem kept up a lively correspondence with him throughout the 1950s. Three days after the conclusion of the Battle for Saigon, Diem wrote Mansfield to "tell you that the people of Vietnam appreciate very much your firm stand. . . . If I am permitted to quote Confucius, the sage said: 'Only in winter do we know which trees are evergreen.' Figuratively speaking, you are the evergreen, as luxuriant as always."[150]

The Diem–Mansfield exchange of letters was distinguished by a tone indicative of the importance of religion in the senator's interpretation of events in Vietnam. Mansfield concluded his earliest surviving letter to Diem with "may God continue to guide you in the great task you have undertaken and may He continue to give you courage and understanding in the difficult days ahead."[151] After the climax of the Battle for Saigon, Mansfield was one of the first Americans to extend his congratulations to Diem, exulting, "We are very proud that, throughout this entire struggle, you have stood steady as a rock in behalf of your God. . . . I hope this letter finds you in good health and that God in His wisdom will be kind to you. May His hand always guide you. . . . My prayers are with you."[152] In thanking Diem for the Christmas gift of a tablecloth, Mansfield promised that "when grace is said over it, it will be with a special prayer that your country will continue to advance toward freedom."[153] An abortive attempt on Diem's life by a Buddhist student in February 1957 drew the following response from Mansfield: "I am thankful that God in His wisdom spared you. . . . It is to be devoutly hoped that you will have many long years ahead."[154] Diem reciprocated Mansfield's sentiments, assuring the senator shortly after the Battle for Saigon that "your work in the United States has produced many fortunate effects in Vietnam. . . . Often I have thought of, and prayed for, the American people."[155]

Similar rhetoric characterized Mansfield's many pronouncements in support of Diem throughout the mid- to late fifties. In a representative address, "American Foreign Policy in the Far East," the senator insisted that policymaking "must develop in accord with the religious and moral principles of the nation. . . . As Pope Pius XII said in his Christmas message in 1948: 'A people threatened with unjust aggression or already its victim may not remain passively indifferent, if it would think and act as befits a Christian.'" Mansfield seized upon the case of Diem as an alternative to such passive indifference. "At the eleventh hour, when the Indochinese situation was almost beyond retrieving," the senator declared, "a government of honest, respectable caliber was installed in the Vietnamese capital of Saigon. It was headed by Ngo Dinh Diem, a Vietnamese patriot of great religious convictions."[156] On another occasion, Mansfield declaimed from the floor of Congress, "Diem is not only the savior of his own country, but, in my opinion, he is the savior of all Southeast Asia." The senator gave "the chief credit" in "defeating communism in Southeast Asia" to "the determination, the courage, the incorruptibility, and the integrity of President Diem."[157]

Given Mansfield's role in promoting the Miracle Man legend, it is perhaps fitting that his files contain some of the sharpest assaults on that legend that the researcher can discover in the period of maximum Diem boosterism. The voices that protested loudest against Diem's abuse of power were Vietnamese. The Dai Viet leader Nguyen Ton Hoan wrote Mansfield in late 1955 that Diem had "managed to wreck whatever unity there was in South Vietnam and turn democracy into a farce." Although "the overwhelming majority of the people in South Vietnam are non-Catholic," Hoan noted, "Diem has chosen to favor non-southerners and Catholics. . . . His bigoted approach in government has unnecessarily stirred popular resentment against Catholics." As if to reassure Mansfield that he did not share this resentment, Hoan pointed out, "I am a Vietnamese Catholic." Still, he insisted, "time is fast running out in South Vietnam. For the sake of its own good name, the United States must stop Diem's experiment in despotism."[158] Huynh Sanh Thong, a South Vietnamese dissident whom Mansfield met in 1956, complained of "the lack of freedom and justice in my country, South Vietnam. . . . How much longer can our American friends afford to stand politely by and allow Diem to carry his experiment in tyranny to its logical conclusion?" Mansfield's assistant Francis Valeo attached a note to Thong's letter stating, "I don't think this should be answered," and apparently it was not.[159] Grievances from other South Vietnamese dissidents likewise went unanswered.[160]

"Partisans of Diem the Man rather than South Vietnam the Country"

Hoan and Thong's fulminations against the Diem regime could be safely kept from public view in the recesses of Mansfield's files. The senator and the AFV were faced with a less easily resolvable dilemma when the *American Mercury* published an article by Hilaire du Berrier entitled "Report from Saigon." Du Berrier, an OSS officer during World War II, had worked under Bao Dai and acted as an adviser to Diem until the premier began his antisect campaign, which du Berrier thought diverted attention from the communist threat. Du Berrier's influence was restricted by his extremist politics and the archconservative journals that carried his work; only the far-right *Mercury* would touch "Report from Saigon." Nonetheless, du Berrier's broadside was the first informed indictment in the American media, not only of Diem's police state, but of the AFV as well.[161]

In damning detail, du Berrier ticked off Diem's crimes against the people of South Vietnam, from "order[ing] all political opposition . . . hacked to pieces" to "forcing nationality on all foreigners born in the country." "No honest, informed authority can say that this sprawling police state machine . . . has hindered the communists at all," du Berrier attested. "What it has done is permit an unwanted dictator to remain in power. He was imposed on a people who never wanted him. . . . The American public would have prevented this if the American public had been told the truth." Why had they not been told the truth? "A propaganda agency . . . has produced articles in magazines, books, meetings, and lectures to perpetuate a false picture of Ngo Dinh Diem and the situation in his country," du Berrier charged. "Now, when disillusionment comes, it will be the more brutal. . . . [M]any more millions of Asiatics are going to atone in chains for our misguided meddling."[162]

The *Mercury* did not wish to associate its name too closely with du Berrier's views, and its editors ran a disclaimer shortly thereafter. Noting that "[m]any informed anti-communist readers strongly differed with Mr. du Berrier's conclusions," they announced that the *Mercury* had invited AFV Chairman O'Daniel to contribute a "different viewpoint."[163] In his rebuttal, O'Daniel praised "the wise, decisive, and farsighted leadership of President Ngo Dinh Diem. . . . More than any other human being I have met, President Ngo knows his people and his country." It was this knowledge, O'Daniel contended, that enabled Diem to take an "anarchic" country, "isolated from the benefits of modern science and technology . . . by a traditional Oriental system" and transform it into "the Free World's bulwark in Southeast Asia." O'Daniel considered it "the great fortune of Vietnam and of the entire Free World that, during her most critical hour, Free Vietnam produced such a dynamic leader." O'Daniel then turned his attention to du Berrier: "A few foreign observers (some with personal axes to grind) have criticized the Diem government for not moving fast enough in the civil liberties area. This indicates an astounding political naïveté when one realizes that Vietnam has almost no tradition of democratic institutions."[164]

O'Daniel's article was littered with inaccuracies, not least of which was his labeling of du Berrier, who was born in North Dakota, as a foreigner, but the journalist had been put in his place. Still, du Berrier continued to denounce Diem and the AFV, usually in publications with limited circulation. "The story of democracy's failure in South Vietnam is also the story of President Ngo Dinh Diem," du Berrier proclaimed in the newsletter of the archconservative National Economic Council. He called the AFV "partisans of Diem the man rather than South Vietnam the country" and warned of widespread Vietnamese "hatred of America . . . for having imposed and supported" an autocrat.[165] In the even less widely distributed bulletin "H. du B. Reports," du Berrier assailed the AFV's "insinuation that dictatorship for a former colonial country is a necessity . . . during that country's transition to independence."[166] Du Berrier kept up a steady stream of letters to prominent policymakers, especially Mansfield, begging for a change in stance on South Vietnam. "Isn't there something we can do about Diem?" he asked Mansfield in one epistle. "You have no idea to what extent Europe and the rest of the world look to you as the author of our policy vis-à-vis Diem, and look to you to get us all out of it before the dilemma which is inevitably approaching . . . arrives."[167]

Mansfield occasionally replied to du Berrier's letters, but with little more than a paraphrase of what he had already said in speeches and articles about the miracle Diem had wrought. "I cannot help but be impressed by the progress made by this remarkable man," the senator wrote du Berrier. "It is true that he may be stubborn, . . . but it is a fact that a free Vietnam exists at the present time and that in large part this free entity is the result of the efforts of Mr. Diem."[168] After a number of these rebuffs, du Berrier sent a missive to several Montana newspapers in the hopes of defeating Mansfield's bid for reelection in 1958. Rambling, grammatically flawed, racist—and, in view of Mansfield's landslide victory, unsuccessful—this letter remains a valid contemporary assessment of the senator's contribution to an American tragedy. "I am interested in the forthcoming senatorial election in Montana," du Berrier declared, citing his "very great fear that you Republicans out there won[']t find a way to get Mike Mansfield back to teaching school, where, aside from doing the sort of deformation job on the minds of his pupils that Mangbetu Africans do to their skulls, he will be comparatively harmless." Du Berrier observed that Mansfield's "stubborn insistence on forcing Ngo Dinh Diem down the throats of a nation that does not and never did want him is costing us all of Southeast Asia" and warned of "the price America and the Free World is going to have to pay someday, because a Montana Democrat took it upon himself to decide who the South Vietnamese should and should not have as their chief of state."[169]

If du Berrier was a straggler in an American fourth estate marching in lockstep to the battle hymn of Diem's miracle, Norman Thomas played a similar role in the ranks of the AFV. When Thomas read John Osborne's article "The Tough Miracle Man of Vietnam" in the 13 May 1957 issue of *Life,* a passage struck him. Osborne's treatment of Diem was in the main positive, but he conceded that "Diem could easily be mistaken for just another dictator. . . . Behind the façade of photographs, flags, and slogans, there is a grim structure of decrees, political prisons, concentration camps, milder 're-education' centers, secret police."[170] Thomas immediately wrote to O'Daniel. "I have been proud to be a member of the American Friends of Vietnam," he declared. "But in that capacity I have been deeply troubled by an article in the current issue of *Life.* . . . I have never approved or condoned totalitarian tactics practiced by non-communist governments, and I don't want to seem to begin to do so now."[171]

There is evidence that the AFV shifted its heretofore-uncritical stance toward Diem in order to keep Thomas's name on its masthead. In October 1957, the executive committee issued a plea to Diem not to carry out the executions of eight Binh Xuyen commandos captured during the Battle for Saigon. "If this sentence were to be executed more than two years after the actual event had taken place," the committee noted, "such executions would be generally regarded . . . by the American public as a sign of insecurity and extremely harsh action."[172] Diem partially relented, executing two of the Binh Xuyen prisoners and commuting the sentences of the other six to life imprisonment.[173] Thomas remained skeptical. Writing to O'Daniel on another occasion, he asserted, "I think we Americans cannot be true to our own convictions about democracy and freedom if we pass over in silence acts done by our friends which we would strongly condemn if done by our enemies." From what he had learned of circumstances in South Vietnam, Thomas argued, they "hardly justified the seemingly unconditional praise that Henry Luce has bestowed on Ngo Dinh Diem."[174]

Thomas also wrote to Secretary of State Dulles, protesting that "I do not see . . . that [South Vietnam's] security requires this kind of high-handed action against individual liberty. . . . [W]e Americans are put in a very bad position when our friends . . . ape our enemies in the denial of liberty."[175] Dulles, who disdained in equal measure socialists, critics of Diem, and dilettantes who presumed to instruct him on foreign policy, blandly responded, "In 1954, it was widely considered a matter of time before the communists would gain control of all of Vietnam, but Diem appears to have succeeded in establishing a stable government."[176] A wavering Thomas retained his membership in the AFV until January 1958, when, distressed by reports of increasing repression in South Vietnam, he resigned.[177] He was unable to persuade other AFV members to join him but left behind a record of principled dissent that holds up very well.

"One of the Great Figures of the Twentieth Century"

State Department records indicate that on at least two occasions in 1955, Angier Biddle Duke, head of the AFV's executive committee, tried to persuade department officials to invite Diem to visit the United States. On both occasions, the officer solicited by Duke felt such an invitation would be premature in light of Diem's tenuous hold on power.[178] These objections no longer applied in 1957, after Diem had succeeded in killing, jailing, exiling, or terrifying into submission all political rivals. When the South Vietnamese president hinted in February 1957 that he would like to tour America, Ambassador Reinhardt affirmed American eagerness to welcome him.[179]

The Eisenhower administration prepared fastidiously for Diem's arrival. A memorandum from the State Department's Office of Protocol instructed department personnel on such points of ceremonialism as the correct pronunciation of the visitor's name—"NGO: N-O as in 'no' with a nasal N ('NHHO')"—and the proper order of "formal toasts"— "First toast must always be made by the host. . . . Subsequent toasts, if any, may be made to persons in declining order of importance."[180] The Office of Protocol also issued a briefing book to "all relevant staff" detailing the South Vietnamese president's eccentricities. "Ngo Dinh Diem is a short, stocky, physically unimpressive man," department officers were informed. "He is an introverted, lonely figure. . . . He is, however, a man with an almost messianic sense of mission." The office warned that "Diem can be both intransigent and almost brutal in pursuing and applying policies he has decided upon, and, when aroused, has a violent temper." Notwithstanding such foibles, the book observed, "his honesty and integrity are unquestionable. . . . A devout Roman Catholic, he lives as a celibate and practices the utmost discipline in his private life. . . . Both he and his brother, Bishop Thuc, are good friends of Francis Cardinal Spellman." As for Diem's refusal to permit any dissenting voices in his country, the Office of Protocol explained that "Vietnam in its present situation and given its own heritage is not yet ready for a democratic government as it is known in the West. . . . The interplay of all shades of opinion in the policy-making process . . . is considered a luxury Vietnam cannot yet afford." The office recommended that administration representatives avoid any criticism of Diem's mode of governance: "He is most sensitive to such charges."[181]

The AFV went into promotional overdrive in the days preceding Diem's arrival in Washington. O'Daniel sent a telegram to over one hundred publishers and editors, urging them to accord Diem "the warmest welcome" with "positive editorial comment."[182] Media response to news of Diem's approaching visit exceeded the AFV's most

26. Diem (center) shakes President Eisenhower's hand as Secretary of State Dulles looks on. © AP/WORLDWIDE PHOTOS, 9 May 1957

soaring expectations. Under the headline "Welcome to a Champion," the *Washington Evening Star* called Diem "a valiant and effective fighter against communism." The *Boston Globe* dubbed him "Vietnam's Man of Iron." The *Washington Post* ran a four-page story titled "Diem— Symbol of Free New Asia." The *New York Times* hailed Diem for "advanc[ing] the cause of freedom and democracy in Asia" and voiced the "hope that he can feel the friendly warmth of our reception as we greet a good friend." The *Washington News* offered a thinly disguised slap at neutralist Asian heads of state like Indonesia's Achmed Sukarno, observing, "Unlike some other state visitors we have had from his part of the world, Ngo Dinh Diem can be counted upon to stand by his word." The *New York Journal-American* noted Diem's "invigorating contempt for Prime Minister Jawaharlal Nehru of India" and "other Asian statesmen mouthing stale pacifist platitudes." "While bigger and edgier countries seek protection behind the cloak of neutralism," the *Journal-American* observed, "Diem boldly proclaims his faith and confidence in the United States. South Vietnam stands as a rugged sentinel of hope projected against the darkening panorama of communist Asia."[183]

The Miracle Man's arrival in the United States was properly triumphal. The day after being greeted by Eisenhower at the airport, Diem stood before both Houses of Congress and received a standing ovation. His address drew thunderous applause at several points. Diem gave credit to "generous American aid" for rescuing his nation "at its moment of absolute peril" and went on to enunciate the principles that were the basis of South Vietnam's government:

> We affirm that the sole legitimate object of the state is to protect the fundamental rights of human beings to existence, to the free development of his [sic] intellectual, moral, and spiritual life. . . . We affirm that democracy is neither material happiness nor the supremacy of numbers. Democracy is essentially a permanent effort to find the right political means in order to assure to all citizens the right of free development and the maximum initiative, responsibility, and spiritual life.[184]

This elucidation was high on spirit but low on specifics and did not accord with most Americans' conception of democracy. If a key tenet of representative government was not "supremacy of numbers," then what was the point of holding elections? Still, editorial response was positive. The *New York Times* quoted Diem's remark that "democracy is neither material happiness nor the supremacy of numbers" and concluded, "With such a declaration, we believe, Thomas Jefferson would have no quarrel. . . . Diem has added a strongly spiritual, rather than political, note to his definition of 'democracy.' This could have been expected from a man of deep religious bent." The *Washington Post* applauded "President Diem's devotion to the spiritual as well as economic welfare of his country." Neal Stanford of the *Christian Science Monitor* felt that the address to Congress demonstrated "President Diem's devotion to the democratic way of life, to the Western way of life" and observed that "Ngo Dinh Diem stole Washington's spotlight—and its heart."[185]

Diem made an even stronger impression on his third day in the nation's capital. In an appearance before the National Press Club, he upbraided those "Asian statesmen" who favored nonalignment in the cold war.[186] When asked why he opposed "neutralism as a policy," he replied, "Since communism is not neutral, we cannot be neutral."[187] The *New York Times* acclaimed this as "straight talk from a courageous man. It is welcome here and it should be heard in some other quarters." *America* approvingly noted that "in contrast to the nervous tightrope

27. Diem addresses a joint session of Congress. Seated behind him are Vice President Richard Nixon (left) and Speaker of the House Sam Rayburn. © AP/WORLDWIDE PHOTOS, 9 May 1957

posturing . . . of other Asian leaders, . . . President Ngo left no doubt that he stands with the Free World." Marguerite Higgins of the *New York Herald Tribune* was astonished by Diem's frankness, judging it a welcome change from "Asian leaders who punctuate smiles and protocol politeness with pointed reminders of their neutralist creed." After visits by the "anti-American" Nehru and Sukarno, Higgins wrote, "it is a refreshing—almost startling—experience to hear this Asian hero assert forthrightly: 'communism isn't neutral, therefore we cannot be neutral.' . . . He made himself unique among recent Asian visitors . . . by the decisiveness with which he publicly chose up sides with the United States and against the communists."[188] The AFV recognized the propaganda value of Diem's apothegm and began citing it in mass mailings as evidence of their man's contempt for "the neutralist approach, so much the vogue throughout contemporary Asia."[189]

Diem's reply to another question had a similarly electrifying impact. Toward the end of the Press Club luncheon, a reporter asked Diem, "What is your religion and have you found it a help or a hindrance in performing your task as head of your country?" The Catholic columnist

John O'Brien indignantly noted that "one cannot . . . imagine a similar question, touching on a matter as personal as one's religion, being asked of a head of a Western state in the Orient." Diem's response, however, delighted O'Brien. "I am a Roman Catholic," Diem declared. "I have always found the principles of my religion a great inspiration, and, if I have achieved anything in my political career, I owe it all to those principles." The statement made headlines in Catholic papers: " 'Faith Inspired Me,' Viet President Says"; "Vietnam President Tells the Press He Owes All to His Catholic Faith"; "Diem Answers a Question." The *Universe-Bulletin* proudly attested that "Diem would hardly have lasted a day in office if he were not the Catholic he is. . . . From his religious faith, he has drawn courage in resisting atheistic communism."[190]

Eisenhower informed the Washington press corps prior to Diem's arrival that the South Vietnamese president's visit was to be "principally ceremonial."[191] No reexaminations of America's policies toward South Vietnam were undertaken during Diem's four days in Washington, although the administration did pledge a steep increase in financial assistance.[192] A comic vignette ensued when Dulles attempted to engage Diem in a discussion about land reform; as Assistant Secretary Robertson recalled, "Secretary Dulles and I went over to see Diem at Blair House, and he just wouldn't stop talking. We couldn't get in a word. And as we came out, Secretary Dulles turned to me and said, 'Wouldn't you think that, here in Washington, he might be interested in what our secretary of state had to say?' "[193] Before Diem took his leave on 11 May, the White House issued a communiqué praising him for "the remarkable achievements of the Republic of Viet-Nam under his leadership."[194] The Miracle Man then left for New York City.

New York's welcome made the Washington reception seem tepid. Diem arrived at LaGuardia Airport on the *Columbine III* and was whisked in a seven-car motorcade to St. Patrick's Cathedral, where the Most Reverend Joseph Flannelly delayed the mass for half an hour and waited for Diem by the great bronze doors. Flannelly's tribute to his guest was vintage fifties. After leading Diem to a place of honor in the sanctuary, the bishop trumpeted, "We are delighted and we are proud to see in the Sanctuary of our Cathedral of New York the president of the Republic of Vietnam, His Excellency Ngo Dinh Diem. The whole world acclaimed him when this God-fearing anti-communist and courageous statesman saved Vietnam! . . . [Y]our fellow Catholics join our hearts and souls with you at this altar of God."[195] That afternoon, Diem

28. Diem shakes hands with Speaker of the House Sam Rayburn after his speech to Congress. © AP/WORLDWIDE PHOTOS, 9 May 1957

paid a visit to his alma mater, the Maryknoll Seminary, where, the *New York Times* recorded, "students, dressed identically in their black cassocks, gave him a rousing welcome."[196] Diem next went to South Orange, New Jersey, where he received an honorary law degree from Seton Hall University. In its citation, Seton Hall affirmed that Diem, "more than anyone else, stopped the communists in their hour of partial conquest of Vietnam."[197]

The following day witnessed a ticker tape parade from Lower Broadway to City Hall, as a crowd 250,000 strong cheered for Diem and threw bunting, confetti, and streamers at the motorcade that took the Miracle Man to meet Mayor Robert Wagner. The mayor called Diem "a man to whom freedom is the very breath of life," referred to South Vietnam as a "political miracle," and declared, "Certainly, the principal credit for this miracle should go to President Ngo Dinh Diem, a man history may yet adjudge as one of the great figures of the twentieth century." Diem accepted Wagner's presentation of the city's Medal of Honor and a scroll for "Distinguished and Exceptional Service."[198] After praising New York as "the most impressive image of economic dynamism and political idealism in America," Diem made a speech in which he contrasted "the exceptional character" of the Vietnamese with "features of other Asian countries." The Vietnamese were more "dynamic," Diem said. "Through centuries, we have successfully resisted the expansion of the immense Chinese mass. . . . Thus we have enough confidence in ourselves not to take refuge behind communism and economic autarky."[199] The audience went wild. Then it was off to a meeting with the Council on Foreign Relations, where Diem again stressed Vietnamese industriousness and concern for the bottom line. "You will not find the kind of elaborate temples, palaces, and ancient monuments in Vietnam that dot the jungles of our South Asian neighbors," he proclaimed. "My explanation for this is simple: My Vietnamese ancestors were practical people, too busy tilling their rice fields, building their homes, harnessing the rivers, to put their savings and toil into beautiful but nonproductive monuments. Perhaps it is no accident of history that today rice fields dot our country while . . . the jungle has swallowed up those other civilizations!"[200]

That evening, Diem attended a dinner in his honor at the Ambassador Hotel. The AFV and IRC had chosen this occasion to present Diem with an award commemorating Richard Byrd, the polar explorer who served as the honorary chairman of the IRC's board of directors from 1949 until his death in 1957.[201] Fittingly, Henry Luce chaired the dinner, and Cardinal Spellman delivered the invocation. Guests included John D. Rockefeller, Senators Mansfield and Kennedy, Eleanor Roosevelt, and William Randolph Hearst Jr.[202] Diem accepted the Byrd Award on behalf of "the entire Vietnamese people" and thanked "Mr. Henry Luce, for all that he and his publications have done to create better American understanding of Vietnam." He claimed that America's greatest "gift" to his country was its "magnificent friendship. . . . The word *friends* should be my theme for tonight. . . . Looking at the newspapers since I have arrived in your country, one would think that everybody in America is now a friend of Vietnam."[203] The crowning moment of the evening came when Leo Cherne read the guests a telegram from Eisenhower that praised Diem for exhibiting "the highest qualities of heroism and statesmanship."[204] For the second time, Eisenhower had graced an AFV-sponsored event on Diem's behalf with a presidential message. It was an intoxicating triumph for the organization.

The day after his fete at the Ambassador Hotel, Diem attended a mass at Cardinal Spellman's residence and a luncheon at the Waldorf-Astoria hosted by the Far East-America Council of Commerce and Industry. In his address at the Waldorf, Diem again made the argument that South Vietnam provided an ideal site for American economic investment because the Vietnamese were not like other Asians. "Let me say to you here and now that my government and the Vietnamese people do not share the hostility toward the West which is so much the vogue in Asia today," Diem declared. "Further, and in contrast to other Asian nations, we do not regard American private investment as a threat to our national integrity."[205] Diem then boarded a plane for Detroit, where he received an honorary degree from Michigan State University, the institution that had hosted him at Wesley Fishel's behest in the early 1950s. In his acceptance speech, Diem called the warm reception extended him "symbolic of the new era that has begun in the relations between the East and the West."[206] From Michigan the Diem party set out for Knoxville, Tennessee, and then on to Los Angeles, where a banquet was staged for them by the Los Angeles World Affairs Council.[207]

Everywhere the Miracle Man went, the press was adulatory. Diem was hailed as "An Asian Liberator" whose "life—all of it—is devoted to God"; "a stalwart champion of freedom"; "the authentic symbol of Vietnamese nationalism, . . . capable of fighting Ho Chi Minh to a standstill." Reporters marveled at how "this remarkable man" had brought "Western-style democracy" to a "divided and polyglot country that had to absorb nearly a million refugees." The *Washington News* noted that Diem's "secret weapon, if any, is fearlessness. . . . He has set his course toward the twin goals of freedom for his country along Christian lines and resolute opposition to the communist menace." Joseph Lash of the *New York Post* overheard a photographer exclaim after snapping Diem's picture, "That head! There's the man's biography." Lash agreed: "It is a fact that Diem, a stubby, chunk man, conveys a sense of will and inner peace. . . . President Ngo Dinh Diem is mankind's latest demonstration that 'lost causes' can be salvaged when there are men of tenacity to lead them."[208]

After ten days of accolades, Diem left America on 19 May, a date almost certainly chosen deliberately. It was Ho Chi Minh's birthday, and the Miracle Man was throwing this at Ho as a parting shot. Just prior to boarding Eisenhower's plane for the long flight home, Diem declared to the assembled press that his visit had "convinced [him] that the American people are as rich in moral strength and spiritual values as they are in material prosperity." He praised Eisenhower and Dulles as "men of generosity, farsightedness, and integrity." His final words, punctuated with a salute, were, "God bless you!"[209]

Diem's exultation at this moment can be imagined. He had experienced a reception in the most powerful nation on earth that seemingly vindicated decades of struggle and disappointment. Three years earlier, he had been unknown, a pauper living in Paris with three shirts to his name. Now he could savor success of a magnitude virtually unprecedented among heads of state in the third world. With absolute authority in his native country and a superpower patron that believed he could do no wrong, his reign seemed destined to last indefinitely.

Conclusion

America's intervention in Vietnam has often been compared to the Civil War in terms of the disunity it engendered among the American people.[1] Fittingly, it was a Civil War general who best perceived the impact of nonmaterial factors in bringing about military defeat—an issue that historians of the Vietnam War inevitably confront. When an admirer asked the Confederate commander Robert E. Lee how his Army of Northern Virginia managed to overwhelm a much larger and better-equipped force led by the diffident Union general George McClellan in the Peninsular Campaign of 1862, Lee responded, "McClellan brought the mightiest army ever mustered on North American soil to the gates of Richmond. But he also brought himself."[2]

American policymakers brought the might of history's greatest economic and military superpower to the task of creating and preserving a noncommunist nation in South Vietnam. Five presidential administrations pumped billions of dollars into America's Southeast Asian client and sent thousands of experts to tutor the South Vietnamese on every aspect of national superintendence. The American military performed logistical miracles, constructing airfields and harbors and distributing tons of equipment to field U.S. and native forces. In terms of material wealth and brute force, the United States overshadowed North Vietnam as completely as one belligerent has ever dwarfed another. But American policymakers also brought themselves to Vietnam—their ethnocentrism and parochialism, political arrogance and cultural blindness, all the mental baggage that had accumulated in their minds since childhood. Specifically, they brought interdependent ideologies of religion and race that, analyzed in conjunction with the anticommunist hysteria of the early cold war, can help historians answer Robert Wiebe's anguished question of why "sophisticated advisers . . . thought they could create a nation of South Vietnam through a puppet Catholic in Saigon and forced relocation in the countryside."[3] To respond to Wiebe according to his convention: those advisers—Secretary of State John Foster Dulles, Senator Mike Mansfield, and others—thought they could accomplish this feat because they believed a puppet Catholic was preferable to any non-Christian Vietnamese with indigenous support. Moreover, they viewed Asians as malleable naïfs who accommodated, indeed invited, Western management of their national destiny, even if this entailed abandoning ancestral homelands, surrendering previously sacrosanct privileges of village autonomy, and enduring a succession of human-rights abuses that no U.S. policymaker would have tolerated if inflicted upon the citizenry of a European ally. Cold war panic combined with religious bigotry and racist preconceptions to bring forth what George Kahin deems "the most fundamental decision of [America's] thirty-year involvement [in Vietnam]—the critical prerequisite to the subsequent incremental steps that culminated in President Johnson's famous escalation a decade later": the policy of "sink or swim with Ngo Dinh Diem."[4]

Harold Isaacs, whose *Scratches on Our Minds* I have cited several times in this work, concludes that classic study with the following observation: "I have never discovered any reason to credit the government policy maker as a type with any superior mental discipline. . . . I think of him as quite an ordinary man [who] has images floating around loosely in his head, even as you or I."[5] With regard to the religious faith of most Vietnamese, the images floating around loosely in Dwight Eisenhower's head were limited to sketches like the one prepared by the operations coordinating board in June 1956, titled "Problem: To Determine the Advisability of a Presidential Message on the Occasion of the 2500th Anniversary of the Buddha." The board concluded that the president *should* deliver some kind of announcement but cautioned Eisenhower that "the Christian belief that 'there is a higher law than that made by man alone' would not be acceptable to most Buddhists, *especially those whom we wish to reach in Southeast Asia.*"[6]

From Eisenhower's perspective, Buddhism's refusal to acknowledge any such higher law was equally unacceptable to an America engaged in a duel to the death with godless communism. For a chief executive who publicly affirmed that "our system demands the Supreme Being," Buddhism's lack of a celestial protagonist served to reduce it to something less than a legitimate religion and its adherents to less than righteous people. "Religion" in Eisenhower's America must be understood as a narrow-gauged category comprising only the major organized churches of "the West": *Protestant-Catholic-Jew,* to cite the title of Will Herberg's best-seller of 1955. It did not include such ostensibly "Eastern" faiths as

Buddhism, Taoism, and Confucianism. Eisenhower underscored this precept when he declared to an audience in Harlem during the presidential campaign of 1952, "I do not care whether you be Baptists, whether you be Jews, whether you be Catholics or Protestants. . . . There *must* be a feeling that man is made in the image of his Maker."[7] The Republican candidate would have cared had his listeners been atheists, had they subscribed to a creed that deviated from a monotheistic core, or had the deity they worshiped borne little resemblance to the Judeo-Christian God Eisenhower designated as indispensable to the American way of life. When Justice William O. Douglas wrote in his majority opinion in the Supreme Court case of *Zorach v. Clauson* (1952) that "we are a religious people whose institutions presuppose a Supreme Being," he implicitly endorsed Eisenhower's view that presupposition of a Supreme Being was the sine qua non of the condition "religious." Any system of beliefs lacking that doctrinal prerequisite could at best be designated a "philosophy" or "theory"—at worst, to borrow the terminology employed by Mansfield and others during the Battle for Saigon, it was "witchcraft."

If one interprets Eisenhower's expression "our system" broadly, as encompassing not just America's domestic institutions but the global network of alliances forged by the United States in the early years of the cold war, then the significance of the president's seemingly trite declaration becomes manifest. Eisenhower announced in his first inaugural address that "forces for good and evil are massed and armed and opposed as rarely before in our history. . . . Freedom is pitted against slavery; lightness against the dark."[8] In such a contest, with such stakes, the United States needed allies who possessed a variant of what Dulles termed America's "dynamic" faith. "We must act," the secretary of state once declared. "Christ did not teach a purely contemplative religion."[9] Devout patriots like Eisenhower and Dulles could not risk America's security on clients whose faiths were characterized in official documents and the media as passive and fatalistic. As the president proclaimed to the World Council of Churches in 1954, "Our interest in religion is serious and genuine, not merely theoretical."[10] America would expect the same evangelic earnestness from its allies.

There is evidence that Ngo Dinh Diem understood this. On the eve of his triumphal tour of the United States in 1957, Diem wrote a letter to Dulles that acknowledged the role played by religion in American policy making:

My dear Mr. Secretary of State,

About two years ago, when almost all material forces in Viet-Nam seemed against me, when I wondered whether I could last a week longer and whether Viet-Nam was not going to fall into communist hands like a rotten fruit, you gave me new courage. . . .

Indeed, Mr. Secretary of State, it is the good fortune of myself and my country that you and I have so many things in common: We both strongly believe in God; your son is a priest, and I have the honor of being a bishop's brother; we both strongly believe in moral forces and the dignity of man. . . . I propose a toast to Secretary of State Dulles, to President Eisenhower, and to the noble American people![11]

Diem paid no lip service to representative government or civil liberties in his letter. While he was occasionally obliged to mouth the rhetoric of democracy in his dealings with the American press and lower-level administration officials, no senior U.S. policymaker expected him to relax his iron grip on every aspect of South Vietnam's political life. In fact, Washington would have viewed such a development as counterproductive. Frederick Reinhardt, J. Lawton Collins's successor as top U.S. diplomat in Saigon, expressed a key tenet of American racism when he issued a report on Diem's first two years in office. "While [Diem] has been criticized by his opponents for his tactics in quelling political opposition, dictatorial hiring and firing of officials, censorship of the press, and arrests on political grounds, it was probably unrealistic to expect anything else," Reinhardt informed the State Department. "The development of a truly democratic government is not a realistic objective at the present stage of this country's development."[12] Reinhardt's dismissal of a catalog of offenses that he himself labeled "dictatorial" was of a piece with American views of the Far East. From the vantage point of statesmen and scholars like Eisenhower, Dulles, Joseph Buttinger, and Wesley Fishel, Asians were not only unqualified to govern themselves; they had no desire to do so, preferring dictatorships to pluralist systems. As Fishel argued in an oxymoronic essay titled "Vietnam's Democratic One-Man Rule" (1959), "The peoples of Southeast Asia should not be expected to understand, let alone embrace, the difficult articles of our democratic faith and practice. . . . Their independence could not have been achieved and cannot be maintained, under present conditions, without strong leadership."[13] It followed, therefore, that Diem's centralization of power was not only understandable but necessary.

The Vietnamese whom Americans encountered in the print media, in newsreels and on television, and in best-selling books like Tom Dooley's *Deliver Us from Evil* and William Lederer's and Eugene Burdick's *The Ugly American* reinforced American presumptions of Asian political immaturity. Emily Rosenberg notes that "women, nonwhite races, and tropical countries" have traditionally been "accorded the same kinds of symbolic characterization from white, male policymakers: emotional, irrational, irresponsible, unbusinesslike, unstable, childlike. These naturally dependent peoples could be expected to exhibit the same kinds of natural responses to patriarchal tutelage. They were assumed, if behaving properly, to be loving, grateful, happy, and appreciative of paternal protection."[14] Rosenberg could be describing Dooley's fawning refugees or the Catholics who thronged around Cardinal Spellman during his frequent visits to Saigon. American policymakers never entertained the possibility that such infantile supplicants could run their own affairs, absent an autarch or "savior." As Dulles declared in making his case for Diem at the Paris Conference in May 1955, "In that part of the world there is no such thing as a 'coalition' government, only one-man governments."[15]

With the United States committed to its survival, Diem's one-man government endured, lavishly subsidized and virtually unchallenged, for the remainder of the 1950s. On the fifth anniversary of South Vietnam's founding, Eisenhower saluted Diem for "the progress made by Viet-Nam in the years since you assumed leadership. . . . We in the United States are aware of your own indispensable role in bringing about this remarkable progress."[16] Four hundred prominent Americans, among them Senator Mansfield, Justice Douglas, and Cardinal Spellman, signed a "message of congratulation."[17] Mansfield proclaimed in a Senate speech that the South Vietnamese were "fortunate in having a man of Diem's vision, strength, and selflessness as their leader."[18] The crimes of the Diem regime, including torture, mass imprisonment, and execution without trial, were not reported in America's mainstream newspapers and magazines until the early 1960s. As late as 1959, the *New York Times* lauded Diem for building "a constitutional democracy," and *Newsweek*'s senior editor Ernest Lindley enthused, "South Vietnam has made more striking progress in more ways than any other Asian nation I have so far visited. For this, credit must go to . . . a dedicated, canny, indefatigable, invincible man, President Ngo Dinh Diem."[19]

As for the Diem regime's increasingly anti-Buddhist policies, the American press was mute and the administration indifferent. Dooley fielded a question on the subject during a fund-raising tour of the United States but brushed it aside condescendingly: "If President Diem has jailed a Buddhist priest in South Vietnam, good lady, you can rest assured he had good reason for doing so."[20] South Vietnam's Buddhists lacked defenders even among those few Americans disposed to find fault with the Eisenhower administration's Miracle Man. As detailed in chapter 6, Hilaire du Berrier was Diem's most persistent critic throughout the 1950s, years ahead of other reporters in his denunciation of the police state America supported. Yet du Berrier shared the religious bigotry of the age. Looking back on Saigon's civil war during the early months of Diem's premiership, the gadfly journalist wrote,

> The one group [in Vietnam] from which no one expected anything, then or ever, was the Buddhists. . . . Buddhism had slowly foundered into a mire of Oriental somnolence. To its followers it offered inertia and called it wisdom. Buddhism did nothing, and graced it with such adorning names as "reflection" and "tolerance." . . . [W]hether it was a family-type Buddhism or the ascetic with precious names such as "the perfumed lotus of the Jade fountain," Buddhism represented no threat of force.[21]

The extent to which du Berrier and others overlooked the iron discipline beneath the placid exterior became evident when a brilliantly organized campaign by Saigon's Buddhists brought about the fall of the Diem government in November 1963. Ironically, one of Diem's most dependable allies played a role in the success of the Buddhist revolt. Images disseminated by the U.S. mass media, including Henry Luce's *Life* and *Time* magazines, made it impossible for Diem and his American apologists to package this uprising as they had the triumph over the Binh Xuyen in 1955. Until monks began self-immolating in the streets of Saigon, the dramatis personae with whom Americans interested in South Vietnam were familiar included Diem, his brother Nhu, possibly Bao Dai, and a few "racketeers" and "witch doctors." The rest of the South Vietnamese were a faceless horde. For all practical purposes, Diem was the only South Vietnamese *visible* to Americans until, on 11 June 1963, the Buddhist monk Thich Quang Duc knelt on Pham Dinh Phung Boulevard, permitted himself to be doused with gasoline, and lit a match. He had alerted members of the international press before

29. A Buddhist monk burns himself alive to protest Diem's repressive policies. ©
Bettmann/CORBIS, 5 October 1963

taking his life, and pictures of his burning body spread across the world
wire services. A series of Buddhist torch suicides came in rapid succession, the horrific images captured on film and broadcast in the United
States.[22]

The sudden intrusion of new characters on the scene compelled
many Americans to reconsider their impressions of Diem's government.
President John F. Kennedy, for one, is reported to have been so appalled
by a photo of Duc's martyrdom that he bolted from the room.[23] Kennedy
later informed Ambassador Henry Cabot Lodge that "no news picture in
history has generated so much emotion around the world as that one."[24]
It was Diem's misfortune to be confronted with the rebellion of Saigon's
Buddhists at the same time Martin Luther King Jr. sat in an Alabama jail
and Birmingham police turned attack dogs and fire hoses on hundreds
of praying, hymn-singing marchers—all while television cameras rolled
and photographers focused their lenses. Buddhism's nonviolent approach to confronting injustice looked more morally muscular to Americans in the summer and fall of 1963 than it had in the mid-1950s. Senator
Frank Church, in a striking choice of words, expressed his revulsion with
the images emanating from Saigon by declaiming to his colleagues on
the Foreign Relations Committee, "Such grisly scenes have not been
witnessed since the Christian martyrs walked hand-in-hand into the

Roman arenas."[25] Within less than a decade, the witch doctors of the Eisenhower years had become the moral equivalent of Christian martyrs in the estimation of at least one prominent American policymaker.

Further damaging Diem's cause was the fact that America, and especially Washington, had cast off much of the fervent religiosity of the 1950s by the time the Buddhist crisis occurred. Policy making was more overtly secular under Kennedy than under Eisenhower. As Loren Baritz observes of JFK's New Frontiersmen, "The memory of John Foster Dulles made them cringe. They thought of themselves as muscular realists, disciplined, potent, demanding hard facts—never pieties."[26] Pieties played beautifully in the mid-1950s, when an ally's Judeo-Christian faith could be decisive in procuring American patronage. Diem's staunch Catholicism, an asset in the Eisenhower era, worked against him with Kennedy. As the first Catholic president in American history, JFK went to great lengths to quell any suspicions that his judgment was colored by religious affiliation. Throughout the presidential campaign of 1960, Kennedy repeatedly denied that his faith impaired his fitness for office, at one point facing down the Houston Ministerial Association with the avowal, "I believe in an America where the separation of church and state is absolute. I am *not* the Catholic candidate for president. I am the . . . candidate . . . who happens to be Catholic."[27]

Moreover, the straitlaced Puritanism that Dulles personified and that was so much a feature of the 1950s religious revival slackened when Kennedy's Camelot seized the imagination of America. JFK's youth, cosmopolitanism, and virility could not have been further removed from Eisenhower's grandfatherly geniality or Dulles's humorless moralizing. Diem must have believed he was still dealing with men in Dulles's mold when he proclaimed to the U.S. ambassador in Saigon during the Buddhist crisis in 1963 that "the Buddhist pagodas had been turned into bordellos, that government troops had found a great deal of female underwear, love letters, and obscene photographs. That the virgins were being despoiled there. That the government knew of one Buddhist priest who had despoiled thirteen virgins!"[28] Kennedy, who had despoiled his share, was not likely to be scandalized by these revelations, assuming he believed them. Any implicit plea by Diem to a fellow Catholic for solidarity against the debauched, pagan Buddhists did not find a sympathetic audience in JFK's White House.

As important as the self-sacrifice of Saigon's Buddhists, the waning of America's theological renaissance, and the inauguration of a Catholic president was the fact that, by the time Kennedy took office, Diem had begun to lose battles in the field. Until Ho Chi Minh authorized the formation of a native South Vietnamese communist insurgency, the National Liberation Front (NLF), in 1960, Diem and his supporters could plausibly claim he was a popular leader with no significant indigenous opposition to his government. By 1961, such conceits had been demolished, as the NLF dealt the Army of the Republic of Vietnam several humiliating defeats.[29] For the first five years of Diem's rule, Ho had concentrated on domestic problems in North Vietnam; he did not even press hard for compliance with the Geneva Conference's stipulation for all-Vietnam elections in 1956, preferring to devote his energies to implementing a land reform program to compensate for the loss of the South's rice supply.[30] Ho's time-buying strategy, combined with the billions of dollars in U.S. aid to South Vietnam, enabled Diem to preside over a more-or-less peaceful, stable nation whose hearty façade masked its internal decay. The bubble of Diem's miracle began to burst around the time Eisenhower handed responsibility for sustaining America's outpost in Southeast Asia over to Kennedy. From 1961 on, South Vietnam went into a tailspin, prompting a reevaluation of U.S. policy toward the regime in Saigon.

Despite the outcome of America's Diem experiment, few of Diem's supporters ever admitted that their lobbying for him had been an error. Buttinger was an exception. The founder of the American Friends of Vietnam resigned from that organization in 1962, declaring in a letter to Chairman Mike O'Daniel that "I no longer believe that the regime of President Diem is capable of defeating the communists without drastic political reform, which the president and his advisers refuse to permit."[31] Days before Diem's assassination, Buttinger called the South Vietnamese leader a "liar" for insisting there was "no religious oppression in Vietnam." Tellingly, however, Buttinger did not view the Buddhist crisis as deriving principally from Diem's religious intolerance. As he wrote to a colleague, "Whatever discrimination there is against the Buddhists, and whatever favors the Catholics can expect under this regime, neither the one nor the other is done in the name of religion or for religious purposes. These acts of discrimination and favoritism are politically inspired, and their purpose is to maintain the present regime in power. ... Diem fights the Buddhists not because he is a Catholic, but because he is a dictator."[32] Buttinger formally apologized for sponsoring Diem in his appositely titled book *Vietnam: The Unforgettable Tragedy*, in which he confessed, "My support of the regime of Ngo Dinh Diem . . . was a serious political mistake, for which I . . . must assume responsibility."[33]

The rest of Diem's Eisenhower-era champions were ambivalent. Edward Lansdale, the premier's closest American adviser during the Battle for Saigon, disclaimed any responsibility for what happened in South Vietnam after he departed. "I left organizations intact," Lansdale tersely observed in 1984. "I don't know what happened."[34] In 1969, Sol Sanders, who had lauded Diem in the pages of the *New Leader* in the 1950s, wrote a bitter account of the Buddhist uprising that toppled his protégé's government. Calling the conflict a "phony 'religious war,'" Sanders complained that Washington never understood that "[m]ost Vietnamese are not believers in the sense we know the concept in the West. . . . Buddhism in Vietnam was . . . a communist-front organization."[35] In 1966, although by then one of the most outspoken critics of U.S. intervention in Vietnam, Mansfield defended his commitment to Diem as "a wise choice," given that, in his view, Diem's overthrow marked "the turning point in the worsening of affairs in South Vietnam."[36]

The Catholic conservatives who made up Diem's most uncritical bloc of American backers were least prone to second thoughts. James Burnham sounded the collusive themes of race and religion in a series of editorials for *National Review* in the wake of Diem's murder. "Diem is the best that has been available in South Vietnam, and a damn sight better than we had any right to expect," Burnham snarled. "What sort of political cretins can they be who think South Vietnam can be ruled like England or Switzerland? South Vietnam isn't even a nation, and not within ten light years of being a constitutional republic."[37] As for Diem's alleged religious prejudice, Burnham affirmed that "throughout Asia today, Buddhism functions as a cover for anti-Westernism, and has been seductively cultivated for many years by Russia and China. . . . The Diem regime represented the only serious and cohesive anti-communist formation in South Vietnam—nor is it by mere chance that Christians were so prominent within it."[38] Anthony Bouscaren, a regular contributor to *National Review* and the author of several pro-Diem articles in the 1950s,[39] published an adulatory biography of the Miracle Man less than two years after Diem's assassination. In it he condemned Vietnamese Buddhism as "a very heterogeneous religious alloy . . . having neither boundaries, gospels, sacraments, hierarchies, registers, or discipline." "Suppose that fifteen villagers gathered around an improvised clay figure have a vision," Bouscaren sniffed, "or that they suddenly feel 'love for all living creatures,' so off they go, paint some ramshackle hut, place bent nails on the roof to ward off some evil spirits, offer up a prayer, and there you have a Pagoda! . . . The informal Buddhist atmosphere makes it easy for the communists to infiltrate."[40] Bouscaren did not draw an explicit comparison between the Buddhism he imagined and the American Catholic Church in the years before Vatican II—that is, a seemingly monolithic institution wherein, on questions of faith and morals, lay-people were expected to regard the hierarchy, headed by an infallible pontiff, as beyond challenge. Still, one suspects that Bouscaren's readers took the hint.

One of the most revealing postmortems on the Diem experiment was articulated by John Hanes, an aide to Dulles throughout his tenure at the State Department. Hanes granted an interview to the journalist Richard Crowl in August 1966, over a year after President Lyndon Johnson had escalated the number of U.S. ground combat forces in South Vietnam and ordered the bombing of the North. Protest against America's intervention in Vietnam was widespread: an antiwar march in Washington in April 1965 drew over thirty thousand people; all-night "teach-ins" at American universities from New York to Madison to Berkeley attracted dozens of celebrity intellectuals who argued in favor of U.S. withdrawal; and, most distressing from the perspective of President Johnson and his advisers, the Senate Foreign Relations Committee began in early 1966 to hold televised hearings on the administration's war policy, thereby giving opponents of the war a platform within the political system from which to disseminate their views.[41] Although the stormiest conflicts between hawks and doves lay several years in the future, *Vietnam* was beginning to display those features that would render it, in Norman Podhoretz's words, "the most negatively charged political symbol in American history."[42] Much of Crowl's interview with Hanes was accordingly given over to ascertaining the Eisenhower administration's role in cementing the U.S. alliance with Diem and laying the foundation for America's Vietnam dilemma.

When Crowl asked "to what extent" Washington had backed Diem in the mid- to late 1950s, Hanes replied, "I would say to every feasible extent—economic aid, political advice, some military aid . . . and a good deal of covert assistance . . . to help him maintain his base." Crowl began to ask another question, but Hanes, his mood darkening, interrupted.

"As a footnote to this," he declared, "I still think that probably one of the most stupid, as well as the most shameful, instances in our policy was our cutting up of Diem a couple of years ago . . . without an alternative. I'm no great moralist, and I assume the Diem regime was many of the things that people said about it. So are a lot of regimes around the world. But to take a reasonably strong regime, to have no alternative, and to abandon it . . . is sheer stupidity. And if we bail out of Vietnam now, having done this, then we don't deserve it!" Hanes charged those "rather fuzzy newspaper people" who clamored for Diem's removal— correspondents like David Halberstam, Neil Sheehan, and Charles Mohr—with being "ignorant of the true bases of foreign policy." "Diem wasn't perfect," Hanes acknowledged. "We knew damned well he wasn't perfect. . . . But he was the best thing around. . . . As to whether or not he was beautiful in face, in feature, in objective, or in morals, I would submit, is irrelevant. And I think it was irrelevant to the secretary [Dulles]. His only interest was could this guy survive and could he build a free government." Sensing that Crowl was about to object to his use of the word "free," Hanes launched a preemptive strike: "In this case, 'free' means non-communist, because 'free' in Vietnam doesn't mean a democracy of the United States type, any more than it does in Cuba or in Ghana or in any place that's at a different stage of development."[43]

Hanes's exchange with Crowl in the summer of 1966 revisited much of the Eisenhower administration's internal debate as it forged a futile, tragic partnership that alienated South Vietnamese from their government, increased the State of Vietnam's vulnerability to communism, and ultimately drew the United States into the longest war in its history. The paternalism—"we don't deserve it," as if Vietnam were an American possession to lose or retain—and ethnocentrism—"different stage of development"—were typical of the attitudes expressed in government correspondence and the national press, as was the self-imprisonment in the "we-have-no-alternative" argument that Hanes repeatedly, and erroneously, advanced. In fact, America had multiple alternatives to Diem when the fatal commitment was made. Policymakers held fast to the Diem experiment because certain religious and racial beliefs predisposed them to interpret developments in Vietnam in such a manner as to rule out abandonment of their ill-starred surrogate. Men like Eisenhower, Dulles, and Mansfield did what they did, in short, because of who they were: culturally conditioned personalities largely incapable of seeing possibilities outside the dominant ideological framework. Henry

Kissinger observes that the "convictions that leaders have formed before reaching high office are the intellectual capital they will consume as long as they continue in office."[44] With regard to Vietnam, American policymakers' intellectual capital proved not only unhelpful but deadly.

John Foster Dulles would not live to witness the results of his Vietnam policy, but he would see the winding down of the sociological phenomenon whose pacesetter he had been. The great religious revival of the 1950s reached its peak in the mid-fifties—roughly contemporaneous with the inception of the Diem experiment—and waned in the latter half of the decade. By the time Dulles died of cancer in 1959, rock 'n' roll had driven popular religious music off the airwaves, sales of religious books had leveled off, books and articles critical of popular religion had begun to appear in greater numbers, and the percentage of Americans attending church each Sunday had declined to 47 percent.[45] Sinclair Lewis even came back into vogue; in 1959 the movie version of *Elmer Gantry,* featuring Burt Lancaster as Lewis's skirt-chasing, alcoholic evangelist, played to packed theaters and won several Academy Awards. One of the most striking indications of the American public's reordering of priorities was the turn for the worse in Dulles's reputation. As mentioned in chapter 2, only 4 percent of Americans polled on their "attitudes toward the secretary of state" in 1953 registered a negative response; by the late 1950s, Richard Immerman notes, "Dulles had come to personify the shortcomings of America's affairs of state, the symbol of misguided and mismanaged foreign policy. In large part he owed his declining popularity to his public image, that of a Presbyterian moralist ever ready—and eager—to do battle with the devil."[46] Yet this was the same public image that had made Dulles so widely respected and his appointment as secretary of state such a foregone conclusion in the early fifties. Dulles never changed; the world around him did.

The same could be said of Diem. In late 1963, as Buddhist monks burned themselves alive in the streets to draw U.S. attention to religious discrimination in South Vietnam and as American reporters in Saigon clamored for an end to the Diem dictatorship, the South Vietnamese president made what was for him a conciliatory gesture. He sent an American journalist a quotation from the teachings of Buddha:

The Wise Man who fares strenuously apart,
Who is unshaken in the midst of praise or blame . . .
A leader of others, not by others led . . .

A note from one of Diem's attendants read, "President Diem thought you would be interested in the fact that an *Oriental* like Buddha had ideas about the nature of a wise ruler that are not unlike his own."[47]

Such tactics did not reassure the Kennedy administration as to Diem's capacity to defuse the Buddhist crisis. Shortly thereafter, Washington gave the go-ahead for the coup that toppled its ally. America would struggle for the next twelve years to bring order to South Vietnam's chaotic government. Amid the recurrent cabinet realignments that followed Diem's downfall, there would be only one U.S.-sponsored chief executive whose tenure in office lasted nearly as long as the Diem experiment: Nguyen Van Thieu. By 1970, American journalists stationed in South Vietnam joked that the strategy of "Sink or swim with Ngo Dinh Diem" had given way to "See it through with Nguyen Van Thieu." Thieu, although a suppler politician than Diem and less of a zealot, was also Catholic. The ideological predispositions that informed America's support for South Vietnam's first president persisted, if in muted form, into the administration of its last.[48]

Notes

INTRODUCTION

1   Anthony Bouscaren, *The Last of the Mandarins* (Pittsburgh, 1965), 122–23; Fox Butterfield, "Man Who Sheltered Diem Recounts '63 Episode," *New York Times*, 4 November 1971; Ellen Hammer, *A Death in November* (New York, 1987), 298; Howard Jones, *Death of a Generation* (New York, 2003), 428–29; Stanley Karnow, *Vietnam: A History* (New York, 1983), 325–26.

2   Malcolm Browne, "Coup Leaders Report Deaths of Diem and Brother Nhu," *Washington Post*, 3 November 1963; David Halberstam, "Suicides Doubted," *New York Times*, 3 November 1963; John Mecklin, *Mission in Torment* (Garden City, N.Y., 1965), 276; Robert Shaplen, *The Lost Revolution* (New York, 1965), 111.

3   Roy Essoyan, "Celebration in Saigon Exuberant and Rowdy," *Washington Star*, 2 November 1963.

4   "Joyous Viet Crowds Burn Nhu Homes," *Boston Globe*, 2 November 1963; "Jubilant Saigon Crowds Cheer Military Seizure," *Washington Post*, 3 November 1963; "Seventeen Hours that Destroyed Diem," *Life* 55 (15 November 1963): 36–40; "Welcome Coup in Vietnam," *Washington Star*, 3 November 1963; Beverly Deepe, "The Fall of the House of Ngo," *Newsweek* 62 (11 November 1963): 28; David Halberstam, "Thousands Join in Saigon Rejoicing," *Boston Herald*, 4 November 1963; Stanley Karnow, "The Fall of the House of Ngo Dinh," reprinted in *Reporting Vietnam: Part One* (New York, 1998), 105–6.

5   Frances FitzGerald, *Fire in the Lake* (Boston, 1972), 171.

6   John Osborne, "The Tough Miracle Man of Vietnam," *Life* 42 (13 May 1957): 156–76; Robert Alden, "City Accords Diem a Warm Welcome," *New York Times*, 14 May 1957.

7   Cited in David Halberstam, *The Best and the Brightest* (New York, 1969), 191.

8   This argument is made implicitly by Chester Cooper, *The Lost Crusade* (New York, 1970), 144–47; and explicitly by George Kahin, *Intervention* (New York, 1986), 66. Even Gabriel Kolko, who does not customarily assign much significance to the traits of an individual historical actor, notes, "Little did the United States realize in 1954 how momentous a decision it had made when it chose to back Ngo Dinh Diem. That it would usher in a major phase of American history, shaped to a considerable extent by the strengths, desires, and weaknesses of one man, seemed unimaginable. And that the United

States's advancement of its own objectives and interests would depend on this exotic figure revealed . . . the extent of caprice in the conduct of its foreign policy." Kolko, *Anatomy of a War* (New York, 1985), 83.

9 For examples of this thesis, see Thomas Boettcher, *Vietnam: The Valor and the Sorrow* (Boston, 1985), 141; Cecil Currey, *Edward Lansdale: The Unquiet American* (Boston, 1988), 150; Hammer, *Death in November*, 50; James Harrison, *The Endless War* (New York, 1982), 209; Karnow, *Vietnam*, 214; Paul Kattenberg, *The Vietnam Trauma in American Foreign Policy* (New Brunswick, N.J., 1980), 51–52; Alexander Kendrick, *The Wound Within* (Boston, 1974), 96; Harry Maurer, *Strange Ground* (New York, 1989), 80–81. Joseph Buttinger, one of America's leading authorities on Vietnam for decades, flatly asserts that "Washington never considered supporting another man. The explanation is simple: Diem was the only Vietnamese leader who had made himself known in the United States." Buttinger, *Vietnam: A Dragon Embattled* (London, 1967), 2:850.

10 Barbara Tuchman, *The March of Folly* (New York, 1984), 4.

11 Michael Hunt, *Ideology and U.S. Foreign Policy* (New Haven, Conn., 1987), 3–7; Anders Stephanson, "Commentary: Ideology and Neorealist Mirrors," *Diplomatic History* 17 (spring 1993): 285.

12 Frank Ninkovich, "Interests and Discourse in Diplomatic History," *Diplomatic History* 13 (spring 1989): 159.

13 Terry Eagleton, *Ideology: An Introduction* (London, 1991), xiii.

14 David McLellan notes that "Ideology is the most elusive concept in the whole of social science." McLellan, *Ideology* (Minneapolis, 1995), 1.

15 Willard Mullins, "On the Concept of Ideology in Political Science," *American Political Science Review* 66 (June 1972): 498–510. Terry Eagleton lists sixteen meanings for the term and suggests that ideology is like bad breath: it is "what the other person has." Eagleton, *Ideology*, 2.

16 William Appleman Williams, *The Tragedy of American Diplomacy* (New York, 1972), esp. chap. 2. For penetrating analyses of Williams as practitioner of ideological history, see Hunt, *Ideology and U.S. Foreign Policy*, 9–11; Michael Latham, *Modernization as Ideology* (Chapel Hill, N.C., 2000), 14.

17 Eric Foner, *Free Soil, Free Labor, Free Men* (New York, 1995), 4. Harold Lasswell casts his net even more broadly, defining ideology as "the thoughts, feelings, and conduct of human beings." Cited in Richard Burks, "A Conception of Ideology for Historians," *Journal of the History of Ideas* 10 (1949): 183.

18 Latham, *Modernization as Ideology*, 13. See also Emily Rosenberg, *Spreading the American Dream* (New York, 1982), 7.

19 See for example Gail Bederman, *Manliness and Civilization* (Chicago, 1995), 10; Mary Renda, *Taking Haiti* (Chapel Hill, N.C., 2001), 23, 26; Anders Stephanson, *Manifest Destiny* (New York, 1995), xiv.

20 Bederman, *Manliness and Civilization*, 24.

21   Robert Packenham, *Liberal America and the Third World* (Princeton, N.J., 1973), xix. Michael Shafer comes to a similar conclusion in his analysis of America's antiguerrilla efforts in the third world. See Shafer, *Deadly Paradigms* (Princeton, N.J., 1988), esp. part 2.

22   David Anderson, "Why Vietnam?: Postrevisionist Answers and a Neorealist Suggestion," *Diplomatic History* 13 (summer 1989): 427.

23   Stephanson, *Manifest Destiny*, xiv.

24   I. F. Stone, *The Hidden History of the Korean War* (New York, 1952); Paul Robeson Testimony, 12 June 1956, in *Thirty Years of Treason*, ed. Eric Bentley (New York, 2002), 770–89; Hans Morgenthau, *In Defense of the National Interest* (New York, 1951); Wilson cited in James Arnold, *The First Domino* (New York, 1991), 159–60, 235–36; Anthony Short, *The Origins of the Vietnam War* (New York, 1989), 195.

25   Clifford Geertz, "Ideology as a Cultural System," in *Ideology and Discontent*, ed. David Apter, 64–65 (New York, 1964).

26   Michael Hunt, "Ideology," in *Explaining the History of American Foreign Relations*, ed. Michael Hogan and Thomas Paterson, 193–94 (Cambridge, 1991). See also idem, *Ideology and U.S. Foreign Policy*, xi.

27   See Richard Immerman, *John Foster Dulles: Piety, Pragmatism, and Power in U.S. Foreign Policy* (Wilmington, Del., 1999); Michael Guhin, *John Foster Dulles: A Statesman and His Times* (New York, 1972); Frederick Marks, *Power and Peace: The Diplomacy of John Foster Dulles* (Westport, Conn., 1993); Ronald Pruessen, *John Foster Dulles* (New York, 1982).

28   Dulles address: "Principles in Foreign Policy," 11 April 1955, John Foster Dulles Papers, Seeley Mudd Library, Princeton University, Princeton, N.J. [hereafter Dulles Papers], box 335.

29   The most useful text, for my purposes, has been James Hudnut-Beumler, *Looking for God in the Suburbs* (New Brunswick, N.J., 1994). A. Roy Eckardt, *The Surge of Piety in America* (New York, 1958), offers an excellent contemporary account of the religious revival of the 1950s. Will Herberg's classic *Protestant-Catholic-Jew* (Garden City, N.Y., 1955) is indispensable reading. Other notable works are Sydney Ahlstrom, *A Religious History of the American People* (New Haven, Conn., 1972); Paul Boyer, *When Time Shall Be No More* (Cambridge, Mass., 1992); George Marsden, *Religion and American Culture* (San Diego, 1990); Mark Noll, ed., *Religion and American Politics* (New York, 1990); Mark Silk, *Spiritual Politics* (New York, 1988); J. Paul Williams, *What Americans Believe and How They Worship* (New York, 1962); Garry Wills, *Under God* (New York, 1990); Robert Wuthnow, *The Restructuring of American Religion* (Princeton, N.J., 1988).

30   Indeed, George Kennan once admonished Dulles, "Let us keep our morality to ourselves. With regard to other nations let us not judge, that we be not judged. Let us not attempt to constitute ourselves the guardian of everyone

else's virtue; we have enough trouble to guard our own." Cited in John Lewis Gaddis, *Strategies of Containment* (New York, 1982), 132. Wise counsel, although it might be argued that Kennan's words sat uncomfortably in the mouth of the man who closed his famous "X" article in 1947 by expressing "a certain gratitude to . . . Providence." George Kennan, "The Sources of Soviet Conduct," reprinted in *American Diplomacy, 1900–1950* (Chicago, 1951), 106.

31   Cited in Douglas Miller and Marion Nowak, *The Fifties: The Way We Really Were* (Garden City, N.Y., 1977), 92.

32   Ambassador George Allen, to whom Dulles directed this riposte, recalled that the secretary spoke "as if he had his own line to God" and that "he was getting his instructions from a very high source." Cited in Leonard Mosley, *Dulles* (New York, 1978), 256.

33   John Foster Dulles, "Faith of Our Fathers," in *The Spiritual Legacy of John Foster Dulles*, ed. Henry P. Van Dusen, 9 (Philadelphia, 1959); idem, "World Brotherhood through the State," ibid., 111. See also Thomas Kane, "The Missionary Theme in the Rhetoric of John Foster Dulles" (Ph.D. diss., University of Pittsburgh, 1968), 98–99. Dean Acheson, Dulles's predecessor as secretary of state, drew the same parallel, noting in his memoirs, "The threat to Western Europe seemed to me singularly like that which Islam had posed centuries before, with its combination of ideological zeal and fighting power." Acheson, *Present at the Creation* (New York, 1969), 490. Eisenhower sounded a similar theme in an address to the World Council of Churches in 1954. The president underscored the importance of "faith" in overcoming a redoubtable foe like the Soviet Union by reminding his audience of "just one instance: the First Crusade—1096. Five columns of individuals, starting in Europe, out of a great burst of faith in their ability to rescue the Holy Land from the infidel." Address at the Second Assembly of the World Council of Churches, Evanston, Ill., 19 August 1954, *Public Papers of the Presidents: Dwight D. Eisenhower, 1954* (Washington, 1955), 734–40. One wonders what Gamal Abdel Nasser or the Shah of Iran thought of Eisenhower's parallelism.

34   Townsend Hoopes, *The Devil and John Foster Dulles* (Boston, 1973), 255–56.

35   Cited in Stephen Whitfield, *The Culture of the Cold War* (Baltimore, 1996), 87.

36   Gordon Craig observes, "To establish the relationship between ideas and foreign policy is always a difficult task, and it is no accident that it has attracted so few historians." Craig, "Political and Diplomatic History," in *Historical Studies Today*, ed. Felix Gilbert and Stephen Graubard, 362 (New York, 1972).

37   H. W. Brands, *The Devil We Knew* (New York, 1993), 56.

38   Melani McAlister, *Epic Encounters* (Berkeley, Calif., 2001), 8–12. See also Douglas Little, *American Orientalism* (Chapel Hill, N.C., 2002); Edward Said, *Orientalism* (New York, 1979).

39 Barbara Fields, "Ideology and Race in American History," in *Region, Race, and Reconstruction*, ed. J. Morgan Kousser and James McPherson, 143–77 (New York, 1982).

40 Kennan, *American Diplomacy*, 96. In a 1942 lecture, Kennan asserted that communism had caused the Russians to "regress into a semi-Asiatic people." Cited in Frank Costigliola, " 'Unceasing Pressure for Penetration': Gender, Pathology, and Emotion in George Kennan's Formation of the Cold War," *Journal of American History* 86 (March 1997): 1323. For Kennan's attitude toward China, Korea, and mainland Asia in general, see Bruce Cumings, *The Origins of the Korean War* (Princeton, N.J., 1991), 2:55–56.

41 To cite just one example: Dulles's intimate collaboration with several Asian statesmen in forging the treaty of 1950 officially ending the Pacific War did not preclude him from observing on the occasion of the treaty's signing, "The Oriental mind . . . was always more devious than the Occidental mind." Dulles's remark is even more revealing when one considers he was addressing Wellington Koo, the ambassador from Nationalist China. Cited in John Dower, *War without Mercy* (New York, 1986), 310.

42 Renda, *Taking Haiti*, 303–4. See also Dower, *War without Mercy*; Richard Drinnon, *Facing West* (Minneapolis, 1980).

43 Wesley Fishel, "Vietnam's Democratic One-Man Rule," *New Leader* 42 (2 November 1956): 10–13.

44 Cited in telegram from the Ambassador in France to the Department of State, 11 May 1955, *Foreign Relations of the United States, 1955–57* (Washington, 1985), 1:393–99 [hereafter *FRUS*, followed by year and volume].

45 Marguerite Higgins, "Little Diem Called Big in Importance," *New York Herald Tribune*, 12 May 1957.

46 Cited in Drinnon, *Facing West*, 420.

47 Cited in Hammer, *Death in November*, 35.

48 Cited in Halberstam, *Best and the Brightest*, 147.

49 Cited in Eric Goldman, *The Crucial Decade and After* (New York, 1960), 116.

50 For examples of this kind of scholarship, see George Herring, *America's Longest War* (New York, 1986); Kahin, *Intervention*; Robert Schulzinger, *A Time for War* (New York, 1987).

51 Bruce Cumings, "The Poverty of Theory in Diplomatic History," reprinted in *America in the World*, ed. Michael Hogan, 35 (Cambridge, 1995).

52 See chapters 4 and 6.

53 See chapters 1 and 5.

54 Dower, *War without Mercy*, x.

55 Ibid., 69–71, 302.

56 Bederman, *Manliness and Civilization*, 10.

57 Robert McMahon review of Lloyd Gardner's *Approaching Vietnam* in *American Historical Review* 94 (December 1989): 1505–6.

58 Richard Slotkin, *Gunfighter Nation* (New York, 1993), 5.

59 Laura McEnaney, "He-Men and Christian Mothers: The America First Movement and the Gendered Meanings of Patriotism and Isolationism," *Diplomatic History* 18 (winter 1994): 47–57; Kristin Hoganson, *Fighting for American Manhood* (New Haven, Conn., 1998); Mary Dudziak, "Desegregation as a Cold War Imperative," *Stanford Law Review* 41 (November 1988): 61–121; Michelle Mart, "Tough Guys and American Cold War Policy: Images of Israel, 1948–1960," *Diplomatic History* 20 (summer 1996): 357–80; Geoffrey Smith, "National Security and Personal Isolation: Sex, Gender, and Disease in the Cold War United States," *International History Review* 14 (spring 1992): 307–37; Penny Von Eschen, *Race against Empire* (Ithaca, N.Y., 1996); Brenda Gayle Plummer, *Rising Wind* (Chapel Hill, N.C., 1996); Emily Rosenberg, " 'Foreign Affairs' after World War II: Connecting Sexual and International Politics," *Diplomatic History* 18 (winter 1994): 59–70; Robert Dean, *Imperial Brotherhood* (Amherst, Mass., 2001); Andrew Rotter, *Comrades at Odds* (Ithaca, N.Y., 2000).

60 Loren Baritz, *Backfire* (New York, 1985), 10.

61 Dower, *War without Mercy*, 157.

62 Clifford Geertz, *The Interpretation of Cultures* (New York, 1973), 232.

1. MR. DIEM GOES TO WASHINGTON

1 Cited in Denis Warner, *The Last Confucian* (New York, 1963), 98–99.

2 Graham Greene, "The Patriot Ruined by the West," *New Republic* 129 (16 May 1955): 13. For the *"My-Diem"* epithet, see Robert Scigliano, *South Vietnam* (Boston, 1963), 206–16; Neil Sheehan, *A Bright Shining Lie* (New York, 1988), 192.

3 The Chargé at Saigon to the Secretary of State, 23 June 1950, *FRUS, 1950*, 6:829. See also Secret Memo: The Catholic Position in Indo-China, 25 March 1950, Record Group 59, National Archives II, College Park, Md. [hereafter RG 59], 751G.00/3-2550; Bond to Neal, 18 May 1950, RG 59, 751G.00/5-1850.

4 Cited in Joseph Morgan, *The Vietnam Lobby* (Chapel Hill, N.C., 1997), 3.

5 John Cooney, *The American Pope* (New York, 1984), 240–41.

6 The Acting Secretary of State to the Legation at Saigon, 28 September 1950, *FRUS, 1950*, 6:885–86. See also the Secretary of State to the Legation in Saigon, 25 October 1950, ibid., 909–10; Little to McCune, 13 September 1950, box 10, lot 54D190, RG 59. Michigan State professor Wesley Fishel, who later became one of Diem's most effective American backers, advised the State Department in early 1951 that "Bishop Thuc is the better informed of the two and may well be the driving force behind Diem." Fishel found Diem "vague and general in his comments." Cited in Coors, Memorandum of Conversation with Wesley Fishel, 8 January 1951, RG 59, 751G.00/1-851.

7   Diem's plans in late 1950 are discussed in Memorandum of Conversation, Leader of Vietnamese Catholic Party, 15 January 1951, RG 59, 751G.00/1-1551.

8   Rusk to McGuire, 2 November 1950, RG 59, 851G.413/10-250. In 1956, McGuire informed the chairman of the American Friends of Vietnam (AFV), a pro-Diem organization, that "Ngo Dinh Diem is a friend of six years standing. In 1950, I did my best to have our State Department recognize his worth." McGuire to O'Daniel, 1 May 1956, American Friends of Vietnam Papers, Vietnam Archive, Texas Tech University, Lubbock [hereafter AFV Papers], box 4.

9   There are currently two full-length biographies of Diem, both badly flawed. Denis Warner's *Last Confucian* provides little information on its subject's early years, and Anthony Bouscaren's *Last of the Mandarins* is sheer hagiography. Both works were written decades before most key government documents relating to the Diem commitment were declassified. They remain useful sources of information and anecdote.

10 Bouscaren, *Last of the Mandarins*, 13.

11 Warner, *Last Confucian*, 88.

12 James Olson and Randy Roberts, *Where the Domino Fell* (New York, 1996), 56–57.

13 "South Vietnam: The Beleaguered Man," *Time* 65 (4 April 1955): 23–24.

14 Cited in Karnow, *Vietnam: A History*, 215.

15 Warner, *Last Confucian*, 90–91.

16 Karnow, *Vietnam: A History*, 215; Currey, *Edward Lansdale*, 376.

17 Boettcher, *Vietnam: The Valor and the Sorrow*, 106–7.

18 Cited in Bernard Fall, *The Two Viet-Nams* (New York, 1963), 239. See also Bruce McFarland Lockhart, *The End of the Vietnamese Monarchy* (New Haven, Conn., 1993), 81–84.

19 Edward Miller, "Confucianism and 'Confucian Learning' in South Vietnam during the Diem Years" [unpublished paper in author's possession]; Shaplen, *Lost Revolution*, 108–9; Sheehan, *Bright Shining Lie*, 176–77.

20 Lockhart, *End of the Vietnamese Monarchy*, 131–33; Olson and Roberts, *Where the Domino Fell*, 58.

21 Cited in Karnow, *Vietnam: A History*, 216–17. See also Marguerite Higgins, *Our Vietnam Nightmare* (New York, 1965), 46.

22 Lockhart, *End of the Vietnamese Monarchy*, 171; Shaplen, *Lost Revolution*, 111.

23 FitzGerald, *Fire in the Lake*, 103.

24 Morgan, *Vietnam Lobby*, 3.

25 The Secretary of State to the Legation in Saigon, 16 January 1951, *FRUS, 1951*, 7:348.

26 Coors Memorandum for the Record, 30 January 1951, RG 59, 751G.00/1-3051.

27 Hoey Memorandum for the Record, 15 January 1951, RG 59, Records of the Philippine and Southeast Asian Division, Country Files, 1923–53, box 7.

28 The Chargé in Saigon to the Secretary of State, 24 January 1951, *FRUS, 1951,* 7:360. See also Coors to Lyndman, 8 January 1951, RG 59, 751G.00/1-851; Cory to Ross, 21 July 1951, RG 59, 751G.00/7-2151.

29 Cooney, *American Pope,* 241, 243–44.

30 FitzGerald, *Fire in the Lake,* 123.

31 Cited in Mecklin, *Mission in Torment,* 31.

32 "South Vietnam: The Beleaguered Man," 23.

33 Hilaire du Berrier, *Background to Betrayal* (Belmont, Mass., 1965), 29; Fall, *Two Viet-Nams,* 238.

34 David Halberstam, *The Making of a Quagmire* (New York, 1988), 46–47.

35 For the clash of anticommunist and anticolonialist policy-making agendas in the Eisenhower administration, see Walter LaFeber, *America, Russia, and the Cold War, 1945–1992* (New York, 1993), 152–55.

36 Morgan, *Vietnam Lobby,* 12.

37 James Thomson et al., *Sentimental Imperialists* (New York, 1981), 310.

38 "'Two Go with Dulles: Senators Smith and Mansfield to Be Far East Advisers," *New York Times,* 20 August 1954; Press Release, 20 August 1954, Dulles Papers, box 84; Dulles address, 15 September 1954, Dulles Papers, box 87.

39 Senator H. Alexander Smith, Chairman, Subcommittee on the Far East, Senate Committee on Foreign Relations, "The Far East and South Asia," 25 January 1954, Douglas Pike Collection, Vietnam Archive, Texas Tech University, Lubbock [hereafter Pike Collection], unit III—Legislature, box 48.

40 Cory, Memorandum of Conversation with Mr. Ngo Dinh Diem, 21 July 1951, RG 59, 751G.00/7-2651.

41 Cited in Morgan, *Vietnam Lobby,* 4. See also James Fisher, *Dr. America* (Amherst, Mass., 1997), 105–6.

42 Patrick Allitt, *Catholic Intellectuals and Conservative Politics in America* (Ithaca, N.Y., 1991), 38.

43 Peter White, "An American in Vietnam," *Jubilee* 8 (July/August 1956): 7–14. See also idem, "American Mother," *Jubilee* 5 (October 1953): 6–15.

44 Cited in Morgan, *Vietnam Lobby,* 5. For background information on Emmet, see William Brownell, "The Vietnam Lobby" (Ph.D. diss., Columbia University, 1993), 144–46. Emmet drafted the official "Statement of Purpose" for the AFV. See Statement of Purpose, undated, AFV Papers, box 1.

45 Memorandum of Conversation, by the Deputy Assistant Secretary of State for Far Eastern Affairs, 8 August 1951, *FRUS, 1951,* 7:479–80. See also Kelly statement in support of Diem, submitted to the *Congressional Record,* 3 May 1956, AFV Papers, box 9; Oram to Kelly, 4 January 1956, ibid.; Kelly to Buttinger, 24 January 1955, Joseph Buttinger Papers, Harvard-Yenching Library, Harvard University, Cambridge, Mass. [hereafter Buttinger Papers].

46 Cited in David Anderson, *Trapped by Success* (New York, 1991), 75. For reviews of "Third Force" philosophy, see Mark Epstein, "The Third Force"

(Ph.D. diss., University of North Carolina, 1971); Packenham, *Liberal America and the Third World*. For contemporary examples of the theory's application to Southeast Asia, see Edwin Halsey, "The Third Force," *Integrity* 5 (May 1951): 33–39; Sol Sanders, "Viet Nam *Has* a Third Force," *New Republic* 125 (30 July 1951): 14–15.

47 For Fishel's role in Diem's rise to power, see John Ernst, *Forging a Fateful Alliance* (East Lansing, Mich., 1998), 8–16. See also *Final Report Covering Activities of the Michigan State Vietnam Advisory Group* (Saigon, 1962); Warren Hinkle et al., "The University on the Make," *Ramparts* 5 (25 January 1968): 58–60.

48 Chester Cooper briefly addresses Sacks's relationship with Diem in *Lost Crusade*, 125. See also Joseph Buttinger, *Vietnam: The Unforgettable Tragedy* (New York, 1977), 59. De Jaegher's close acquaintance with the future South Vietnamese premier is discussed in Minutes of Executive Committee Meeting, 28 September 1956, AFV Papers, box 1.

49 Morgan, *Vietnam Lobby*, 6.

50 Sol Sanders, *A Sense of Asia* (New York, 1969), 149–64; idem, "Crisis in Indo-China," *New Leader* 38 (21 March 1955): 3–5; idem, "My Friend Nguyen," *New Leader* 37 (26 July 1954): 11–12; idem, "One Way to Save Indo-China," *New Leader* 34 (27 August 1951): 8–9; Gouverneur Paulding, "Little Mr. Diem," *The Reporter* 11 (2 December 1954): 4.

51 Cited in Fisher, *Dr. America*, 107.

52 Brownell, "Vietnam Lobby," 173–74.

53 Philip Catton, *Diem's Final Failure* (Lawrence, Kans., 2002), 41–50. For other useful examinations of personalism, see Ashoka Chowdry, "President Diem's Political Philosophy," *Vietnam through Indian Eyes* (Saigon, 1960), 1–12; John Donnell, "Personalism in Vietnam," in *Problems of Freedom*, ed. Wesley Fishel, 27–69 (New York, 1961); Dennis Duncanson, *Government and Revolution in Vietnam* (New York, 1968), 215–19; FitzGerald, *Fire in the Lake*, 118–22; M. K. Haldar, *Asia: Challenge at Dawn* (Delhi, 1961); Neil Jamieson, *Understanding Vietnam* (Berkeley, Calif., 1993), 234; Ralph Johnson, "Confucian Political Influence on the South Vietnamese Government of Ngo Dinh Diem" (M.A. thesis, American University, 1978), 124–28; Nguyen Thai, "The Government of Men in the Republic of Vietnam" (Ph.D. diss., Michigan State University, 1962), 213–35.

54 Cited in Harrison, *Endless War*, 208.

55 Nguyen Khac Vien, "Confucianism and Marxism in Vietnam," in *Tradition and Revolution in Vietnam*, ed. David Marr and Jayne Werner, 17 (Berkeley, Calif., 1975).

56 Hammer, *Death in November*, 50.

57 See for example Herring, *America's Longest War*, 53. Kahin, *Intervention*, 93; William Turley, *The Second Indochina War* (Boulder, Colo., 1987), 13.

58 Catton, *Diem's Final Failure*, 35, 37.

59 Miller, "Confucianism and 'Confucian Learning' in South Vietnam."

60 Catton, *Diem's Final Failure*, 36. For the extent to which Vietnamese communists tried to attract a larger following by drawing parallels between Confucianism and Marxism, see David Marr, *Vietnamese Tradition on Trial* (Berkeley, Calif., 1984), 130–34; William Duiker, *Ho Chi Minh: A Biography* (New York, 2000), 63, 135–36, 555; Vien, "Confucianism and Marxism in Vietnam," 46–52.

61 Cited in Higgins, *Our Vietnam Nightmare*, 166.

62 Catton, *Diem's Final Failure*, 41–42.

63 The Ambassador in Saigon to the Department of State, 22 December 1958, *FRUS, 1958–60*, 1:109–13.

64 Cited in FitzGerald, *Fire in the Lake*, 109; Halberstam, *Making of a Quagmire*, 47.

65 Harold Isaacs, *Scratches on Our Minds* (Westport, Conn., 1958), 11–22, 274–75, 55, 220.

66 Walter Hixson, *Parting the Curtain* (New York, 1997), 25.

67 White House Office, National Security Council Staff: Papers, 1948–61, OCB Central File Series: Special Committee Report on Southeast Asia, 5 April 1954: box 79, Dwight D. Eisenhower Library, Abilene, Kansas [hereafter EL].

68 White House Office, National Security Council Staff: Papers, 1948–61, OCB Central File Series: Application of "Project Action"—Vietnam, 24 May 1955: box 39, EL.

69 *Executive Sessions of the Senate Foreign Relations Committee*, "Report on Indochina," 83d Cong., 2d Sess., 16 February 1954 (Washington, 1977), 6:143–44.

70 AFV Circular, 1957, AFV Papers, box 11. For Buttinger's scholarly reputation during the Eisenhower years, see Mark Bradley, *Imagining Vietnam and America* (Chapel Hill, N.C., 2000), 213.

71 Graves to Mansfield, 1 December 1954, Mike Mansfield Papers, Maureen and Mike Mansfield Library, University of Montana, Missoula [hereafter Mansfield Papers], series XIII, box 6.

72 "Special Study Mission to Southeast Asia and the Pacific," 29 January 1954, Pike Collection, unit III—Legislature, box 48.

73 Cited in Paul Carter, *Another Part of the Fifties* (New York, 1983), 117–26.

74 William O. Douglas, *North from Malaya* (Garden City, N.Y., 1953), 180–81.

75 Cited in Morgan, *Vietnam Lobby*, 10. See also James Simon, *Independent Journey* (New York, 1980), 324–25.

76 Gregory Olson, *Mansfield and Vietnam* (East Lansing, Mich., 1995), 12. See also Louis Baldwin, *Hon. Politician* (Missoula, Mont., 1989), 13–18; Don Oberdorfer, *Senator Mansfield* (Washington, 2003), 78–81; Francis Valeo, *Mike Mansfield, Majority Leader* (Armonk, N.Y., 1999), 184–92.

77 Cited in William Conrad Gibbons, *The U.S. Government and the Vietnam War* (Princeton, N.J., 1986), 1:52.

78 "Lecture Notes on Indo-China," undated, Mansfield Papers, series IV, box 6.

79 Cited in Olson, *Mansfield and Vietnam*, 11.

80 For a vivid example of this rhetorical inclination, see Mansfield address: "American Foreign Policy in the Far East," 22 May 1955, Mansfield Papers, series XXI, box 37.

81 Cited in Michael Charlton and Richard Moncrieff, *Many Reasons Why* (New York, 1977), 54. See also Oberdorfer, *Senator Mansfield*, 118. In fact, Justice Douglas was not Catholic. William Brennan Jr. was the only Catholic on the Supreme Court at the time.

82 Douglas, *North from Malaya*, 188.

83 I am indebted to Dr. Shibusawa for alerting me to this case. All of the press quotes are from her book *America's Geisha Ally* (Cambridge, Mass., forthcoming), 316–42.

84 Nguyen-Thai to Mansfield, 17 March 1954, plus enclosed *Shield* article, 15 October 1953, Mansfield Papers, series XIII, box 8.

85 Mansfield to Nguyen-Thai, 19 March 1954, Mansfield Papers, series XIII, box 8.

86 For the dismal state of American knowledge with regard to Vietnam, see White House Central Files, Confidential File, Subject Series, Department of State: Pruett to Edman, 5 August 1953: box 67, EL. See also Mill to Mansfield, 16 December 1954, Mansfield Papers, series XIII, box 6; Graves to Mansfield, 1 December 1954, ibid.

87 Bradley, *Imagining Vietnam and America*, 207.

88 Virginia Thompson, *French Indochina* (New York, 1968), 248, 43, 357–58, 469–71, 333, 47, 474.

89 Thomas Ennis, *French Policy and Developments in Indochina* (New York, 1936), 192, 134. For use of Ennis's works by the U.S. diplomatic corps, see Bradley, *Imagining Vietnam and America*, 207. Mona Gardner's *Menacing Sun*, another ostensibly authoritative work on Indochina by a veteran Asia correspondent, also dwelled upon the peculiar inertia of the Vietnamese. Gardner described "weak husks of men who seem like stagnant blots. . . . Everyone, even the children, moves with a queer devitalized motion. . . . [T]hey seem too finely bred, as though the long civilization behind them has made them tired, too tired to change, and that in the process strong emotions and passion have been drained from them." Gardner, *Menacing Sun* (London, 1939), 16.

90 Memorandum of Conversation by Edmund A. Gullion of the Policy Planning Staff, 7 May 1953, *FRUS, 1952–54*, 13:553–54.

91 Cooper, *Lost Crusade*, 122–24.

92 The best military account of the Franco–Viet Minh war is Phillip Davidson, *Vietnam at War* (New York, 1991), 35–311.

93 *Executive Sessions of the Senate Foreign Relations Committee*, "Report on a Study Mission to the Associated States of Indochina," 83d Cong., 2d Sess., 16 February 1954, 6:46–53.

94 The classic history of the battle of Dien Bien Phu is Bernard Fall, *Hell in a Very Small Place* (New York, 1968). See also Donald Simpson, *Dien Bien Phu* (Washington, 1994).

95 Mansfield speech: "The Western Pacific Perspective and Prospective," 25 May 1967, Mansfield Papers, series XII, box 76.

96 See Melanie Billings-Yun, *Decision against War* (New York, 1988); John Burke and Fred Greenstein, *How Presidents Test Reality* (New York, 1989), 28–115, 256–300; George Herring and Richard Immerman, "Eisenhower, Dulles, and Dien Bien Phu: 'The Day We Didn't Go to War' Revisited," *Journal of American History* 71 (September 1984): 343–63.

97 Anderson, *Trapped by Success*, 65, 200.

98 Minutes of National Security Council Meeting, 4 February 1954, *FRUS, 1952–54*, 13:1014–15.

99 Cited in John Newhouse, *War and Peace in the Nuclear Age* (Garden City, N.Y., 1985), 59.

100 *Executive Sessions of the Senate Foreign Relations Committee*, "Report on Indochina," 83d Cong., 2d Sess., 16 February 1954, 143.

101 Arnold, *First Domino*, 342.

102 White House National Security Staff, Papers, 1948–61: OCB Central File Series: "Recommendations Concerning Study of Religious Factors in International Strategy," 13 April 1955: box 2, EL.

103 For the Eisenhower administration's "psywar" activities, see Stephen Ambrose, *Ike's Spies* (Garden City, N.Y., 1980); Blanche Weisen Cook, *The Declassified Eisenhower* (Garden City, N.Y., 1981).

104 Tuchman, *March of Folly*, 265.

105 White House National Security Staff, Papers, 1945–61: OCB Central Files Series: "Proposals Regarding U.S. Relations with Therawada Buddhist Countries," early draft, undated: box 2, EL.

106 White House National Security Staff, Papers, 1945–61: OCB Central Files Series: Memorandum of Meeting, Committee on Buddhism, 31 May 1956: box 2, EL.

107 White House National Security Staff, Papers, 1945–61: OCB Central Files Series: Young to Landon, 26 August 1956: box 2, EL.

108 White House National Security Staff, Papers, 1945–61: OCB Central Files Series: Outline Plan Regarding Buddhist Organizations [final draft], 16 January 1957: box 2, EL.

109 McClintock to Dulles, 6 May 1954, RG 59, 751G.00/5-654; McClintock to Dulles, 9 June 1954, RG 59, 751G.00/6-954. See also Reinhardt to Dulles, 13 October 1955, RG 59, 751G.00/10-1355.

110 U.S. Department of State Working Paper: "North Vietnamese Role in the War in South Vietnam," October 1955, Pike Collection, unit VI—Republic of Vietnam, box 12.

111 State Department Intelligence Report No. 6431: "Major Non-Communist Political Parties and Religious and Armed Groups in the State of Vietnam," 28 September 1953, RG 59, General Records of the Department of State, Research and Analysis Branch (OSS) and Bureau of Intelligence and Research, Intelligence Reports, October 1941–August 1961, box 299. See also "Programs for the Implementation of U.S. Policy Towards South Vietnam," 22 April 1955, RG 59, 751G.00/4-2255.

112 Stuart to Hoey, 10 May 1954, RG 59, 751G.00/5-1154. See also Drumright to Murphy, 11 May 1954, RG 59, 751G.00/5-1154.

113 Cited in Kidder report: "Political Conditions in Vietnam," 5 May 1954, RG 59, 751G.00/5-554.

114 McClintock to Dulles, 27 June 1954, RG 59, 751G.00/6-2754.

115 For examples of this argument, see Anderson, *Trapped by Success*, 52–57; Cooper, *Lost Crusade*, 126–28; Lloyd Gardner, *Approaching Vietnam* (New York, 1988), 292–93; Herring, *America's Longest War*, 49–50.

116 Heath to Dulles, 4 July 1954, RG 59, 751G.00/7-454.

117 Cited in the Ambassador in France to the Department of State, 20 June 1954, *FRUS, 1952–54*, 13:1725–27. Maurice DeJean, former French commissioner general in Indochina, characterized Diem as "too narrow, too rigid, too unworldly, and too pure to have any chance of creating an effective government in Vietnam." Cited in the Chargé at Saigon to the Department of State, 13 June 1954, *FRUS, 1952–54*, 13:1685. The archival record indicates that French civilian and military authorities unanimously disapproved of Diem's appointment.

118 Jean Sainteny, *Ho Chi Minh and His Vietnam*, trans. Herma Briffault (Chicago, 1972), 107–8.

119 The Ambassador in Saigon to the Department of State, 24 January 1951, *FRUS, 1951*, 6:359.

120 Cited in Anderson, *Trapped by Success*, 54. The South Vietnamese politician Phan Huy Quat advised U.S. Ambassador to Cambodia Robert McClintock that "Diem has been appointed because Bao Dai expected that this appointment would bring immediate direct American aid." Cited in McClintock to Dulles, 5 June 1954, RG 59, 751G.00/6-554. See also Lockhart, *End of the Vietnamese Monarchy*, 172–73.

121 Smith to Dulles, 17 May 1954, RG 59, 751G.00/5-1754.

122 Memorandum of Conversation, 18 May 1954, RG 59, 751G.00/5–1854. Luyen bore a letter from Bao Dai empowering him "to provide and receive on my behalf any information, explanation, or proposal." The Chief of the State of Vietnam to His Excellency the Chief of the Delegation of the United States of America to the Geneva Conference, 13 May 1954, RG 59, 751G.00/5-1354.

123 Bonsal to Smith, 19 May 1954, RG 59, 751G.00/5-1954.

124 Bonsal Memorandum of Conversation with Luyen, 20 May 1954, *FRUS, 1952–54*, 16:859–62.

125 Cited in Anderson, *Trapped by Success*, 55.

126 The Secretary of State to the United States Delegation, 22 May 1954, *FRUS, 1952–54*, 16:892. See also Heath to Bonsal, 25 May 1954, RG 59, 751G.00/5-2554.

127 Duff to Dulles, 6 January 1953, Dulles Papers, box 69.

128 Dulles to Duff, 28 January 1953, Dulles Papers, box 69.

129 Interview with John Hanes, 29 January and 12 August 1966, John Foster Dulles Oral History Project, Seeley Mudd Library, Princeton University, Princeton, N.J. [hereafter DOHP].

130 Cited in Anderson, *Trapped by Success*, 55.

131 Heath Memorandum of Conversation, 24 April 1954, *FRUS, 1952–54*, 13:1384–85.

132 Cooper, *Lost Crusade*, 126–27.

133 USARMLO to Dulles, 1 June 1954, RG 59, 751G.00/6-154.

134 Anderson, *Trapped by Success*, 55; Du Berrier, *Background to Betrayal*, 29.

135 Cameron to Dulles, 26 May 1954, RG 59, 751G.00/5-2654.

136 McClintock to Dulles, 25 May 1954, RG 59, 751G.00/5-2554.

137 Dillon to Dulles, 9 June 1954, RG 59, 751G.00/6-954. See also Bedell Smith to Dulles, 25 May 1954, RG 59, 751G.00/5-2554; McClintock to Dulles, 27 May 1954, RG 59, 751G.00/5-2755; Cameron to Dulles, 5 June 1954, RG 59, 751G.00/6-554; Heath to Dulles, 21 June 1954, RG 59, 751G.00/6-2154.

138 Cited in Heath to Dulles, 11 March 1954, RG 59, 751G.00/3-1154.

139 Memorandum of Meeting, 14 June 1954, *FRUS, 1952–54*, 16:1134–36.

140 Dillon to Dulles, 25 May 1954, RG 59, 751G.00/5-2554.

141 Free Translation, Message from Bao Dai to the Vietnamese People Issued at Paris, 17 June 1954, on the Occasion of a Change in Premiership in Vietnam, RG 59, 751G.00/6-1754.

142 McClintock to Dulles, 18 June 1954, RG 59, 751G.00/6-1854.

143 Karnow, *Vietnam: A History*, 218. Diem himself noted in an interview years later that when he returned to Vietnam, it "looked like France at the time of Joan of Arc." Cited in Shaplen, *Lost Revolution*, 113.

144 Collins Papers: USARMA Saigon to DEPTAR Washington, 25 August 1954: box 26, EL.

145 Du Berrier, *Background to Betrayal*, 29.

146 Buttinger, *Vietnam: A Dragon Embattled*, 851.

147 Edward Lansdale, *In the Midst of Wars* (New York, 1972), 156–57.

148 Warner, *Last Confucian*, 90.

2. AMERICA'S THIRD GREAT AWAKENING

1 Cited in LaFeber, *America, Russia, and the Cold War*, 66.

2 Cited in Andrew Rotter, "Christians, Muslims, and Hindus: Religion and U.S.-South Asian Relations, 1947–1954," *Diplomatic History* 24 (fall 2000): 596.

3 Cited in Hudnut-Beumler, *Looking for God*, 50.

4 John Winthrop, "A Model of Christian Charity," in *The Boisterous Sea of Liberty*, ed. David Brion Davis and Steven Mintz, 65–66 (New York, 1998).

5 Cited in Wills, *Under God*, 218.

6 "President Woodrow Wilson's War Message, 1917," *Major Problems in American Foreign Relations*, ed. Dennis Merrill and Thomas Paterson, 2:38–40 (Boston, 2000); "Roosevelt's War Message, 1941," ibid., 131–32.

7 Ronald Oakley, *God's Country* (New York, 1986).

8 Cited in Mark Toulouse, *The Transformation of John Foster Dulles* (Macon, Ga., 1985), 217.

9 Cited in Piero Gheddo, *The Cross and Bo-Tree*, trans. Charles Quinn (New York, 1970), 115.

10 Robert Handy, "The American Religious Depression, 1925–1935," *Church History* 29 (March 1960): 3–16.

11 "Humanist Manifesto," in *American Political Theology*, ed. Charles Dunn, 98–100 (New York, 1984).

12 Cited in Handy, "American Religious Depression," 7.

13 "Protestant Architect," *Time* 62 (19 April 1954): 62.

14 Cited in Miller and Nowak, *Fifties*, 84; William O'Neill, *American High* (New York, 1986), 212.

15 Miller and Nowak, *Fifties*, 87; Oakley, *God's Country*, 326.

16 "Growth of U.S. Churches," *Time* 57 (2 April 1951): 81.

17 Leo Ribuffo, "God and Contemporary Politics," *Journal of American History* 80 (March 1993): 1517–18.

18 Cited in Miller and Nowak, *Fifties*, 85.

19 "I Believe . . . ," *Newsweek* 40 (20 October 1952): 106. See also "The Proof of God," *Time* 65 (10 January 1955): 60.

20 Cited in O'Neill, *American High*, 212.

21 See for example Warren Weaver, "Peace of Mind," *Saturday Review* 38 (11 December 1954): 11, 47–50; Harry Meserve, "The New Piety," *Atlantic Monthly* 196 (June 1955): 34–38.

22 Herberg, *Protestant-Catholic-Jew*, 54.

23 Reinhold Niebuhr, "Varieties of Religious Revival," *New Republic* 129 (6 June 1955): 13–16.

24 Cited in Paul Hutchinson, "Have We a 'New' Religion?" *Life* 38 (11 April 1955): 140.

25 Cited in Oakley, *God's Country*, 320.

26 "Dial-A-Prayer," *Newsweek* 49 (4 July 1955): 23.

27 Cited in "Dial Trinity 5-7561," *Newsweek* 51 (3 September 1956): 56.

28 Hutchinson, "Have We a 'New' Religion?" 138–42.

29 Stanley Rowland, "Suburbia Buys Religion," *Nation* 184 (28 July 1956): 79.

30 Hudnut-Beumler, *Looking for God*, 47.

31 Cited in "Power of Prayer," *Newsweek* 42 (14 January 1952): 75.

32 Cited in Hutchinson, "Have We a 'New' Religion?" 139.

33 Gordon Gow, *Hollywood in the Fifties* (New York, 1971), 11–37. See also Alan Nadel, "God's Law and the Wide Screen," in *Containment Culture*, ed. Alan Nadel, 90–116 (Durham, N.C., 1995).

34 Cited in McAlister, *Epic Encounters*, 44.

35 Whitfield, *Culture of the Cold War*, 86.

36 Cited in Eric Goldman, "Goodbye to the Fifties—and Good Riddance," *Harper's* 214 (January 1960): 28–29.

37 Eddie Cantor, "Greater Than the H-Bomb," *Reader's Digest* 65 (September 1953): 7.

38 A. Roy Eckardt, "The New Look in American Piety," *Christian Century* 71 (17 November 1954): 1395.

39 Oakley, *God's Country*, 320.

40 Cited in Arthur Shulman and Roger Youman, *How Sweet It Was* (New York, 1966), 301. For Sheen's television career, see James Breig, "Fulton Sheen: And Now a Word with His Sponsor," *U.S. Catholic* 45 (February 1980): 24–28; Kathleen Fields, "Bishop Fulton J. Sheen: An American Response to the Twentieth Century" (Ph.D. diss., University of Notre Dame, 1988); Jeffrey Hadden and Charles Swann, *Prime Time Preachers* (Reading, Mass., 1981); D. P. Noonan, *Missionary with a Mike* (New York, 1968).

41 Whitfield, *Culture of the Cold War*, 84.

42 In 1953, Peale's self-help gospel sold more copies than any other book, fiction or nonfiction, except the Bible. William Miller, "Some Negative Thinking about Norman Vincent Peale," *Reporter* 13 (7 January 1955): 19.

43 Hudnut-Beumler, *Looking for God*, 48, 60.

44 Cited in Miller and Nowak, *Fifties*, 87.

45 Gerald Weales, "The Family that Prays Together Weighs Together," *New Republic* 131 (25 March 1957): 19–20; "The Power of the Brief Burst," *Time* 73 (13 April 1959): 95–96.

46 Hudnut-Beumler, *Looking for God*, 47.

47 Walter Ong, *Frontiers in American Catholicism* (New York, 1957), 32. For the

extent to which Luce shaped popular opinion in the early cold war years, see James Baughman, *Henry R. Luce and the Rise of the American News Media* (Boston, 1987); John Kobler, *Luce: His Time, Life, and Fortune* (New York, 1968); W. A. Swanberg, *Luce and His Empire* (New York, 1972). For Wallace's impact, see John Heidenry, *Theirs Was the Kingdom* (New York, 1993); Samuel Schreiner Jr., *The Condensed World of the Reader's Digest* (New York, 1977); Joanne Sharp, *Condensing the Cold War* (Minneapolis, 2000).

48 Henry Luce, "A Path to Peace through Prayer," *Life* 35 (13 September 1954): 48. Such Madison Avenue proselytism inspired the Jewish theologian Milton Rosenberg to pen the following couplet: *"Luce does more than Niebuhr can / To justify God's ways to man."* Cited in Martin Marty, *The New Shape of American Religion* (New York, 1959), 17.

49 Henry Luce, "The Churches of America," *Life* 34 (6 April 1953): 24.

50 "Mighty Wave Over the U.S.," *Life* 39 (26 December 1955): 45.

51 Cited in Miller and Nowak, *Fifties*, 90.

52 Whitfield, *Culture of the Cold War*, 88.

53 Norman Rosenberg and Emily Rosenberg, *In Our Times* (Englewood Cliffs, N.J., 1995), 64.

54 Inaugural address, 20 January 1953, *Public Papers of the Presidents: Dwight D. Eisenhower, 1953* (Washington, 1954), 1–6.

55 Cited in James Patterson, *Grand Expectations* (New York, 1996), 329.

56 Message to the National Conference of Christians and Jews, 9 July 1953, *Public Papers of the Presidents: Dwight D. Eisenhower, 1953*, 489–90.

57 Remarks Recorded for the "Back to God" Program of the American Legion, 20 February 1955, *Public Papers of the Presidents: Dwight D. Eisenhower, 1955* (Washington, 1956), 273–74.

58 Carter, *Another Part of the Fifties*, 125.

59 Stanley High, "What the President Wants," *Reader's Digest* 65 (April 1953): 2–4.

60 Elinor Smith, "Won't Somebody Please Tolerate Me?" *Harper's* 212 (August 1956): 36–38.

61 George Kennan, "Overdue Changes in Our Foreign Policy," ibid., 27–33.

62 Cited in Carter, *Another Part of the Fifties*, 114.

63 Remarks to the Daughters of the American Revolution, 22 April 1954 in *Public Papers of the Presidents: Dwight D. Eisenhower, 1954*, 403.

64 "The Testimony of a Devout President," *Life* 39 (26 December 1955): 12–13.

65 Message for the Fourth of July Ceremonies at Independence Hall, 4 July 1954 in *Public Papers of the Presidents: Dwight D. Eisenhower, 1954*, 617. For Eisenhower's post-oration activities, see William Miller, *Piety along the Potomac* (Boston, 1964), 42.

66 Hunt, *Ideology and U.S. Foreign Policy*, 15.

67 Samuel Flagg Bemis, preface to Louis Gerson, *John Foster Dulles* (New York, 1967), xi.

68   Hoopes, *Devil and John Foster Dulles*, 184–85, 491.

69   Cited in Anthony Eden, *Full Circle* (Boston, 1960), 71; John Moran, *Winston Churchill and the Struggle for Survival* (London, 1966), 508.

70   Cited in David Finlay et al., *Enemies in Politics* (Chicago, 1967), 37.

71   Roscoe Drummond, *Duel at the Brink* (New York, 1960), 76–77.

72   Among the religious figures who attest to advising Dulles from 1953 until the secretary's death in 1959 are Roswell Barnes: Interview, 24 July 1964; Yaacov Herzog: Interview, 27 May 1964; Henry Leiper: Interview, 7 May 1965; Frederick Nolde: Interview, 2 June 1965, DOHP.

73   Cited in Bemis, preface to Gerson, *John Foster Dulles*, xi.

74   Address at the First Presbyterian Church, Watertown, N.Y., 11 October 1953, Dulles Papers, box 309.

75   Cited in Hoopes, *Devil and John Foster Dulles*, 11. See also Immerman, *John Foster Dulles*, 2–3.

76   Pruessen, *John Foster Dulles*, 11. Dulles's close friend once remarked, "Foster, your mother must have been terribly disappointed when you didn't become a minister." Dulles responded, "Nearly broke her heart." Cited in Van Dusen, *Spiritual Legacy of John Foster Dulles*, xxii.

77   John Foster Dulles, "Moral Force in World Affairs," *Presbyterian Life* 1 (10 April 1948): 13. See also idem, "I Was a Nominal Christian," *Challenge* 4 (January-March 1942): 45–49; "The Churches and World Order," 20 May 1951, Dulles Papers, box 290; "Faith of Our Fathers," 1 January 1954, Dulles Papers, box 58.

78   See for example John Foster Dulles, "Challenge of Today," *Department of State Bulletin* 24 (11 June 1951): 935–37; "A Diplomat and His Faith," *Christian Century* 69 (19 March 1952): 336–38; "Foreign Policy: Ideals Not Deals," *Commercial and Financial Chronicle* 165 (20 February 1947): 996; "Moral Leadership," *Vital Speeches of the Day* 14 (15 July 1948): 581–83.

79   Toulouse, *Transformation of John Foster Dulles*, 61.

80   John Foster Dulles, *War, Peace, and Change* (New York, 1939), 12–19.

81   Report to Federal Council of Churches, August 1942, Dulles Papers, box 282.

82   Dulles address: "The Church's Role in Developing the Bases of a Just and Durable Peace," 28 May 1941, Dulles Papers, box 290.

83   Richard Goold-Adams, *John Foster Dulles: A Reappraisal* (London, 1974), 31.

84   John Foster Dulles, *War or Peace* (New York, 1950), 7–19.

85   John Foster Dulles, "A Righteous Faith," *Life* 13 (28 December 1942): 49–51. See also idem, "How to Take the Offensive for Peace," *Life* 29 (24 April 1950): 130–36; "A Policy of Boldness," *Life* 33 (19 May 1952): 146–61; "Thoughts on Soviet Foreign Policy and What to Do About It: Part I," *Life* 21 (3 June 1946): 113–26; "Thoughts on Soviet Foreign Policy and What To Do About It: Part II," *Life* 21 (10 June 1946): 119–30.

86   Henry Van Dusen observes that "a study of John Foster Dulles's vocabulary,

particularly at those times when he was speaking from central conviction and to the crucial point, discovers a single phrase occurring over and over again like a reiterated refrain: 'a *righteous* and *dynamic* faith.' . . . '*Dynamic*.' One of the great, recurring words. . . . Dynamic—the very temper of the Pilgrim." Van Dusen, *Spiritual Legacy of John Foster Dulles*, xiv.

87   Dulles address: "Is Containment Enough?" 9 October 1952, Dulles Papers, box 309.

88   Transcript of address in Hartford *Courant*, 12 October 1949, Dulles Papers, box 289.

89   Dulles address: "Freedom and Its Purpose," 11 December 1952, Dulles Papers, box 309; Dulles, "Moral Force in World Affairs," 29.

90   Dulles, "A Policy of Boldness," 146–61.

91   Dulles address before the Foreign Policy Association, 16 February 1955, Dulles Papers, box 98.

92   Cited in Hagerty Papers, Diary Entries: 23 May 1954: box 1a, EL.

93   Dulles, "Moral Force in World Affairs," 31. "To the extent that the Western powers have any policy at all to counter, in Asia, the revolutionary threat of Soviet communism," Dulles once attested, "they can thank the Christian missionaries." Dulles address: "The Spiritual Bases of Peace," 9 January 1950, Dulles Papers, box 301.

94   Cited in Marks, *Power and Peace*, 33.

95   Eisenhower revisionism has become a cottage industry. For a synopsis, see Stephen Rabe, "Eisenhower Revisionism: The Scholarly Debate," in *America in the World*, ed. Michael Hogan, 300–326 (Cambridge, 1995). See also Vincent DeSantis, "Eisenhower Revisionism," *Review of Politics* 38 (April 1976): 190–207. The classic texts of Eisenhower revisionism are Stephen Ambrose, *Eisenhower*, vol. 2 (New York, 1984); Robert Divine, *Eisenhower and the Cold War* (New York, 1981); Fred Greenstein, *The Hidden-Hand Presidency* (New York, 1982).

96   Ambrose, *Eisenhower*, 2:10.

97   Arthur Schlesinger Jr., *The Cycles of American History* (Boston, 1986), 394, 390.

98   Hans-Jurgen Grabbe, "Konrad Adenauer, John Foster Dulles, and West German-American Relations," in *John Foster Dulles and the Diplomacy of the Cold War*, ed. Richard Immerman, 109–32 (Princeton, 1990).

99   Cited in Immerman, introduction, *John Foster Dulles and the Diplomacy of the Cold War*, 3–4.

100   The President's News Conference of 30 January 1957, *Public Papers of the Presidents: Dwight D. Eisenhower, 1957* (Washington, 1958), 100–101.

101   Interview with Henry Luce, 28 July 1965, DOHP.

102   John Foster Dulles, "The Power of Moral Forces," *Spiritual Legacy of John Foster Dulles*, 223.

103 Thomas McAvoy, *A History of the Catholic Church in the United States* (South Bend, Ind., 1969), 445.

104 James Hennesey, *American Catholics* (New York, 1981), 283–84. See also Patrick Carey, *The Roman Catholics in America* (Westport, Conn., 1996), 93.

105 Charles Morris, *American Catholic* (New York, 1997), 223. A census of 1957 estimated that 26 percent of American households were Catholic. Cited in David Caute, *The Great Fear* (New York, 1978), 108.

106 For a detailed statistical analysis of the baby boom phenomenon, see Richard Easterlin, *Birth and Fortune* (New York, 1980).

107 Morris, *American Catholic*, 223.

108 Cited in Hennesey, *American Catholics*, 286.

109 Carey, *Roman Catholics in America*, 93–94.

110 John Ellis, "American Catholics and Intellectual Life," *Thought* 30 (Autumn 1955): 351.

111 Dolan, *American Catholic Experience*, 400.

112 Morris, *American Catholic*, 224.

113 Carey, *Roman Catholics in America*, 108–9.

114 Marty, *New Shape of American Religion*, 74.

115 Morris, *American Catholic*, 224.

116 Paul Blanshard, *American Freedom and Catholic Power* (Boston, 1949), 269–70.

117 James Fisher, *The Catholic Counterculture in America* (Chapel Hill, N.C., 1989), 158.

118 Morris, *American Catholic*, 247.

119 Ibid., 225.

120 Dolan, *American Catholic Experience*, 392–94.

121 Oakley, *God's Country*, 323.

122 James Fisher, *Communion of Immigrants* (New York, 2002), 127–28.

123 Marty, *New Shape of American Religion*, 74.

124 Patrick Allitt, *Catholic Intellectuals and Conservative Politics in America* (Ithaca, N.Y., 1993), 23.

125 David O'Brien, *American Catholics and Social Reform* (New York, 1968), 82. See also Robert Frank, "Prelude to Cold War: American Catholics and Communism," *Journal of Church and State* 86 (winter 1992): 39–56.

126 David Valaik, "American Catholics and the Second Spanish Republic," *Journal of Church and State* 58 (winter 1968): 13–28.

127 George Sirgiovanni, *An Undercurrent of Suspicion* (New Brunswick, N.J., 1990), 151. For Catholic attitudes toward Mussolini, see John Diggins, "American Catholics and Italian Fascism," *Journal of Contemporary History* 2 (October 1967): 51–68. For American Catholic attitudes toward Nazi Germany, see Edward Cuddy, "Pro-Germanism and American Catholicism," *Catholic Historical Review* 54 (October 1968): 427–54; Thomas McAvoy,

"American Catholics and the Second World War," *Review of Politics* 69 (April 1954): 131–50.

128 Nathan Glazer and Daniel Patrick Moynihan, *Beyond the Melting Pot* (Cambridge, Mass., 1970), 271. James Fisher, whose treatment of Catholic anticommunism is the best in the literature, notes, "One thing which can be said for certain (and that definitely could not be said with respect to other Christian denominations) is that no one in America in the 1940s and early 1950s believed it was possible to be at once a Catholic and a communist, socialist, or self-styled Marxist of any flavor." Fisher, *Catholic Counterculture in America*, 152.

129 Cited in Fisher, *Catholic Counterculture in America*, 154.

130 O'Brien, *American Catholics and Social Reform*, 96.

131 The best biography of Spellman is Robert Gannon, *The Cardinal Spellman Story* (New York, 1963). For representative treatments of Spellman in the mid-1950s, see John Cogley, "Who Will Be the Next Pope?" *Collier's* 131 (14 March 1953): 22–36; "Fast-Traveling Cardinal: His Fast-Growing Church," *Newsweek* 44 (24 May 1954): 57.

132 Cited in Whitfield, *Culture of the Cold War*, 96.

133 Cited in Gannon, *Cardinal Spellman Story*, 338.

134 Cited in Cooney, *American Pope*, 165.

135 Whitfield, *Culture of the Cold War*, 96.

136 Louis Budenz, *This Is My Story* (New York, 1947). For an account of Budenz's career, see Herbert Packer, *Ex-Communist Witnesses* (Stanford, Calif., 1962), 121–77.

137 For the Catholic component in McCarthy's popular support, see David Oshinsky, *A Conspiracy So Immense* (New York, 1983), 305–7.

138 Donald Crosby, *God, Church, and Flag* (Chapel Hill, N.C., 1978), 231. Crosby belittles this statistic, asking, "Can anyone seriously argue that a spread of 10 points constitutes a major difference?" In fact, it does constitute a major difference. Ten points higher in America's largest denomination translates into a formidable number of people.

139 William F. Buckley and Brent Bozell, *McCarthy and His Enemies* (Washington, 1953), 335. See also Vincent De Santis, "American Catholics and McCarthyism," *Catholic Historical Review* 51 (April 1965): 1–30.

140 Cooney, *American Pope*, 216–20.

141 James Miller, "Taking off the Gloves: The United States and the Italian Elections of 1948," *Diplomatic History* 7 (winter 1983): 35–55; Wendy Wall, "America's 'Best Propagandists': Italian Americans and the 1948 'Letters to Italy' Campaign," in *Cold War Constructions*, ed. Christian Appy, 89–109 (Amherst, Mass., 2000).

142 Garry Wills, *Nixon Agonistes* (New York, 1970), 26–30.

143 Morris, *American Catholic*, 246–49, 466.

144 Walter Lippmann, *The Public Philosophy* (New York, 1955), 11.

145 Cited in Ronald Steel, *Walter Lippmann and the American Century* (New York, 1980), 491.

146 Lippmann, *Public Philosophy*, 133.

147 Steel, *Walter Lippmann and the American Century*, 491. See also Allitt, *Catholic Intellectuals*, 7–8.

148 Cited in Carter, *Another Part of the Fifties*, 126.

149 Morris, *American Catholic*, ix.

150 Cited in Miller and Nowak, *Fifties*, 91.

151 Cited in Toulouse, *Transformation of John Foster Dulles*, 221.

152 See John McGreevy, "Thinking on One's Own: Catholicism in the American Intellectual Imagination, 1928–1960," *Journal of American History* 84 (June 1997): 97–131; Barbara Welter, "From Maria Monk to Paul Blanshard," in *Uncivil Religion*, ed. Robert Bellah and Frederick Greenspan, 43–71 (New York, 1987).

153 Cited in Bradley, *Imagining Vietnam and America*, 183.

154 Paul Blanshard, *Communism, Democracy, and Catholic Power* (Boston, 1951), 234.

3. AMERICA'S "ASIA" AT MIDCENTURY

1 For a detailed narrative of this turbulent time, see David McCullough, *Truman* (New York, 1992), 749–856.

2 Kobler, *Luce: His Time, Life, and Fortune*, 2. Luce scholarship largely sustains Kobler's verdict. In addition to the studies of Luce's impact on American attitudes and policies cited in chapter 2, see James Aaronson, *The Press and the Cold War* (Indianapolis, 1970); David Cort, *The Sin of Henry R. Luce* (Secaucus, N.J., 1974); Robert Elson, *The World of Time, Inc.* (New York, 1973); David Halberstam, *The Powers That Be* (New York, 1979); Robert Hertzstein, *Henry Luce* (New York, 1994); John Hohenberg, *Between Two Worlds* (New York, 1967); John Jessup, *The Ideas of Henry Luce* (New York, 1969); Michael Leigh, *Mobilizing Consent* (Westport, Conn., 1976); William Rivers, *The Opinion-makers* (Boston, 1965); Loudon Wainwright, *The Great American Magazine* (New York, 1986).

3 For the debate between "Asia-firsters" and "Europe-firsters" in the late 1940s and early 1950s, see LaFeber, *America, Russia, and the Cold War*, 86–93, 130–37.

4 Patricia Neils, *China Images in the Life and Times of Henry Luce* (Lanham, Md., 1990), 190–295.

5 Christina Klein, *Cold War Orientalism* (Berkeley, Calif., 2003), 123–24; Karen Janis Leong, "The China Mystique" (Ph.D. diss., University of California, Berkeley, Calif., 1999), 57–114, 268–351.

6 George Becker, *James A. Michener* (New York, 1983), 1.

7 Hugh Fordin, *Getting to Know Him* (New York, 1977), 281–82; John Hayes, "James Michener: An American Writer" (Ph.D. diss., Temple University, 1984), 177–235.

8 For Michener's extraordinary literary output, see F. X. Roberts and C. D. Rhine, *James A. Michener: A Checklist of His Works* (Westport, Conn., 1995).

9 "James Michener: Again the Warm Voice of Asia," *Newsweek* 43 (25 January 1954): 92–95.

10 James Michener, "Blunt Truths about Asia," *Life* 9 (4 June 1951): 96–118.

11 For Luce's lifelong interest in China and how this shaped his politics during the cold war, see Michael Hunt, "East Asia in Henry Luce's 'American Century,'" in *The Ambiguous Legacy*, ed. Michael Hogan, 232–78 (Cambridge, 1999). See also John Hersey, "Henry Luce's China Dream," *New Republic* 165 (2 May 1983), 27–32; Stephen MacKinnon and Oris Friesen, *China Reporting* (Berkeley, Calif., 1987); Hollington Tong, *Dateline—China* (New York, 1972). For analyses of the China Lobby, see Stanley Bachrack, *Committee of One Million* (New York, 1976); Floyd Goodno, "Walter H. Judd: Spokesman for China" (Ph.D. diss., Oklahoma State University, 1970); Joseph Keeley, *The China Lobby Man* (New Rochelle, N.Y., 1969); Ross Koen, *The China Lobby in American Politics* (New York, 1960).

12 Michener, "Blunt Truths about Asia," 118–21.

13 Bederman, *Manliness and Civilization*, 109; William Roseberry, "The Unbearable Lightness of Anthropology," *Radical History Review* 65 (spring 1996): 10–14; Vernon Williams, *Rethinking Race* (Lexington, Ky., 1996), 1–36.

14 Klein, *Cold War Orientalism*, 121, 129.

15 Shibusawa, *America's Geisha Ally*, 7.

16 Classic works on modernization theory include Cyril Black, *The Dynamics of Modernization* (New York, 1966); Daniel Leaner, *The Passing of Traditional Society* (New York, 1958); Walt Rostow, *The Stages of Economic Growth* (Cambridge, 1960). For the origins of modernization theory in the immediate postwar years, see Nils Gilman, "Paved with Good Intentions" (Ph.D. diss., University of California, Berkeley, 2000).

17 Latham, *Modernization as Ideology*, 14–17. See also Reginald Horsman, *Race and Manifest Destiny* (Cambridge, Mass., 1981); Klein, *Cold War Orientalism*, 198–99; Jonathan Nashel, "The Road to Vietnam," in *Cold War Constructions*, ed. Appy, 132–54.

18 Cited in John Dower, *Embracing Defeat* (New York, 1999), 550–51.

19 Shibusawa, *America's Geisha Ally*, esp. chap. 2.

20 Cited in Bradley, *Imagining Vietnam and America*, 168.

21 The Secretary of State to the Embassy in France, 13 May 1947, *FRUS, 1947*, 6:96.

22 The Consul at Saigon to the Secretary of State, 14 June 1947, *FRUS, 1947*, 6:105.

Over twenty years later, America's commander in Vietnam, General William Westmoreland, drew upon the same logic of paternalism when he remarked to a documentary filmmaker, "You know, Vietnam reminded me of a child, the developing of a child. . . . The child has to sit up before it crawls. It has to crawl before it walks. It has to walk before it runs." Cited in *Hearts and Minds*, 1973, directed by Peter Davis. For popular views of America's colonial project in the Philippines, see Bradley, *Imagining Vietnam and America*, 53–54, 66–67.

23 Klein, *Cold War Orientalism*, 8.

24 John Belton, *Widescreen Cinema* (Cambridge, 1992), 69, 70–75; David Bordwell, Janet Staiger, and Kristin Thompson, *The Classical Hollywood Cinema* (New York, 1985), 331–32, 358–61; John Izod, *Hollywood and the Box Office, 1895–1986* (New York, 1988), 134, 139–40; Miller and Nowak, *Fifties*, 314–43.

25 For the frequency with which American films "employed Asian themes, Asian actors, or Asian actresses" from 1930 to 1975, see Eugene Franklin Wong, "On Visual Media Racism" (Ph.D. diss., University of Denver, 1977), 188–246. See also Anand Yang, "Images of Asia," *History Teacher* 15 (May 1980): 351–69.

26 Christina Klein, "Cold War Orientalism" (Ph.D. diss., Yale, 1997), 213.

27 Margaret Landon, *Anna and the King of Siam* (New York, 1944). Ironically, Margaret Landon was the wife of Kenneth Landon, the operations coordinating board representative whose "Committee on Buddhism" (1956–57) is discussed in chapter 1. Bradley, *Imagining Vietnam and America*, 222.

28 James Parish and Michael Pitts, *The Great Hollywood Musical Pictures* (Mentuchen, N.J., 1992), 354–57. See also Rock Brynner, *Yul—The Man Who Would Be King* (New York, 1989).

29 Chalermsri Thuriyanoda Chantasingh, "The Americanization of *The King and I*" (Ph.D. diss., University of Kansas, 1999), 160–62; Cobbett Steinberg, *Film Facts* (New York, 1980), 22, 51, 227–28.

30 See for example Chula Chakrabongse, *Lords of Life* (London, 1986), 178–215; B. J. Terwiel, *A History of Modern Thailand, 1767–1942* (London, 1983), 162–203; David Wyatt, *Thailand: A Short History* (New Haven, Conn., 1984), 181–222.

31 *The King and I*, 1956, directed by Walter Lang; Richard Rodgers and Oscar Hammerstein II, *The King and I*, in *Six Plays by Rodgers and Hammerstein* (New York, 1953), 404–29.

32 Hoey to Kocher: O'Daniel's Appearance before the House Foreign Affairs Committee, 2 March 1956, RG 59, 751G.00/3-256. See chapter 6 for a fuller account of O'Daniel's prescriptions for manipulating Asians.

33 Cited in Jonathan Nashel, *Edward Lansdale and the End of American Innocence* (Amherst, Mass., forthcoming), 196.

34 Rodgers and Hammerstein, *Six Plays*, 385.

35 For a provocative reading of this scene, see Danielle Glassmeyer, "Sentimental Orientalism and American Intervention in Vietnam" (Ph.D. diss., Loyola University, 2001), 113–19, 126–28.

36   *The King and I*, 1956, directed by Walter Lang; Rodgers and Hammerstein, *Six Plays*, 446–47.

37   Rodgers and Hammerstein, *Six Plays*, 444.

38   I am indebted to Danielle Glassmeyer for drawing my attention to this theatrical device. Glassmeyer, "Sentimental Orientalism," 153–54.

39   See chapter 4 for a detailed analysis of Tom Dooley and the image of Asia he conveyed to a mass audience.

40   Christina Klein, "Family Ties and Political Obligation," in *Cold War Constructions*, ed. Appy, 51–52.

41   Rodgers and Hammerstein, *Six Plays*, 345–47; Richard Rodgers, *Musical Stages* (New York, 1975), 261–62.

42   *South Pacific*, 1958, directed by Joshua Logan; Rodgers and Hammerstein, *Six Plays*, 293, 359–60.

43   Glassmeyer, "Sentimental Orientalism," 93; Shibusawa, *America's Geisha Ally*, 4–6.

44   *The Geisha Boy*, 1958, directed by Frank Tashlin.

45   *Steel Helmet*, 1951, directed by Samuel Fuller; *Battle Hymn*, 1956, directed by Douglas Sirk; *Three Stripes in the Sun*, 1955, directed by Richard Murphy.

46   *Sayonara*, 1957, directed by Joshua Logan.

47   *The Teahouse of the August Moon*, 1956, directed by Daniel Mann; *My Geisha*, 1962, directed by Jack Cardiff.

48   *The Bridge on the River Kwai*, 1957, directed by David Lean.

49   Miller and Nowak, *Fifties*, 362.

50   Karla Rae Fuller, "Creatures of Good and Evil," in *Classic Hollywood/Classic Whiteness*, ed. Daniel Bernardi, 281–300 (Minneapolis, 2001); Charles Higham and Joel Greenberg, *Hollywood in the Forties* (New York, 1968), 98; Dorothy Jones, *The Portrayal of China and India on the American Screen* (Cambridge, Mass., 1955), 197–99.

51   Wong, "On Visual Media Racism," 96–109. See also Frank Chin, "Charlie Chan and the Hollywood Image of Asians," *Ramparts* 11 (March 1973): 41–48; Sandra M. Hawley, "The Importance of Being Charlie Chan," in *America Views China*, ed. Jonathan Goldstein, Jerry Israel, and Hilary Conroy, 132–47 (London, 1991).

52   *The Big Picture*, ABC-TV, re-released on Marathon Music and Video, 1998.

53   For an account of the writing, publication, and critical reception of *The Voice of Asia*, see Hayes, "James A. Michener," 177–87.

54   James Michener, *The Voice of Asia* (New York, 1951), 180–81.

55   See chapter 1 for a fuller discussion of the lack of reliable scholarship on Vietnam in the 1950s.

56   For representative analyses dealing with both texts, see Clive Christie, *The Quiet American and the Ugly American* (Canterbury, 1989), 36–70; Renny Christopher, *The Vietnam War/The American War* (Amherst, Mass., 1995),

154–63, 192–201; Nashel, *Edward Lansdale*, 226–81. For treatments of *The Quiet American*, see Miriam Allott, "The Moral Situation in *The Quiet American*," in *Graham Greene: Some Critical Considerations*, ed. Miriam Allott, 188–206 (Lexington, Mass., 1963); Robert Hoskins, *Graham Greene: An Approach to the Novels* (New York, 1999), 155–64; Michael Shelden, *Graham Greene: The Man Within* (London, 1994), 382–405; Norman Sherry, *The Life of Graham Greene* (London, 1994), 2:359–434. For *The Ugly American*, see Dean, *Imperial Brotherhood*, 172–78; Drinnon, *Facing West*, 374; John Hellmann, *American Myth and the Legacy of Vietnam* (New York, 1986), 15–38; Klein, *Cold War Orientalism*, 85–91; Slotkin, *Gunfighter Nation*, 441–61.

57 Graham Greene, *The Quiet American* (New York, 1955), 53.

58 Ibid., iii.

59 Nashel, *Edward Lansdale*, 227.

60 For a particularly fervent tribute to Greene on this score, see Baritz, *Backfire*, 23–25.

61 Greene, *Quiet American*, 4, 74, 108–9.

62 Ibid., 84–96, 126, 170.

63 Ibid., 119, 92, 101.

64 Christopher, *Vietnam War/The American War*, 159–60; Nashel, *Edward Lansdale*, 230–33; Richard West, "Graham Greene and *The Quiet American*," *New York Review of Books*, 16 May 1991, 49–52.

65 Greene, *Quiet American*, 88.

66 Waugh cited in Sherry, *Life of Graham Greene*, 2:472; "This Man's Caricature of the American Abroad," *Newsweek* 47 (2 January 1956): 58–59; "When Greene Is Red," *Newsweek* 48 (1 October 1956): 94–96; A. J. Liebling, "A Talkative Something-or-Other," *New Yorker* 167 (7 April 1956): 148–54.

67 For an outline of *The Quiet American* as rewritten by Mankiewicz, see Mankiewicz, "Synopsis," undated, AFV Papers, box 14.

68 Mankiewicz cited in Katz to Oram, 2 May 1956, AFV Papers, box 1.

69 Reinhardt to Duke, 1 May 1956, AFV Papers, box 9.

70 For Mankiewicz's intentions of casting Clift, see Katz to Oram, 2 May 1956, AFV Papers, box 1. For O'Daniel's stumping for Murphy, see Brownell, "Vietnam Lobby," 232.

71 For Murphy's remarkable career, see Charles Whiting, *No Name on the Bullet* (New York, 1989).

72 Cited in Nashel, *Edward Lansdale*, 256–57. For Mankiewicz's views on adapting Greene's book, see Kenneth Geist, *Pictures Will Talk* (New York, 1978), 268–76.

73 *The Quiet American*, 1958, directed by Joseph Mankiewicz. I am indebted to Julian Smith for drawing my attention to this dialogue. Smith, *Looking Away*, (New York, 1975), 110. For a superb cinematic analysis of *The Quiet American*, see Gene Phillips, *Graham Greene: The Films of His Fiction* (New York, 1974), 135–46.

74 For reference to Lansdale's input, see Jonas to Marks, 20 September 1957, AFV Papers, box 14. For the "Lansdale as Pyle" myth, see Nashel, *Edward Lansdale*, 242–48.

75 See Movie Premiere of *The Quiet American*: Rights to the Premiere, Mail Sales, Box Office, Free Tickets, etc., undated, AFV Papers, box 14; Statement of General John W. O'Daniel in Regard to the World Premiere of the Motion Picture *The Quiet American*, undated, ibid.; Suggested Draft Invitation to Benefit Premiere of *The Quiet American*, 12 November 1957, ibid.

76 Graham Greene, "To the Editor," *Le Monde*, 7 February 1958, translation in Buttinger Papers.

77 Hellmann, *American Myth and the Legacy of Vietnam*, 19.

78 Dean, *Imperial Brotherhood*, 172–73.

79 Yvonne Daily, "The Persistence of the Ugly American," *Boston Globe Magazine*, 2 December 2001, 12, 22; Fisher, *Dr. America*, 69–70, 175–76.

80 William Lederer and Eugene Burdick, *The Ugly American* (New York, 1958), 7, 14, 21.

81 Cited in Daily, "Persistence of the Ugly American," 23. See also Nashel, "Road to Vietnam," 135.

82 Nashel, *Edward Lansdale*, 264.

83 Lederer and Burdick, *Ugly American*, 107, 39, 282.

84 See chapter 4 for the Lansdale-Hillandale controversy.

85 Lederer and Burdick, *Ugly American*, 110–14.

86 Ibid., 174–88.

87 Ibid., 205–31.

88 Ibid., 232–38.

89 Ibid., 271–85.

90 In one of the book's key scenes, Suzie's Western inamorato caught her turning tricks and spanked her like a naughty child; she remained faithful thereafter. Richard Mason, *The World of Suzie Wong* (London, 1957), 121–26. For the extent to which "Suzie Wong" became a pop culture phenomenon in the 1950s and 1960s, see Gary McDonogh and Cindy Hing-Yuk Wong, "Orientalism Abroad," in *Classic Hollywood/Classic Whiteness*, ed. Bernardi, 210–42.

91 *The World of Suzie Wong*, 1960, directed by Richard Quine.

92 James Michener, *The Bridges at Toko-Ri* (New York, 1953), 71.

93 James Michener, *Sayonara* (New York, 1954), 81, 86, 91. Lloyd Gruver, *Sayonara*'s protagonist and narrator, noted that "Joe, being a good Catholic, was repelled when Katsumi established in their home a Shinto shrine, complete with symbols to be prayed to. There were some heated words, and the shrine came down." Joe's statuette of the Madonna, readers could assume, remained on display. Ibid., 112.

94 James Michener, *Return to Paradise* (New York, 1951), 4.

95 Hayes, "James A. Michener," 186; *Until They Sail*, 1957, directed by Robert Wise; *Return to Paradise*, 1953, directed by Mark Robson.

96 Michener, *Return to Paradise*, 434–35.

97 "Abandoning Asia," *New Leader* 40 (4 January 1954): 31.

98 Cited in Ray Moore and Donald Robinson, *Partners for Democracy* (New York, 2002), 39–45.

99 For the best study of how Chiang was perceived in the United States during this crucial period, see Christopher Jespersen, *American Images of China, 1931–1949* (Stanford, Calif., 1996).

100 David Halberstam, *The Fifties* (New York, 1993), 56–57; Gayle Montgomery and James Johnston, *One Step from the White House* (Berkeley, Calif., 1998), 84–131; Patterson, *Grand Expectations*, 170–73. President Eisenhower and Secretary of State John Foster Dulles were more lavish in their praise of Chiang than the outgoing Truman administration had been; they also appeared far more willing to risk nuclear war to defend the generalissimo's island fortress and repeatedly threatened to "unleash" his Nationalist army against the mainland. See Andrew Berding, *Dulles on Diplomacy* (Princeton, 1965), 56–70; Mosley, *Dulles*, 304–6; Nancy Bernkopf Tucker, "John Foster Dulles and the Taiwan Roots of the 'Two Chinas' Policy," in *John Foster Dulles and the Diplomacy of the Cold War*, ed. Immerman, 235–62.

101 "A President Is Baptized," *Time* 16 (3 November 1930): 25. See also "Chinese President Embraces Christianity; Move Startles China, Which Sees Blow to Reds," *New York Times*, 24 October 1930; Brian Crozier, *The Man Who Lost China* (New York, 1976), 46; Emily Hahn, *Chiang Kai-shek* (Garden City, N.Y., 1955), 147; Robert Payne, *Chiang Kai-shek* (New York, 1969), 136–37; Yuwu Song, "Madame Chiang Kai-shek and Her Two Worlds" (Ph.D. diss., University of Alabama, 1999), 42–43.

102 "Chiang Dares," *Time* 28 (9 November 1936): 18–20; "Dictator Un-kidnapped," *Time* 29 (4 January 1937): 18; "Japan Conquers North, South, and Central China and Chiang Kai-shek Becomes a 'Lost Cause,'" *Life* 5 (7 November 1938): 75; Theodore White, "Chiang Kai-shek," *Life* 12 (2 March 1942): 80. The hugely popular *Why We Fight* documentaries, directed by the Hollywood legend Frank Capra and produced by the War Department Signal Corps for the Morale Services Division, played up Chiang's religious devotion in *The Battle of China*, number six in a series of seven informational films. Capra cut between footage of "heathen" Japanese brutality on the battlefield and scenes of a Chinese Christian church complete with a cloth poster of Jesus hanging from a balcony. *The Battle of China*, directed by Frank Capra, re-released by MPI Home Video, 1984.

103 Chiang Kai-shek, "What the Sufferings of Jesus Mean to Me," *Christian Century*, 12 May 1937, 611–12; idem, "Why I Believe in Jesus," *Christian Century*, 8 June 1938, 723–24.

104 Jesperson, *American Images of China*, 201.

105 Halberstam, *Powers That Be*, 74–87; Jespersen, *American Images of China*, 115–22.

106 "The 1949 China 'White Paper,' " in *The Truman Administration*, ed. Barton Bernstein and Allen Matusow, 300–309 (New York, 1966).

107 Cited in Neils, *China Images*, 147.

108 Cited in Jespersen, *American Images of China*, 81.

109 "Man of the Single Truth," *Time* 65 (18 April 1955): 32–39.

110 James Cromwell, "What Happens Next?" reprinted in *Syngman Rhee through Western Eyes* (Seoul, 1954), 129; William Bullitt, "The Story of Syngman Rhee," *Reader's Digest* 63 (September 1953): 107–11; Robert Oliver, *Syngman Rhee* (New York, 1955), 62–63.

111 Frederick Harris, "The Portrait of a Man," *Washington Sunday Star*, 14 December 1952; James A. Van Fleet, "The Truth about Korea. Part II," *Life*, 33 (18 May 1953), 162–63; "The Walnut," *Time* 61 (9 March 1953): 30–34.

112 Hunt, "East Asia in Henry Luce's 'American Century,' " 243.

113 Nashel, *Edward Lansdale*, 165–69; Lansdale, *In the Midst of Wars*, 20–59; Sheehan, *Bright Shining Lie*, 187–90.

114 For useful reviews of Magsaysay's reign, see James Hamilton-Paterson, *America's Boy* (New York, 1998), 159–87; Stanley Karnow, *In Our Image* (New York, 1989), 346–55; Sung Yong Kim, "United States–Philippine Relations during the Magsaysay Administration" (Ph.D. diss., University of Michigan, 1959).

115 See for example "Magsaysay Wins in a Landslide," *Life* 35 (23 November 1953): 40–42; "Peace under the Palms," *Time* 60 (11 August 1952): 40; "Men Who Came to Dinner," *Time* 61 (6 April 1953): 40–41; " 'Lastly! Lastly!,' " *Time* 61 (20 April 1953): 42–43; "Unanimous," *Time* 61 (1 June 1953): 32; "The People's Choice," *Time* 63 (23 November 1953): 36–37.

116 Carlos Romulo, *Crusade in Asia* (New York, 1955); Alvin Scaff, *The Philippine Answer to Communism* (Stanford, Calif., 1955); Robert Smith, *Philippine Freedom* (New York, 1958).

117 Carlos Romulo, *The Magsaysay Story* (New York, 1956), 49.

118 Cited in Mosley, *Dulles*, 256.

119 Toasts of the President and President Rhee of Korea at the White House, 26 July 1954, *Public Papers of the Presidents: Dwight D. Eisenhower, 1954*, 656.

120 Ann Whitman File, DDE Diary Series: Eisenhower to Churchill, 22 July 1954: box 7, EL.

121 Eisenhower used to welcome visitors to the White House by having a band play "Oh, What a Beautiful Morning" from *Oklahoma*. Paul Goodman, *Growing Up Absurd* (New York, 1960), 109.

122 For Eisenhower's anti-intellectualism, see Peter Lyon, *Eisenhower: Portrait of the Hero* (Boston, 1974), 383; Herbert Parmet, *Eisenhower and the American Crusades* (New York, 1972), 15.

123 "Michener: Again the Warm Voice of Asia," 92.

124 Michener, *Voice of Asia*, 331–32.

125 James Michener, *Tales of the South Pacific* (New York, 1946), 139.

126 James Michener, *The World Is My Home* (New York, 1992), 149.

4. DOOLEY AND THE REFUGEES

1 Christopher, *Vietnam War/American War*, 192; Fisher, *Dr. America*, 175; Hellmann, *American Myth and the Legacy of Vietnam*, 126; Slotkin, *Gunfighter Nation*, 447.

2 Heidenry, *Theirs Was the Kingdom*, 471–81; Sharp, *Condensing the Cold War*, 83–106.

3 William Lederer, "They'll Remember the *Bayfield*," *Reader's Digest* 67 (March 1955): 1–8.

4 See chapter 3 for a discussion of *The Ugly American* and its proposals for fighting communism in Asia.

5 Christopher, *Vietnam War/American War*, 195.

6 Lederer, "*Bayfield*," 3.

7 Oakley, *God's Country*, 15.

8 See James Cable, *The Geneva Conference of 1954 on Indochina* (London, 1986); Robert Randle, *Geneva 1954: The Settlement of the Indochina War* (Princeton, 1969).

9 Short, *Origins of the Vietnam War*, 155.

10 The Department of State to the Embassy in Paris, 28 June 1954, *FRUS, 1952–54*, 16:1256–58. See also Ann Whitman File, Dulles-Herter Series: Dillon to Dulles, 2 July 1954: box 2, EL.

11 The Ambassador in Saigon to the Department of State, 23 July 1954, *FRUS, 1952–54*, 13:1872.

12 Louis Weisner, *Victims and Survivors* (Westport, Conn., 1988), 3–5.

13 Gheddo, *The Cross and Bo-Tree*, 57–61.

14 The Ambassador in Saigon to the Department of State, 5 August 1954, *FRUS, 1952–54*, 13:1921–22; Heath to Dulles, 6 August 1954, RG 59, 751G.00/8-654.

15 See "The Role of the United States Navy," in *Viet-Nam: The First Five Years*, ed. Richard Lindholm, 45–103 (East Lansing, Mich., 1959); Eric Chester, *Covert Network* (Armonk, N.Y., 1995), 143–56; Eileen Egan, *For Whom There Is No Room* (New York, 1995), 317–54; Aaron Levenstein, *Escape to Freedom* (Westport, Conn., 1983), 203–8; Gertrude Samuels, "Passage to Freedom," *National Geographic* 107 (June 1955): 858–74; Weisner, *Victims and Survivors*, 1–18. See also White House Office, National Security Council Staff: Papers, 1948–61, OCB Central File Series: Kenneth Landon, "Narrative of Evacuation Operations in Viet-Nam," 24 May 1955: box 39, EL; Collins Papers: "Summary of the Refugee Situation in Viet-Nam," 3 November 1954: box 25, EL.

16   Wiesner, *Victims and Survivors*, 17.

17   See Joseph Harnett, "The Work of Roman Catholic Groups," in *Viet-Nam: The First Five Years*, ed. Lindholm, 77–103.

18   Harnett to Swanstrom, 19 September 1954, Monsignor Joseph Harnett Papers, Hesburgh Library, University of Notre Dame, South Bend, Ind. [hereafter Harnett Papers], box 2; Harnett to Swanstrom, 30 August 1954, ibid.

19   Ken Post, *Revolution, Socialism, and Nationalism in Vietnam* (Brookfield, Vt., 1989), 1:224.

20   See White House Press Release, 22 August 1954, *FRUS, 1952–54*, 13:1972–73; McClintock to Dulles, 25 May 1954, RG 59, 751G.00/5-2555; McClintock to Hagerty, 14 August 1954, RG 59, 751G.00/8-1454.

21   Bouscaren, *Last of the Mandarins*, 35.

22   Cited in Jeffrey Race, *War Comes to Long An* (Berkeley, Calif., 1972), 32.

23   Cooper, *Lost Crusade*, 130.

24   Lansdale appeared in Lederer's and Burdick's book as Colonel Hillandale. Greene allegedly modeled his central character, the idealistic Alden Pyle, after Lansdale. Nashel, *Edward Lansdale*, 226–81.

25   Cited in Gibbons, *U.S. Government and the Vietnam War*, 1:265.

26   Cited in *The Pentagon Papers as Published by the New York Times* (New York, 1971), 17.

27   B. S. N. Murti, *Vietnam Divided* (New York, 1964), 83.

28   Currey, *Edward Lansdale*, 156–66; Lansdale Team's Report on Covert Saigon Mission in 1954 and 1955, *The Pentagon Papers (Gravel Edition)* (Boston, 1971), 1:573–83; Lansdale, *In the Midst of Wars*, 165–72.

29   Cited in Gheddo, *Cross and Bo-Tree*, 68.

30   The figure of eighty-nine dollars comes from Robert Scheer, *How the United States Got Involved in Vietnam* (Santa Barbara, Calif., 1965), 21.

31   *Pentagon Papers (Gravel Edition)*, 1:248.

32   "Flight from Communism—Vietnam Refugees," *New York Times Magazine*, 10 October 1954; "Pilgrims of the East," *Newsweek* 45 (24 January 1955): 42; excerpt from *March of Time* newsreel, *Vietnam: A Television History*, Episode Three: "America's Mandarin" (1985); Leo Cherne, "To Win in Indochina, We Must Win These People," *Look* 19 (25 January 1955): 33–39.

33   "Retreat from Nam Dinh," *Time* 64 (12 July 1954): 25; "Bug-out in the Delta," *Life* 37 (12 July 1954): 13; Earl Voss, "Catholics Form Backbone of Resistance to Viet Minh," *Washington Sunday-Star*, 22 November 1954.

34   Ellen Hammer, *The Struggle for Indochina, 1940–1955* (Stanford, Calif., 1966), 284–85, 347–48.

35   Joseph Breig, "Flight of the 800,000," *Catholic Bulletin*, 21 May 1955; Fred Sparks, "Besieged Bishop," *Jubilee* 6 (May 1954): 9; "Flight to Freedom," *Catholic Digest* 19 (January 1955): 94–101; "Confession of the Faith," *Ave Maria* 79 (26 March 1955): 3.

36 This is confirmed by a review of the microfilm holdings for 1954–55 at Notre Dame's Hesburgh Library, which contains the largest collection of American Catholic newspapers in the world.

37 Frank Hall, director of the Far Eastern staff of the NCWC News Service, revealed in 1955 that O'Connor "has often been chosen by the secular reporters to be their 'pool' representative on one-man assignments to stories. Thus he has represented all the world's leading wire services." Cited in "Hits Author's Slur on U.S. Priest-Reporter," *Catholic Universe Bulletin*, 20 May 1955; "Graham Greene Slurs Work of Father O'Connor in Far East," *Catholic Herald Citizen*, 21 May 1955; "Nips New Greene Slur on Catholic Priest-Reporter," *Catholic Universe Bulletin*, 10 June 1955.

38 Patrick O'Connor, "Grab Babies from Catholic Mothers' Arms to Stop Their Departure," *New World*, 10 December 1954; "Viet Minh Prisons Graveyards for Priests and Nuns," *Catholic Herald-Citizen*, 4 December 1954; "Blood Flows as Red Troops Attack Thousands of Refugees," *Catholic Herald-Citizen*, 27 November 1954; "Goodbye to Hanoi: Neck-Deep in Tears," *Catholic Digest*, October 1954, 79–82. For more O'Connor extracts from NCWC reports, see *Terror in Vietnam: Record of Another Broken Pledge*, distributed by the NCWC and located in Mansfield Papers, series XIII, box 8; *Exodus—Report on a Voluntary Mass Flight to Freedom*, ibid. For O'Connor's lobbying efforts on behalf of Diem in the United States, see McGuire to O'Daniel, 1 May 1956, AFV Papers, box 4. The reports of O'Connor and other journalists prompted the annual convocation in Washington of Roman Catholic bishops to petition the administration for a public denunciation of Viet Minh "trickery, pressure, and the most brutal violence." The White House, State Department, and Senate were deluged with telegrams protesting the treatment of Vietnamese Catholic refugees. See Collins Papers: Saltzman to AmEmbassies Saigon, Hanoi, Paris, Warsaw, New Delhi, Ottawa, and New York, 26 November 1954: box 32, EL. See also Ann Whitman File, Legislative Meetings Series: Memorandum of Bipartisan Briefing of Congressional Leaders on Foreign Policy, 12 November 1954: box 1, EL.

39 O. Edmund Clubb, "Divided Vietnam: Second Korea?" *Progressive* 19 (December 1955): 19.

40 Cooney, *American Pope*, 241.

41 Kidder to Dulles, 6 December 1954, RG 59, 751G.00/12-654.

42 See Heath to Dulles, 17 January 1955, RG 59, 751G.00/1-1755; Reuters Report, 17 January 1955, RG 59, 751G.00/1-1755; Kidder to Dulles, 29 January 1955, RG 59, 751G.00/1-2955; International Commission for Supervision and Control Report on Balang Incident, 7 February 1955, RG 59, 751G.00/2-755; Collins to Dulles, 13 March 1955, RG 59, 751G.00/3-1355; Anderson to Dulles, 20 May 1957, RG 59, 751G.00/5-2057.

43 Collins Papers: Corcoran to Dulles, 6 January 1955: box 31, EL. See also

Corcoran to Dulles, 28 January 1955, RG 59, 751G.00/1-2855; Collins Papers: Corcoran to Dulles, 4 February 1955: box 32, EL; Corcoran to Dulles, 23 April 1955, RG 59, 751G.00/4-2355; Corcoran to Dulles, 29 April 1955, RG 59, 751G.00/4-2955; Corcoran to Dulles, 15 May 1955, RG 59, 751G.00/5-1555; Corcoran to Dulles, 24 May 1955, RG 59, 751G.00/5-2455.

44　"Most Esteemed Men," *Honolulu Star-Bulletin*, 23 January 1961; "He Gave His Life," *Indianapolis News*, 20 January 1961.

45　Daniel Boorstin, *The Image* (New York, 1961), 54.

46　Gottwald eulogy reprinted as "Final Tribute to Dr. Dooley," *Tablet*, 23 January 1961.

47　Eisenhower to Agnes Dooley [undated], Thomas A. Dooley Papers, Western Historical Manuscript Collection, University of Missouri at St. Louis [hereafter Dooley Papers], series II—Vietnam.

48　Fisher, *Dr. America*, 262–63.

49　Agnes Dooley, *Promises to Keep* (New York, 1962); Teresa Gallagher, *Give Joy to My Youth* (New York, 1965).

50　Fisher, *Catholic Counterculture in America*, 202.

51　Ibid., 174.

52　Diana Shaw, "The Temptation of Tom Dooley," *Los Angeles Times Magazine*, 15 December 1991, 80.

53　Cited in Fisher, *Catholic Counterculture in America*, 168.

54　Nicholas von Hoffman, "Hang Down Your Head, Tom Dooley," *Critic* 5 (November-December 1969): 16–23.

55　See for example Herring, *America's Longest War*; Kahin, *Intervention*; Karnow, *Vietnam: A History*; Michael Maclear, *The Ten Thousand Day War* (New York, 1981); Marilyn Young, *The Vietnam Wars* (New York, 1991).

56　The sole exception was a study of Dooley's debate skills by a student in the Speech Department at the University of Oregon. See Dale Warren Mark, "The Rhetoric of Thomas A. Dooley, M.D." (Ph.D. diss., University of Oregon, 1971).

57　Fisher, *Dr. America*, 34–35.

58　Von Hoffman, "Hang Down Your Head, Tom Dooley," 16.

59　Arthur Shay, "Dr. Dooley's Mission of Love," *Chicago Sun-Times*, 25 May 1958.

60　Cited in Richard Guilderson, "Deliver Us from Evil," *Information* 3 (September 1956): 7.

61　Cited in "Navy Doctor-Hero Tells Mom: 'Teach Your Child About God,'" *St. Louis Register*, 4 May 1956.

62　Miller, *Piety along the Potomac*, 34.

63　Cited in Miller and Nowak, *Fifties*, 90.

64　Christopher, *Vietnam War/American War*, 128.

65　Letter from Laos, 1 August 1957, Dooley Papers, series III—Laos, 1955–60.

66   Dooley, *Promises to Keep*, 61.

67   Cited in Shaw, "Temptation of Tom Dooley," 80.

68   Robert Allen, "The Amazing Doctor Dooley," *Catholic Digest* 22 (October 1958): 28.

69   Cited in Fisher, *Catholic Counterculture in America*, 132.

70   Fisher, *Dr. America*, 19.

71   Cited in Shaw, "Temptation of Tom Dooley," 44.

72   Brownell, "Vietnam Lobby," 275–79; Fisher, *Dr. America*, 19–33; idem, *Catholic Counterculture in America*, 142.

73   Fisher, *Dr. America*, 36.

74   Cited in Fisher, *Catholic Counterculture in America*, 165.

75   Cited in Richard Schickel, "The Splendid American," *Look* 23 (August 1959): 151.

76   Tom Dooley to Agnes Dooley, 15 August 1954, Dooley Papers, series II—Vietnam. [Letters from Dooley to his mother hereafter cited as TD to AD.]

77   TD to AD, 11 November 1954, Dooley Papers, series II—Vietnam.

78   TD to AD, 15 August 1954, Dooley Papers, series II—Vietnam. See also TD to AD, 18 August 1954; TD to AD, 15 January 1955; TD to AD, 22 February 1955; TD to AD, 23 February 1955; TD to AD, 24 March 1955; TD to AD, 27 September 1956, ibid.

79   TD to AD, 29 October 1954, Dooley Papers, series II—Vietnam.

80   TD to AD, 28 August 1954, Dooley Papers, series II—Vietnam.

81   TD to AD, 1 September 1954, Dooley Papers, series II—Vietnam. See also TD to AD, 8 September 1954, ibid.

82   Amberson, Operation "Passage to Freedom," 1 June 1956, Dooley Papers, series II—Vietnam.

83   TD to AD, 22 September 1954, Dooley Papers, series II—Vietnam; TD to AD, 11 October 1954; TD to AD, 18 October 1954, ibid.

84   TD to AD, 13 October 1954, Dooley Papers, series II—Vietnam.

85   Dooley, "Passage to Freedom," 21 August 1954, Dooley Papers, series II—Vietnam.

86   TD to AD, 23 November 1954, Dooley Papers, series II—Vietnam.

87   TD to AD, 12 February 1955, Dooley Papers, series II—Vietnam.

88   TD to AD, 28 November 1954, Dooley Papers, series II—Vietnam. See also TD to AD, 5 January 1955, ibid.

89   Shaw, "Temptation of Tom Dooley," 45.

90   Cited in Brownell, "Vietnam Lobby," 294.

91   Thomas Dooley, *Deliver Us from Evil* (New York, 1956), 115.

92   Cited in Brownell, "Vietnam Lobby," 294.

93   Dooley, *Deliver Us from Evil*, 190.

94   TD to AD, 12 February 1955, Dooley Papers, series II—Vietnam. Just before receiving the Legion of Merit, Dooley wrote to his mother, "There is some-

thing new in the wind in the way of the Navy's recognition that I can't write of now[,] . . . but it will show a few people who didn't believe in me." TD to AD, 18 February 1955, ibid.

95   TD to AD, 22 September 1954, Dooley Papers, series II—Vietnam.

96   TD to AD, 11 December 1954, Dooley Papers, series II—Vietnam. See also Dooley to Gilmore, 13 May 1955, ibid.

97   TD to AD, 18 December 1954, Dooley Papers, series II—Vietnam.

98   TD to AD, 18 October 1954, Dooley Papers, series II—Vietnam.

99   TD to AD, Thanksgiving Day, 1954, Dooley Papers, series II—Vietnam.

100 Cited in Fisher, *Dr. America*, 69.

101 Dooley, "Treatment for Terror," Dooley Papers, series II—Vietnam. For an earlier incarnation of this speech, probably composed in October 1954, see Dooley, "History of Indochina for Those Taking Part in the Refugee Resettlement," Thomas A. Dooley Collection, Pius XII Library, St. Louis University, St. Louis, Mo. [hereafter Dooley Collection], Teresa Gallagher File. "I have given several lectures which are always received with much applause and awaited with great expectancy," a proud Dooley wrote in January 1955. TD to AD, 29 January 1955, Dooley Papers, series II—Vietnam.

102 TD to AD, 1 January 1955, Dooley Papers, series II—Vietnam.

103 TD to AD, 1 May 1955, Dooley Papers, series II—Vietnam. Dooley had been submitting accounts of his adventures to his hometown newspaper since Passage to Freedom began, but the *St. Louis Post-Dispatch* declined to publish them until the wayward native son began appearing in other papers; then, in an about-face, the *Post-Dispatch* ran a feature that lauded him as "a modern Doctor Livingstone." TD to AD, 28 August 1954, Dooley Papers, series II—Vietnam; TD to AD, 4 December 1954, ibid; Larry Allen, "Lt. Dooley's Heroic Role," *St. Louis Post-Dispatch*, 16 May 1955.

104 Cited in Fisher, *Dr. America*, 70.

105 TD to AD, 12 May 1955, Dooley Papers, series II—Vietnam.

106 Diem Citation, 12 May 1955, Dooley Papers, series II—Vietnam.

107 TD to AD, 12 May 1955, Dooley Papers, series II—Vietnam. Had Dooley been less euphoric he might have sensed something awry in the fact that Diem's citation was in flawless English, which neither the premier nor any of his entourage could compose. The citation had in fact been written on Colonel Edward Lansdale's manual typewriter. Lansdale informed the historian William Brownell that he once took the wind out of Dooley's sails by inviting him to compare the typescript on the citation with that of other communications produced on the colonel's typewriter. Brownell, "Vietnam Lobby," 291. See also Scheer, *How the United States Got Involved in Vietnam*, 29.

108 TD to AD, 9 June 1955, Dooley Papers, series II—Vietnam.

109 Dooley, *Deliver Us from Evil*, 213.

110 TD to AD, 5 June 1955, Dooley Papers, series II—Vietnam.

111 TD to AD, 10 June 1955, Dooley Papers, series II—Vietnam; Lederer to Dooley, 28 July 1955, ibid.

112 TD to AD, 8 June 1955, Dooley Papers, series II—Vietnam.

113 Fisher, *Dr. America*, 68–77; Dooley, *Deliver Us from Evil*, 37.

114 James Monahan, *Before I Sleep* (New York, 1961), vii.

115 Brownell, "Vietnam Lobby," 300–301.

116 "Dooley to Discuss Flight of Refugees," *Charlottesville Cavalier*, 24 April 1956.

117 The price of the full-length version is quoted in *Reader's Digest* 68 (April 1956): 42.

118 Wallace to Dooley, 24 August 1956, Dooley Collection—"Lectures I" Scrapbook.

119 Dooley, *Deliver Us from Evil*, 204, 125.

120 Ibid., 22–23, 25–30, 205.

121 Ibid., 209.

122 Ibid., 175–77.

123 TD to AD, 18 February 1955, Dooley Papers, series II—Vietnam.

124 Dooley, *Deliver Us from Evil*, 183.

125 Ibid., 181–82.

126 Ibid., 146, 52.

127 Ibid., 129–30, 188, 69.

128 Ibid., 185, 210.

129 "Books: Briefly Noted," *New Yorker*, 5 May 1956; "Navy Doctor and Red Plague," *Washington Post*, 15 April 1956; Peggy Durdin, "Mission of Mercy Accomplished," *New York Times*, 19 August 1956; Hogan cited in Dooley, *Promises to Keep*, 102; Edwin Stanton, "When 600,000 Vietnamese Took the Way to Freedom," *New York Herald Tribune*, 15 April 1956.

130 Irene Kuhn, "Finding Maturity in Others' Trials," *San Diego Union*, 6 May 1956; "Indochina Hero to Speak Here Tonight," *Helena Register*, 22 April 1956; "Samaritan in Vietnam," *America's Book-Log*, June 1956; "Middlebrow's Bookshelf," *Ogden Standard-Examiner*, 3 June 1956; "Sermon in the East," *Hollywood Citizen-News*, 16 April 1956; Barbara Shaughnessy, "Doctor Dooley of Viet Nam," *Extension*, August 1956, 10; "Ideas of Communists as Bad as Their Cruelties," *Catholic View*, 13 May 1956; B. Haskins, "Did You Know," *Pomeroy Sentinel*, 18 April 1956.

131 James Murphy, Book Reviews, *American Ecclesiastical Review* 127 (September 1957): 214–15; *Spiritual Life* cited in Fisher, *Catholic Counterculture in America*, 164; "Deliver Us from Evil," *Catholic Review Service*, 30 April 1956; "Book About Vietnam Makes One Exclaim: 'Would That There Were More Tom Dooleys!,'" *Catholic Free Press*, May Book Supplement, 1956; Mark Heath, "Book Reviews," *Torch*, June–July 1956. Handwritten on a clipping

of the Heath article is "Favorite review so far!" Dooley Collection—"Deliver Us from Evil II" Scrapbook.

132 A copy of Mansfield's remarks in the *Congressional Record* 102 (9 April 1956) is in Dooley Collection—"Lectures I" Scrapbook.

133 Cited in Lawrence Elliot, *The Legacy of Tom Dooley* (New York, 1969), xii.

134 Eisenhower to Dooley, 18 April 1956, Dooley Collection—"Lectures I" Scrapbook; Roosevelt to Dooley, 18 April 1956; Spellman to Dooley, 24 February 1956, ibid.; Warren to Dooley, 17 December 1956, Dooley Papers, series III—Laos.

135 Diem to Dooley, 25 June 1956, Dooley Collection—"Lectures I" Scrapbook.

136 Chuong to Dooley, 21 February 1956, Dooley Collection—"Lectures I" Scrapbook.

137 Dooley, *Promises to Keep*, 64.

138 Gallagher, *Give Joy to My Youth*, 175–76.

139 Cited in Brownell, "Vietnam Lobby," 304.

140 Cited in Dooley, *Promises to Keep*, 102.

141 Cited in Brownell, "Vietnam Lobby," 327.

142 Norton to Hogan, 23 April 1956, Dooley Collection—"Lectures I" Scrapbook.

143 Leslie to Dooley, 21 February 1956, Dooley Collection—"Deliver Us from Evil I" Scrapbook.

144 Cited in "An American Doctor and 500,000 Refugees," *Catholic View*, May 1956.

145 Cited in Brownell, "Vietnam Lobby," 310–11.

146 "The People Choose Eisenhower as the 'Most Admired Man,'" *Worcester Daily Telegram*, 26 August 1956; "Selections Are Announced for Ten Outstanding Young Men," *Future*, January 1957.

147 TD to AD, 28 August 1956, Dooley Papers, series II—Vietnam.

148 Fisher, *Dr. America*, 82–89; idem, *Catholic Counterculture in America*, 167–70; Randy Shilts, *Conduct Unbecoming* (New York, 1993), 24–26.

149 Cited in Joe Aaron, "Anxious to Return to 'Filthy Country,'" *Evansville Courier*, 26 July 1956.

150 "Man With a Mission," *Hollywood Citizen-News*, 12 April 1956; "Deliver Us from Evil," *Washington Daily News*, 20 April 1956.

151 Fisher, *Dr. America*, 98–99. See also Minutes of AFV Executive Committee Meeting, 14 February 1956, AFV Papers, box 1; TD to AD, May 18, 1957, Dooley Papers, series III—Laos.

152 See for instance TD to AD, 28 August 1954, Dooley Papers, series II—Vietnam; TD to AD, 9 September 1954; TD to AD, 9 January 1955; Dooley to Gilmore, 25 August 1955, ibid.

153 Transcript of interview, 18 March 1958, Dooley Collection—"Laos II" Scrapbook. See also Elliot, *Legacy of Tom Dooley*, 2.

154 Plans for the Medical Mission to the Kingdom of Laos, undated, Dooley Papers, series III—Laos.

155 Fisher, *Dr. America*, 128.

156 Rex Davis, Introduction, "That Free Men May Live" [hereafter TFMML], 26 January 1957, Dooley Papers, series VII—Tapes.

157 TFMML, 25 May 1957, Dooley Papers, series VII—Tapes.

158 TFMML, 12 January 1957, Dooley Papers, series VII—Tapes.

159 TFMML, 22 June 1957, Dooley Papers, series VII—Tapes.

160 TFMML, 23 November 1960, Dooley Collection—Teresa Gallagher File.

161 TFMML, 1 May 1950, Dooley Collection—Teresa Gallagher File.

162 TFMML, 31 October 1956, Dooley Papers, series VII—Tapes.

163 TFMML, 6 July 1957, Dooley Papers, series VII—Tapes.

164 See Don Dunham, "America's Doctor Schweitzer," *Detroit News*, 5 August 1957; Vincent X. Flaherty, "He Sells Peace With Medicine," *Los Angeles Examiner*, 13 July 1958; "Dooley Stresses Personal Touch in Providing Foreign Assistance," *Honolulu Star-Bulletin*, 22 July 1958; Pat Carson, "A Jungle Doctor's Motives," *Detroit News*, 5 September 1958.

165 TFMML, 5 April 1960, Dooley Collection—Teresa Gallagher File.

166 TFMML, 24 April 1960, Dooley Collection—Teresa Gallagher File.

167 Cited in "U.S. Lives in Mansion amidst World Slum," *Saint Louis Post-Dispatch*, 25 May 1958.

168 Dooley, "The role of MEDICO," Address to the Society, 22 November 1959, *John Carroll Quarterly*, spring 1960. Clipping in Dooley Collection—"Lectures III" Scrapbook.

169 Dooley, "Foreign Aid—The Human Touch," *New York Times Magazine*, 20 April 1958, 11.

170 "Two Outstanding Men," *Redbook*, November 1960, 52.

171 Dooley, "Project Laos," *Journal of American Medicine* 161 (1 September 1956): 41.

172 Mansfield to Dooley, 14 June 1956, Dooley Collection—"Lectures I" Scrapbook.

173 A copy of Humphrey's remarks in the *Congressional Record* 58 (10 March 1958) is in Dooley Collection—"Laos II" Scrapbook.

174 "Voice in the Wilderness," *Tablet*, 26 December 1959.

175 "Excerpts from Letters to Doctor Dooley," August 1959, Dooley Collection—"Deliver Us from Evil II" Scrapbook.

176 Cited in Fisher, *Dr. America*, 232.

177 Nashel, "Modernization Theory in Fact and Fiction" in *Cold War Constructions*, ed. Appy, 136–39.

178 Finian "was largely inspired by Lederer's idealized version of Dooley's work," Fisher notes. "Finian, like Dooley, is an ardent anti-communist who

—virtually alone among the American community—wins the natives' love and loyalty." Fisher, *Catholic Counterculture in America*, 175.

179 Lederer and Burdick, *Ugly American*, 51–55.

180 William Lederer and Eugene Burdick, "Salute to Deeds of Non-Ugly Americans," *Life* 46 (7 December 1959): 157–58.

181 TD to AD, 15 May 1957, Dooley Papers, series III—Laos; Dooley to Gilmore, 10 January 1957, ibid.

182 TD to AD, 13 April 1957, Dooley Papers, series III—Laos.

183 "Letter from the Editor," *Natchez Register*, 27 August 1959.

184 Fisher, *Dr. America*, 202–24.

185 Monahan, *Before I Sleep*, 219.

186 Hersted to Dooley, 30 August 1959, Dooley Papers, series III—Laos.

187 Shilts, *Conduct Unbecoming*, 21.

188 Dooley, *Deliver Us from Evil*, 214.

189 Shilts, *Conduct Unbecoming*, 736; Fisher, *Dr. America*, 252–64.

190 Gottwald eulogy reprinted as "Final Tribute to Dr. Dooley," *Tablet*, 21 January 1961.

191 TFMML, 22 May 1960, Dooley Collection—Teresa Gallagher File.

192 "Dr. Tom Dooley's Plea," *Honolulu Star-Bulletin*, January 23, 1961.

193 Edward Said, "Through Gringo Eyes," *Harper's* 244 (April 1988): 72.

194 Cited in Brownell, "Vietnam Lobby," 347–48.

195 Thomas A. Dooley, "Deliver Us from Evil," *Reader's Digest* 68 (May 1956): 43. See also Dooley, *Deliver Us from Evil*, 20.

5. COLLINS AND THE BATTLE FOR SAIGON

1 Collins Papers: Collins to Gruenther, 4 January 1955: box 17, EL.

2 The most comprehensive treatment of the Collins mission is Anderson, *Trapped by Success*, 91–119. See also idem, "J. Lawton Collins, John Foster Dulles, and the Eisenhower Administration's 'Point of No Return' in Vietnam," *Diplomatic History* 12 (spring 1988): 127–48; Arnold, *First Domino*, 249–89; J. Lawton Collins, *Lightning Joe* (Baton Rouge, La., 1979), 378–411; Daniel Greene, "Tug of War" (Ph.D. diss., University of Texas at Austin, 1990), 287–433; Ronald Spector, *Advice and Support* (New York, 1985), 231–54.

3 Collins, *Lightning Joe*, 378. See also Collins Papers: Memorandum for the Record, 31 October, 1954: box 25, EL.

4 Benedict Anderson, *Imagined Communities* (London, 1983).

5 For the disposition of power in postwar South Vietnam, see Sergei Blagov, *Honest Mistakes* (Huntington, N.Y., 2001), 17–25, 45–56; Bernard Fall, *Viet-Nam Witness* (New York, 1966), 141–60; Hammer, *Struggle for Indochina*,

346–50; David Marr, *Vietnamese Tradition on Trial* (Berkeley, Calif., 1981), 288–326; Ralph Smith, *Viet-Nam and the West* (Ithaca, N.Y., 1971), 70–85.

6   Olson and Roberts, *Where the Domino Fell*, 54–55; Warner, *Last Confucian*, 99–105.

7   McClintock to Dulles, 22 May 1954, RG 59, 751G.00/5-2254; The Ambassador in Saigon to the State Department, 4 July 1954, *FRUS, 1952–54*, 13:1460; Fall, *Viet-Nam Witness*, 155.

8   "Sin Is the Target," *Newsweek* 45 (24 January 1955): 42; Alsop cited in Robert Merry, *Taking on the World* (New York, 1994), 282; Homer Bigart, "Viet Nam Premier Would End Vice," *New York Herald Tribune*, 22 December 1954.

9   Heath to Dulles, 27 August 1954, RG 59, 751G.00/8-2754.

10   McClintock to Dulles, 4 July 1954, RG 59, 751G.00/7-454.

11   Cited in Heath to Dulles, 7 August 1954, RG 59, 751G.00/8-754.

12   Joseph Buttinger, *Vietnam: A Political History* (New York, 1968), 393. See also Heath to Dulles: Transcript of Hinh Radio Broadcast, 28 October 1954, RG 59, 751G.00/10-2854.

13   Buttinger, *Vietnam: A Dragon Embattled*, 2:851–65; Lansdale, *In the Midst of Wars*, 159–75.

14   The Ambassador in Vietnam to the Department of State, 29 September 1954, *FRUS, 1952–54*, 13:2092–93.

15   Cited in Warner, *Last Confucian*, 101.

16   Dulles Papers, White House Memoranda Series: Memorandum of Conversation with the President, 30 October 1954: box 1, EL.

17   Arnold, *First Domino*, 249; Collins, *Lightning Joe*, 198–377.

18   Dwight D. Eisenhower, Pre-Presidential Papers, Principal File: Eisenhower to Collins, 20 February 1948: box 25, EL.

19   Cited in Collins, *Lightning Joe*, 378.

20   Collins Papers: Memorandum of Conference at the Residence of Mr. John Foster Dulles, Secretary of State, 31 October 1954: box 25, EL. See also White House Office, Office of the Special Assistant for National Security Affairs, NSC Series, Briefing Notes Subseries: Memorandum of Conversation, 31 October 1954: box 11, EL.

21   White House Central Files, Confidential File, Subject Series, Department of State: Press Release, 3 November 1954: box 69, EL.; Collins Papers: Eisenhower to Collins, 3 November 1954: box 25, EL. See also "President Names Collins Special Aide in Vietnam," *New York Times*, 4 November 1954.

22   Collins Papers: Notes Made During State Department Conference on Indochina, 1 November 1954: box 25, EL.

23   Collins Papers: Briefing Book on Vietnam for General Collins, 3 November 1954—U.S. Policy for Post-Armistice Vietnam, 19 August 1954: box 25, EL. I am indebted to Gregory Olson for pointing out the "American/Christian" bias in Collins's briefing book. Olson, *Mansfield and Vietnam*, 44–45. For the

famine that swept northern Vietnam at the close of World War II, see David Marr, *Vietnam, 1945* (Berkeley, Calif., 1995), 96–107.

24 Collins Papers: Briefing Book on Vietnam for General Collins, 3 November 1954—Report on Indochina by Senator Mike Mansfield, 15 October 1954: box 25, EL.

25 Anderson, *Trapped by Success*, 83; Victor Bator, *Vietnam: A Diplomatic Tragedy* (Dobbs Ferry, N.Y., 1965), 183; *Pentagon Papers: Gravel Edition*, 1:222.

26 Office of the Special Assistant for National Security Affairs: Memorandum of Conference, 31 October 1954: box 11, EL.

27 Cited in Hammer, *Death in November*, 71.

28 Collins Papers: Collins to Dulles, 10 November 1954: box 25, EL.

29 Collins Papers: Collins to Dulles, 13 November 1954: box 25, EL.

30 Collins Papers: Briefing Points on South Vietnam, 2 November 1954: box 25, EL. See also Collins Papers: Joint State-Defense Message to Saigon, 22 October 1955: ibid.

31 Collins Papers: Collins to Dulles, 13 November 1954: box 31, EL. The second highest-ranking American in Vietnam, General "Iron Mike" O'Daniel, shared Collins's opinion of Hinh; while Iron Mike would go on to become one of Diem's staunchest advocates, he is on record as remarking to Heath in early September 1954 that he preferred "Hinh to Diem should he have to make a choice between the two men." Cited in Heath to Dulles, 16 September 1954, *United States-Vietnam Relations, 1945–1971* [hereafter *U.S.-VN Relations*] (Washington, 1971), 10:753–55.

32 Collins, *Lightning Joe*, 385–86; Shaplen, *Lost Revolution*, 119; Collins Papers: Accomplishments, 19 November 1954: box 25, EL.

33 Translations from French News Sources: General Hinh Protests against Statement of Senator Mansfield, 15 October 1954, Mansfield Papers, series XIII, box 7.

34 Cited in Telegram from the Ambassador in Phnom Penh to the Department of State, 10 June 1954, *FRUS, 1952–54*, 13:1737–38.

35 Dulles to Eisenhower—Subject: General Collins's Recommendations Regarding Force Levels, 17 November 1954, RG 59, 751G.00/11-1754.

36 Collins, *Lightning Joe*, 385–87; Spector, *Advice and Support*, 232–43. See also Dulles Press Conference, 11 December 1954, Dulles Papers, box 82.

37 Telegram from the Special Representative in South Vietnam to the Department of State, 3 January 1955, *FRUS, 1955–57*, 1:9. I am indebted to James Arnold for drawing my attention to this cable. Arnold, *First Domino*, 259. In a subsequent report, Collins reiterated that there was "never any question of submitting [the] Minute of Understanding to [the] Vietnamese Govt. for its approval." Collins Papers: Collins to Dulles, 5 January 1955: box 25, EL.

38 Collins Papers: Meeting between Ambassador Collins and General Ely at the Commissariat General at 10:30 A.M., 3 December 1954: box 25, EL.

39   Collins Papers: Collins to Dulles, 6 December 1954: box 25, EL.

40   Collins, *Lightning Joe*, 389–90.

41   The Ambassador in Saigon to the Department of State, 29 March 1955, *FRUS*, *1955–57*, 1:155–57.

42   Hammer, *Struggle for Indochina*, 348.

43   Collins Papers: Report on Vietnam for the National Security Council, 20 January 1955: box 25, EL.

44   See for example Graham Greene, "Last Act in Indo-China," *New Republic* 129 (9 May 1955): 10–11; Bernard Fall, "The Political-Religious Sects of Vietnam," *Pacific Affairs* 28 (September 1955): 235–53; Peter Schmid, "Free Indo-China Fights against Time," *Commentary* 20 (January 1955): 24–25.

45   For analyses of Cao Daism, see Victor Oliver, *Cao Dai Spiritualism* (Leiden, 1976); Hue Tam Ho Tai, *Millenarianism and Peasant Politics in Vietnam* (Cambridge, Mass., 1983), esp. chaps. 5 and 6; Jayne Werner, "The Cao Dai" (Ph.D. diss., Cornell University, 1976); idem, *Peasant Politics and Religious Sectarianism* (New Haven, Conn., 1981). See also Gerald Hickey, *Village in Vietnam* (New Haven, Conn., 1964), 66–73, 290–94; Marr, *Vietnam, 1945*, 83–84, 110–12; Archimedes Patti, *Why Vietnam?* (Berkeley, Calif., 1980), 212, 257–58, 277, 500–503.

46   Collins Papers: Collins to Dulles, 23 November 1954: box 25, EL.

47   NIE: Probable Developments in South Vietnam, Laos, and Cambodia through July 1956, 23 November 1954, *FRUS*, *1952–54*, 13:2286–90.

48   Collins Papers: Collins to Dulles, 1 December 1954: box 25, EL.

49   Collins, *Lightning Joe*, 390. See also Collins Papers: Memorandum for the Record: Phan Huy Quat—His Ideas Re: A National Assembly, 24 November 1954: box 29, EL.

50   Anderson, *Trapped by Success*, 49–50; Bui Diem and David Chanoff, *In the Jaws of History* (Boston, 1987), 62–89.

51   Cited in Collins Papers: Collins to Dulles, 20 November 1954: box 31, EL.

52   Collins Papers: Collins to Dulles, 11 December 1954: box 31, EL; Collins Papers: Collins to Dulles, 11 December 1954: box 29, EL; Collins Papers: Collins to Dulles, 12 December 1954: box 25, EL; Collins Papers: Collins to Dulles, 6 December 1954: ibid.

53   Cited in Memorandum of Conversation, 7 December 1954, RG 59, 751G.00/12-754.

54   The Secretary of State to the Embassy in Vietnam, 9 December 1954, *FRUS*, *1952–54*, 13:2356–57.

55   Collins Papers: Fishel to Collins, 11 December 1954: box 29, EL.

56   Collins Papers: Collins to Dulles, 13 December 1954: box 29, EL.

57   Collins Papers: Collins to Dulles, 16 December 1954: box 25, EL.

58   The Acting Secretary of State to the Embassies in Paris and Saigon, 17 December 1954, *FRUS*, *1952–54*, 13:2393–94.

59   Collins Papers: Dulles to Collins, 24 December 1954: box 25, EL.

60 See Collins to Dulles, 6 December 1954, RG 59, 751G.00/12-654; Collins Papers: Collins to Dulles, 6 April 1955: box 26, EL; Collins to Dulles, 10 May 1955, RG 59, 751G.00/3-1055.

61 Collins Papers: Spellman to Amembassy Saigon, 15 December 1954: box 31, EL; Collins to Spruance, 16 December 1954, ibid.

62 Collins Papers: Kidder to Collins, 17 December 1954: box 31, EL.

63 Cited in Collins Papers: Memorandum of Staff Meeting, 4 January 1955: box 25, EL.

64 Cited in Collins Papers: Sturm to Collins, 24 December 1954: box 29, EL.

65 Handbill: "Here is Premier Diem's True Face," submitted by Kidder to Dulles, 13 February 1955, RG 59, 751G.00/2-1555. See also Viet Nam Quoc Dan Dang (VNQDD) broadsheet: "A Dictatorship by Catholics—A New Kind of Fascism," 8 July 1955, RG 59, 751G.00/7-855; Cao Dai handbill: "A Government of Religion and Family," 30 December 1954, RG 59, 751G.00/12-3054.

66 Cited in Collins Papers: Collins to Dulles, 12 February 1955: box 31, EL.

67 Cited in Collins Papers: Collins to Dulles, 18 February 1955: box 31, EL.

68 Fishel to Collins, 6 March 1955, RG 59, 751G.00/3-55.

69 Harnett to Swanstrom, 16 January 1955, Harnett Papers, box 2.

70 "Viet Refugees Hail Cardinal Spellman," *Catholic Universe-Bulletin*, 14 January 1955. See also "Medal from Vietnam," *New World*, 12 January 1955. For a detailed account of another Spellman visit to South Vietnam, see Catholic Relief Services—National Catholic Welfare Conference, Viet-Nam Mission, Monthly Narrative Report, 31 January 1956, Mansfield Papers, series XIII, box 8.

71 Cited in Kidder to Dulles, 18 April 1955, RG 59, 751G.0/4-1855.

72 Report on Vietnam for the National Security Council by General J. Lawton Collins, 20 January 1955, RG 59, 751G.00/1-2055.

73 Collins, *Lightning Joe*, 397.

74 Collins Papers: Eisenhower to Diem, 3 February 1955: box 25, EL. See also Diem to Eisenhower, 23 January 1955, Vietnam Collection, George Kahin Donation, National Security Archives, George Washington University, Washington [hereafter Kahin Donation], box 1.

75 Cited in Clyde Pettit, *The Experts* (Secaucus, N.J., 1975), 84.

76 Mecklin, *Mission in Torment*, 159; Olson, *Mansfield and Vietnam*, 42–45; Sheehan, *Bright Shining Lie*, 143–44. A Buddhist anti-Diem group calling itself the "Committee of Popular Conciliation" warned U.S. Embassy Chargé Randolph Kidder of "a strong feeling among the people that everything is being done for the northern refugees and virtually nothing for the local population." Cited in Kidder to Dulles, 29 April 1955, RG 59, 751G.00/4-2955. See also Collins Papers: Collins to Dulles, 17 February 1955: box 31, EL.

77 "South Vietnam: The Beleaguered Man," 22; Tillman Durdin, "Indochina Political Feuds Threaten Diem's Regime," *New York Times*, 27 March 1955; "U.S. in Middle of Gang War," *U.S. News and World Reports* 38 (13 May 1955):

39–41; Schmid, "Free Indo-China Fights Against Time," 24–25; Patrick O'Connor, "Vietnam 'Sects' Aren't Religious," *Tablet*, 2 April 1955; "Religious Sects?" *Ave Maria* 81 (23 April 1955): 6; "Sects Mentioned in Vietnam News Are Irreligious," *Catholic Bulletin*, 2 April 1955.

78 "Buddhism," *Life* 38 (7 March 1955): 100–103.

79 Frank Meyer, "Principles and Heresies," reprinted in *The Times They Were A'Changing*, ed. Irwin Unger and Debi Unger, 100–101 (New York, 1998); Tillman Durdin, "Reds Have Margin in Indochina Despite Even Split Under Truce," *New York Times*, 21 July 1954; "The *Atlantic* Report on the World Today: Cambodia," *Atlantic Monthly* 208 (October 1955): 18.

80 "Buddhist Priest Sought Certainty," *Our Sunday Visitor*, 18 July 1954; "From Buddhism to Catholicism," *Tablet*, 26 March 1955; "Buddhism to the Faith," *New World*, 18 March 1955; "From Buddha to Christ," *Catholic Herald-Citizen*, 16 April 1955; "Lay Missionary," *Catholic Universe Bulletin*, 11 March 1955; Julius Dorszynski, "In Indonesia It's Buddha or Christ," *Catholic Herald-Citizen*, 26 March 1955.

81 Henri de Lubac, *Aspects of Buddhism* (New York, 1953), 51–52, 41, 49, 127. For the paucity of scholarship on Buddhism in mid-1950s America, see Patricia Armstrong Vessie, *Zen Buddhism: A Bibliography of Books and Articles in English, 1892–1975* (Ann Arbor, 1976), 1–39.

82 Isaacs, *Scratches on Our Minds*, 11, 45, 86, 82, 259, 353–54.

83 Collins Papers: Collins to Dulles, 6 December 1954: box 25, EL.

84 Buttinger, *Vietnam: A Dragon Embattled*, 2:865–71; Collins, *Lightning Joe*, 397–98; Lansdale, *In the Midst of Wars*, 228–40.

85 Collins Papers: Proclamation of the Binh Xuyen, Cao Dai, and Hoa Hao Sects, 4 March 1955: box 30, EL.

86 Collins, *Lightning Joe*, 398.

87 Collins Papers: Voice of the Unified Front of All the Nationalist Forces, 21 March 1955: box 30, EL.

88 Telegram from the Special Representative in Saigon to the Department of State, 22 March 1955, *FRUS, 1955–57*, 1:140–41.

89 Collins, *Lightning Joe*, 399.

90 Collins Papers: Collins to Dulles, 23 March 1955: box 31, EL.

91 Buttinger, *Vietnam: A Dragon Embattled*, 2:871. See also Collins to Dulles, 30 March 1955, RG 59, 751G.00/3-3055.

92 Collins Papers: Collins to Dulles, 31 March 1955: box 25, EL.

93 Dulles Papers, Telephone Calls Series: Dulles to Eisenhower, 1 April 1955: box 10, EL; Ann Whitman File, Dwight D. Eisenhower, Papers as President, DDE Diary Series, 1 April 1955: box 9, EL.

94 Olson, *Mansfield and Vietnam*, 61. See also Oberdorfer, *Senator Mansfield*, 132–35.

95 Mike Mansfield Interview, 28 September 1966, DOHP.

96   Memorandum of Conversation, 1 April 1955, Mansfield Papers, series XXII, box 107. See also Dulles Papers, Telephone Calls Series: Mansfield to Dulles, 1 April 1955: box 3, EL.

97   Collins Papers: Dulles to Collins, 1 April 1955: box 26, EL.

98   Cooper, *Lost Crusade*, 140–43; Shaplen, *Lost Revolution*, 120–21.

99   Lansdale, *In the Midst of Wars*, 272.

100   "South Vietnam: The Beleaguered Man," cover page and 22–27.

101   See for example Collins Papers: Collins to Dulles, 1 April 1955: box 32, EL; Collins Papers: Collins to Dulles, 2 April 1955: ibid.; Collins Papers: Collins to Dulles, 2 April 1955: box 26, EL; Collins Papers: Collins to Dulles, 4 April 1955: ibid.; Collins Papers: Collins to Dulles, 5 April 1955: ibid.; Collins Papers: Collins to Dulles, 6 April 1955: ibid.

102   Ambrose, *Eisenhower: The President*, 231–45; Bennett Rushkoff, "Eisenhower, Dulles, and the Quemoy-Matsu Crisis, 1954–1955," *Political Science Quarterly* 96 (fall 1981): 465–80.

103   For Eisenhower's preoccupation with the Formosa crisis and Dulles's control of America's Vietnam policy during the early months of 1955, see Anderson, *Trapped by Success*, 117; Daniel Greene, "John Foster Dulles and the End of the Franco-American Entente in Indochina," *Diplomatic History* 20 (spring 1996): 557.

104   Press and Radio News Conference, Tuesday, 15 March 1955, 11:00 A.M. EST, Dulles Papers, box 93.

105   Collins Papers: Dulles to Collins, 6 April 1955: box 26, EL.

106   Cited in Collins Papers: Collins to Dulles, 7 April 1955: box 26, EL.

107   Collins Papers: Collins to Dulles, 7 April 1955: box 26, EL.

108   These meetings were referred to but not discussed in depth in a conversation between Dulles and White House Chief of Staff Sherman Adams. Dulles Papers, Telephone Calls Series: Dulles to Adams, 8 April 1955: box 10, EL.

109   Dulles Papers, Telephone Calls Series: Dulles to Dulles, 11 April 1955: box 3, EL.

110   Anderson, *Trapped by Success*, 104–5; Oberdorfer, *Senator Mansfield*, 136–37; Olson, *Mansfield and Vietnam*, 56.

111   Cited in Young to Dulles, 8 April 1955, RG 59, 751G.00/4-855.

112   Collins Papers: Dulles to Collins, 8 April 1955: box 26, EL; Collins Papers: Collins to Dulles, 9 April 1955: ibid.

113   Collins Papers: Dulles to Collins, 9 April 1955: box 26, EL.

114   Collins Papers: Collins to Dulles, 10 April 1955: box 26, EL.

115   Draft Telegram from the Secretary of State to the Embassy in Vietnam, 11 April 1955; Revised Draft Telegram from the Secretary of State to the Embassy in Vietnam, 11 April 1955, *FRUS, 1955–57*, 1:236–38; Dulles Papers, White House Memoranda Series: Memorandum of Meeting with the President, 12 noon, 11 April 1955: box 3, EL.

116 Dulles Papers, Telephone Calls Series: Dulles to Robertson, 3:57 P.M., 11 April 1955: box 3, EL.
117 Memorandum of Conversation, 4:00 P.M., 11 April 1955, RG 59, 751G.00/4-1155.
118 Dulles Papers, Telephone Calls Series: Dulles to George, 4:41 P.M., 11 April 1955: box 3, EL.
119 Young to Robertson, 11 April 1955, RG 59, 751G.00/4-1155.
120 The Secretary of State to the Embassy in Vietnam, 11 April 1955, *FRUS, 1955–57*, 1:239–41.
121 Dulles speech: "Principles in Foreign Policy," 11 April 1955, Dulles Papers, box 335. See the introduction for a fuller analysis of the secretary's address.
122 Telegram from the Special Representative in Vietnam to the Department of State, 12 April 1955, *FRUS, 1955–57*, 1:242–44.
123 Collins to Dulles, 13 April 1955, RG 59, 751G.00/4-1355.
124 Cited in Collins Papers: Collins to Dulles, 19 April 1955: box 26, EL.
125 Dulles Papers, White House Memoranda Series: Memorandum of Conversation with the President, 16 April 1955: box 3, EL. See also Dulles Papers, Telephone Calls Series: Dulles to Eisenhower, 16 April 1955: box 10, EL.
126 Collins Papers: Dulles to Collins, 16 April 1955: box 25, EL. See also Hagerty Papers, Diary Entries: 12–20 April 1955: box 1a, EL.
127 Collins Papers: Collins to Dulles, 19 April 1955: box 26, EL.
128 Sebald to Dulles, 23 April 1955, RG 59, 751G.00/4-2355.
129 White House Office, Office of the Special Assistant for National Security Affairs, Special Assistant Series, Chronological Subseries: Memorandum for the Record: South Vietnam—General Joe Collins's Comments, 22 April 1955: box 1, EL.
130 Cited in Shaplen, *Lost Revolution*, 122.
131 White House Office, Office of the Special Assistant for National Security Affairs, Special Assistant Series, Chronological Subseries: Memorandum for the Record: South Vietnam—General Joe Collins's Comments, 22 April 1955: box 1, EL.
132 USARMA Saigon to Dulles, 20 April 1955, RG 59, 751G.00/4-2055; USARMA Saigon to Dulles, 23 April 1955, RG 59, 751G.00/4-2355.
133 A. M. Rosenthal, "Vietnam's Rebels Cool to Peace Bid," *New York Times*, 24 April 1955.
134 Kidder to Dulles, 22 April 1955, RG 59, 751G.00/4-2255.
135 Hensel to Robertson, 24 April 1955, RG 59, 751G.00/4-2455.
136 Ann Whitman File, Legislative Meetings Series: Legislative Leadership Meeting, Supplementary Notes, 26 April 1955: box 1, EL. See also White House Office Papers, Office of the Staff Secretary Records, Legislative Meeting Series: Memorandum for the Record, 26 April 1955: box 2, EL.
137 Summary of Remarks of General J. Lawton Collins, 27 April 1955, Mansfield Papers, series XXII, box 107. For Collins's account of the meeting, see Col-

lins Papers: Staff Meeting, 3 May 1955: box 25, EL. There is no record of Collins's appeals to the congressional committees, but it became apparent within a few days that most committee members were not won over by his presentation of the case for removing Diem.

138   Cited in Olson, *Mansfield and Vietnam*, 59.

139   Young to Robertson, 30 April 1955, *U.S.-VN Relations*, 10:945–47.

140   Collins Papers: Dulles to Kidder/Dillon: Deptel 3828, 27 April 1955: box 25, EL; Collins Papers: Dulles to Kidder/Dillon: Deptel 3829, 27 April 1955: ibid.

141   Some, like James Arnold, argue that "Diem learned of Washington's decision [to replace him], and decided to precipitate a crisis." Arnold, *First Domino*, 276. See also Anderson, *Trapped by Success*, 111; Schulzinger, *A Time for War*, 74; Short, *Origins of the Vietnam War*, 206; Warner, *Last Confucian*, 103. Others contend that it was Bay Vien, not Diem, who started the battle—even though, had Vien simply stayed his hand for a few hours, the Americans would have done his dirty work for him. See for example Clark Dougan, Edward Doyle, Samuel Lipsman, and Stephen Weiss, *The Vietnam Experience* (Boston, 1982), 2:128; Herring, *America's Longest War*, 53–54; Shaplen, *Lost Revolution*, 123.

142   Shaplen, *Lost Revolution*, 122–23.

143   "All-Out Civil War Rages in Saigon; Palace Is Shelled, Area Set Afire," *New York Herald Tribune*, 29 April 1955; "100 Killed in Saigon as Rebel Sect Forces Open War on Premier," *Washington Post-Herald*, 29 April 1955; "Saigon Battle Renewed, 100 Dead," *Boston Globe*, 29 April 1955; "Saigon Is Two Cities, and One Is Dying," *New York Times*, 30 April 1955. For detailed treatments of the Battle for Saigon, see Blagov, *Honest Mistakes*, 143–94; Currey, *Edward Lansdale*, 176–82; Lansdale, *In the Midst of Wars*, 282–311.

144   Collins Papers: Dulles to Kidder/Dillon, 27 April 1955: box 25, EL.

145   "Conditions in South Vietnam," *Congressional Record* 101 (2 May 1955): 5288–91.

146   Cited in Pettit, *Experts*, 87.

147   "Collins's Removal as Aide in Asia Urged by Dodd," *Washington Post*, 2 May 1955.

148   For reference to the leak, see Young to Sebald, 29 April 1955, RG 59, 751G.00/4-2955.

149   Mansfield speech, 2 May, "But Which He Made Available Today," 29 April 1955, Mansfield Papers, series XXI, box 37.

150   Collins Papers: Dulles to Kidder/Dillon, 30 April 1955: box 25, EL.

151   Young to Robertson, 30 April 1955, RG 59, 751G.00/4-3055.

152   In the months following his defeat of the Binh Xuyen, Diem sent his troops to eliminate disloyal Cao Dai and Hoa Hao strongholds in the Mekong Delta, but these were little more than cleanup operations that occurred well

after the Battle for Saigon had ended. During the pivotal days of late April and early May 1955, there was hardly any armed combat between VNA soldiers and the troops of the two religious groups. Robert MacAlister, a Diem supporter who was in Saigon at the time, concludes that "in terms of fighting forces, the Binh Xuyen stood pretty much alone." MacAlister, "The Great Gamble" (M.A. thesis, University of Chicago, 1958), 109. See also Arnold, *First Domino*, 276–79; Buttinger, *Vietnam: A Dragon Embattled*, 2:878–85; Collins, *Lightning Joe*, 406; Lansdale, *In the Midst of Wars*, 291–309.

153 Mansfield speech: "American Foreign Policy in the Far East," 22 May 1955, Mansfield Papers, series XXI, box 37.

154 Dulles address to the Washington Council of Governors, 2 May 1955, Dulles Papers, box 99.

155 "South Vietnam: The Beleaguered Man," 22; "U.S. in Middle of Gang War," *U.S. News and World Report* 38 (13 May 1955): 39–41; Max Lerner, "Chaos in Vietnam," *New York Post*, 14 March 1955; "Tragedy in Saigon," *New York Times* 30 May 1955; "Trouble in Vietnam," *New York Times*, 6 April 1955; Howard Simpson, "Showdown in Saigon," *Commonweal* 62 (12 May 1955): 140; idem, "Last Hope in Viet-Nam," *Commonweal* 62 (25 March 1955): 650–52; Robert Crane, "Dilemma in Indo-China," *Christian Century* 72 (5 May 1955): 587; "Who's Fighting Whom in Saigon?" *Christian Century* 72 (18 May 1955): 620–22.

156 Henry Luce, "Revolution in Vietnam," *Life* 38 (16 May 1955): 3.

157 Calvin Trillin, *Remembering Denny* (New York, 1993), 7.

158 Collins Papers: Dillon to Dulles, 6 May 1955: box 26, EL.

159 "U.S. Friend Wins Saigon Fight," *Boston Herald*, 2 May 1955.

160 Cited in Harold Callender, "Vietnamese Army Winning Fight With Rebels," *New York Times*, 30 April 1955.

161 Kidder to Dulles, 8 May 1955, RG 59, 751G.00/5-855.

162 "They Are Going to Hit . . . Sooner or Later," *Life* 38 (9 May 1955): 28.

163 Cited in "U.S. v. the French," *Time* 65 (16 May 1955): 37.

164 "Manifesto of the Revolutionary Committee in Free Viet-Nam," 1 May 1955, Pike Collection, unit VI—Republic of Vietnam, box 12.

165 Collins Papers: Kidder to Dulles, 1 May 1955: box 26, EL.

166 The Secretary of State to the Embassy in Vietnam, 1 May 1955, *FRUS, 1955–57*, 1:344–45.

167 Collins, *Lightning Joe*, 407.

168 Dana Adams Schmidt, "Collins's Advice Awaited," *New York Times*, 21 April 1955. See also Collins Papers: Dulles to State Department, 16 March 1955: box 25, EL.

169 Dulles Papers, Telephone Calls Series: Dulles to Eisenhower, 6 May 1955: box 10, EL.

170 Republican National Committee, White House Press Releases: Hagerty Statement, 10 May 1955: box 96, EL. See also Dulles Press Conference, 13 May 1955, Dulles Papers, box 99.

171 Collins Papers: Collins to Dulles, 5 May 1955: box 26, EL.

172 Young to Dulles/Robertson, 6 May 1955, RG 59, 751G.00/5-655.

173 Dulles Papers, White House Memoranda Series: Memorandum of Conversation with the President, 6 May 1955: box 3, EL.

174 The Secretary of State to the Department of State, 8 May 1955, *FRUS, 1955–57*, 1:372–76.

175 The Secretary of State to the Department of State, 8 May 1955, *FRUS, 1955–57*, 1:377.

176 The Ambassador in Saigon to the Embassy in France, 9 May 1955, *FRUS, 1955–57*, 1:382–85.

177 Hoey to Dulles, 9 May 1955, RG 59, 751G.00/5-955. I am indebted to Daniel Greene for drawing my attention to this document. Greene, "Tug of War," 441–42.

178 Bonesteel memorandum, 9 May 1955, *U.S.-VN Relations*, 10:975.

179 *Pentagon Papers (Gravel Edition)*, 1:304.

180 Dulles to Hoover, 8 May 1955, *U.S.-VN Relations*, 10:964–66.

181 Cited in the Ambassador in France to the Department of State, 11 May 11 1955, *FRUS, 1955–57*, 1:393–99.

182 Cited in Greene, "Tug of War," 372.

183 Cited in Aldrich to Dulles, 15 May 1955, RG 59, 751G.00/5-1555.

184 The Secretary of State to the Department of State, 13 May 1955, *FRUS, 1955–57*, 1:408.

185 Greene, "Tug of War," 421–89; idem, "End of the Franco-American Entente," 551–71; Hoopes, *Devil and John Foster Dulles*, 259–61; Shaplen, *Lost Revolution*, 127–28.

186 Dulles Papers, Subject Series: Memorandum of Conversation, 11 May 1955: box 9, EL; Telegram from the Ambassador in France to the Department of State, 11 May 1955, *FRUS, 1955–57*, 1:398; Memo of U.S.-French Meeting at Hotel Matignon, 11 May 1955, Kahin Donation, box 1.

187 Minutes of the 249th Meeting of the National Security Council, 19 May 1955, *FRUS, 1955–57*, 1:415.

188 Kidder to Dulles, 30 April 1955, RG 59, 751G.00/4-3055.

189 Memorandum of Conversation, 3 May 1955, RG 59, 751G.00/5-355.

190 Collins to Dulles, 15 May 1955, RG 59, 751G.00/5-1555. Diem's official statement to his people upon presenting the new cabinet did not smack of town hall democracy. "[The] government will not permit misled elements to provoke disorder, weaken independence, or prevent social reform," the premier proclaimed. "Regardless of personal convictions, individuals can only suitably defend Free Vietnam by accepting [the] government's decisions

without reservation." Cited in Collins to Dulles, 11 May 1955, RG 59, 751G.00/5-1155.

191   Dulles to Reinhardt, 13 May 1955, RG 59, 751G.00/5-1355.

192   Cited in Cooper, *Lost Crusade*, 148.

193   Collins, *Lightning Joe*, 410.

194   Dulles to Collins, 3 June 1955, Dulles Papers, box 90.

6. THE VIETNAM LOBBY

1   Ambrose, *Eisenhower*, 2:384.

2   "The King Comes West," *Time* 69 (28 January 1957): 27–33.

3   "Welcome, President Diem," *New York Times*, 8 May 1957.

4   Andrew Tully, "A Shy Little Man, But Full of Dignity," *Washington News*, 9 May 1957.

5   Remarks of Welcome to Ngo Dinh Diem at the Washington National Airport, 8 May 1957, *Public Papers of the Presidents: Dwight D. Eisenhower, 1957* (Washington, 1958), 334. Remarks of Welcome to President Eisenhower, ibid.

6   Cited in "President Hails Viet Nam Chief," *Washington Evening Star*, 8 May 1957.

7   Russell Baker, "Eisenhower Greets Vietnam President, Lauds Patriotism," *New York Times*, 9 May 1957. See also "Red Carpet for Mr. Diem," *U.S. News and World Report* 42 (17 May 1957): 20.

8   Address by John Foster Dulles, 8 May 1955, Dulles Papers, box 98.

9   Address by the Assistant Secretary of State for Far Eastern Affairs, Washington, 1 June 1956, *Pentagon Papers (Gravel Edition)*, 1:610–11.

10   Toasts of the President and President Diem of Viet-Nam, 8 May 1957, *Public Papers of the Presidents: Dwight D. Eisenhower, 1957*, 334–35.

11   Bowles Address: "The Future of Free Asia," 17 April 1959, Leo Cherne Papers, Special Collections and Archives, Mugar Library, Boston University, Boston, Massachusetts [hereafter Cherne Papers], box 17.

12   Patrick O'Connor, "World Indebted to Vietnam Head," *Tablet*, 20 April 1957; "A Hero Comes to the U.S.," *Catholic Universe Bulletin*, 5 May 1957; Freda Utley, "The Amazing Mr. Diem," *National Review* 2 (24 November 1956): 16.

13   Luce Circular, 23 April 1957, AFV Papers, box 11.

14   John Osborne, "The Tough Miracle Man of Vietnam," *Life* 42 (13 May 1957): 156–76; Ernest Lindley, "A Friend Named Diem," *Newsweek* 49 (20 May 1957): 40; Philip Cook, "Miracle Maker from Asia—Diem of South Vietnam," *New York Herald Tribune*, 9 May 1957; William Randolph Hearst, "South Viet-Nam Boldly Supports America," *New York Journal-American*, 13 April 1956; "Anniversary in Vietnam," *New York Times*, 7 July 1959; Ed-

ward Murrow Interview with CBS Correspondent, Extract in Duke to Editors of *Reporter*, 15 March 1963, AFV Papers, box 11.

15 Dwayne Bess, "Bright Spot in Asia," *Saturday Evening Post* 224 (15 September 1956): 229; "Another Place Where the Reds Are Losing," *U.S. News and World Report* 42 (1 March 1957): 47; "Country at Peace," *Time* 69 (11 February 1957): 30–31; "Signs of Progress," *Time* 70 (30 December 1957): 24; O. K. Armstrong, "Biggest Little Man in Asia," *Reader's Digest* 68 (February 1956): 144–48.

16 William Henderson, "South Vietnam Finds Itself," *Foreign Affairs* 35 (January 1957): 283–86; Guy Pauker, "The Future of Vietnam," *Foreign Policy Bulletin* 36 (1 November 1956): 29–32; Francis Corley, "Viet-Nam since Geneva," *Thought* 33 (winter 1958–59), 515–68; Ellen Hammer, "Progress Report on Southern Viet Nam," *Pacific Affairs* 30 (September 1957): 221–35.

17 Morgan, *Vietnam Lobby*, 27–28.

18 Fisher, *Dr. America*, 99–100.

19 Joseph Lash, "Vietnam Isn't a Lost Cause," *New York Post*, 14 January 1955; Gouverneur Paulding, "Little Mr. Diem," *Reporter* 11 (2 December 1954): 4; Howard Simpson, "Last Hope in Vietnam," *Commonweal* 61 (25 March 1955): 652.

20 Cited in Brownell, "Vietnam Lobby," 170.

21 Letter from the Elders Addressed to President Ngo-Dinh-Diem, 7 June 1956, RG 59, 751G.00/6-756.

22 Anderson to Dulles, 12 July 1956, RG 59, 751G.00/7-1256.

23 Joseph Amter, *Vietnam Verdict* (New York, 1984), 30–31; Duiker, *Ho Chi Minh*, 472–73; Kolko, *Anatomy of a War*, 89.

24 Fall, *Viet-Nam Witness*, 235; Karnow, *Vietnam: A History*, 227.

25 For the "self-containment" of Vietnamese villages, see Bernard Fall, "Representative Government in the State of Vietnam," *Far Eastern Survey* 23 (August 1954): 122–25; FitzGerald, *Fire in the Lake*, 53–56, 147; Paul Mus, "The Role of the Village in Vietnamese Politics," *Pacific Affairs* 22 (September 1949): 266–67.

26 Dennis Duncanson, *Government and Revolution in Vietnam* (New York, 1968), 211–28; Kahin, *Intervention*, 96–101; Scigliano, *South Vietnam*, 54.

27 Cited in Dillon to Dulles, 19 October 1955, RG 59, 751G.00/10-1955.

28 The Secretary of State's Press Conference, 7 August 1955, Dulles Papers, box 93.

29 Cited in Maclear, *Ten Thousand Day War*, 53.

30 Herring, *America's Longest War*, 55.

31 Cited in Reinhardt to Dulles, 21 October 1955, RG 59, 751G.00/10-2155. See also Anderson to Dulles, 18 October 1955, RG 59, 751G.00/10-1855.

32 "Westerners See Victory for Diem in Viet Nam Vote," *Washington Daily News*, 19 October 1955.

33 Reinhardt to Dulles, 25 October 1955, RG 59, 751G.00/10-2555.

34 Anderson to Dulles, 29 November 1955, RG 59, 751G.00/11-2955.

35 See especially Wesley Fishel, "Problems of Democratic Growth in Free Viet-Nam," *New Leader* 40 (7 December 1957): 16–21. Fishel praised Diem's "rule by law, in distinction to Ho Chi Minh's rule by terrorism."

36 The Constitution of the Republic of Vietnam, 26 October 1956, Pike Collection, unit IV—Republic of Vietnam, box 13. See also Catton, *Diem's Final Failure*, 13; J. A. C. Grant, "The Vietnamese Constitution of 1956," *American Political Science Review* 83 (June 1959): 329–62.

37 Warner, *Last Confucian*, 107–14.

38 Wilfred Burchett, *The Furtive War* (New York, 1963), 44–45.

39 Olson and Roberts, *Where the Domino Fell*, 66; Jamieson, *Understanding Vietnam*, 236–37.

40 Gheddo, *Cross and Bo-Tree*, 146–51.

41 Cited in FitzGerald, *Fire in the Lake*, 565–66.

42 Anderson to Dulles: President Diem's Political Philosophy, 8 August 1956, RG 59, 751G.00/8-856.

43 Ambassador Lodge to State Department, 19 September 1963, *Pentagon Papers: New York Times Edition*, 228–29.

44 Robert Scheer and Warren Hinkle, "The Vietnam Lobby," *Ramparts* 3 (July 1965): 16–24.

45 Scheer and Hinkle, "The Vietnam Lobby: Part II," *Ramparts* 7 (January 1969): 32.

46 Herring, *America's Longest War*, 57.

47 Morgan, *Vietnam Lobby*, xii.

48 Anderson, *Trapped by Success*, 118.

49 Buttinger, *Vietnam: A Dragon Embattled*, 2:1109. Emphasis added.

50 Leo Cherne to Members of the Research Institute, 13 September 1954, Cherne Papers, box 17; Cherne to Stassen, 30 September 1954, Cherne Papers, box 37; Stassen to Cherne, 6 October 1954, ibid.; Cherne to Diem, 7 October 1954, ibid.

51 Cited in Morgan, *Vietnam Lobby*, 18.

52 Joseph Buttinger, *In the Twilight of Socialism* (New York, 1953).

53 Transcript of IRC Board of Directors Meeting, 6 October 1954, Cherne Papers, box 28.

54 Excerpts from Cherne Press Conference after Returning from Indo-China, undated, Cherne Papers, box 57; Cherne Memorandum for Dorothy Houghton, 20 October 1954, Cherne Papers, box 37.

55 Cherne to Diem, 12 October 1954, Buttinger Papers. Cherne wrote Ambassador Donald Heath that Buttinger's "helpful . . . attributes" included "his own Austrian-Catholic background." Cherne to Heath, 12 October 1954, Cherne Papers, box 37.

56 Cooper, *Lost Crusade*, 132.

57 Diary Entry, 27 October 1954, Buttinger Papers.

58 Buttinger to Cherne, 21 November 1954, Buttinger Papers.

59 Diary Entry, 14 December 1954, Buttinger Papers.

60 Buttinger to Cherne, 4 December 1954, Buttinger Papers.

61 Buttinger: Memorandum on Indochina, 22 December 1954, Buttinger Papers.

62 Diary Entry, 20 November 1954, Buttinger Papers.

63 Diary Entries: 29 November, 13 December, 17 December, 18 December 1954, Buttinger Papers.

64 Suggested Form Letter to Senators, Newspapers, Government Officials, Etc., undated, Buttinger Papers.

65 Diary Entry, 20 November 1954, Buttinger Papers. This officer was almost certainly Colonel Edward Lansdale, the CIA operative whose work in Vietnam is addressed in chapter 4. Buttinger subsequently mentioned Lansdale by name in his Saigon journal. See Diary Entry, 2 December 1954.

66 Buttinger to Diem, 11 December 1954, Buttinger Papers.

67 Buttinger, *Vietnam: The Unforgettable Tragedy*, 69.

68 Buttinger to Oram, 22 April 1954, Buttinger Papers.

69 Oram to Chuong, 2 September 1955, Buttinger Papers. See also Oram to Diem, undated, ibid.

70 Oram Memorandum: "Summary of Expenses to be Incurred in the Proposed Public Relations Campaign on Behalf of the Government of South Vietnam," 25 May 1955, Buttinger Papers.

71 Buttinger to Fairbanks, 26 September 1963, Buttinger Papers.

72 Morgan, *Vietnam Lobby*, 21–22.

73 Young to Robertson, with attached Memorandum on Indochina by Buttinger, 6 January 1955, RG 59, 751G.00/1-655. See also Oram to Dulles, with attached Memorandum by Buttinger, 3 June 1955, RG 59, 751G.00/6-355; Buttinger to Dulles, 21 January 1955, Dulles Papers, box 99.

74 Dulles to Buttinger, 16 February 1955, Buttinger Papers; Chester, *Covert Network*, 163.

75 Buttinger to Mansfield, 21 February 1975, Mansfield Papers, series XXII, box 55. See also Buttinger to Mansfield, 8 February 1955, Mansfield Papers, series XIII, box 8.

76 "Hope in Vietnam?" *New York Times*, 29 January 1955; Joseph Buttinger, "Our Policy toward Vietnam," *New York Times*, 30 January 1955. I am indebted to Gregory Olson for pointing out the appearance of these two *Times* pieces shortly after the Buttinger interview. Olson, *Mansfield and Vietnam*, 52.

77 Joseph Buttinger, "An Eyewitness Report on Vietnam," *Reporter* 12 (20 January 1955): 19–20. See also idem, "Saigon: Intrigue," *New Republic* 132 (28 February 1955): 9–10; "Are We Saving South Vietnam?" *New Leader* 38 (27 June 1955): 53–59, 510–15.

78 Martin to Buttinger, 24 February 1955, Buttinger Papers.

79 Complete List of AFV Members, 7 May 1956, AFV Papers, box 4.

80 James Aronson, *The Press and the Cold War* (Indianapolis, 1970), 184–86; Scheer, *How the United States Became Involved in Vietnam*, 34–37.

81 Cited in Brownell, "Vietnam Lobby," 140–42. George Kahin concurs with Cherne's recollection, observing, "There were so few Vietnam specialists in the U.S. [that] Diem's advocates had an almost open field and exerted a disproportionate influence on American opinion." George Kahin and John Lewis, *The United States in Vietnam* (New York, 1967), 80.

82 Fisher, *Dr. America*, 109.

83 Thomas to Oram, 21 October 1955, AFV Papers, box 9.

84 Thomas to O'Daniel, February 1958, AFV Papers, box 4.

85 "Statement of Purpose of the American Friends of Vietnam," 20 October 1955, AFV Papers, box 1.

86 Cited in Oram to Chuong, 19 July 1956, Buttinger Papers.

87 Ann Whitman File, Names Series: Donovan to Eisenhower, 5 February 1956: box 8, EL; Eisenhower to Donovan, 7 February 1956, ibid.

88 Minutes of the First Meeting of the Executive Committee, 8 December 1955, AFV Papers, box 1.

89 Department of Defense, Office of Public Information, Press Branch: General John O'Daniel, USA [undated], AFV Papers, box 11.

90 O'Daniel's Report on Inspection Tour of Indochina, 13 March 1954, Kahin Donation, box 1.

91 Heath to State Department, 16 September 1954, *U.S.-VN Relations*, 10:753–55.

92 Heath to Bonsal, 2 February 1954, RG 59, 751G.00/2-254.

93 Cited in Shaplen, *Lost Revolution*, 123.

94 Cited in du Berrier, *Background to Betrayal*, 94.

95 O'Daniel to Oram, 14 June 1957, Buttinger Papers.

96 This conversation is alluded to in Minutes of the First Meeting of the Executive Committee, 8 December 1955, AFV Papers, box 1.

97 Duke to O'Daniel, 14 December 1955, AFV Papers, box 11.

98 White House Central Files, President's Personal File: Persons to O'Daniel, 20 February 1956: box 764, EL.

99 O'Daniel to the American Friends of Vietnam, 1 March 1956, AFV Papers, box 11.

100 John O'Daniel, *The Nation That Refused to Starve* (New York, 1960), 65, 117.

101 Cited in Buttinger, *Vietnam: The Unforgettable Tragedy*, 156.

102 Admiral Ulysses Sharp, the U.S. commander in chief, Pacific (CINCPAC), advised the State Department in late 1955 that "O'Daniel, perhaps more than any other individual, has a keen understanding of the situation in Indochina" and "an intimate knowledge of the Vietnam [*sic*]." Sharp affirmed his "utmost confidence" in O'Daniel's "judgment" and declared that

"full support in implementing his recommendations will be in the best interests of the United States." CINCPAC to DEPTAR WASH, 11 August 1955, Kahin Donation, box 1.

103 Poster: "General John Wilson 'Iron Mike' O'Daniel, Lecture Subjects: 'The War against Communism in Southeast Asia,' 'Combat Principles of the Cold War,' and 'Viet Nam's Fight for Independence,'" 1956, AFV Papers, box 11.

104 Transcript of Conference "The Economic Needs of Vietnam," 17 March 1957, AFV Papers, box 5.

105 O'Daniel, "Brief Concerning the Situation in Vietnam," 1957, AFV Papers, box 13.

106 O'Daniel to Robertson, 31 October 1956, RG 59, 751G.00/10-3155.

107 O'Daniel, "Military Training and Assistance in Vietnam," 1957, AFV Papers, box 11.

108 O'Daniel to the Editor of the *Chicago Sun-Times*, 15 March 1956, AFV Papers, box 11.

109 AFV Publicity: "O'Daniel Praises South Vietnam's Efforts," 27 July 1958, AFV Papers, box 4.

110 O'Daniel memo, 17 April 1956, AFV Papers, box 13.

111 O'Daniel to Oram, 14 June 1957, Buttinger Papers.

112 Hoey to Kocher: O'Daniel's Appearance before the House Foreign Affairs Committee, 2 March 1956, RG 59. 751G.00/3-256.

113 Hanes to Robertson: Extract from Dulles Memorandum, 28 December 1956, RG 59, 751G.00/12-2856. See also Ann Whitman File, International Series: O'Daniel Brief for the President, 2 March 1956: box 50, EL.

114 Diem to O'Daniel, 1 July 1957, AFV Papers, box 11.

115 Minutes of Executive Committee Meeting, 14 February 1956, AFV Papers, box 1; Minutes of Executive Committee Meeting, 14 March 1956, ibid.

116 Minutes of Executive Committee Meeting, 8 May 1956, AFV Papers, box 1.

117 Cited in Jonas to Duke, 25 April 1956, AFV Papers, box 4.

118 Robertson to Duke, 17 May 1956, AFV Papers, box 4.

119 Duke to Mansfield, 17 April 1956, AFV Papers, box 4; Duke to Kennedy, 25 April 1956; Kennedy to O'Daniel, 17 May 1956, ibid.; Mansfield to O'Daniel, 9 May 1956, Mansfield Papers, series XIII, box 8.

120 AFV Press Release, undated, AFV Papers, box 4.

121 Reinhardt to Dulles, 6 May 1956, RG 59, 751G.00/5-656.

122 Dulles to Reinhardt, 10 May 1956, RG 59, 751G.00/5-1056. See also O'Daniel to Jonas, 10 May 1956, AFV Papers, box 4.

123 O'Daniel, "Keynote and Welcome," Transcript of Conference, 1 June 1956, AFV Papers, box 4.

124 Kennedy, "America's Stake in Vietnam," Transcript of Conference, 1 June 1956, AFV Papers, box 4.

125 Robertson, "United States Policy towards Vietnam," Transcript of Conference, 1 June 1956, AFV Papers, box 4.

126 Cherne, "Vietnam's Economy," Transcript of Conference, 1 June 1956, AFV Papers, box 4.

127 Dooley, "Delivering the Refugees," Transcript of Conference, 1 June 1956, AFV Papers, box 4.

128 Harnett, "Refugee Resettlement," Transcript of Conference, 1 June 1956, AFV Papers, box 4.

129 Judd, "Review of American Policy in Asia," Transcript of Conference, 1 June 1956, AFV Papers, box 4.

130 Eisenhower Telegram, Transcript of Conference, 1 June 1956, AFV Papers, box 4.

131 Dulles Telegram, Transcript of Conference, 1 June 1956, AFV Papers, box 4.

132 White House Central Files, President's Personal File: O'Daniel to Persons, 11 June 1965: box 784, EL.

133 Buu Hoan, Review of "America's Stake in Vietnam: A Symposium," *Pacific Affairs* 29 (September 1956): 185–87.

134 John F. Kennedy, "America's Stake in Vietnam," *Vital Speeches of the Day* 22 (1 August 1956): 617–19.

135 This passage from the *Congressional Record* is in Mansfield Papers, series XIII, box 7.

136 Oram's memorandum is discussed in Minutes of Executive Committee Meeting, 28 September 1956, AFV Papers, box 1.

137 Diem cited in Jonas to Executive Committee Members, 11 October 1956, AFV Papers, box 1. See also mailing list, undated, ibid.

138 O'Daniel Form Letter, 10 December 1956, AFV Papers, box 11.

139 Transcript of Conference, 15 March 1957, AFV Papers, box 5. See also Diem to AFV Conference on Investment Conditions, 8 March 1957, AFV Papers, box 4.

140 Joseph Lash, "The Man Who Wouldn't Give Up," *New York Post*, 19 May 1957.

141 Memorandum of Interview with President Diem, 4 December 1956, Buttinger Papers.

142 Chuong Address, 11 April 1957, AFV Papers, box 9.

143 Minutes of Executive Committee Meeting, 12 April 1957, AFV Papers, box 1.

144 Mike Mansfield, "Reprieve in Viet-Nam," *Harper's* 212 (January 1956): 45.

145 Letter from Laos, 1 August 1957, Dooley Papers, series III—Laos, 1955–60.

146 Mansfield, "Reprieve in Viet Nam," 45–51.

147 Interview with Joseph Alsop, 4 March 1966, DOHP.

148 Editor's Note, *Harper's* 212 (January 1956): 3.

149 "Mansfield to Visit Indo-China," *Economist*, 27 August 1955. This verdict is sustained by much Vietnam War scholarship. See Anderson, *Trapped by*

Success, 83; Cooper, *Lost Crusade,* 134; Oberdorfer, *Senator Mansfield,* 138–41; Olson, *Mansfield and Vietnam,* 61.

150   Diem to Mansfield, 5 May 1955, Mansfield Papers, series XXII, box 95.

151   Mansfield to Diem, 13 January 1955, Mansfield Papers, series XIII, box 8.

152   Mansfield to Diem, 17 May 1955, Mansfield Papers, series XXII, box 95.

153   Mansfield to Diem, 12 January 1956, Mansfield Papers, series XII, box 95.

154   Mansfield to Diem, 26 February 1957, Mansfield Papers, series XXII, box 95.

155   Diem to Mansfield, 4 May 1955, Mansfield Papers, series XXII, box 95.

156   Mansfield Speech: "American Foreign Policy in the Far East," 22 May 1955, Mansfield Papers, series XXI, box 37.

157   Mansfield Remarks, *Congressional Record* 103 (13 May 1957). Clipping in Pike Collection, unit IV—Republic of Vietnam, box 12.

158   Hoan to Mansfield, 14 September 1955, Mansfield Papers, series XIII, box 8. See also Hoan to Eisenhower, undated, RG 59, 751G.00/00-00.

159   Thong to Mansfield, with Valeo attachment, 1 February 1957, Mansfield Papers, series XIII, box 8.

160   See Nguyen Thai Binh to Mansfield, 6 March 1956, Mansfield Papers, series XIII, box 8; Tran Van Tung to Mansfield, 12 April 1956, ibid.

161   Brownell, "Vietnam Lobby," 177–84.

162   Hilaire du Berrier, "Report from Saigon," *American Mercury* 87 (September 1958): 43–51.

163   Editor's Note, *American Mercury* 88 (February 1959): 147.

164   John O'Daniel, "Free Vietnam: Modern Miracle," *American Mercury* 88 (February 1959): 146–51.

165   Hilaire du Berrier, "The South Vietnam Americans Never Hear Of," National Economic Council newsletter, December 1957, Pike Collection, unit VI—Republic of Vietnam, box 12.

166   Hilaire du Berrier, "H. du B. Reports" newsletter, 28 October 1957, Buttinger Papers; du Berrier, "H. du B. Reports" newsletter, 16 September 1957, ibid.

167   Du Berrier to Mansfield, 3 July 1956, Mansfield Papers, series XIII, box 6. See also du Berrier to Mansfield, 19 October 1954, ibid.; du Berrier to Mansfield, 29 July 1959, Mansfield Papers, series XIV, box 40; du Berrier to Cherne, 7 January 1957, Buttinger Papers; du Berrier to Cherne, 31 January 1957, ibid.

168   Mansfield to du Berrier, 3 July 1956, Mansfield Papers, series XIII, box 6.

169   Du Berrier to Scanian, 27 August 1958, Mansfield Papers, series XIV, box 40.

170   Osborne, "The Tough Miracle Man of Vietnam," 156–76.

171   Thomas to O'Daniel, 13 May 1957, AFV Papers, box 1.

172   Duke/Cherne/Buttinger to Diem, 12 September 1957, AFV Papers, box 9.

173   Diem's response to the AFV's entreaty is discussed in Minutes of Executive Committee Meeting, 4 December 1957, AFV Papers, box 1.

174   Thomas to O'Daniel, 24 June 1957, AFV Papers, box 11.

175   Thomas to Dulles, 26 July 1957, RG 59, 751G.00/7-2657.

176 Dulles to Thomas, 17 August 1957, RG 59, 751G.00/8-1757.

177 Thomas to O'Daniel, 23 January 1958, AFV Papers, box 4.

178 See Collins to Young, 26 January 1955, RG 59, 751G.00/1-2655; Young to Reinhardt, 3 November 1955, box 5, lot 58D207, Records of Southeast Asia Affairs, RG 59.

179 For reference to the conversation between Reinhardt and Diem, see Robertson to Dulles, 11 February 1957, *FRUS, 1955–57*, 1:762–63.

180 Office of the Chief of Protocol's "Information for Use During the Visit to the United States of His Excellency Ngo Dinh Diem," 13 May 1957, Pike Collection, unit IV—Republic of Vietnam, box 12.

181 White House Central Files, Confidential File, 1953–61, Subject Series: Briefing Book: Ngo Dinh Diem, undated: box 73, EL.

182 O'Daniel to Publishers and Editors, 7 May 1957, plus attached list of recipients, AFV Papers, box 11.

183 "Welcome to a Champion," *Washington Evening Star*, 8 May 1957; "Vietnam's Man of Iron," *Boston Globe*, 6 May 1957; Chalmers Roberts, "Diem—Symbol of Free New Asia," *Washington Post and Times Herald*, 8 May 1957; "Welcome, President Diem," *New York Times*, 8 May 1957; "A Welcome Visitor," *Washington News*, 7 May 1957; William Randolph Hearst Jr., "South Vietnam Boldly Supports America," *New York Journal-American*, 13 April 1957.

184 Address before a Joint Meeting of the Congress, 9 May 1957, *The Emergence of Free Viet-Nam* (Saigon, 1957), 7–11.

185 "Diem on Democracy," *New York Times*, 12 May 1957; "Diem Grateful to U.S. for Aid to Vietnam," *Washington Post*, 10 May 1957; Neal Stanford, "Diem Holds Spotlight in Talk to Congress," *Christian Science Monitor*, 9 May 1957.

186 Speech before the National Press Club, Washington, 10 May 1957, *Emergence of Free Viet-Nam*, 15–18.

187 Cited in "Diem Bids for Increase in U.S. Aid," *Washington Post and Times Herald*, 11 May 1957.

188 "Diem on Democracy," *New York Times*, 12 May 1957; "No Neutrality for Ngo," *America* 97 (25 May 1957): 251; Marguerite Higgins, "Little Diem Called Big in Importance," *New York Herald Tribune*, 12 May 1957.

189 O'Daniel Standard Form Letter to Contributors, 10 June 1957, AFV Papers, box 7; O'Daniel to "Friends," undated, AFV Papers, box 2.

190 "'Faith Inspired Me,' Viet President Says," *Catholic Bulletin*, 17 May 1957; John O'Brien, "Vietnam President Tells the Press He Owes All to His Catholic Faith," *Catholic Bulletin*, 18 May 1957; idem, "Diem Answers a Question," *Catholic Universe Bulletin*, 17 May 1957; Patrick O'Connor, "Vietnam's Diem Guest of Ike," *Catholic Universe Bulletin*, 10 May 1957.

191 Cited in Russell Baker, "Eisenhower Greets Vietnam President," *New York Times*, 9 May 1957.

192 Ann Whitman File, Dulles-Herter Series: Memorandum of Conversation, 9 April 1957: box 10, EL.

193 "John Foster Dulles and the Far East": Transcript of a Special Meeting of the Advisory Committee, 17 July 1964, DOHP.

194 White House Central Files, Confidential File, 1953–1961, Subject Series: Joint Communiqué, 12 May 1957: box 73, EL.

195 Cited in Philip Cook, "City Greets Diem, Here for 3 Days," *New York Herald Tribune*, 13 May 1957.

196 Robert Alden, "Diem, Here for Visit, Relives His Exile at Maryknoll," *New York Times*, 13 May 1957.

197 Address at Seton Hall, 12 May 1957, *Emergence of Free Viet-Nam*, 19.

198 Cited in Robert Alden, "City Accords Diem a Warm Welcome," *New York Times*, 14 May 1957.

199 Address by His Excellency Ngo Dinh Diem, 13 May 1957, Pike Collection, unit IV—Republic of Vietnam, box 12.

200 Address before Council on Foreign Relations, 13 May 1957, Buttinger Papers.

201 Minutes of Executive Committee Meeting, 12 May 1957, AFV Papers, box 11.

202 Guest List, undated, AFV Papers, box 11.

203 Diem Address, Transcript of Dinner in Honor of Ngo Dinh Diem, 13 May 1957, AFV Papers, box 11.

204 Eisenhower Telegram, Transcript of Dinner in Honor of Ngo Dinh Diem, 13 May 1957, AFV Papers, box 11.

205 Diem Address to the Far East-America Council of Commerce and Industry, 14 May 1957, Pike Collection, unit IV—Republic of Vietnam, box 12.

206 Address at Michigan State University, 15 May 1957, *Emergence of Free Viet-Nam*, 41–43.

207 Program for the Visit to the United States by Ngo Dinh Diem, May 6 to 18, Buttinger Papers.

208 "An Asian Liberator," *New York Times*, 10 May 1957; "Mr. Diem in Washington," *Christian Science Monitor*, 10 May 1957; Ernest Lindley, "A Friend Named Diem," *Newsweek* 49 (20 May 1957): 40; "Visitor from Viet Nam," *Washington Post*, 8 May 1957; "A Welcome Visitor," *Washington News*, 7 May 1957; Joseph Lash, "The Man Who Wouldn't Give Up," *New York Post*, 19 May 1957.

209 President Ngo's Farewell Message, 19 May 1957, Pike Collection, unit VI— Republic of Vietnam, box 12.

1   For two recent instances of historians drawing this parallel, see Fredrik Log-
    evall, *Choosing War* (Berkeley, Calif., 1999), xiii; H. R. McMaster, *Dereliction
    of Duty* (New York, 1997), ix.

2   Cited in *The Civil War*, Episode II: "A Very Bloody Affair," directed by Ken
    Burns, 1989.

3   Robert Wiebe, *Self-Rule* (Chicago, 1995), 261.

4   Kahin, *Intervention*, 66.

5   Isaacs, *Scratches on Our Minds*, 405.

6   White House Office, National Security Council Staff, Papers, 1948–1961, OCB
    Central File Series: Landon to Eisenhower, 22 May 1956: box 2, EL. Emphasis
    added.

7   Cited in Carter, *Another Part of the Fifties*, 125.

8   Inaugural Address, 20 January 1953, *Public Papers of the Presidents: Dwight D.
    Eisenhower, 1953*, 1–3.

9   Dulles address, "A Righteous Faith," October 1942, Dulles Papers, box 282.

10 Address to the Second Assembly of the World Council of Churches, 19 August
    1954, *Public Papers of the Presidents: Dwight D. Eisenhower, 1954*, 736.

11 Diem to Dulles, 9 May 1957, Dulles Papers, box 115.

12 Reinhardt to Dulles, 10 June 1956, RG 59, 751G.00/6-1056; Reinhardt to Dul-
    les, 6 February 1956, RG 59, 751G.00/2-656.

13 Fishel, "Vietnam's Democratic One-Man Rule," 10–13.

14 Emily Rosenberg, "Walking the Borders," in *Explaining the History of Ameri-
    can Foreign Relations*, ed. Hogan and Paterson, 32–33.

15 John Foster Dulles Papers, Subject Series: Dulles Memorandum of Conversa-
    tion with Faure, 11 May 1955: box 9, EL.

16 Message to President Diem, 11 July 1959, *Public Papers of the Presidents:
    Dwight D. Eisenhower, 1959* (Washington, 1960), 519.

17 Message of Congratulation to His Excellency Ngo Dinh Diem, 15 July 1959,
    AFV Papers, box 4.

18 Mansfield Speech, 7 July 1959, AFV Papers, box 4.

19 "Anniversary in Vietnam," *New York Times*, 7 July 1959; Ernest Lindley, "An
    Ally Worth Having," *Newsweek* 72 (29 June 1959): 31.

20 Cited in du Berrier, *Background to Betrayal*, 182.

21 Ibid., 120.

22 The best account of the Buddhist crisis of 1963 may be found in Hammer,
    Death in November, 103–279.

23 Halberstam, *Best and the Brightest*, 260.

24 Cited in Schulzinger, *A Time for War*, 120.

25 Cited in Tad Szulc, "Kennedy Warns the Diem Regime U.S. Will Oppose All
    Divisive Actions," *New York Times*, 13 September 1963.

26 Baritz, *Backfire*, 89.
27 Cited in Richard Reeves, *President Kennedy* (New York, 1993), 15; John Morton Blum, *Years of Discord* (New York, 1991), 18–19.
28 Cited in Reeves, *President Kennedy*, 593.
29 For an excellent account of one of these triumphs—the Battle of Ap Bac—see Sheehan, *Bright Shining Lie*, 212–65.
30 Duiker, *Ho Chi Minh*, 462–514.
31 Buttinger to O'Daniel, 15 March 1962, AFV Papers, box 7.
32 Buttinger to Fairbanks, 26 September 1963, Buttinger Papers.
33 Buttinger, *Vietnam: The Unforgettable Tragedy*, 39.
34 Cited in Currey, *Edward Lansdale*, 185.
35 Sol Sanders, *A Sense of Asia* (New York, 1969), 158–59.
36 Interview with Mike Mansfield, 28 September 1966, DOHP.
37 James Burnham, "What Chance in Vietnam?" *National Review* 13 (8 October 1963): 304.
38 James Burnham, "The Revolution on the Mekong," *National Review* 13 (3 December 1963): 436.
39 *American Catholic Who's Who* (Grosse Point, Mich., 1964), 32.
40 Bouscaren, *Last of the Mandarins*, 102.
41 The best account of domestic dissent in 1965–66 is Tom Wells, *The War Within* (Berkeley, Calif., 1994), 9–114.
42 Norman Podhoretz, *Why We Were in Vietnam* (New York, 1982), 10.
43 Interview with John Hanes, 29 January and 12 August, DOHP.
44 Henry Kissinger, *White House Years* (Boston, 1979), 54.
45 Williams, *What Americans Believe and How They Worship*, 474.
46 Richard Immerman, introduction, *John Foster Dulles and the Diplomacy of the Cold War*, 3.
47 Cited in Hammer, *Death in November*, 53.
48 Diem, *In the Jaws of History*, 166.

Bibliography

PRIMARY SOURCES

Archival, Manuscript, and Oral History Sources

American Friends of Vietnam Papers, Vietnam Archive, Texas Tech University, Lubbock, Texas.

Joseph Buttinger Papers, Harvard-Yenching Library, Harvard University, Cambridge, Massachusetts.

Leo Cherne Papers, Archives and Special Collections, Mugar Memorial Library, Boston University, Boston, Massachusetts.

Thomas A. Dooley Collection, Pius XII Library, Saint Louis University, Saint Louis, Missouri.

Thomas A. Dooley Papers, Western Historical Manuscript Collection, University of Missouri-Saint Louis, Saint Louis, Missouri.

Allen Dulles Papers, Seeley Mudd Library, Princeton University, Princeton, New Jersey.

John Foster Dulles Oral History Project, Seeley Mudd Library, Princeton University, Princeton, New Jersey.

John Foster Dulles Papers, Seeley Mudd Library, Princeton University, Princeton, New Jersey.

Dwight D. Eisenhower Library, Abilene, Kansas
    J. Lawton Collins Papers
    John Foster Dulles Papers
    Eisenhower Papers, Ann Whitman File
    Eisenhower Records, White House Central Files
    Andrew Goodpaster Oral History
    James C. Hagerty Diary
    C. D. Jackson Papers
    National Security Council Staff Records
    News Clippings, 1932–1963
    Office of the Special Assistant for National Security Affairs
    Office of the Staff Secretary Records
    Republican National Committee
    White House Press Releases

Monsignor Joseph Harnett Papers, Theodore M. Hesburgh Library, University of Notre Dame, South Bend, Indiana.

George Kahin Donation, National Security Archives, George Washington University, Washington, D.C.

Michael J. Mansfield Papers, Maureen and Mike Mansfield Library, University of Montana, Missoula.

National Archives II, College Park, Maryland

Intelligence Reports, October 1941–August 1961

Record Group 59: General Records of the State Department (Microfilm)

Records of the Bureau of Far Eastern Affairs, 1955

Records of the Department of State, Research and Analysis Branch (OSS) and Bureau of Intelligence and Research

Douglas Pike Collection, Vietnam Archive, Texas Tech University, Lubbock.

Government Publications

Executive Sessions of the Senate Foreign Relations Committee. Volume 6. Eighty-third Congress, Second Session, 1954. Washington: Government Printing Office, 1977.

Executive Sessions of the Senate Foreign Relations Committee. Volume 7. Eighty-fourth Congress, First Session, 1955. Washington: Government Printing Office, 1978.

Public Papers of the Presidents: Dwight D. Eisenhower, 1953. Washington: Government Printing Office, 1954 [hereafter *PPP:DDE*].

PPP:DDE, 1954. Washington: Government Printing Office, 1955.

PPP:DDE, 1955. Washington: Government Printing Office, 1956.

PPP:DDE, 1956. Washington: Government Printing Office, 1957.

PPP:DDE, 1957. Washington: Government Printing Office, 1958.

PPP:DDE, 1958. Washington: Government Printing Office, 1959.

PPP:DDE, 1959. Washington: Government Printing Office, 1960.

U.S. Department of State. *Foreign Relations of the United States, 1950.* Volume 7. *Asia and the Pacific.* Washington: Government Printing Office, 1976 [hereafter *FRUS*].

——. *FRUS, 1951.* Volume 6. *Asia and the Pacific.* Washington: Government Printing Office, 1977.

——. *FRUS, 1952–1954.* Volume 13. *Indochina.* Washington: Government Printing Office, 1982.

——. *FRUS, 1952–1954.* Volume 14. *The Geneva Conference.* Washington: Government Printing Office, 1982.

——. *FRUS, 1955–1957.* Volume 1. *Vietnam.* Washington: Government Printing Office, 1985.

——. *FRUS, 1958–1960.* Volume 1. *Vietnam.* Washington: Government Printing Office, 1988.

United States-Vietnam Relations, 1945–1971. Volume 10. Washington: Government Printing Office, 1971.

Newspapers
Army Times [Springfield, Va.]
Baltimore Sun
Boston Globe
Boston Herald
Brooklyn Tablet
Catholic Free Press [Worcester, Mass.]
Catholic Review Service [Baltimore]
Catholic View [Schiller Park, Ill.]
Charlottesville [Va.] *Cavalier*
Chicago New World
Chicago Sun-Times
Chicago Tribune
Christian Science Monitor [Boston]
Cleveland Catholic Universe Bulletin
Detroit News
Evansville [Ill.] *Courier*
Evansville [Ill.] *Press*
Helena [Mont.] *Register*
Hollywood [Calif.] *Citizen-News*
Honolulu Star-Bulletin
Indianapolis News
Los Angeles Examiner
Los Angeles Mirror
Milwaukee Catholic Herald Citizen
Nashville [Tenn.] *Register*
Natchez [Miss.] *Register*
New York Daily News
New York Herald Tribune
New York Journal American
New York Post
New York Times
New York World Telegram and Sun
Ogden [Utah] *Standard-Examiner*
Our Sunday Visitor [Huntington, Ind.]
Philadelphia Inquirer
Pomeroy [Ohio] *Sentinel*
Rochester [N.Y.] *Catholic Courier Journal*
St. Louis Post-Dispatch
St. Paul [Minn.] *Catholic Bulletin*
San Diego Union
San Francisco Monitor

Times of Vietnam [Saigon, South Vietnam, now Ho Chi Minh City, Vietnam]
Wall Street Journal
Washington Daily News
Washington Post
Washington Star
Worcester [Mass.] *Daily Telegram*

Periodicals
America
American Mercury
America's Book-Log
Atlantic Monthly
Ave Maria
Catholic Digest
Challenge
Christian Century
Collier's
Commentary
Commercial and Financial Chronicle
Commonweal
Critic
Department of State Bulletin
Ecclesiastical Book Review
Economist
Extension
Foreign Affairs
Foreign Policy Bulletin
Future
Harper's
Information
John Carroll Quarterly
Journal of American Medicine
Jubilee
Library Journal
Life
Look
Los Angeles Times Magazine
Nation
National Geographic
National Review
New Leader
New Republic

Newsweek
New Yorker
New York Times Magazine
Notre Dame Magazine
Pacific Affairs
Presbyterian Life
Progressive
Ramparts
Reader's Digest
Redbook
Reporter
Saturday Review
Scholastic
Spiritual Life
Time
Torch
U.S. News And World Report
Vital Speeches of the Day
Yale Review

SECONDARY SOURCES AND PUBLISHED MEMOIRS

Aaronson, James. *The Press and the Cold War*. Indianapolis: Bobbs-Merrill, 1970.

Acheson, Dean. *Present at the Creation: My Years in the State Department*. New York: W. W. Norton, 1969.

Adams, Sherman. *Firsthand Report*. New York: Harper and Row, 1961.

Ahlstrom, Sydney H. *A Religious History of the American People*. New Haven, Conn.: Yale University Press, 1972.

Alexander, Charles C. *Holding the Line: The Eisenhower Era, 1952–1961*. Bloomington: Indiana University Press, 1975.

Allitt, Patrick. *Catholic Intellectuals and Conservative Politics in America, 1950–1985*. Ithaca, N.Y.: Cornell University Press, 1991.

Ambrose, Stephen A. *Eisenhower: Soldier, General of the Army, President-Elect*. New York: Simon and Schuster, 1983.

——. *Eisenhower: The President*. New York: Simon and Schuster, 1984.

——. *Ike's Spies: Eisenhower and the Espionage Establishment*. Garden City, N.Y.: Doubleday, 1981.

American Catholic Who's Who. Grosse Pointe, Mich.: Walter Romig, 1964.

Amter, Joseph A. *Vietnam Verdict: A Citizen's History*. New York: Free Press, 1984.

Anderson, Benedict. *Imagined Communities: Reflections on the Origins and Spread of Nationalism*. London: Verso, 1983.

Anderson, David L. "J. Lawton Collins, John Foster Dulles, and the Eisenhower

Administration's 'Point of No Return' in Vietnam." *Diplomatic History* 12 (spring 1988): 134–48.

——. *Trapped by Success: The Eisenhower Administration and Vietnam, 1953–1961.* New York: Columbia University Press, 1991.

——. "Why Vietnam?: Postrevisionist Answers and a Neorealist Suggestion." *Diplomatic History* 13 (summer 1989): 423–29.

Appy, Christian G., ed. *Cold War Constructions: The Political Culture of United States Imperialism, 1945–1966.* Amherst: University of Massachusetts Press, 2000.

Apter, David E., ed. *Ideology and Its Discontents.* London: Routledge, 1964.

Arnold, James R. *The First Domino: Eisenhower, the Military, and America's Intervention in Vietnam.* New York: William Morrow, 1991.

Bachrack, Stanley. *Committee of One Million: "China Lobby" Politics, 1953–1971.* New York: Columbia University Press, 1976.

Baldwin, Louis. *Hon. Politician: Mike Mansfield of Montana.* Missoula, Mont.: Mountain Press, 1979.

Baritz, Loren. *Backfire.* New York: William Morrow, 1985.

Bator, Victor M. *Vietnam: A Diplomatic Tragedy.* Dobbs Ferry, N.Y.: Oceana Publications, 1965.

Baughman, James L. *Henry R. Luce and the Rise of the American News Media.* Boston: Twayne, 1987.

Beale, John R. *John Foster Dulles: A Biography.* New York: Harper and Row, 1957.

Becker, George J. *James A. Michener.* New York: Frederick Ungar, 1983.

Bederman, Gail. *Manliness and Civilization: A Cultural History of Gender and Race in the United States, 1880–1917.* Chicago: University of Chicago Press, 1995.

Bellah, Robert N. *Varieties of Civil Religion.* New York: Harper and Row, 1980.

Bellah, Robert N., and Frederick E. Greenspan, eds. *Uncivil Religion: Interreligious Hostility in America.* New York: Columbia University Press, 1987.

Belton, John. *Widescreen Cinema.* Cambridge: Cambridge University Press, 1992.

Bentley, Eric, ed. *Thirty Years of Treason: Excerpts from Hearings before the House Committee on Un-American Activities.* New York: Viking Press, 1971.

Berding, Andrew H. *Dulles on Diplomacy.* Princeton: D. Van Nostrand, 1965.

Bernardi, Daniel, ed. *Classic Hollywood/Classic Whiteness.* Minneapolis: University of Minnesota Press, 2001.

Bernstein, Barton J., and Allen J. Matusow. *The Truman Administration: A Documentary History.* New York: Coward-McCann, 1968.

Billings-Yun, Melanie. *Decision Against War: Eisenhower and Dien Bien Phu, 1954.* New York: Columbia University Press, 1988.

Black, Cyril. *The Dynamics of Modernization: A Study in Comparative History.* New York: Harper and Row, 1966.

Black, Jan Knippers. *Development in Theory and Practice: Bridging the Gap.* Boulder: Westview Press, 1991.

Blagov, Sergei. *Honest Mistakes: The Life and Death of Trinh Minh Thé.* Huntington, N.Y.: New Science Publishers, 2001.

Blanshard, Paul. *American Freedom and Catholic Power.* Boston: Beacon Press, 1949.

——. *Communism, Democracy, and Catholic Power.* Boston: Beacon Press, 1951.

Blum, John Morton. *Years of Discord: American Politics and Society, 1961–1974.* New York: Simon and Schuster, 1991.

Bodard, Lucien. *The Quicksand War: Prelude to Vietnam.* Translated by Patrick O'Brian. London: Faber and Faber, 1967.

Boettcher, Thomas D. *Vietnam: The Valor and the Sorrow.* Boston: Little, Brown, 1986.

Boorstin, Daniel J. *The Image: A Guide to Pseudo-Events in America.* New York: Simon and Schuster, 1961.

Bordwell, David, Janet Staiger, and Kristin Thompson. *The Classical Hollywood Cinema: Film Style and Mode of Production to 1960.* New York: Columbia University Press, 1985.

Bouscaren, Anthony T. *The Last of the Mandarins: Diem of Vietnam.* Pittsburgh: Duquesne University Press, 1965.

Boyer, Paul. *When Time Shall Be No More: Prophecy Belief in Modern American Culture.* Cambridge, Mass.: Belknap Press of Harvard, 1992.

Bradley, Mark. *Imagining Vietnam and America: The Making of Postcolonial Vietnam, 1919–1950.* Chapel Hill., N.C.: University of North Carolina Press, 2000.

Brands, H. W. *Cold Warriors: Eisenhower's Generation and American Foreign Policy.* New York: Columbia University Press, 1988.

——. *The Devil We Knew: Americans and the Cold War.* New York: Oxford University Press, 1993.

Brownell, William. "The Vietnam Lobby: The Americans Who Lobbied for a Free and Independent South Vietnam in the 1940s and 1950s." Ph.D. dissertation, Columbia University, 1993.

Brynner, Rock. *Yul—The Man Who Would Be King: A Memoir of Father and Son.* New York: Simon and Schuster, 1989.

Buckley, William F., and L. Brent Bozell. *McCarthy and His Enemies: The Record and Its Meaning.* Washington, D.C.: Henry Regnery, 1953.

Budenz, Louis. *Men without Faces: The Communist Conspiracy in the USA.* New York: Harper and Row, 1950.

——. *The Techniques of Communism.* Washington: Henry Regnery, 1954.

——. *This Is My Story.* New York: McGraw-Hill, 1947.

Bui Diem, with David Chanoff. *In the Jaws of History.* Boston: Houghton Mifflin, 1987.

Burchett, Wilfred G. *The Furtive War: The United States in Vietnam and Laos.* New York: International Publishers, 1963.

Burke, John P., and Fred I. Greenstein, with the collaboration of Larry Berman and

Richard Immerman. *How Presidents Test Reality: Decisions and Vietnam, 1954 and 1965*. New York: Russell Sage Foundation, 1989.

Buttinger, Joseph. *In the Twilight of Socialism: A History of the Revolutionary Socialists in Austria*. New York: Praeger, 1953.

———. *Vietnam: A Dragon Embattled*. 2 volumes. London: Pall Mall Press, 1967.

———. *Vietnam: A Political History*. New York: Praeger, 1968.

———. *Vietnam: The Unforgettable Tragedy*. New York: Horizon Press, 1977.

Buu Hoan. "Review of *America's Stake in Vietnam: A Symposium.*" *Pacific Affairs* 29 (September 1956): 185–87.

Cable, James. *The Geneva Conference of 1954 on Indochina*. New York: Oxford University Press, 1986.

Cable, Larry. *Conflict of Myths: The Development of American Counterinsurgency Doctrine and the Vietnam War*. New York: New York University Press, 1988.

Carey, Patrick W. *The Roman Catholics in America*. New York: Praeger, 1996.

Carter, Paul A. *Another Part of the Fifties*. New York: Columbia University Press, 1983.

Catton, Philip E. *Diem's Final Failure: Prelude to America's War in Vietnam*. Lawrence: University Press of Kansas, 2002.

Caute, David. *The Great Fear: Under Truman and Eisenhower*. New York: Simon and Schuster, 1978.

Chakrabongse, Chula. *Lords of Life: A History of the Kings of Thailand*. London: Alvin Redman, 1986.

Chantasingh, Chalermsri Thuriyanoda. "The Americanization of *The King and I:* The Transformation of the English Governess into an American Legend." Ph.D. dissertation, University of Kansas, 1999.

Charlton, Michael, and Richard Moncrieff. *Many Reasons Why: The American Involvement in Vietnam*. New York: Hill and Wang, 1977.

Chester, Eric Thomas. *Covert Network: Progressives, the International Rescue Committee, and the* CIA. Armonk, N.Y.: M. E. Sharp, 1995.

Christie, Clive. *The Quiet American and the Ugly American: Western Literary Perspectives on Indo-China in a Decade of Transition, 1950–1960*. University of Kent at Canterbury, Occasional Paper #10, 1989.

Christopher, Renny. *The Vietnam War/The American War: Images and Representations in Euro-American and Vietnamese Exile Narratives*. Amherst: University of Massachusetts Press, 1995.

Cogley, John, ed. *Religion in America*. New York: Oxford University Press, 1958.

Collins, J. Lawton. *Lightning Joe: An Autobiography*. Baton Rouge: Louisiana State University Press, 1979.

Comfort, Mildred Houghton. *John Foster Dulles: Peacemaker*. Minneapolis: T. S. Denison, 1960.

Cook, Blanche Weisen. *The Declassified Eisenhower: A Divided Legacy*. Garden City, N.Y.: Doubleday, 1981.

Cooney, John. *The American Pope: The Life and Times of Francis Cardinal Spellman.* New York: Times Books, 1984.

Cooper, Chester L. *The Lost Crusade: America in Vietnam.* New York: Dodd, Meade, 1970.

Corley, Francis J. "The Constitution in the Republic of Vietnam." *Pacific Affairs* 34 (summer 1961): 165–74.

——. "Vietnam since Geneva." *Thought* 33 (winter 1958–59): 515-68.

Cort, David. *The Sin of Henry R. Luce: An Anatomy of Journalism.* Secaucus, N.J.: Lyle Stuart, 1974.

Costigliola, Frank. " 'Unceasing Pressure for Penetration': Gender, Pathology, and Emotion in George Kennan's Formation of the Cold War." *Journal of American History* 86 (March 1997): 1309–39.

Couto, Maria. *Graham Greene: On the Frontier.* New York: St. Martin's Press, 1988.

Craig, Gordon A. *War, Politics, and Diplomacy.* New York: Praeger, 1966.

Crosby, Donald F. *God, Church, and Flag: Senator Joseph R. McCarthy and the Catholic Church, 1950–1957.* Chapel Hill, N.C.: University of North Carolina Press, 1978.

Crozier, Brian. *The Man Who Lost China.* New York: Charles Scribner's Sons, 1976.

Cuddy, Edward. "Pro-Germanism and American Catholicism." *Catholic Historical Review* 54 (October 1968): 427–54.

Cumings, Bruce. *The Origins of the Korean War.* Volume 2: *The Roaring of the Cataract.* Princeton: Princeton University Press, 1991.

Currey, Cecil B. *Edward Lansdale: The Unquiet American.* Boston: Houghton Mifflin, 1988.

Dalloz, Jacques. *The War in Indo-China, 1945–1954.* Translated by Josephine Bacon. Savage, Md.: Barnes and Noble Ltd., 1990.

Davidson, Phillip B. *Vietnam at War: The History, 1946–1975.* New York: Oxford University Press, 1991.

Davis, David Brion, and Steven Mintz, eds. *The Boisterous Sea of Liberty: A Documentary History of America from the Discovery through the Civil War.* New York: Oxford University Press, 1998.

Dean, Robert. *Imperial Brotherhood: Gender and the Making of the Cold War.* Amherst: University of Massachusetts Press, 2000.

De Lubac, Henri. *Aspects of Buddhism.* New York: Sheed and Ward, 1953.

De Santis, Vincent P. "American Catholics and McCarthyism." *Catholic Historical Review* 51 (April 1965): 1–30.

——. "Eisenhower Revisionism." *Review of Politics* 38 (April 1976): 190–207.

Devillers, Philippe, and Jean Lacoutre. *End of a War: Indochina 1954.* Translated by Alexander Lieven and Adam Roberts. New York: Praeger, 1969.

Diggins, John P. "American Catholics and Italian Fascism." *Journal of Contemporary History* 2 (October 1967): 51–68.

Divine, Robert. *Eisenhower and the Cold War.* New York: Oxford University Press, 1981.

Dolan, Jay P. *The American Catholic Experience: A History from Colonial Times to the Present*. Garden City, N.Y.: Doubleday, 1985.

Dooley, Agnes. *Promises to Keep*. New York: Farrar, Straus, and Cudahy, 1962.

Dooley, Thomas A. *Deliver Us from Evil: The Story of Viet Nam's Flight to Freedom*. New York: Farrar, Straus, and Cudahy, 1956.

Dougan, Clark, Edward Doyle, Samuel Lipsman, and Stephen Weiss. *The Vietnam Experience*. Volume 2: *Passing the Torch*. Boston: Boston Publishing, 1983.

Douglas, William O. *North from Malaya: An Adventure on Five Fronts*. Garden City, N.Y.: Doubleday, 1953.

Dower, John W. *Embracing Defeat: Japan in the Wake of World War II*. New York: W. W. Norton, 1999.

——. *War without Mercy: Race and Power in the Pacific War*. New York: Pantheon Books, 1986.

Drinnon, Richard. *Facing West: The Metaphysics of Indian Hating and Empire Building*. Minneapolis: University of Minnesota Press, 1980.

Drummond, Roscoe. *Duel at the Brink: John Foster Dulles's Command of American Power*. Garden City, N.Y.: Doubleday, 1960.

Du Berrier, Hilaire. *Background to Betrayal: The Tragedy of Vietnam*. Belmont, Mass.: Western Islands Press, 1965.

Dudziak, Mary. "Desegregation as a Cold War Imperative." *Stanford Law Review* 41 (November 1988): 61–121.

Duiker, William J. *Ho Chi Minh: A Life*. New York: Hyperion, 2000.

Dulles, John Foster. *War or Peace*. New York: Macmillan, 1950.

——. *War, Peace, and Change*. New York: Harper and Brothers, 1939.

Duncanson, Dennis J. *Government and Revolution in Vietnam*. New York: Oxford University Press, 1968.

Dunn, Charles W., ed. *American Political Theology: Historical Perspective and Theoretical Analysis*. New York: Praeger, 1984.

Eagleton, Terry. *Ideology: An Introduction*. London and New York: Verso, 1991.

——, ed. *Ideology*. London and New York: Verso, 1994.

Easterlin, Richard. *Birth and Fortune: The Impact of Numbers on Personal Welfare*. New York: Basic Books, 1980.

Eckardt, A. Roy. *The Surge of Piety in America: An Appraisal*. New York: Association Press, 1958.

Eden, Anthony. *Full Circle: The Memoirs of Anthony Eden*. Boston: Houghton Mifflin, 1960.

Egan, Eileen. *For Whom There Is No Room: Scenes from the Refugee World*. New York: Paulist Press, 1995.

Eggleston, Noel Clinton. "The Roots of Commitment: United States Policy toward Vietnam, 1945–1950." Ph.D. dissertation, University of Georgia, 1977.

Eisenhower, Dwight D. *Mandate for Change, 1953–1956*. Garden City, N.Y.: Doubleday, 1963.

———. *The White House Years: Waging Peace, 1956–1961.* Garden City, N.Y.: Doubleday, 1965.

Ellis, John Tracy. "American Catholics and Intellectual Life." *Thought* 30 (autumn 1955): 353–86.

Elson, Robert. *The World of Time Inc.: An Intimate History of a Publishing Enterprise.* New York: Atheneum, 1973.

The Emergence of Free Viet-Nam: Major Addresses Delivered by President Ngo Dinh Diem during His Official Visit to the United States of America. Saigon: Presidency of the Republic of Viet-Nam Press Office, 1957.

Epstein, Mark. "The Third Force: Liberal Ideology in a Revolutionary Age, 1945–1950." Ph.D. dissertation, University of North Carolina at Chapel Hill, 1971.

Ernst, John. *Forging a Fateful Alliance: Michigan State University and the Vietnam War.* East Lansing: Michigan State University Press, 1998.

Fall, Bernard B. *Hell in a Very Small Place: The Siege of Dien Bien Phu.* New York: Vintage Books, 1968.

———. "The Political-Religious Sects of Vietnam." *Pacific Affairs* 28 (September 1955): 235–53.

———. "Representative Government in the State of Vietnam." *Far Eastern Survey* 23 (August 1954): 122–25.

———. *The Two Viet-Nams: A Political and Military Analysis.* New York: Praeger, 1963.

———. *Viet-Nam Witness, 1933–1966.* New York: Praeger, 1966.

Fifield, Russell H. *Americans in Southeast Asia: The Roots of Commitment.* New York: Thomas Y. Crowell, 1973.

Finlay, David J., Ole R. Holsti, and Richard R. Fagan. *Enemies in Politics.* Chicago: Rand McNally, 1967.

Fishel, Wesley R., ed. *Problems of Freedom: South Vietnam since Independence.* New York: Free Press of Glencoe, 1961.

———, ed. *Vietnam: Anatomy of a Conflict.* Itasca, Minn.: F. E. Peacock, 1968.

Fisher, James T. *The Catholic Counterculture in America, 1933–1962.* Chapel Hill, N.C.: University of North Carolina Press, 1989.

———. *Communion of Immigrants: A History of Catholics in America.* New York: Oxford University Press, 2002.

———. *Dr. America: The Lives of Thomas A. Dooley, 1927–1961.* Amherst: University of Massachusetts Press, 1997.

FitzGerald, Frances. *Fire in the Lake: The Vietnamese and the Americans in Vietnam.* Boston: Little, Brown, 1972.

Foner, Eric. *Free Soil, Free Labor, Free Men: The Ideology of the Republican Party before the Civil War.* New York: Oxford University Press, 1995.

Fordin, Hugh. *Getting to Know Him: A Biography of Oscar Hammerstein II.* New York: Frederick Ungar, 1977.

Frank, Robert P. "Prelude to Cold War: American Catholics and Communism." *Journal of Church and State* 86 (winter 1992): 39–56.

Gaddis, John Lewis. *Strategies of Containment: A Critical Appraisal of Postwar American National Security Policy*. New York: Oxford University Press, 1982.

Gallagher, Teresa. *Give Joy to My Youth: A Memoir of Tom Dooley*. New York: Farrar, Straus, and Cudahy, 1965.

Gannon, Robert I. *The Cardinal Spellman Story*. New York: Pocket Books, 1963.

Gardner, Lloyd C. *Approaching Vietnam: From World War II through Dien Bien Phu*. New York: W. W. Norton, 1988.

Gardner, Mona. *Menacing Sun*. London: John Murray, 1939.

Garside, B. A. *One Increasing Purpose: The Life of Henry Winters Luce*. New York: Fleming H. Revell, 1948.

Gaustad, Edwin, ed. *A Documentary History of Religion in America*. Volume 2. Grand Rapids, Mich.: William B. Eerdmans, 1982.

Geertz, Clifford. *The Interpretation of Cultures*. New York: Basic Books, 1973.

Gerson, Louis L. *John Foster Dulles*. New York: Cooper Square Publishers, 1967.

Gettleman, Marvin E., Jane Franklin, Marilyn Young, and H. Bruce Franklin, eds. *Vietnam and America*. Second Edition. New York: Grove Press, 1995.

Gheddo, Piero. *The Cross and Bo-Tree: Catholics and Buddhists in Vietnam*. Translated by Charles Underhill Quinn. New York: Sheed and Ward, 1970.

Gibbons, William Conrad. *The U.S. Government and the Vietnam War: Executive and Legislative Roles and Relationships*. 10 volumes. Originally Prepared for the Committee on Foreign Relations of the United States Senate. Princeton, N.J.: Princeton University Press, 1986.

Gilbert, Felix, and Stephen R. Crawford, eds. *Historical Studies Today*. New York: Columbia University Press, 1972.

Gilman, Nils. "Paved with Good Intentions: The Genesis of Modernization Theory." Ph.D. dissertation: University of California, Berkeley, 2000.

Glassmeyer, Danielle S. "Sentimental Orientalism and American Intervention in Vietnam." Ph.D. dissertation, Loyola University, 2001.

Glazer, Nathan, and Daniel Patrick Moynihan. *Beyond the Melting Pot: The Negroes, Puerto Ricans, Jews, Italians, and Irish of New York City*. Second Edition. Cambridge, Mass.: MIT Press, 1970.

Gleason, Philip. "In Search of Unity: American Catholic Thought, 1920–1960." *Catholic Historical Review* 65 (April 1979): 185–205.

Goldman, Eric F. *The Crucial Decade—And After: America, 1945–1960*. New York: Vintage Books, 1960.

Goldstein, Jonathan, Jerry Israel, and Hilary Conroy, eds. *America Views China: American Images of China Then and Now*. London: Associated U Presses, 1991.

Goodno, Floyd Russell. "Walter H. Judd: Spokesman for China in the United States House of Representatives." Ph.D. dissertation, Oklahoma State University, 1970.

Goold-Adams, Richard. *John Foster Dulles: A Reappraisal*. London: Weidenfield and Nicolson, 1974.

Gow, Gordon. *Hollywood in the Fifties*. New York: Random House, 1971.

Grant, J. A. C. "The Vietnam Constitution of 1956." *American Political Science Review* 83 (June 1958): 437–63.

Greene, Daniel P. O'C. "John Foster Dulles and the End of the Franco-American Entente in Indochina." *Diplomatic History* 20 (spring 1996): 549–61.

——. "Tug of War: The Eisenhower Administration and Vietnam, 1953-1955." Ph.D. dissertation, University of Texas at Austin, 1990.

Greene, Graham. *The Quiet American*. New York: Penguin, 1956.

Greenstein, Fred I. *The Hidden-Hand Presidency: Eisenhower as Leader*. New York: Basic Books, 1982.

Guhin, Michael A. *John Foster Dulles: A Statesman and His Times*. New York: Columbia University Press, 1972.

Hadden, Jeffrey K., and Charles E. Swann. *Prime Time Preachers: The Rising Power of Televangelism*. Reading, Mass.: Addison-Wesley, 1981.

Hagerty, James C. *The Diary of James C. Hagerty: Eisenhower in Mid-Course, 1953– 1954*. Edited by Robert H. Ferrell. Bloomington: Indiana University Press, 1983.

Hahn, Emily. *Chiang Kai-shek: An Unauthorized Biography*. Garden City, N.Y.: Doubleday, 1955.

Halberstam, David. *The Best and the Brightest*. New York: Random House, 1969.

——. *The Fifties*. New York: Villard Books, 1993.

——. *The Making of a Quagmire: America and Vietnam during the Kennedy Era*. Revised Edition. New York: Alfred A. Knopf, 1988.

——. *The Powers that Be*. New York: Alfred A. Knopf, 1979.

Haldar, M. K. *Asia: Challenge at Dawn*. Delhi: Ascension, 1961.

Hamilton-Paterson, James. *America's Boy: A Century of American Colonialism in the Philippines*. New York: Henry Holt, 1998.

Hammer, Ellen. *A Death in November*. New York: Dutton Press, 1987.

——. *The Struggle for Indo-China, 1940–1954*. Stanford, Calif.: Stanford University Press, 1966.

Handy, Robert T. "The American Religious Depression, 1925–1935." *Church History* 29 (March 1960): 3–16.

Harrison, James P. *The Endless War: Vietnam's Struggle for Independence*. New York: Columbia University Press, 1989.

Hayes, John P. "James Michener: An American Writer." Ph.D. dissertation, Temple University, 1984.

Hearden, Patrick J. *The Tragedy of Vietnam*. New York: HarperCollins, 1991.

Heidenry, John. *Theirs Was the Kingdom: Lila and DeWitt Wallace and the Story of the Reader's Digest*. New York: Simon and Schuster, 1993.

Heller, Dean, and David Heller. *John Foster Dulles: Soldier for Peace*. New York: Holt, Rinehart, and Winston, 1960.

Hellmann, John. *American Myth and the Legacy of Vietnam*. New York: Columbia University Press, 1986.

Hennesey, James. *American Catholics: A History of the Roman Catholic Community in the United States*. New York: Oxford University Press, 1981.

Henning, Joseph M. *Outposts of Civilization: Race, Religion, and the Formative Years of American-Japanese Relations*. New York: New York University Press, 2000.

Herberg, Will. *Protestant-Catholic-Jew: An Essay in American Religious Sociology*. Garden City, N.Y.: Doubleday, 1955.

Herring, George C. *America's Longest War: The United States and Vietnam, 1945–1975*. Second Edition. New York: McGraw-Hill, 1986.

Herring, George C., and Richard Immerman. "Eisenhower, Dulles, and Dien Bien Phu: 'The Day We Didn't Go to War' Revisited." *Journal of American History* 71 (September 1984): 343–63.

Herzstein, Robert E. *Henry Luce: A Political Portrait of the Man Who Created the American Century*. New York: Charles Scribner's Sons, 1994.

Hess, Gary R. "The First American Commitment in Indochina: Acceptance of the Bao Dai Solution, 1950." *Diplomatic History* 2 (fall 1978): 331–35.

Hickey, Gerald Cannon. *Village in Vietnam*. New Haven, Conn.: Yale University Press, 1964.

Higgins, Marguerite. *Our Vietnam Nightmare*. New York: McGraw-Hill, 1965.

Higham, Charles, and Joel Greenberg. *Hollywood in the Forties*. New York: A. S. Barnes, 1968.

Hixson, Walter. *Parting the Curtain: Propaganda, Culture, and the Cold War, 1945–1961*. New York: St. Martin's Press, 1997.

Hogan, Michael J., ed. *The Ambiguous Legacy: U.S. Foreign Relations in the "American Century."* Cambridge: Cambridge University Press, 1999.

——, ed. *America in the World: The Historiography of United States Foreign Relations since 1941*. Cambridge: Cambridge University Press, 1995.

Hogan, Michael J., and Thomas G. Paterson, eds. *Explaining the History of American Foreign Relations*. Cambridge: Cambridge University Press, 1991.

Hoganson, Kristin. *Fighting for American Manhood: How Gender Politics Provoked the Spanish-American and Philippine-American Wars*. New Haven, Conn.: Yale University Press, 1998.

Hohenberg, John. *Between Two Worlds: Policy, Press, and Opinion in Asian-American Relations*. New York: Praeger, 1967.

Hooper, Edwin Bickford, Dean C. Allard, and Oscar P. Fitzgerald. *The United States Army and the Vietnam Conflict*. Volume 1: *Setting the Stage to 1959*. Washington, D.C.: U.S. Government Printing Office, 1976.

Hoopes, Townsend. *The Devil and John Foster Dulles*. Boston: Little, Brown, 1973.

Horsman, Reginald. *Race and Manifest Destiny: The Origins of American Racial Anglo-Saxonism*. Cambridge, Mass.: Harvard University Press, 1981.

Hoskins, Robert. *Graham Greene: An Approach to the Novels*. New York: Garland, 1999.

Hudnut-Beumler, James. *Looking for God in the Suburbs: The Religion of the Ameri-

can Dream and Its Critics, 1945–1965. New Brunswick, N.J.: Rutgers University Press, 1994.

Hudson, Winthrop, ed. *Nationalism and Religion in America: Concepts of American Identity and Mission.* New York: Harper and Row, 1970.

Hughes, Emmet John. *The Ordeal of Power: A Political Memoir of the Eisenhower Years.* New York: Atheneum, 1963.

Hunt, Michael H. *Ideology and U.S. Foreign Policy.* New Haven, Conn.: Yale University Press, 1987.

Immerman, Richard H. *John Foster Dulles: Piety, Pragmatism, and Power in U.S. Foreign Policy.* Wilmington, Del.: Scholarly Resources, 1999.

——, ed. *John Foster Dulles and the Diplomacy of the Cold War.* Princeton: Princeton University Press, 1990.

Investment Conditions in the Republic of Vietnam: A Symposium. New York: American Friends of Vietnam, 1958.

Iriye, Akira. *Across the Pacific: The Inner History of American–East Asian Relations.* New York: Harcourt Brace Jovanovich, 1967.

Isaacs, Harold. *Scratches on Our Minds: American Images of China and India.* Westport, Conn.: Greenwood Press, 1958.

Isaacson, Walter, and Evan Thomas. *The Wise Men: Six Friends and the World They Made.* New York: Simon and Schuster, 1986.

Jacobs, Seth. " 'Our System Demands the Supreme Being': The U.S. Religious Revival and the 'Diem Experiment,' 1954–55." *Diplomatic History* 25 (fall 2001): 589–624.

——. " 'Sink or Swim with Ngo Dinh Diem': Religion, Orientalism, and United States Intervention in Vietnam, 1950–1957." Ph.D. dissertation, Northwestern University, 2000.

Jamieson, Neil L. *Understanding Vietnam.* Berkeley: University of California Press, 1993.

Jespersen, Christopher. *American Images of China, 1931–1949.* Stanford, Calif.: Stanford University Press, 1996.

Jessup, John K. *The Ideas of Henry Luce.* New York: Atheneum, 1969.

Johnson, Ralph. "Confucian Political Influence on the South Vietnamese Government of Ngo Dinh Diem." M.A. thesis, American University, 1978.

Jones, Dorothy. *The Portrayal of China and India on the American Screen, 1896–1955.* Cambridge, Mass.: MIT Press, 1955.

Jones, Howard. *Death of a Generation: How the Assassinations of Diem and JFK Prolonged the Vietnam War.* New York, Oxford University Press: 2003.

Kahin, George McT. *Intervention: How America Became Involved in Vietnam.* New York: Anchor Books, 1986.

——, ed. *Governments and Politics of Southeast Asia.* Ithaca, N.Y.: Cornell University Press, 1964.

Kahin, George McT., and John W. Lewis. *The United States in Vietnam.* New York: Dial Press, 1967.

Kane, Thomas. "The Missionary Theme in the Rhetoric of John Foster Dulles." Ph.D. dissertation, University of Pittsburgh, 1968.

Karnow, Stanley. *In Our Image: America's Empire in the Philippines*. New York: Penguin Books, 1987.

———. *Vietnam: A History*. New York: Viking Press, 1983.

Kattenburg, Paul M. *The Vietnam Trauma in American Foreign Policy, 1945–1975*. New Brunswick, N.J.: Transaction Books, 1980.

Keeley, Joseph C. *The China Lobby Man: The Story of Alfred Kohlberg*. New Rochelle, N.Y.: Arlington House, 1969.

Kempton, Murray. *America Comes of Middle Age: Columns, 1950–1962*. Boston: Little, Brown, 1963.

Kendrick, Alexander. *The Wound Within: America in the Vietnam Years, 1945–1974*. Boston: Little, Brown, 1974.

Kennan, George F. *American Diplomacy, 1900–1950*. Chicago: University of Chicago Press, 1951.

Keyser, Barbara. *Hollywood and the Catholic Church: The Image of Roman Catholicism in American Movies*. Chicago: Loyola University Press, 1984.

Kim, Sung Yong. "United States–Philippine Relations during the Magsaysay Administration." Ph.D. dissertation, University of Michigan, 1959.

Kimball, Jeffrey P., ed. *To Reason Why: The Debate about the Causes of U.S. Intervention in the Vietnam War*. New York: McGraw-Hill, 1990.

Kissinger, Henry. *Diplomacy*. New York: Random House, 1994.

———. *White House Years*. Boston: Little, Brown, 1979.

Klein, Christina. *Cold War Orientalism: Asia in the Middlebrow Imagination, 1945–1961*. Berkeley: University of California Press, 2003.

———. "Cold War Orientalism: Musicals, Travel Narratives, and Middlebrow Culture in Postwar America." Ph.D. dissertation, Yale University, 1997.

Klunk, Brian Edward. "The Idea of America's Mission and Its Role in the Beliefs and Diplomacy of John Foster Dulles and Jimmy Carter." Ph.D. dissertation, University of Virginia, 1985.

Kobler, John. *Luce: His Time, Life, and Fortune*. New York: Random House, 1968.

Koen, Ross Y. *The China Lobby in American Politics*. New York: Macmillan, 1960.

Kolko, Gabriel. *Anatomy of a War: Vietnam, the United States, and the Modern Historical Experience*. New York: Pantheon Books, 1985.

Kousser, John, and James McPherson, eds. *Region, Race, and Reconstruction*. New York: Oxford University Press, 1991.

Kselman, Thomas A., and Stephen Avella. "Marian Piety and the Cold War in the United States." *Catholic Historical Review* 72 (July 1986): 403–24.

Lacoutre, Jean. *Vietnam: Between Two Truces*. Translated by Konrad Kellen and Joel Carmichael. New York: Random House, 1966.

LaFeber, Walter. *America, Russia, and the Cold War, 1945–1992*. Seventh Edition. New York: HarperCollins, 1993.

Lancaster, Donald. *The Emancipation of French Indochina*. London: Oxford University Press, 1961.

Landon, Margaret. *Anna and the King of Siam*. New York: John Day, 1944.

Lansdale, Edward Geary. *In the Midst of Wars: An American's Mission to Southeast Asia*. New York: Harper and Row, 1972.

Larson, Dana B. "In Search of the Third Force: The American Lobby for Ngo Dinh Diem." M.A. thesis, University of Arizona, 1985.

Latham, Michael A. *Modernization as Ideology: American Social Science and Nation Building in the Kennedy Era*. Chapel Hill, N.C.: University of North Carolina Press, 2000.

Leaner, Daniel. *The Passing of Traditional Society: Modernizing the Middle East*. New York: Free Press, 1958.

Lederer, William J., and Eugene Burdick. *The Ugly American*. New York: W. W. Norton, 1958.

Leong, Karen Janis. "The China Mystique: Mayling Soong Chiang, Pearl Buck, and Anna May Wong in the American Imagination." Ph.D. dissertation, University of California, Berkeley, 1999.

Levenstein, Aaron. *Escape to Freedom: The Story of the International Rescue Committee*. Westport, Conn.: Greenwood Press, 1983.

Lewy, Guenter. *America in Vietnam*. New York: Oxford University Press, 1978.

Lindholm, Richard W., ed. *Vietnam, the First Five Years: An International Symposium*. East Lansing: Michigan State University Press, 1959.

Lippmann, Walter. *The Public Philosophy*. Boston: Little, Brown, 1955.

Lockhart, Bruce McFarland. *The End of the Vietnamese Monarchy*. New Haven, Conn.: Yale Center for International and Area Studies, 1993.

Logevall, Fredrik. *Choosing War: The Lost Chance for Peace and the Escalation of War in Vietnam*. Berkeley: University of California Press, 1999.

Lomperis, Timothy J. *The War Everyone Lost—and Won: American Intervention in Vietnam's Twin Struggles*. Washington: CQ Press, 1987.

Lyon, Peter. *Eisenhower: Portrait of a Hero*. Boston: Little, Brown, 1974.

MacAlister, Robert J. "The Great Gamble: United States Policy toward South Viet Nam from July 1954 to July 1956." M.A. thesis, University of Chicago, 1958.

MacKinnon, Stephen R., and Oris Friesen. *China Reporting: An Oral History of American Journalism in the 1930s and 1940s*. Berkeley: University of California Press, 1987.

Maclear, Michael. *The Ten Thousand Day War: Vietnam, 1945–1975*. New York: Avon, 1981.

Major Policy Speeches by President Ngo Dinh Diem. Third Edition. Saigon: Presidency of the Republic of Viet-Nam Press Office, 1957.

Mardsden, George M. *Religion and American Culture*. San Diego, Calif.: Harcourt Brace Jovanovich, 1990.

Mark, Dale Warren. "The Rhetoric of Thomas A. Dooley, M.D." Ph.D. dissertation, University of Oregon, 1971.

Marks, Frederick W. *Power and Peace: The Diplomacy of John Foster Dulles*. New York: Praeger, 1993.

Marr, David G. *Vietnam 1945: The Quest for Power*. Berkeley: University of California Press, 1995.

———. *Vietnamese Anticolonialism, 1885–1925*. Berkeley: University of California Press, 1971.

———. *Vietnamese Tradition on Trial, 1920–1945*. Berkeley: University of California Press, 1984.

Marr, David G., and Jayne Susan Werner, eds. *Tradition and Revolution in Vietnam*. Berkeley, Calif.: Indochina Resource Center, 1975.

Mart, Michelle. "Tough Guys and American Cold War Policy: Images of Israel, 1948–1960." *Diplomatic History* 20 (summer 1996): 357–80.

Marty, Martin. *Modern American Religion*. Volume 3: *Under God, Indivisible, 1941–1960*. Chicago: University of Chicago Press, 1996.

———. *The New Shape of American Religion*. New York: Harper and Row, 1959.

———. *Religion in America: 1950 to the Present*. New York: Harper and Row, 1979.

Mason, Richard. *The World of Suzie Wong*. London: William Collins Sons, 1957.

Maurer, Harry. *Strange Ground: Americans in Vietnam, 1945–1975: An Oral History*. New York: Henry Holt, 1989.

McAlister, John T., and Paul Mus. *The Vietnamese and Their Revolution*. New York: Harper and Row, 1970.

McAlister, Melani. *Epic Encounters: Culture, Media, and U.S. Interests in the Middle East*. Berkeley: University of California Press, 2001.

McAvoy, Thomas T. "American Catholics and the Second World War." *Review of Politics* 69 (April 1954): 131–50.

———. *A History of the Catholic Church in the United States*. South Bend, Ind.: University of Notre Dame Press, 1969.

McCullough, David. *Truman*. New York: Simon and Schuster, 1992.

McEnaney, Laura. "He-Men and Christian Mothers: The America First Movement and the Gendered Meanings of Patriotism and Isolationism." *Diplomatic History* 18 (winter 1994): 47–57.

McLellan, David. *Ideology*. Second Edition. Minneapolis: University of Minnesota Press, 1995.

McLoughlin, William G., and Robert N. Bellah, eds. *Religion in America*. Boston: Houghton Mifflin, 1968.

McMahon, Robert J. "Review of Lloyd Gardner's *Approaching Vietnam: From World War II through Dien Bien Phu*." *American Historical Review* 94 (December 1989): 1505–6.

———, ed. *Major Problems in the History of the Vietnam War*. Second Edition. Lexington, Mass.: D. C. Heath, 1995.

Mecklin, John. *Mission in Torment: An Intimate Account of the U.S. Role in Vietnam*. Garden City, N.Y.: Doubleday, 1965.

Melanson, Richard A., and David Mayers, eds. *Reevaluating Eisenhower: American Foreign Policy in the 1950s*. Urbana: University of Illinois Press, 1987.

Merry, Robert W. *Taking On the World: Joseph and Stewart Alsop—Guardians of the American Century*. New York: Penguin Books, 1994.

Meyer, Donald. *The Positive Thinkers: Religion as Pop Psychology from Mary Baker Eddy to Oral Roberts*. Garden City, N.Y.: Doubleday, 1980.

Michener, James. *The Bridges at Toko-Ri*. New York: Random House, 1953.

———. *Return to Paradise*. New York: Random House, 1951.

———. *Sayonara*. New York: Ballantine Books, 1954.

———. *Tales of the South Pacific*. New York: Macmillan, 1946.

———. *The Voice of Asia*. New York: Random House, 1951.

———. *The World Is My Home: A Memoir*. New York: Random House, 1992.

Miller, Douglas T., and Marion Nowak. *The Fifties: The Way We Really Were*. Garden City, N.Y.: Doubleday, 1977.

Miller, Edward G. "Confucianism and 'Confucian Learning' in South Vietnam during the Diem Years." Unpublished paper in possession of the author.

Miller, James E. "Taking Off the Gloves: The United States and the Italian Elections of 1948." *Diplomatic History* 7 (winter 1983): 35–55.

Miller, William Lee. *Piety Along the Potomac*. Boston: Little, Brown, 1964.

Miscamble, Wilson D. "Catholics and American Foreign Policy from McKinley to McCarthy." *Diplomatic History* 4 (summer 1980): 223–40.

Monahan, James. *Before I Sleep: The Last Days of Doctor Tom Dooley*. New York: Farrar, Straus, and Cudahy, 1961.

Montgomery, Gayle B., and James W. Johnston. *One Step from the White House: The Rise and Fall of Senator William Knowland*. Berkeley: University of California Press, 1998.

Montgomery, John D. *The Politics of Foreign Aid: The American Experience in Southeast Asia*. New York: Praeger, 1962.

Moore, Ray A., and Donald L. Robinson. *Partners for Democracy: Crafting the New Japanese State under MacArthur*. New York: Oxford University Press, 2002.

Moran, John W. *Winston Churchill and the Struggle for Survival, 1940–1965*. London: Westbrook, 1966.

Morgan, Joseph G. *The Vietnam Lobby: The American Friends of Vietnam, 1955–1975*. Chapel Hill, N.C.: University of North Carolina Press, 1997.

Morgenthau, Hans J. *In Defense of the National Interest*. New York: McGraw-Hill, 1951.

Morris, Charles R. *American Catholic: The Saints and Sinners Who Built America's Most Powerful Church*. New York: Random House, 1997.

Mosley, Leonard R. *Dulles: A Biography of Eleanor, Allen, and John Foster Dulles and Their Family Network*. New York: Dial Press, 1978.

Moss, George Donelson. *Vietnam: An American Ordeal*. Englewood Cliffs, N.J.: Prentice-Hall, 1990.

Mullins, Willard. "On the Concept of Ideology in Political Science." *American Political Science Review* 66 (June 1972): 498–510.

Murti, B. S. N. *Vietnam Divided: The Unfinished Struggle*. New York: Longman, 1964.

Nadel, Alan, ed. *Containment Culture: American Narratives, Postmodernism, and the Atomic Age*. Durham, N.C.: Duke University Press, 1995.

Nashel, Jonathan. "Edward Lansdale and the American Attempt to Remake Southeast Asia, 1945–1965." Ph.D. dissertation, Rutgers University, 1994.

———. *Edward Lansdale, the Cold War, and the End of American Innocence*. Amherst: University of Massachusetts Press, forthcoming.

Neils, Patricia. *China Images in the Life and Times of Henry Luce*. Lanham, Md.: Rowman and Littlefield, 1990.

Newhouse, John. *War and Peace in the Nuclear Age*. Garden City, N.Y.: Doubleday, 1985.

Nguyen Cao Ky. *Twenty Years and Twenty Days*. New York: Stein and Day, 1976.

Nguyen Thai. "The Government of Men in the Republic of Vietnam." Ph.D. dissertation, Michigan State University, 1962.

Nicasio, Lino. "The Rhetoric of Fulton J. Sheen: A Fantasy Theme Analysis of the Television Speeches on Russia and Communism." Ph.D. dissertation, Indiana University, 1991.

Ninkovich, Frank. "Interests and Discourse in Diplomatic History." *Diplomatic History* 13 (spring 1989): 135–61.

Noll, Mark A., ed. *Religion and American Politics: From the Colonial Period to the 1980s*. New York: Oxford University Press, 1990.

Oakley, J. Ronald. *God's Country: America in the Fifties*. New York: Dembner Books, 1986.

Oberdorfer, Don. *Senator Mansfield: The Extraordinary Life of a Great American Statesman and Diplomat*. Washington: Smithsonian Books, 2003.

O'Brien, David. *American Catholics and Social Reform*. New York: Oxford University Press, 1968.

O'Daniel, John W. *The Nation That Refused to Starve: The Challenge of the New Vietnam*. New York: Coward-McCann, 1960.

Oliver, Robert T. *Syngman Rhee: The Man behind the Myth*. New York: Dodd, Mead, 1955.

Oliver, Victor L. *Cao Dai Spiritualism: A Study of Religion in Vietnamese Society*. Leiden: E. J. Brill, 1976.

Olson, Gregory A. *Mansfield and Vietnam: A Study in Rhetorical Adaptation*. East Lansing: Michigan State University Press, 1995.

Olson, James, and Randy Roberts. *Where the Domino Fell: America and Vietnam, 1945–1990*. New York: St. Martin's Press, 1996.

O'Neill, William L. *American High: The Years of Confidence, 1945–1960*. New York: Free Press, 1986.

Ong, Walter J. *Frontiers in American Catholicism: Essays on Ideology and Culture.* New York: Macmillan, 1957.

Oshinsky, David. *A Conspiracy So Immense: The World of Joe McCarthy.* New York: Free Press, 1983.

Packenham, Robert L. *Liberal America and the Third World: Political Development Ideas in Foreign Aid and Social Science.* Princeton, N.J.: Princeton University Press, 1973.

Packer, Herbert L. *Ex-Communist Witnesses: Four Studies in Fact Finding.* Stanford, Calif.: Stanford University Press, 1962.

Parish, James R., and Michael R. Pitts. *The Great Hollywood Musical Pictures.* Mentuchen, N.J.: Scarecrow Press, 1992.

Parker, Everett C., David W. Barry, and Dallas W. Smythe. *The Television-Radio Audience and Religion.* New York: Harper and Brothers, 1955.

Parmet, Herbert. *Eisenhower and the American Crusades.* New York: Macmillan, 1972.

Paterson, Thomas G., and Dennis Merrill, eds. *Major Problems in American Foreign Policy.* Lexington, Mass.: D. C. Heath, 1984.

Patterson, James T. *Grand Expectations: The United States, 1945–1974.* New York: Oxford University Press, 1996.

Patti, Archimedes L. A. *Why Vietnam?* Berkeley: University of California Press, 1980.

Payne, Robert. *Chiang Kai-shek.* New York: Weybright and Talley, 1969.

Peale, Norman Vincent. *The Power of Positive Thinking.* New York: Prentice-Hall, 1952.

The Pentagon Papers as Published by The New York Times. New York: Quadrangle Books, 1971.

The Pentagon Papers: The Defense Department History of United States Decisionmaking on Vietnam, Senator Gravel Edition. 5 volumes. Boston: Beacon Press, 1971.

Pettit, Clyde Edwin. *The Experts.* Secaucus, N.J.: Lyle Stuart, 1975.

Pike, Douglas. *Viet Cong: The Organization and Techniques of the National Liberation Front of South Vietnam.* Cambridge, Mass.: MIT Press, 1966.

Plummer, Brenda Gayle. *Rising Wind: Black Americans and U.S. Foreign Affairs, 1935–1960.* Chapel Hill, N.C.: University of North Carolina Press, 1996.

Podhoretz, Norman. *Why We Were in Vietnam.* New York: Simon and Schuster, 1982.

Popkin, Samuel L. *The Rational Peasant: The Political Economy of Rural Society in South Vietnam.* Berkeley: University of California Press, 1979.

Porter, Gareth, ed. *Vietnam: The Definitive Documentation of Human Decisions.* 2 volumes. Stanfordville, N.Y.: Earl M. Coleman, 1979.

Post, Ken. *Revolution, Socialism, and Nationalism in Vietnam.* Brookfield, Vt.: Dartmouth Press, 1989.

Prados, John. *The Sky Would Fall: Operation Vulture—The U.S. Bombing Mission in Indochina, 1954*. New York: Dial Press, 1983.

President Ngo Dinh Diem. Saigon: Presidency of the Republic of Viet-Nam Press Office, 1957.

President Ngo Dinh Diem on Asia: Extracts from Speeches by President Ngo Dinh Diem. Saigon: Presidency of the Republic of Viet-Nam Press Office, 1957.

The Problem of the Reunification of Viet-Nam. Saigon: Ministry of Information, 1958.

Pruessen, Ronald W. *John Foster Dulles: The Road to Power*. New York: Free Press, 1982.

Quigley, Thomas E. *American Catholics and Vietnam*. Grand Rapids, Mich.: William B. Eerdmans, 1968.

Rabe, Stephen. "Eisenhower Revisionism: A Decade of Scholarship." *Diplomatic History* 17 (winter 1993): 97–115.

Race, Jeffrey. *War Comes to Long An: Revolutionary Conflict in a Vietnamese Province*. Berkeley: University of California Press, 1972.

Randle, Robert F. *Geneva 1954: The Settlement of the Indochinese War*. Princeton, N.J.: Princeton University Press, 1969.

Reeves, Richard C. *President Kennedy: Profile of Power*. New York: Simon and Schuster, 1993.

Renda, Mary A. *Taking Haiti: Military Occupation and the Culture of U.S. Imperialism*. Chapel Hill, N.C.: University of North Carolina Press, 2001.

Reporting Vietnam, Part One: Journalism 1959–1969. New York: Library of America, 1998.

Reston, James. *Artillery of the Press: Its Influence on American Foreign Policy*. New York: Harper and Row, 1966.

Ribuffo, Leo P. "God and Contemporary Politics." *Journal of American History* 80 (March 1993): 1515–33.

Rivers, William L. *The Opinion-Makers*. Boston: Beacon Press, 1965.

Roberts, F. X., and C. D. Rhine. *James A. Michener: A Checklist of His Works with a Selected, Annotated Bibliography*. Westport, Conn.: Greenwood Press, 1995.

Rodgers, Richard. *Musical Stages: An Autobiography*. New York: Random House, 1975.

Rodgers, Richard, and Oscar Hammerstein. *Six Plays by Rodgers and Hammerstein*. New York: Random House, 1953.

Romulo, Carlos P. *Crusade in Asia*. New York: John Day, 1955.

——. *The Magsaysay Story*. New York: John Day, 1956.

Roseberry, William. "The Unbearable Lightness of Anthropology." *Radical History Review* 65 (spring 1996): 10–14.

Rosenberg, Emily S. " 'Foreign Affairs' After World War II: Connecting Sexual and International Politics." *Diplomatic History* 18 (winter 1994): 59–70.

——. *Spreading the American Dream: American Economic and Cultural Expansion, 1890–1945*. New York: Hill and Wang, 1982.

Rosenberg, Norman L., and Emily S. Rosenberg. *In Our Times: America since World War II*. Englewood Cliffs, N.J.: Prentice-Hall, 1995.

Rostow, Walt. *The Stages of Economic Growth: A Non-Communist Manifesto*. Cambridge: Cambridge University Press, 1960.

Rotter, Andrew J. "Christians, Muslims, and Hindus: Religion and U.S.–South Asian Relations, 1947–1954." *Diplomatic History* 24 (fall 2000): 593–613.

———. *Comrades at Odds: The United States and India, 1947–1964*. Ithaca, N.Y.: Cornell University Press, 2000.

———. "Gender Relations, Foreign Relations: The United States and South Asia, 1947–1964." *Journal of American History* 81 (September 1994): 518–42.

Said, Edward W. *Orientalism*. New York: Vintage Books, 1979.

———. "Through Gringo Eyes: With Conrad in Latin America." *Harper's* 244 (April 1988): 70–72.

Sainteny, Jean. *Ho Chi Minh and His Vietnam: A Personal Memoir*. Translated by Herma Briffault. Chicago: Cowles, 1972.

Sanders, Sol. *A Sense of Asia*. New York: Charles Scribner's Sons, 1969.

Scaff, Alvin H. *The Philippine Answer to Communism*. Stanford, Calif.: Stanford University Press, 1955.

Scheer, Robert. *How the United States Got Involved in Vietnam*. Santa Barbara, Calif.: Center for the Study of Democratic Institutions, 1965.

Schlereth, Thomas J. *The University of Notre Dame: A Portrait of Its History and Campus*. South Bend, Ind.: University of Notre Dame Press, 1976.

Schlesinger, Arthur M. *The Cycles of American History*. Boston: Houghton Mifflin, 1986.

———. *A Thousand Days: John F. Kennedy in the White House*. Boston: Houghton Mifflin, 1965.

Schreiner, Samuel A. *The Condensed World of the Reader's Digest*. New York: Stein and Day, 1977.

Schulzinger, Robert D. *A Time for War: The United States and Vietnam, 1941–1975*. New York: Oxford University Press, 1997.

Schwab, George, ed. *Ideology and Foreign Policy: A Global Perspective*. New York: Cyrco Press, 1978.

Scigliano, Robert. *South Vietnam: Nation under Stress*. Boston: Houghton Mifflin, 1963.

Scott, James S. *The Moral Economy of the Peasant: Rebellion and Subsistence in Southeast Asia*. New Haven, Conn.: Yale University Press, 1976.

Seven Years of the Ngo Dinh Diem Administration: 1954–1961. Saigon: Republic of Vietnam Government Printing Office, 1961.

Shafer, D. Michael. *Deadly Paradigms: The Failure of U.S. Counterinsurgency Policy*. Princeton: Princeton University Press, 1988.

Shaplen, Robert. *The Lost Revolution*. New York: Harper and Row, 1965.

Sharp, Joanne P. *Condensing the Cold War: Reader's Digest and American Identity*. Minneapolis: University of Minnesota Press, 2000.

Shaw, Diana. "The Temptation of Tom Dooley." *Los Angeles Times Magazine,* 15 December 1991, 43–46, 50, 80.

Sheehan, Neil. *A Bright Shining Lie: John Paul Vann and America in Vietnam.* New York: Random House, 1988.

Shelden, Michael. *Graham Greene: The Man Within.* London: William Heinemann, 1994.

Sherry, Norman. *The Life of Graham Greene.* Volume 2: *1939–1955.* London: Jonathan Cape, 1994.

Shibusawa, Naoko. *America's Geisha Ally: Race, Gender, and Maturity in Reconfiguring the Japanese Enemy, 1945–1964.* Cambridge, Mass.: Harvard University Press, forthcoming.

Shilts, Randy. *Conduct Unbecoming: Lesbians and Gays in the U.S. Military—Vietnam to the Persian Gulf.* New York: St. Martin's Press, 1993.

Short, Anthony. *The Origins of the Vietnam War.* New York: Longman, 1989.

Shulman, Arthur, and Roger Youman. *How Sweet It Was.* New York: Bonanza Books, 1966.

Silk, Mark. *Spiritual Politics: Religion in America since World War II.* New York: Simon and Schuster, 1988.

Simon, James F. *Independent Journey: The Life of William O. Douglas.* New York: Harper and Row, 1980.

Simpson, Donald R. *Dien Bien Phu: The Epic Battle America Forgot.* Washington: Brassey's, 1994.

Simpson, Paul. "The United States and Diem: An Impossible Alliance." M.A. thesis, California State College at Fullerton, 1972.

Sirgiovanni, George. *An Undercurrent of Suspicion: Anti-Communism in America during World War II.* New Brunswick, N.J.: Transaction, 1990.

Slotkin, Richard. *Gunfighter Nation: The Myth of the Frontier in Twentieth- Century America.* New York: Harper Perennial, 1993.

Smith, Geoffrey. "National Security and Personal Isolation: Sex, Gender, and Disease in the Cold War United States." *International History Review* 14 (spring 1992): 307–37.

Smith, Julian. *Looking Away: Hollywood and Vietnam.* New York: Charles Scribner's Sons, 1975.

Smith, Ralph. *Vietnam and the West.* Ithaca, N.Y.: Cornell University Press, 1971.

Smith, Robert. *Philippine Freedom, 1946–1958.* New York: Columbia University Press, 1958.

Song, Yuwu. "Madame Chiang Kai-shek and Her Two Worlds, 1908–1949." Ph.D. dissertation, University of Alabama, 1999.

Spector, Ronald H. *Advice and Support: The Early Years of the U.S. Army in Vietnam, 1941–1960.* New York: Free Press, 1985.

Steel, Ronald. *Walter Lippmann and the American Century.* Boston: Little, Brown, 1980.

Steinberg, Cobbett S. *Film Facts*. New York: Facts on File, 1980.

Stephanson, Anders. "Commentary: Ideology and Neorealist Mirrors." *Diplomatic History* 17 (spring 1993): 285–95.

——. *Manifest Destiny: American Expansion and the Empire of Right*. New York: Hill and Wang, 1995.

Stone, I. F. *The Hidden History of the Korean War*. New York: Monthly Review Press, 1952.

Swanberg, W. A. *Luce and His Empire*. New York: Charles Scribner's Sons, 1972.

Syngman Rhee through Western Eyes. Seoul: Office of Public Information, 1954.

Tai, Hue Tam Ho. *Millenarianism and Peasant Politics in Vietnam*. Cambridge, Mass.: Harvard University Press, 1983.

——. *Radicalism and the Origins of the Vietnamese Revolution*. Cambridge, Mass.: Harvard University Press, 1992.

Terwiel, B. J. *A History of Modern Thailand, 1767–1942*. London: University of Queensland Press, 1983.

Thomson, James C., Peter W. Stanley, and John Curtis Perry. *Sentimental Imperialists: The American Experience in East Asia*. New York: Harper and Row, 1981.

Tong, Hollington. *Dateline—China: The Beginning of China's Press Relations with the World*. New York: Rockport Press, 1972.

Toulouse, Mark G. *The Transformation of John Foster Dulles: From Prophet of Realism to Priest of Nationalism*. Macon, Ga.: Mercer University Press, 1985.

Toward Better Mutual Understanding: Speeches Delivered by President Ngo Dinh Diem during His State Visits to Thailand, Australia, and Korea. Saigon: Presidency of the Republic of Viet-Nam Press Office, 1957.

Trillin, Calvin. *Remembering Denny*. New York: Farrar, Straus, and Giroux, 1993.

Truong Nhu Tang, David Chanoff, and Duong Van Thai. *A Vietcong Memoir*. New York: Harcourt Brace Jovanovich, 1985.

Tuchman, Barbara. *The March of Folly: From Troy to Vietnam*. New York: Random House, 1984.

Turley, William. *The Second Indochina War: A Short Political and Military History, 1954–1975*. Boulder: University of Colorado Press, 1987.

Unger, Irwin, and Debi Unger, eds. *The Times Were A'Changing: The Sixties Reader*. New York: Three Rivers Press, 1998.

Valaik, J. David. "American Catholics and the Second Spanish Republic, 1911–1936." *Journal of Church and State* 54 (winter 1968): 13–28.

Valeo, Francis R. *Mike Mansfield, Majority Leader: A Different Kind of Senate, 1961–1976*. Armonk, N,Y.: M. E. Sharpe, 1999.

Van Dusen, Henry P., ed. *The Spiritual Legacy of John Foster Dulles: Selections from His Articles and Addresses*. Philadelphia: Westminster Press, 1959.

Vessie, Patricia Armstrong. *Zen Buddhism: A Bibliography of Books and Articles in English, 1892–1975*. Ann Arbor: University of Michigan Microfilms International, 1976.

Vietnam through Indian Eyes. Saigon: Consulate General of the Republic of Vietnam, 1960.

Von Der Mehden, Fred R. *Religion and Modernization in Southeast Asia*. Syracuse: Syracuse University Press, 1986.

Von Eschen, Penny M. *Race against Empire: Black Americans and Anticolonialism, 1937–1957*. Ithaca, N.Y.: Cornell University Press, 1996.

Wainwright, Loudon. *The Great American Magazine: An Inside Story of Life*. New York: Alfred A. Knopf, 1986.

Warner, Denis. *The Last Confucian*. New York: Macmillan, 1963.

Weisner, Louis A. *Victims and Survivors: Displaced Persons and Other War Victims in Viet-Nam, 1954–1975*. Westport, Conn.: Greenwood Press, 1988.

Wells, Tom. *The War Within: America's Battle over Vietnam*. Berkeley: University of California Press, 1994.

Werner, Jayne Susan. "The Cao Dai: The Politics of a Vietnamese Syncretic Religious Movement." Ph.D. dissertation, Cornell University, 1976.

———. *Peasant Politics and Religious Sectarianism: Peasant and Priest in the Cao Dai in Viet Nam*. New Haven, Conn.: Yale University Southeast Asia Studies, 1981.

Whitfield, Stephen J. *The Culture of the Cold War*. Second Edition. Baltimore: Johns Hopkins University Press, 1996.

Wiebe, Robert H. *Self-Rule: A Cultural History of American Democracy*. Chicago: University of Chicago Press, 1995.

Williams, J. Paul. *What Americans Believe and How They Worship*. Revised Edition. New York: Harper and Row, 1962.

Williams, Vernon J. *Rethinking Race: Franz Boas and His Contemporaries*. Lexington: University Press of Kentucky, 1996.

Williams, William Appleman. *The Tragedy of American Diplomacy*. Revised Edition. New York: W. W. Norton, 1972.

Wills, Garry. *Under God: Religion and American Politics*. New York: Simon and Schuster, 1990.

Wong, Eugene Franklin. "On Visual Media Racism: Asians in the American Motion Pictures." Ph.D. dissertation, University of Denver, 1977.

Wu, Chi-Wei David. "A Rhetorical Analysis of Selected Speeches by Generalissimo Chiang Kai-shek during the War of Resistance against Japanese Aggression." Ph.D. dissertation, Ohio University, 1986.

Wuthnow, Robert. *The Restructuring of American Religion: Society and Faith since World War II*. Princeton, N.J.: Princeton University Press, 1988.

Wyatt, David K. *Thailand: A Short History*. New Haven, Conn.: Yale University Press, 1984.

Yang, Anand. "Images of Asia: A Passage through Fiction and Film." *The History Teacher* 15 (May 1980): 351–69.

Young, Marilyn B. *The Vietnam Wars*. New York: HarperCollins, 1991.

Audio and Video Sources

Battle Hymn. Directed by Douglas Sirk, 1956.

The Big Picture. ABC-TV, re-released on Marathon Music and Video, 1998.

The Bridge on the River Kwai. Directed by David Lean, 1957.

The Civil War. Directed by Ken Burns. Florentine Films and WETA-TV, 1989.

The Geisha Boy. Directed by Frank Tashlin, 1958.

Hearts and Minds. Directed by Peter Davis, 1973.

The King and I. Directed by Walter Lang, 1956.

My Geisha. Directed by Jack Cardiff, 1962.

On the Waterfront. Directed by Elia Kazan, 1954.

Return to Paradise. Directed by Mark Robson, 1953.

Sayonara. Directed by Joshua Logan, 1957.

South Pacific. Directed by Joshua Logan, 1958.

Steel Helmet. Directed by Samuel Fuller, 1951.

The Teahouse of the August Moon. Directed by Daniel Mann, 1956.

That Free Men May Live broadcasts, 1957–61. Thomas A. Dooley Papers, Western Historical Manuscript Collection, University of Missouri-St. Louis.

Three Stripes in the Sun. Directed by Richard Murphy, 1955.

Until They Sail. Directed by Robert Wise, 1957.

Vietnam: A Television History. Videotape produced by WGBH TV, Boston. New York: Sony, 1983.

Why We Fight. Directed by Frank Capra, re-released by MPI Home Video, 1984.

The World of Suzie Wong. Directed by Richard Quine, 1960.

Index

sage to Freedom, 135–36, 308 nn.37–
38. *See also* Media, American
Catholic Relief Services (CRS), 131, 187–
88
Catholic Universe Bulletin, 220
Catton, Philip, 36
Central Evacuation Committee, 133
Central Intelligence Agency (CIA), 26,
51, 84, 132, 205
Chambers, Whittaker, 84, 89
Cherne, Leo, 134–35, 162, 230–31, 242–
43, 260
Chiang Kai-shek: Christianity of, 12, 13,
119–22; communism and, 41, 121;
criticism of, 121, 123–24, 222; media
coverage of, 88, 119–20, 222; *Time*
on, 88, 119, 120–21, 197; U.S. relations with, 91, 119, 123–24, 304 n.100
Chicago Sun-Times, 141, 239
Childishness (stereotype): America as
parent figure, 15, 115, 116–17, 238,
242, 244, 267, 274; of Asians, 96–105,
107–8, 109, 129, 170, 238; of dissident
generals, 195; in literature, 107–8,
113, 116, 129; of North Vietnamese
refugees, 146; precludes self-
government, 125, 219, 238; Vietnamese and, 107–8, 146, 156–57,
238
China Lobby, 91
Chou En-lai, 235
Christian Century, 79, 120, 208
Christianity: atheism and, 12, 69, 265;
Buddhism and, 12, 16, 118, 122; of
Chiang Kai-shek, 12, 13, 119–22;
church membership, 62–63, 65, 66,
275; communism and, 12, 18, 60, 66–
67, 74, 75, 122, 151, 272; conversion
to, 119, 122; democracy and, 118;
Jehovah's Witnesses, 64, *70*; missionaries, 34, 50, 62, 118, 122, 192; in
print media, 66–67, 69, 70, 79–80;

themes in South Vietnamese consti-
tution, 227
Christian Science Monitor, 256
Christopher, Renny, 129, 142
Church, Frank, 269–70
Church, Marguerite, 40
Churchill, Winston, 72, 124, 130
Clubb, O. Edmund, 137
Collins, J. Lawton (Lightning Joe), *177*,
186; on America's responsibility for
Vietnam, 213; on Binh Xuyen-VNA
cease-fire, 194–95, 202; on cabinet
formation in Diem government,
185, 188, 194, 202, 211, 214–16; on
Cardinal Spellman's visit to Vietnam, 187, 188; Catholicism of, 173,
196; on Diem's removal from office,
4, 11, 195–97, 200–206; on FEC's
importance, 213; John Foster Dulles
and, 188, 198, 201, 216; on Nguyen
Van Hinh, 180; Paul Ely and, 198–
99; Phan Huy Quat supported by,
183–85, 196; *Time* profile of, 197;
Vietnamese National Army (VNA)
and, 180–81. *See also* Ngo Dinh
Diem; Ngo Dinh Diem regime
Commentary, 189
Commonweal, 208, 223
Communism: anti-Diem propaganda
of, 240; Buddhism and, 190, 191,
272–73; Catholicism and, 18–19, 26,
31, 44, 49–50, 80–85, 134–37, 167,
243, 297 n.128; Chiang Kai-shek and,
41, 121; Christianity and, 18, 66–67,
74, 75, 122, 151; Diem opposition to,
3–4, 28–30, 32–33, 55, 85, 221, 247,
249, 258; Dooley on, 141; John Foster
Dulles on, 18–19, 74–75; Hukbalahap rebellion, 123; in Italy, 84; in
Laos, 164; opposition as holy war,
60; public relations of, 28, 112, 115–
16; *Quiet American* and, 109–10; in

Communism (*continued*)
South Vietnam, 188–89; *Ugly American* (Lederer and Burdick) and, 112. *See also* Viet Minh

Coody, Gerry, 65

Cooper, Chester, 46, 55, 132

Coors, Dallas, 31

Corcoran, Thomas, 137

Corley, Francis, 222

Council on Foreign Relations, 260

Couve de Murville, Maurice, 201

Craig, Gordon, 280 n.36

Critic, 140

Cromwell, James, 122

Cronin, John, Father, 84

Crowl, Richard, 273–74

Cumings, Bruce, 19

Dac Khe, 57

Dai Viet Party, 231–32, 249

Davis, Rex, 164

Dean, Robert, 21

De Jaegher, Raymond, 35

DeJean, Maurice, 289 n.117

Deliver Us from Evil (Dooley): as cold war propaganda, 145, 154; "Communist Re-education," 155; cultural narcissism in, 170; epitaph for Dooley in, 169, 171; paternalism in, 145, 154, 156–57; personal transformation described in, 154–55; praise for, 153, 158–60; in *Reader's Digest*, 148–49, 153–54; Vietnam introduced in, 140; writing of, 146, 153, 154

De Lubac, Henri, 192

DeMille, Cecil B., 65, 97

Dewey, Thomas, 73

Diem, Ngo Dinh. *See* Ngo Dinh Diem

Dien Bien Phu, 47–48, 107

Dillon, Douglas, 53, 56–57, 210

Docherty, George, 70

Donovan, William, 35, 235

Dooley, Agnes, 160, 168

Dooley, Tom: American Friends of Vietnam (AFV) and, 162, 229, 234, 242, 243; correspondence of, 140–41, 144–50, 155–56, 161; death of, 139, 168–69; on Diem, 147, 152, 159–60, 164–65, 268, 311 n.107; fundraising tours of United States, 165–66; homosexuality of, 139–40, 161; in Laos, 162–64, 167–68; Medical International Cooperation Organization (MEDICO) and, 139, 161, 170; medical training of, 143–44, 155; motivational speeches of, 150–51, 160–61, 168–69; in Passage to Freedom, 143, 149, 155, 243; paternalism of, 19, 101, 140, 144, 156–57, 162–63, 171, 247; personality of, 138–39, 140–41, 146, 154–55; press coverage of, 140, 141, 158–59; radio broadcasts of, 162, 163–64, 170; on refugees, 144–46, 147, 149, 155; *Ugly American* (Lederer and Burdick) portrayal of, 167, 314 n.178; on Viet Minh atrocities, 147–49, 154, 155–56. *See also Deliver Us from Evil* (Dooley)

Douglas, Kirk, 162, 163

Douglas, William O., 16, 41, 43, 46, 222–23, 265, 267, 287 n.81

Dower, John, 19–20, 21–22

Drummond, Roscoe, 72

Du Berrier, Hilaire, 250–52, 268

Dudziak, Mary, 21

Duff, James, 54–55

Duke, Angier Biddle, 234, 253–54

Dulles, Allen, 48, 199, 233

Dulles, John Foster, 77; American Friends of Vietnam (AFV) and, 244; Chiang Kai-shek supported by, 124; on communism, 18–19, 74–75; on Diem's regime, 54–55, 173, 174, 176, 184–85, 214–16, 253, 267; on Diem's

removal from office, 196, 197, 198, 199–202, 205–6, 211; "dynamism" as theme of, 74, 135, 265, 294 n.86; Eisenhower influenced by, 75–76; on Franco-American alliance, 212–14; J. Lawton Collins and, 188, 198, 201, 216; Kennedy presidency and, 270; on one-man governments, 214–15; paternalism of, 12, 14, 18–19, 281 n.41; religious faith of, 9–12, 18, 71–73, 85–86, 275, 279 n.30, 280 n.32; Syngman Rhee supported by, 124; *Ugly American* (Lederer and Burdick) and, 111; on U.S. unilateral responsibility for Vietnam, 213–14
Durdin, Peggy, 158

Eagleton, Terry, 5
Eden, Anthony, 72
Eisenhower, Dwight D., *68*; American Friends of Vietnam (AFV) and, 244, 260; Article 14(d) Geneva Accords and, 130; Asian culture, knowledge of, 47, 48, 124, 264; Collins meeting with, 177, 203–4; on *Deliver Us from Evil* (Dooley), 159; on Diem's leadership, 196, 199, 201, 203–4, 260, 267; Diem's visit to America and, 217–18, *219*, 254, *255*, 256; Dulles's influence on, 75–76; O'Daniel and, 240; on Phan Huy Quat, 205; on religion, 48–49, 67–69, 70–71, 264–66; on resistance to communism in South Vietnam, 188–89; Rodgers and Hammerstein's musicals and, 124, 305 n.121; *Ugly American* (Lederer and Burdick) and, 111
Eisenhower administration: Dien Bien Phu and, 47–48; Operations Coordinating Board (OCB), 39, 49–50, 51, 52; paternalism of, 14–17, 19, 27, 33, 38–40; religious revivalism in, 11–12,

21, 61, 279 n.29; Vietnam expertise in, 8–9, 59
Elmer Gantry, 275
Elson, Edward, Reverend, 63
Ely, Paul: Binh Xuyen-VNA cease-fire by, 195, 202; departure from Indochina, 214; on Diem regime, 180, 199, 202; J. Lawton Collins and, 180, 198–99; on Passage to Freedom, 130, 131; Vietnamese National Army (VNA) and, 180–81, 195, 213
Emmett, Christopher, 34
Ennis, Thomas, 45, 46

Fall, Bernard, 36
Far East-America Council of Commerce and Industry, 261
Faure, Edgar, 15–16, 212, 213, 214
Federal Council of Churches, 73
Field, Marshall, Jr., 235
Fields, Barbara, 14
Fishel, Wesley, 15, 34, 35, 38, 184, 261, 266, 282 n.6
Fisher, James T., 143, 144, 167, 222, 234, 297 n.128, 314 n.178
FitzGerald, Frances, 2, 32
Fitzpatrick, Francis J., 128
Flannelly, Joseph, Most Reverend, 258
Foner, Eric, 6
Foreign Affairs, 222
Foreign Agents Registration Act, 233
Foreign Missionary Conference of North America, 62
Foreign Policy Association, 75
Foreign Policy Bulletin, 222
Formosa, 119, 122
Fortune, 66
France: Bao Dai and, 30; civil administration of South Vietnam and, 130; colonial government of, 145, 189; Diem and, 15–16, 27–29, 33, 46, 53, 54, 206, 212, 289 n.117; Dien Bien

Ideological history, 5–6, 7, 20

Immerman, Richard, 275

International Control Commission, 130

International Rescue Committee (IRC), 162, 230–31, 234, 260

Isaacs, Harold, 38–39, 192–93, 264

Islam, 12, 280n.33

Italy, elections in, 84

Jehovah's Witnesses, 64, *70*

Johnson, Lyndon B., 4, 16, 206, 273

Jonas, Gilbert, 171, 241

Jubilee, 34, 135

Judd, Walter, 17, 25, 34, 40, 121, 233, 234, 240

Kahin, George, 264

Karnow, Stanley, 28, 58

Katayama, Tetsu, 119

Kattenburg, Paul, 241

Kelly, Edna, 17, 34, 206, 235

Kennan, George, 11, 14, 69, 279 n.30, 281 n.40

Kennedy, John F.: American Friends of Vietnam (AFV) and, 234, 241, 242, 245; Catholicism of, 79, 86–87, 270; Diem and, 4, 43, 46, 260; on Dooley, 139; presidency of, 2, 4, 270–71; on self-immolation of Buddhists, 269

Kidder, Randolph, 52, 137, 186, 204, 210, 215

King, Martin Luther, Jr., 269

King and I, 97–101, 124

Kirk, Russell, 83

Kissinger, Henry, 12, 274–75

Klein, Christina, 96

Kolko, Gabriel, 277 n.8

Korea, 12–13, 27, 53, 88, 102, 122, 230

LaChambre, Guy, 176

Lancaster, Burt, 275

Landon, Kenneth, 51

Laniel, Joseph, 47

Lansdale, Edward: Diem and, 16, 58, 196, 272; Ramon Magsaysay election and, 123; on plebiscite (1955), 225; portrayals of, 110, 132, 167, 307 n.24; propaganda campaign of, 132–33

Laos, 162–64, 167–68, 191

Lash, Joseph, 246, 261

Latham, Michael, 5

Lederer, William, 110–11, 127–29, 143, 149, 151, 153, 167–68

Lee, Robert E., 263

Lerner, Max, 208

Le Van "Bay" Vien , 175, 178, *193*, 194, 323 n.141

Lewis, Jerry, 102, *103*

Lewis, Sinclair, 62, 275

Liebling, A. J., 109

Life: Buddhists' self-immolation reported in, 268; Chiang Kai-shek in, 119, 120; cultural impact of, 209–10; Diem in, 209, 221, 233, 252; Dooley in, 151, 167–68; Michener article in, 88, 90–91; Passage to Freedom coverage by, 134–35; on religious revivalism, 66, 67; on Syngman Rhee, 122–23; "The World's Great Religions" series, 190

Lindbergh, Charles, 20

Lindley, Ernest, 221, 267

Link, Henry, 66

Lippmann, Walter, 84–85

Lodge, Henry Cabot, 159, 228, 229

Look, 134, 151

Luce, Henry: American Friends of Vietnam (AFV) and, 233, 234; anti-communism of, 88–89, 190; Chiang Kai-shek and, 88–89, 119–20; Diem and, 4, 197, 221, 253, 260; on Dulles's statesmanship, 76–77; influence of, 66, 88, 292 n.47; James Michener

126; *Return to Paradise*, 116–17; *Sayonara*, 116, 303 n.93; *Tales of the South Pacific*, 126; on *Ugly American* (Lederer and Burdick), 110–12; *Voice of Asia*, 106; *World is My Home*, 125–26

Michigan State University, 34, 35, 261

Miller, Edward, 37

Mindszenty, Joseph, Cardinal, 82, *86*

Modernization theory, 94, 95

Modern Screen, 65

Mohr, Charles, 274

Montgomery, Bernard, 177

Morgan, Joseph, 33, 229

Morgenthau, Hans, 8, 242

Morison, Samuel Eliot, 234

Morris, Charles, 79, 85

Mounier, Emmanuel, 36

Movie industry, 65, 80, 96–104, 109–10

Moynihan, Daniel Patrick, 81

Muir, Malcolm, 233

Murphy, Audie, 110, 234

Murphy, James, Father, 159

Murrow, Edward R., 221

Nam Phuong, 56

National Catholic Welfare Conference (NCWC), 84, 131, 136, 137, 308 nn.37–38

National Conference of Christians and Jews, 67

National Council of Churches, 74

National Liberation Front (NLF), 224, 271

National Review, 191, 220, 272

National Security Council (NSC), 5–6, 19, 48, 49, 188, 213

Navarre, Henri-Eugene, 47

Nehru, Jawaharlal, 16, 72, 255, 257

New Leader, 15, 35, 118, 233, 272

New Republic, 233

Newsweek: on corruption in Saigon, 175–76; Diem and, 221, 233, 267; on James Michener, 124; Passage to Freedom coverage in, 134, 135; *The Quiet American* reviewed in, 109

New Yorker, 158

New York Herald Tribune, 158, 176, 233, 257

New York Journal-American, 221, 233, 255

New York Post, 208, 223, 246, 261

New York Times: on Buddhist passivity, 191; Cao Dai in, 189; Diem praised in, 217, 221, 233, 256, 267; Dooley in, 166; Passage to Freedom in, 134

Ngo Dinh Diem, *125*; American Friends of Vietnam (AFV) and, 230, 233–34, 241–45, 254–55, 257, 260; in American media, 27, 35, 136, 197–98, 208–9, 220, 222, 245, 254–55, 272; assassination of, 1–2, 237–38, 272; background of, 28, 32, 52, 56, 110, 259; Bao Dai and, 29, 53–55, 176, 195, 200, 224–25, 247; Binh Xuyen and, 195, 196, 202, 204, 206, 223–24; Catholicism of, 25–26, 28, 31, 61–62, 85, 209, 254, 258; communism opposed by, 3–4, 28–30, 32–33, 55, 85, 221, 247, 249, 258; Confucianism of, 36–38; on democratic government in Vietnam, 125, 246, 256, 260, 266; Dooley on, 147, 159–60, 164–65, 268, 311 n.107; elections and, 130, 219, 224–25, 235, 241–42, 244, 247; France and, 15–16, 28–29, 29, 33, 46, 53, 54, 176, 206, 212–13, 289 n.117; Ho Chi Minh and, 29–33, 46, 200, 247, 261; Mike Mansfield's support of, 16–17, 25, 34, 41, 43, 200, 222–23, 247–49; as Miracle Man, 17, 217, 221–22, 238, 249, 252, 256, 261; one-man rule of, 38, 228–29, 231–32; personality of, 4, 15–16, 27–28, 32, 53, 57–59, 222–23,

Ngo Dinh Diem (*continued*)
228, 254; public relations for, 232–35,
237, 245; removal from office, 195–
206, 211, 274; sectarianism of, 36–38,
173, 185–88, 195, 228, 231, 249–50,
275–76; sink or swim policy of
United States and, 2, 3, 13, 21, 264,
276; Cardinal Francis Spellman and,
32, 186–88, 233, 260–61. *See also*
American Friends of Vietnam
(AFV); Battle for Saigon; Dulles,
John Foster; Eisenhower, Dwight D.;
Mansfield, Mike; South Vietnam;
Vietnamese National Army (VNA)
Ngo Dinh Diem regime: Bao Dai in,
54, 55–56, 57–58, 200; cabinet formation in, 185, 188, 194, 202, 211,
214–16, 325 n.190; Catholics in
administration of, 13, 182, 187, 194,
228, 232; civil liberties in, 224, 226–
27, 239–40, 247, 249–50, 267, 271;
economic investment in, 245–46,
261; Kennedy presidency and, 270–
71; leadership alternatives to, 4, 173,
176, 180, 183, 196–97, 199–200, 204,
205; National Liberation Front
(NLF) and, 224, 271; one-man rule
in, 15, 38, 173, 183, 214–16, 223, 228–
32, 240, 252, 267; overthrow of, 1–3,
237–38, 268–72; self-immolation of
Buddhists and, 50, 268–70 (269);
U.S. aid to, 2, 26, 53, 239–40, 273–74;
Viet Minh and, 29, 30, 224. *See also*
Phan Huy Quat
Ngo Dinh Diem's visits to the United
States: academia and, 34–35, 261;
addresses to Congress, 256, 257, 259;
American Friends of Vietnam
(AFV), 254–55; awards during, 259,
260, 261; Catholic community and,
27, 32, 110, 208, 220, 258–61, 272;
Dwight Eisenhower, 217–18, 219, 254,

255, 256; New York City visit, 258–61;
press coverage of, 27, 32, 217, 254–57,
261; speeches during, 256, 257–58,
259, 260–62; State Department
meetings, 26–27, 31, 258; Washing-
ton visits, 26–27, 41, 217–18, 253–58
Ngo Dinh Khoi, 29
Ngo Dinh Luyen, 54
Ngo Dinh Nhu, 210, 223, 268
Ngo Dinh Thuc, Bishop, 26–27, 30,
254, 282 n.6
Nguyen Khac Vien, 37
Nguyen Nhoc Bich, 46
Nguyen-Thai, Augustine, 44–45
Nguyen Thanh Phuong, 187, 194–95
Nguyen Ton Hoan, 249, 250
Nguyen Van Hinh, 4, 176, 180, 197
Nguyen Van Thieu, 276
Niebuhr, Reinhold, 63–64
Ninkovich, Frank, 5
Nixon, Richard, 48, 84, 111
North Atlantic Treaty Organization
(NATO), 27, 65, 76, 172, 177, 211
Norton, James, Reverend, 160

O'Brien, David, 82
O'Brien, John, 257–58
O'Connor, Patrick, 136, 190, 308 nn.37–
38
O'Daniel, John W. ("Iron Mike"):
American Friends of Vietnam (AFV)
and, 234, 235–38; "America's Stake in
Vietnam" conference and, 242; army
career of, 236; Battle for Saigon and,
237; on business investments in
Vietnam, 245; Joseph Buttinger's
resignation from AFV and, 271; Cardinal Spellman's South Vietnam
visit and, 186–88; Diem supported
by, 236–37, 242, 244, 251–53, 317 n.31;
erratic behavior of, 236; House Foreign Affairs Committee address, 239;

on Nguyen Van Hinh, 317 n.31;
paternalism of, 238–39; "Report
from Saigon" rebuttal by, 251; U.S.
Military Assistance and Advisory
Group (MAAG) and, 152, 180, 236,
239; Vietnam expertise of, 238–40,
247, 330 n.102
Office of Philippine and Southeast Asia
Affairs (PSA), 51–52, 95–96, 184,
199–201, 205–7, 211–12, 233
Olson, Gregory, 196
O'Melia, Thomas A., 55
O'Neill, William, 63
Operations Coordinating Board (OCB),
39, 49–50, 51, 52
Oram, Harold, 232–33, 234, 235, 237,
245
Osborne, John, 252
Oursler, Fulton, 66
Our Sunday Visitor, 85, 191

Pacific Affairs, 222, 245
Packenham, Robert, 7
Paris Conference (1955), 211–15, 267
Passage to Freedom: American aid in,
13, 131, *132*, 134, 144, 145; as Catholic-
communist struggle, 134–37, 137,
243; Dooley and, 143, 149, 155, 243;
France and, 130, 131, 145; International Rescue Committee (IRC) and,
230; press coverage of, 134, 135–36.
See also Refugees, North Vietnamese
Paternalism: America as parent figure,
15, 115, 116–17, 238, 242, 244, 267, 274;
Asians and, 95–101, 158, 165, 299
n.22; Buddhism and, 190; deception
as, 238–40; of Ngo Dinh Diem, 125,
156; of Dooley, 19, 101, 144, 156, 158,
165–66; in foreign policy, United
States, 14–17, 19, 33, 38–40; French
colonialism as, 109; in literature,
113–16, 127–29; missionaries and, 34,

50, 62, 118, 122, 192; of John W.
("Iron Mike") O'Daniel, 238–40;
one-man rule and, 173, 183, 214–16,
223–24, 240, 252, 267
Pauker, Guy, 222
Paulding, Gouverneur, 35, 223
Peale, Norman Vincent, 66
Pentagon Papers, 134, 153
Pham Cong Tac , *193*
Pham Quang Dan, 227
Phan Huy Quat: anticommunism of, 4,
183; Buddhism and, 12, 183–84; Col-
lins support of, 183–85, 196, 199, 204;
Diem and, 4, 187, 289 n.120; as viable
leader, 199, 200, 204, 205, 206
Phibun Songhram, 218
Philadelphia Inquirer, 233
Philippines, 96, 113, 123
Plummer, Brenda Gayle, 21
Podhoretz, Norman, 273
Presbyterian Life, 74
Progressive, 137
Provoo, John, 43

Quiet American (Greene): communism
in, 109–10; film version of, 109–10;
French colonialism in, 109; significance of, 106; *Ugly American* (Lederer and Burdick) and, 110–11; Viet
Minh in, 108, 109; Vietnamese stereotyped as children in, 107–8

Rabaut, Louis, 60
Racial stereotypes: anti-Asian prejudice, 25–26, 91–94, 95, 266; of
Eisenhower administration, 14–15,
17, 27, 39–40; of Dooley, 154, 162–63,
167–68; homogenization of cultures
and, 14, 215; Laotians and, 167–68; in
literature, 110–17, 127–29; in modernization theory, 94; in movie
images of Asians, 96–104; in musi-

Wintrebert, Michel, 52
World Conference on Church, Community, and State, 73
World Council of Churches, 265
World War II, 29, 62

Young, Kenneth, 51, 184, 199–201, 207, 211–12, 233

Zablocki, Clement, 40, 43, 234, 240
Zorach v. Clauson (1952), 41, 265

Seth Jacobs is an assistant professor in the
Department of History at Boston College.

Library of Congress Cataloging-in-Publication Data
Jacobs, Seth
America's miracle man in Vietnam : Ngo Dinh Diem, religion, race,
and U.S. intervention in Southeast Asia, 1950–1957 / Seth Jacobs.
p. cm. — (American encounters/global interactions)
Includes bibliographical references and index.
ISBN 0-8223-3429-1 (cloth : alk. paper)
ISBN 0-8223-3440-2 (pbk. : alk. paper)
1. United States—Foreign relations—Vietnam (Republic)
2. Vietnam (Republic)—Foreign relations—United States.
3. Ngô, <ình Diòêm, 1901–1963. 4. United States—Foreign
relations—1953–1961. I. Title. II. Series.
E183.8.V5J33 2004   327.730597'09'045—dc22
2004012452